AF731512

JUDICIARY
—WALLAH—

LAW OF CRIME
(BHARATIYA NYAYA SANHITA)

EDITION: First

Published By: Physicswallah Limited

Physics Wallah Publication

ISBN: 978-93-6034-011-7

MRP: 409/-

Mobile App: Physics Wallah (Available on Play Store)

Website: www.pw.live

Youtube Channels: Physics Wallah - Alakh Pandey

Judiciary by PW (@JudiciarybyPW)

Email: publication@pw.live

Printed by: PWP

(This book shall only be used for educational purposes.)

PREFACE

The judiciary plays a pivotal role in upholding the principles of justice, equality, and fairness in Indian democratic society. Judges are entrusted with the responsibility of interpreting and applying the law impartially, ensuring that rights are protected, disputes are resolved, and justice is served. To become a part of this esteemed profession is not merely a career choice but a commitment to the noble cause of upholding the rule of law and safeguarding the rights of individuals.

The Judicial Service Examination is the gateway to a career in the judiciary. It is a rigorous and competitive examination that tests not only the candidate's knowledge of the law but also their analytical skills, legal reasoning ability, and aptitude for judicial service. As such, thorough preparation is essential to succeed in this examination.

This book on the Law of Crime (BNS) is meticulously crafted to assist aspiring candidates in their journey towards a fulfilling career in the judiciary. Whether you are a law student, a legal practitioner, or someone with a passion for justice and the rule of law, this book is designed to be your steadfast companion as you navigate through the complexities of the judicial service examination.

SALIENT FEATURES OF THE BOOK

- ✔ This book is structured to cover all the essential components of the Judicial Service Examination syllabus comprehensively.
- ✔ It provides in-depth coverage of various topics of the Law of Crime (BNS).
- ✔ Bulletised presentation of content to make the concepts easier to comprehend and recall in the examination.
- ✔ Special emphasis on Bare Provisions, its key ingredients, illustrations, case laws and legal maxims to provide a comprehensive understanding of the concepts.
- ✔ Each chapter is meticulously crafted to provide a conceptual understanding of the law, supplemented with illustrative examples, case studies, and relevant legal provisions.
- ✔ This book is not just about preparing for an examination; it is about nurturing a holistic understanding of the law and cultivating the qualities essential for a successful judicial career.

We trust that this book will serve as a valuable resource not only in your preparation for the Judicial Services Examination but also for other examinations such as Assistant Public Prosecutor, Higher Judicial Services and Specialist Law Officer.

However, this book is not a substitute for diligent study and hard work. Success in the Judicial Service Examination requires dedication, perseverance, and a passion for the law.

We sincerely hope that this book serves as a valuable resource in your journey towards becoming a successful judicial officer. May it inspire you to strive for excellence, uphold the values of justice, and contribute meaningfully to the legal fraternity and society at large. Wishing you the very best for your examination and future endeavors!

ACKNOWLEDGMENT

We would like to express our gratitude to the founder and visionary behind Physics Wallah, whose commitment to education and innovation has provided a platform for the dissemination of knowledge and the empowerment of students across the country.

It is with immense gratitude and heartfelt appreciation that we extend our acknowledgement to all those who have contributed to the publication of the Judicial Services Examination book by Physics Wallah.

This endeavor has been made possible through the collaborative efforts of numerous individuals whose dedication and expertise have played an instrumental role in bringing this book to fruition.

First and foremost, we would like to express our sincere gratitude to the Physics Wallah Judiciary content team whose unwavering commitment to excellence has shaped the intellectual foundation of this book. Their diligent research, meticulous planning, and insightful contributions have ensured that the content is comprehensive, accurate, and relevant to the needs of aspiring judicial officers.

We extend our heartfelt thanks to the DTP team for their exceptional skills and attention to detail in formatting, designing, and arranging the content of this book. Their creative input and technical expertise have enhanced the readability and visual appeal of the book, making it more engaging and user-friendly for readers.

We are deeply grateful to the publishing team for their invaluable support and guidance throughout the publishing process. Their professionalism, efficiency, and dedication have played a vital role in coordinating various aspects of production, from editing and proofreading to printing and distribution, ensuring that the book meets the highest standards of quality and accuracy.

Furthermore, we would like to extend our appreciation to all other individuals who have contributed to this project in various capacities, including researchers, reviewers, proofreaders, and administrative staff. Their collective efforts have been indispensable in bringing this book to fruition.

It is our sincere hope that this book serves as a valuable resource for aspiring judicial officers and contributes to their success not only in the Judicial Services Examination but also for other examinations such as Assistant Public Prosecutor, Higher Judicial Services and Specialist Law Officer.

CONTENTS

COMPARATIVE CHART OF IPC AND BNS

THE INDIAN PENAL CODE, 1860		THE BHARATIYA NYAYA SANHITA, 2023	
Section	**Heading**	**Section**	**Heading**
1 2 3 4 5	Title and extent of operation of the Code	1	Short title, commencement and application
	Some of the General Explanations	2	Definitions
33 32	"Act", "Omission"	2(1)	"Act"
47	"Animal"	2(2)	"Animal"
-	(No Provision)	2(3)	"Child" (New Section)
28	"Counterfeit"	2(4)	"Counterfeit"
20	"Court of Justice"	2(5)	"Court"
46	"Death"	2(6)	"Death"
24	"Dishonestly"	2(7)	"Dishonestly"
29	"Document"	2(8)	"Document" (induding Electronic Record)
25	"Fraudulently"	2(9)	"Fraudulently"
8	"Gender"	2(10)	"Gender"
52	"Good faith"	2(11)	"Good faith"
17	"Government"	2(12)	"Government"
52A	"Harbour"	2(13)	"Harbour"
44	"Injury"	2(14)	"Injury"
43	"Illegal", "legally bound to do"	2(15)	"Illegal" and "legally bound to do"
19	"Judge"	2(16)	"Judge"
45	"Life"	2(17)	"Life"
42	"Local Law"	2(18)	"Local Law"
10	"Man", "Woman"	2(19)	"Man"
49	"Month" and "Year"	2(20)	"Month" and "year"
22	"Movable property"	2(21)	"Movable Property"

THE INDIAN PENAL CODE, 1860		THE BHARATIYA NYAYA SANHITA, 2023	
Section	Heading	Section	Heading
9	"Number"	2(22)	"Number"
51	"Oath"	2(23)	"Oath"
40	"Offence"	2(24)	"Offence"
33	"Act", "Omission	2(25)	"Omission"
11	"Person"	2(26)	"Person"
12	"Public"	2(27)	"Public"
21	"Public servant"	2(28)	"Public"
26	"Reason to believe"	2(29)	"Reason to believe"
41	"Special Law"	2(30)	"Special Law"
30	"Valuable security"	2(31)	"Valuable security"
48	"Vessel"	2(32)	"Vessel"
39	"Voluntarily"	2(33)	"Voluntarily"
31	"A will"	2(34)	"Will"
10	"Man", "Woman"	2(35)	"Woman"
23	"Wrongful gain" "Wrongful loss" Gaining wrongfully and Losing wrongfully	2(36) 2(37) 2(38)	"Wrongful gain" "Wrongful loss" "Gaining wrongfully" and "Losing wrongfully"
-	(No provision)	2(39)	Words and expressions
6 7 27 32 34 35 36 37 38	Definitions in the Code to the understood subject to exceptions Sense of expression once explained Property in possession of wife, clerk or servant Words referring to acts include illegal omissions Acts done by several persons in furtherance of common intention When such an act in criminal by reason of its being done with a criminal knowledge or intention Effect caused partly by act and partly by omission Co-operation by doing one of several acts constituting an offence Persons concerned in criminal act may be guilty of different offences	3(1) 3(2) 3(3) 3(4) 3(5) 3(6) 3(7) 3(8) 3(9)	General explanations

THE INDIAN PENAL CODE, 1860		THE BHARATIYA NYAYA SANHITA, 2023	
Section	Heading	Section	Heading
	Chapter II – of Punishments		**Chapter III – of Punishments**
53	Punishment	4	Punishments
54	Commutation of sentence of death	5	Commutation of sentence
55 55A	Commutation of sentence imprisonment for life		
57	Fractions of terms of punishment	6	Fractions of terms of punishment
60	Sentence may be (in certain cases of imprisonment) wholly or partly rigorous or simple	7	Sentence may be (in certain cases of imprisonment) wholly or partly rigorous or simple
63	Amount of fine	8(1)	Amount of fine, liability in default of payment of fine, etc.
64	Sentence of imprisonment for non-payment of fine	8(2)	
65	Limit to imprisonment for non-payment of fine, when imprisonment and fine awardable	8(3)	
66	Description of imprisonment for non-payment of fine	8(4)	
67	Imprisonment for non-payment of fine, when offence punishable with fine only	8(5)	
68	Imprisonment to terminate on payment of fine	8(6)(a)	
69	Termination of imprisonment on payment of proportional part of fine	8(6)(b)	
70	Fine leviable within six years, of during imprisonment. Death not to discharge property from liability	8(7)	
71	Limit of punishment of offence made up of several offences	9	Limit of punishment of offence made up of several offences
72	Punishment of person guilty of one of several offences, the judgment stating that it is doubtful of which	10	Punishment of person guilty of one of several offences, judgment stating that it is doubtful of which
73	Solitary confinement	11	Solitary confinement
74	Limit of solitary confinement	74	Limit of solitary confinement
75	Enhanced punishment for certain offences under Chapter XII or Chapter XVII after previous conviction	13	Enhanced punishment for certain offences after previous conviction
76	Act by a person bound, or by mistake of fact believing himself bound, by law	14	Act done by a person bound, or by mistake of fact believing himself bound, by law

THE INDIAN PENAL CODE, 1860		THE BHARATIYA NYAYA SANHITA, 2023	
Section	Heading	Section	Heading
77	Act of Judge when acting judicially	15	Act of Judge when acting judicially
78	Act done pursuant to the judgment or order Of Court	16	Act done pursuant to judgment or order of Court
79	Act done by a person justified, or by mistake of fact believing himself and not him self justified, law	17	Act done by a person justified, or by mistake of fact believing himself and not him self justified, law
80	Accident in doing a lawful act	18	Accident in doing a lawful act
81	Act likely to cause harm, but done without criminal intent, and to prevent other harm	19	Act likely to cause harm, but done without criminal intent, and to prevent other harm
82	Act of a child under seven years of age	20	Act of a child under seven years of age
83	Act of a child above seven and under twelve of immature understanding.	21	Act of a child above seven and under twelve years of age of immature understanding
84	Act of a person of unsound mind	22	Act of a person of unsound mind
85	Act of a person incapable of judgment by reason of intoxication caused against his will	23	Act of a person incapable of judgment by reason of intoxication caused against his will
86	Offence requiring a particular intent or knowledge committed by one who is intoxicated	24	Offence requiring a particular intent or knowledge committed by one who is intoxicated
87	Act not intended and not known to be likely to cause death or grievous hurt, done by consent	25	Act not intended and not known to be likely to cause death or grievous hurt, done by consent
88	Act not intended to cause death, done by consent in good faith for person's benefit	26	Act not intended to cause death, done by consent in good faith for person's benefit
89	Act done in good faith for benefit of child or insane person, by or by consent of guardian	27	Act done in good faith for benefit of child or person of unsound mind, by or by consent of guardian.
90	Consent known to be given under fear or misconception.	28	Consent known to be given under fear or misconception
91	Exclusion of acts which are offences independently of harm caused	29	Exclusion of acts which are offences independently of harm caused
92	Act done in good faith for benefit of a person without consent	30	Act done in good faith for benefit of a person without consent
93	Communication made in good faith	31	Communication made in good faith
94	Act to which a person is compelled by threats	32	Act to which a person is compelled by threats
95	Act causing slight harm	33	Act causing slight harm

THE INDIAN PENAL CODE, 1860		THE BHARATIYA NYAYA SANHITA, 2023	
Section	**Heading**	**Section**	**Heading**
96	Things done in private defence	34	Things done in private defence
97	Right of private defence of the body and of property	35	Right of private defence of the body and of property
98	Right of private defence against the act of a person of unsound mind etc.	36	Right of private defence against the act of a person of unsound mind etc.
99	Acts against which there is no right of private defence Extent to which the right may be exercised	37	Acts against which there is no right of private defence
100	When the right of private defence of the body extends to causing death.	38	When right of private defence of body extends to causing death.
101	When such right extends to causing any harm other than death	39	When such right extends to causing any harm other than death
102	Commencement and continuance of the right of private defence of the body	40	Commencement and continuance of right of private defence of the body
103	When the right of private defence of property extends to causing death	41	When right of private defence of property extends to causing death
104	When such right extends to causing any harm other than death	42	When such right extends to causing any harm other than death
105	Commencement and continuance of the right of private defence of property	43	Commencement and continuance of right of private defence of property
106	Right of private defence against deadly assault when there is risk of harm to innocent person	44	Right of private defence against deadly assault when there is risk of harm to innocent person
107	Abetment of a thing	45	Abetment of a thing
108	Abettor	46	Abettor
108A	Abetment in India of offences outside India	47	Abetment in India of offences outside India
-	(No Provision)	48	Abetment outside India for offence in India (New Section)
109	Punishment of abetment if the act abetted is committed in consequence and where no express provision is made for its punishment	49	Punishment of abetment if act abetted is committed in consequence and where no express provision is made for its punishment
110	Punishment of abetment if person abetted does act with different intention from that of abettor	50	Punishment of abetment if person abetted does act with different intention from that of abettor
111	Liability of abettor when one act abetted and different act done	51	Liability of abettor when one act abetted and different act done

THE INDIAN PENAL CODE, 1860		THE BHARATIYA NYAYA SANHITA, 2023	
Section	**Heading**	**Section**	**Heading**
112	Abettor when liable to cumulative punishment for act abetted and for act done	52	Abettor when liable to cumulative punishment for act abetted and for act done
113	Liability of abettor for an effect caused by the act abetted different from that intended by abettor	53	Liability of abettor for an effect caused by the act abetted different from that intended by abettor
114	Abettor present When offence is committed	54	Abettor present when offence is committed
115	Abetment of offence punishable with death or imprisonment for life.—if offence not committed.	55	Abetment of offence punishable with death or imprisonment for life
116	Abetment of offence punishable with imprisonment—if offence be not committed.	56	Abetment of offence punishable with imprisonment
117	Abetting commission of offence by the public or by more than ten persons	57	Abetting commission of offence by public or by more than ten persons
118	Concealing design to commit offence punishable with death or imprisonment for life If offence be committed-if offence be not committed or	58	Concealing design to commit offence punishable with death or imprisonment for life
119	Public servant concealing design to commit offence which it is his duty to prevent	59	Public servant concealing design to commit offence which it is his duty to prevent
120	Concealing design to commit offence punishable with imprisonment	60	Concealing design to commit offence punishable with imprisonment
120A 120B	Definition of criminal conspiracy Punishment of criminal conspiracy	61(1) 61(2)	Criminal conspiracy
511	Punishment for attempting to commit offences punishable with imprisonment for life or other imprisonment	62	Punishment for attempting to commit offences punishable with imprisonment for life or other imprisonment
375	Rape	63	Rape
376	Punishment for rape (Clause 1, 2)	64	Punishment for rape
376(3) 376AB	Punishment for rape Punishment for rape on woman under twelve years of age	65(1) 65(2)	Punishment for rape in certain cases
376A	Punishment for causing death or resulting in persistent vegetative state of victim	66	Punishment for causing death or resulting in persistent vegetative state of victim

THE INDIAN PENAL CODE, 1860		THE BHARATIYA NYAYA SANHITA, 2023	
Section	**Heading**	**Section**	**Heading**
368B	Sexual intercourse by husband upon his wife during separation	67	Sexual intercourse by husband upon his wife during separation
376C	Sexual intercourse by a person in authority	68	Sexual intercourse by a person in authority
-	(No Provision)	69	Sexual intercourse by employing deceitful means, etc. (New Section)
376D 376DA 376DB	Gang rape Punishment for gang rape on woman under 16 years of age Punishment for gang rape on woman under 12 years of age	70	Gang rape
376E	Punishment for repeat offenders	71	Punishment for repeat offenders
228A	Disclosure of identity of the victim of certain offences, etc.	72	Disclosure of identity of victim of certain offences, etc.
228A(3)	Disclosure of identity of the victim of certain offences, etc.	73	Printing or publishing any matter relating to Court proceedings without permission
354	Assault or criminal force to woman with intent to outage her modesty	74	Assault or use of criminal force to woman with intent to outrage her modesty
354A	Sexual harassment and punishment for sexual harassment	75	Sexual harassment
354B	Assault or use of criminal force to woman with intent to disrobe	76	Assault or use of criminal force to woman with intent to disrobe
354C	Voyeurism	77	Voyeurism
354D	Stalking	78	Stalking
509	Word, gesture or a t intended to insult the modesty of a woman	79	Word, gesture or act intended to insult the modesty of a woman
304B	Dowry death	80	Dowry death
493	Cohabitation caused by a man deceitfully inducing belief of lawful marriage	81	Cohabitation caused by a man deceitfully inducing belief of lawful marriage
494 495	Marrying again during lifetime of husband or wife Same offence with concealment of former marriage from person with whom subsequent marriage is contracted	82(1) 82(2)	Marrying again during lifetime of husband or wife
496	Marriage ceremony fraudulently gone through without lawful marriage	83	Marriage ceremony fraudulently gone through without lawful marriage

THE INDIAN PENAL CODE, 1860		THE BHARATIYA NYAYA SANHITA, 2023	
Section	**Heading**	**Section**	**Heading**
498	Enticing or taking away or detaining with criminal intent a married woman	84	Enticing or raking away or detaining with criminal intent a married woman
498A	Husband or relative of husband of a woman subjecting her to cruelty	85	Husband or relative of husband of a woman subjecting her to cruelty
498A	Explanation to Section 498A	86	Cruelty defined
300	Kidnapping, abducting or inducing woman to compel her marriage, etc.	87	Kidnapping, abducting or inducing woman to compel her marriage, etc.
312	Causing miscarriage	88	Causing miscarriage
313	Causing miscarriage without woman's consent	89	Causing miscarriage without woman's consent
314	Death caused by act done with intent to cause miscarriage if act done without woman's consent	90	Death caused by act done with in tent to cause miscarriage
315	Act done with intent to prevent child being born alive or to cause it to die after birth.	91	Act done with intent to prevent child being born alive or to cause to die after birth
316	Causing death of quick unborn child by act amounting to culpable homicide	92	Causing death of quick unborn child by act amounting to culpable homicide
317	Exposure and abandonment of child under twelve years, by parent or person having care of it	93	Exposure and abandonment of child under twelve years, by parent or person having care of it
318	Concealment of birth by secret disposal of dead body	94	Concealment of birth by secret disposal of dead body
-	(No Provision)	95	Hiring, employing or engaging a child to commit an offence (New section)
366A	Procuration of minor girl	96	Procuration of child
369	Kidnapping or abducting child under ten years of age with intent to steal from its person	97	Kidnapping or abducting child under ten years of age with intent to steal from its person
372	Selling minor for purposes of prostitution, etc.	98	Selling child for purposes of prostitution, etc.
373	Buying minor for purposes of prostitution, etc.	99	Buying child for purposes of prostitution, etc.
299	Culpable homicide	100	Culpable homicide
300	Murder	101	Murder
301	Culpable homicide by causing death of person other than person whose death was intended	102	Culpable homicide by causing death of person other than person whose death was intended
302	Punishment for murder	103	Punishment for murder
303	Punishment for murder by life-convict	104	Punishment for murder by life-convict

THE INDIAN PENAL CODE, 1860		THE BHARATIYA NYAYA SANHITA, 2023	
Section	**Heading**	**Section**	**Heading**
304	Punishment for culpable homicide not amounting to murder	105	Punishment for culpable homicide not amounting to murder
304A	Causing death by negligence	106	Causing death by negligence
305	Abetment of suicide of child or insane person	107	Abetment of suicide of child or person of unsound mind
306	Abetment of suicide	108	Abetment of suicide
307	Attempt to murder	109	Attempt to murder
308	Attempt to commit culpable homicide	110	Attempt to commit culpable homicide
-	(No Provision)	111	Organised crime (New section)
-	(No Provision)	112	Petty organised crime (New section)
-	(No Provision)	113	Terrorist act (New section)
319	Hurt	114	Hurt
321 323	Voluntarily causing hurt Punishment for voluntarily causing hurt	115(1) 115(2)	Voluntarily causing hurt
320	Grievous hurt	116	Grievous hurt
322 325	Voluntarily causing grievous hurt Punishment for voluntarily causing grievoushurt	117(1) 117(2)	Voluntarily causing grievous hurt
324 326	Voluntarily causing hurt by dangerous weapons or means Voluntarily causing grievous hurt by dangerous weapons or means	118(1) 118(2)	Voluntarily causing hurt or grievous hurt by dangerous weapons or means
327 329	Voluntarily causing hurt to extort property, or to constrain to an illegal act Voluntarily causing grievous hurt to extort property, or to constrain to an illegal act	119(1) 119(2)	Voluntarily causing hurt or grievous hurt to extort property, or to constrain to an illegal act
330 331	Voluntarily causing hurt to extort confession, or to compel restoration of property Voluntarily causing grievous hurt to extort confession, or to compel restoration of property	120(1) 120(2)	Voluntarily causing hurt to extort confession, or to compel restoration of property
332 333	Voluntarily causing hurt to deter public servant from his duty Voluntarily causing grievous hurt to deter public servant from his duty	121(1) 121(2)	Voluntarily causing hurt or grievous hurt to deter public servant from his duty

THE INDIAN PENAL CODE, 1860		THE BHARATIYA NYAYA SANHITA, 2023	
Section	Heading	Section	Heading
334 335	Voluntarily causing hurt on provocation Voluntarily causing grievous hurt on provocation	122(1) 122(2)	Voluntarily causing hurt or grievous hurt on provocation
328	Causing hurt by means of poison, etc., with intent to commit an offence	123	Causing hurt by means of poison, etc., with intent to commit an offence
326A 326B	Voluntarily causing grievous hurt by use of acid, etc. Voluntarily throwing or attempting to throw acid	124	Voluntarily causing grievous hurt by use of acid, etc.
336 337 338	Act endangering life or personal safety of others Causing hurt by act endangering life or personal safety of others Causing grievous hurt by act endangering life or personal safety of others	125	Act endangering life or personal safety of others
339 341	Wrongful restraint Punishment for wrongful restraint	126	Wrongful restraint
340 342 343 344 345 346 347 348	Wrongful confinement Punishment for wrongful confinement Wrongful confinement for three or more days Wrongful confinement for ten or more days Wrongful confinement of person for whose liberation writ has been issued Wrongful confinement in secret Wrongful confinement to extort property, or constrain to illegal act Wrongful confinement to extort confession, or compel restoration of property	127	Wrongful confinement
349	Force	128	Force
350	Criminal force	129	Criminal force
351	Assault	130	Assault
352	Punishment for assault or criminal force otherwise than on grave provocation	131	Punishment for assault or criminal force otherwise than on grave provocation

THE INDIAN PENAL CODE, 1860		THE BHARATIYA NYAYA SANHITA, 2023	
Section	**Heading**	**Section**	**Heading**
353	Assault or criminal force to deter public servant from discharge of his duty	132	Assault or criminal force to deter public servant from discharge of his duty
355	Assault or criminal force with intent to dishonour person, otherwise than on grave provocation	133	Assault or criminal force with intent to dishonour person, otherwise than on grave provocation
356	Assault or criminal force in attempt to commit theft of property carried by a person	134	Assault or criminal force in attempt to commit theft of property carried by a person
357	Assault or criminal force in attempt to wrongfully confine a person	135	Assault or criminal force in attempt to wrongfully confine a person
358	Assault or criminal force on grave provocation	136	Assault or criminal force on grave provocation
359	Kidnapping	137(1)	Kidnapping
360	Kidnapping from India	137(1)(a)	
361	Kidnapping from lawful guardianship	137(1)(b)	
363	Punishment for kidnapping	137(2)	
362	Abduction	138	Abduction
363A	Kidnapping or maiming a minor for purposes of begging	139	Kidnapping or maiming a child for purposes of begging
364	Kidnapping or abducting in order to murder	140(1)	Kidnapping or abducting in order to murder or for ransom, etc.
364A	Kidnapping for ransom, etc.	142(2)	
365	Kidnapping or abducting with intent secretly and wrongfully to confine person	140(3)	
367	Kidnapping or abducting in order to subject person to grievous hurt, slavery, etc.	140(4)	
366B	Importation of girl from foreign country	141	Importation of girl or boy from foreign country
368	Wrongfully concealing or keeping in confinement, kidnapped or abducted person	142	Wrongfully concealing or keeping in confinement, kidnapped or abducted person
370	Trafficking of person	143	Trafficking of person
370A	Exploitation of a trafficked person	144	Exploitation of a trafficked person
371	Habitual dealing in slaves	145	Habitual dealing in slaves
374	Unlawful compulsory labour	146	Unlawful compulsory labour

THE INDIAN PENAL CODE, 1860		THE BHARATIYA NYAYA SANHITA, 2023	
Section	Heading	Section	Heading
121	Waging, or attempting to wage war, or abetting waging of war, against the Government of India	147	Waging, or attempting to wage war, or abetting waging of war, against the Government of India
121A	Conspiracy to commit offences punishable by section 121	148	Conspiracy to commit offences punishable by section 147
122	Collecting arms, etc., with intention of waging war against the Government of India	149	Collecting arms, etc., with intention of waging war against the Government of India
123	Concealing with intent to facilitate design to wage war	150	Concealing with intent to facilitate design to wage war
124	Assaulting President, Governor, etc., with intent to compel or restrain the exercise of any lawful power	151	Assaulting President, Governor, etc., with intent to compel or restrain the exercise of any lawful power
124A	Sedition	152	Act endangering sovereignty, unity and integrity of India
125	Waging war against any Asiatic power in alliance with the Government of India	153	Waging war against Government of any foreign State at peace with Government of India
126	Committing depredation on territories of power at peace with the Government of India	154	Committing depredation on territories of foreign State at peace with Government of India.
127	Receiving property taken by war 'or' depredation mentioned in sections 125 and 126	155	Receiving property taken by war 'or' depredation mentioned in sections 153 and 154
128	Public servant voluntarily allowing prisoner of State or war to escape	156	Public servant voluntarily allowing prisoner of State or war to escape
129	Public servant negligently suffering such prisoner to escape	157	Public servant negligently suffering such prisoner to escape
130	Aiding escape of, rescuing or harbouring such prisoner	158	Aiding escape of, rescuing or harbouring such prisoner
131	Abetting mutiny, or attempting to seduce a soldier, sailor or airman from his duty	159	Abetting mutiny, or attempting to seduce a soldier, sailor or airman from his duty
132	Abetment of mutiny, if mutiny is committed in consequence there of	160	Abetment of mutiny, if mutiny is committed in consequence there of
133	Abetment of assault by soldier, sailor or airman on his superior officer, when in execution of his office	161	Abetment of assault by soldier, sailor or airman on his superior officer, when in execution of his office
134	Abetment of such assault, if the assault is committed	162	Abetment of such assault, if the assault is committed

THE INDIAN PENAL CODE, 1860		THE BHARATIYA NYAYA SANHITA, 2023	
Section	**Heading**	**Section**	**Heading**
135	Abetment of desertion of soldier, sailor or airman	163	Abetment of desertion of soldier, sailor or airman
136	Harbouring deserter	164	Harbouring deserter
137	Deserter concealed on board merchant vessel through negligence of master	165	Deserter concealed on board merchant vessel through negligence of master
138	Abetment of act of insubordination by soldier, sailor or airman	166	Abetment of act of insubordination by soldier, sailor or airman
139	Persons subject to certain Acts	167	Persons subject to certain Acts
140	Wearing garb or carrying token used by soldier, sailor or airman	168	Wearing garb or carrying token used by soldier, sailor or airman
171A	"Candidate", "Electoral right" defined	169	Candidate, electoral right defined
171B	Bribery	170	Bribery
171C	Undue influence at elections	171	Undue influence at elections
171D	Personation at elections	172	Personation at elections
171E	Punishment for bribery	173	Punishment for bribery
171F	Punishment for undue influence or personation at an election	174	Punishment for undue influence or personation at an election
171G	False statement in connection with an election	175	False statement in connection with an election
171H	Illegal payments in connection with an election	176	Illegal payments in connection with an election
171-I	Failure to keep election accounts	177	Failure to keep election accounts
231 255 489A	Counterfeiting coin Counterfeiting Government stamp	178	Counterfeiting coin, Government stamps, currency-notes or bank-notes
237 238 239 240 241 250	Import or export of counterfeit coin Import or export of counterfeits of the Indian coin Delivery of coin, possessed with knowledge that it is counterfeit Delivery of Indian coin, possessed with knowledge that it is counterfeit Delivery of coin as genuine, which, when first possessed, the deliverer did not know to be counterfeit Delivery of coin, possessed with knowledge that it is altered	179	Using as genuine, forged or counterfeit coin, Government stamp, currency-notes or bank-notes

THE INDIAN PENAL CODE, 1860		THE BHARATIYA NYAYA SANHITA, 2023	
Section	**Heading**	**Section**	**Heading**
251	Delivery of Indian coin, possessed with knowledge that it is altered		
254	Delivery of coin as genuine, which, when first possessed, the deliverer did not know to be altered		
258	Sale of counterfeit Government stamp		
260	Using as genuine a Government stamp known to be counterfeit		
489B	Using as genuine, forged or counterfeit currency-notes or bank notes		
242	Possession of counterfeit coin by person who knew it to be counterfeit when he became possessed thereof	180	Possession of forged or counterfeit coin, Government stamp, currency-notes or bank-notes
243	Possession of Indian coin by person who knew it to be counterfeit when he became possessed thereof		
252	Possession of coin by person who knew it to be altered when he became possessed thereof		
253	Possession of Indian coin by person who knew it to be altered when he became possessed thereof		
259	Having possession of counterfeit Government stamp		
489C	Possession of forged or counterfeit currency-notes or bank-notes		
233	Making or selling instrument for counterfeiting coin	181	Making or possessing instruments or materials for forging or counterfeiting coin Government stamp, currency-notes or bank-notes
234	Making or selling instrument for counterfeiting Indian coin		
235	Possession of instrument or material for the purpose of using the same for counterfeiting coin		
256	Having possession of instrument or material for counterfeiting Government stamp		
257	Making or selling instrument for counterfeiting Government stamp		
489D	Making or possessing instruments or materials for forging or counterfeiting currency notes or bank-notes		

THE INDIAN PENAL CODE, 1860		THE BHARATIYA NYAYA SANHITA, 2023	
Section	**Heading**	**Section**	**Heading**
489E	Making or possessing instruments or materials for forging or counterfeiting currency-notes or bank-notes.	182	Making or using documents resembling currency-notes or bank- notes
261	Effacing writing from substance bearing Government stamp, or removing from document a stamp used for it, with intent to cause loss to Government	183	Effacing writing from substance bearing Government stamp, or removing from document a stamp used for it, with intent to cause loss to Government
262	Using Government stamp known to have been before used	184	Using Government stamp known to have been before used
263	Erasure of mark denoting that stamp has been used	185	Erasure of mark denoting that stamp has been used
263A	Prohibition of fictitious stamps	186	Prohibition of fictitious stamps
244	Person employed in mint causing coin to be of different weight or composition from that fixed by law	187	Person employed in mint causing coin to be of different weight or composition from that fixed by law
245	Unlawfully taking coining instrument from mint	188	Unlawfully taking coining instrument from mint
141	Unlawful assembly	189(1)	Unlawful assembly
142	Being member of unlawful assembly	189(2)	
143	Punishment	189(2)	
145	Joining or continuing in unlawful assembly, knowing it has been commanded to disperse	189(3)	
144	Joining unlawful assembly armed with deadly weapon	189(4)	
151	Knowingly joining or continuing in assembly of five or more persons after it has been commanded to disperse	189(5)	
150	Hiring, or conniving at hiring, of persons to join unlawful assembly	189(6)	
157	Harbouring persons hired for an unlawful assembly	189(7)	
158	Being hired to take part in an unlawful assembly or riot	189(8)	
	or to go armed	189(9)	
149	Every member of unlawful assembly guilty of offence committed in prosecution of common object	190	Every member of unlawful assembly guilty of offence committed in prosecution of common object

THE INDIAN PENAL CODE, 1860		THE BHARATIYA NYAYA SANHITA, 2023	
Section	**Heading**	**Section**	**Heading**
146	Rioting	191(1)	Rioting
147	Punishment for rioting	191(2)	
148	Rioting, armed with deadly weapon	191(3)	
153	Wantonly giving provocation, with intent to cause riot-if rioting be committed-if not committed	192	Wantonly giving provocation with intent to cause riot-if rioting be committed; if not committed
154	Owner or occupier of land on which an unlawful assembly is held	193(1)	Liability of owner, occupier, etc., of land on which an unlawful assembly or riot takes place
155	Liability of person for whose benefit riot is committed	193(2)	
156	Liability of agent of owner or occupier for whose benefit riot is committed	193(3)	
159	Affray	194(1)	Affray
160	Punishment for committing affray	194(2)	
152	Assaulting or obstructing public servant when suppressing riot, etc.	195	Assaulting or obstructing public servant when suppressing riot, etc.
153A	Promoting enmity between different groups on grounds of religion, race, place of birth, residence, language, etc., and doing acts prejudicial to maintenance of harmony Offence committed in place of worship, etc.	196	Promoting enmity between different groups on grounds of religion, race, place of birth, residence, language, etc., and doing acts prejudicial to maintenance of harmony
153B	Imputations, assertions prejudicial to national integration	197	Imputations, assertions prejudicial to national integration
166	Public servant disobeying law, with intent to cause injury to any person	198	Public servant disobeying law, with intent to cause injury to any person
166A	Public servant disobeying direction under law	199	Public servant disobeying direction under law
166B	Punishment for non-treatment of victim	200	Punishment for non-treatment of victim
167	Public servant framing an incorrect document with intent to cause injury	201	Public servant framing an incorrect document with intent to cause injury
168	Public servant unlawfully engaging in trade	202	Public servant unlawfully engaging in trade
169	Public servant unlawfully buying or bidding for property	203	Public servant unlawfully buying or bidding for property
170	Personating a public servant	204	Personating a public servant
171	Wearing garb or carrying token used by public servant with fraudulent intent	205	Wearing garb or carrying token used by public servant with fraudulent intent

THE INDIAN PENAL CODE, 1860		THE BHARATIYA NYAYA SANHITA, 2023	
Section	Heading	Section	Heading
172	Absconding to avoid service of summons or other proceeding	206	Absconding to avoid service of summons or other proceeding
173	Preventing service of summons or other proceeding, or preventing publication thereof	207	Preventing service of summons or other proceeding, or preventing publication thereof
174	Non-attendance in obedience to an order from public servant	208	Non-attendance in obedience to an order from public servant
174A	Non-appearance in response to a proclamation under section 82 of Act 2 of 1974	209	Non-appearance in response to a proclamation under section 84 of Bharatiya Nagarik Suraksha Sanhita, 2023
175	Omission to produce document or electronic record to public servant by person legally bound to produce it	210	Omission to produce document or electronic record to public servant by person legally bound to produce it
176	Omission to give notice or information to public servant by person legally bound to give it	211	Omission to give notice or information to public servant by person legally bound to give it
177	Furnishing false information	212	Furnishing false information
178	Refusing oath or affirmation when duly required by public servant to make it	213	Refusing oath or affirmation when duly required by public servant to make it
179	Refusing to answer public servant authorised to question	214	Refusing to answer public servant authorised to question
180	Refusing to sign statement	215	Refusing to sign statement
181	False statement on oath or affirmation to public servant or person authorised to administer an oath or affirmation	216	False statement on oath or affirmation to public servant or person authorised to administer an oath or affirmation
182	False information, with intent to cause public servant to use his lawful power to injury of another person	217	False information, with intent to cause public servant to use his lawful power to injury of another person
183	Resistance to the taking of property by lawful authority of a public servant	218	Resistance to the taking of property by lawful authority of a public servant
184	Obstructing sale of property offered for sale by authority of public servant	219	Obstructing sale of property offered for sale by authority of public servant
185	Illegal purchase or bid for property offered for sale by authority of public servant	220	Illegal purchase or bid for property offered for sale by authority of public servant
186	Obstructing public servant in discharge of public functions	221	Obstructing public servant in discharge of public functions
187	Omission to assist public servant when bound by law to give assistance	222	Omission to assist public servant when bound by law to give assistance

THE INDIAN PENAL CODE, 1860		THE BHARATIYA NYAYA SANHITA, 2023	
Section	Heading	Section	Heading
188	Disobedience to order duly promulgated by public servant	223	Disobedience to order duly promulgated by public servant
189	Threat of injury to public servant	224	Threat of injury to public servant
190	Threat of injury to induce person to refrain from applying for protection to public servant	225	Threat of jury to induce person to refrain from applying for protection to public servant
-	(No Provision)	226	Attempt to commit suicide to compel or restrain exercise of lawful power (New Section)
191	Giving false evidence	227	Giving false evidence
192	Fabricating false evidence	228	Fabricating false evidence
193	Punishment for false evidence	229	Punishment for false evidence
194	Giving or fabricating false evidence with intent to procure conviction of capital offence	230	Giving or fabricating false evidence with intent to procure conviction of capital offence
195	Giving or fabricating false evidence with intent to procure conviction of offence punishable with imprisonment for life or imprisonment	231	Giving or fabricating false evidence with intent to procure conviction of offence punishable with imprisonment for life or imprisonment
195A	Threatening any person to give false evidence	232	Threatening any person to give false evidence
196	Using evidence known to be false	233	Using evidence known to be false
197	'Issuing or' signing false certificate	234	'Issuing or' signing false certificate
198	Using as true a certificate known to be false	235	Using as true a certificate known to be false
199	False statement made in declaration which is by law receivable as evidence	236	False statement made in declaration which is by law receivable as evidence
200	Using as true such declaration knowing it to be false	237	Using as true such declaration knowing it to be false
201	Causing disappearance of evidence of offence, or giving false information to screen offender	238	Causing disappearance of evidence of offence, or giving false information to screen offender
202	Intentional omission to give information of offence by person bound to inform	239	Intentional omission to give information of offence by person bound to inform
203	Giving false information respecting an offence committed	240	Giving false information respecting an offence committed
204	Destruction of document or electronic record to prevent its production as evidence	241	Destruction of document or electronic record to prevent its production as evidence

THE INDIAN PENAL CODE, 1860		THE BHARATIYA NYAYA SANHITA, 2023	
Section	Heading	Section	Heading
205	False personation for purpose of act or proceeding in suit or prosecution	242	False personation for purpose of act or proceeding in suit or prosecution
206	Fraudulent removal or concealment of property to prevent its seizure as forfeited or in execution	243	Fraudulent removal or concealment of property to prevent its seizure as forfeited or in execution
207	Fraudulent claim to property to prevent its seizure as forfeited or in execution	244	Fraudulent claim to property to prevent its seizure as forfeited or in execution
208	Fraudulently suffering decree for sum not due	245	Fraudulently suffering decree for sum not due
209	Dishonestly making false claim in Court	246	Dishonestly making false claim in Court
210	Fraudulently obtaining decree for sum not due	247	Fraudulently obtaining decree for sum not due
211	False charge of offence made with intent to injure	248	False charge of offence made with intent to injure
212	Harbouring offender	249	Harbouring offender
213	Taking gift, etc., to screen an offender from punishment	250	Taking gift, etc., to screen an offender from punishment
214	Offering gift or restoration of property in consideration of screening offender	251	Offering gift or restoration of property in consideration of screening offender
215	Taking gift to help to recover stolen property, etc.	252	Taking gift to help to recover stolen property, etc.
216	Harbouring offender who has escaped from custody or whose apprehension has been ordered	253	Harbouring offender who has escaped from custody or whose apprehension has been ordered
216A	Penalty for harbouring robbers or dacoits	254	Penalty for harbouring robbers or dacoits
217	Public servant disobeying direction of law with intent to save person from punishment or property from forfeiture	255	Public servant disobeying direction of law with intent to save person from punishment or property from forfeiture
218	Public servant framing incorrect record or writing with intent to save person from punishment or property from forfeiture	256	Public servant framing incorrect record or writing with intent to save person from punishment or property from forfeiture
219	Public servant in judicial proceeding corruptly making report, etc., contrary to law	257	Public servant in judicial proceeding corruptly making report, etc., contrary to law
220	Commitment for trial or confinement by person having authority who knows that he is acting contrary to law	258	Commitment for trial or confinement by person having authority who knows that he is acting contrary to law

THE INDIAN PENAL CODE, 1860		THE BHARATIYA NYAYA SANHITA, 2023	
Section	**Heading**	**Section**	**Heading**
221	Intentional omission to apprehend on part of public servant bound to apprehend	259	Intentional omission to apprehend on part of public servant bound to apprehend
222	Intentional omission to apprehend on part of public servant bound to apprehend person under sentence or lawfully committed	260	Intentional omission to apprehend on part of public servant bound to apprehend person under sentence or lawfully committed
223	Escape from confinement or custody negligently suffered by public servant	261	Escape from confinement or custody negligently suffered by public servant
224	Resistance or obstruction by a person to his lawful apprehension	262	Resistance or obstruction by a person to his lawful apprehension
225	Resistance or obstruction to lawful apprehension of another person	263	Resistance or obstruction to lawful apprehension of another person
225A	Omission to apprehend, or sufferance of escape, on part of public servant, in cases not otherwise provided for	264	Omission to apprehend, or sufferance of escape, on part of public servant, in cases not otherwise provided for
225B	Resistance or obstruction to lawful apprehension or escape or rescue in cases not otherwise provided for	265	Resistance or obstruction to lawful apprehension or escape or rescue in cases not otherwise provided for
227	Violation of condition of remission of punishment	266	Violation of condition of remission of punishment
228	Intentional insult or interruption to public servant sitting in judicial proceeding	267	Intentional insult or interruption to public servant sitting in judicial proceeding
229	Personation of a juror or assessor	268	Personation of assessor
229A	Failure by person released on bail or bond to appear in Court	269	Failure by person released on bail bond or bond to appear in Court
268	Public nuisance	270	Public nuisance
269	Negligent act likely to spread infection of disease dangerous to life	271	Negligent act likely to spread infection of disease dangerous to life
270	Malignant act likely to spread infection of disease dangerous of life	272	Malignant act likely to spread infection of disease dangerous of life
271	Disobedience to quarantine rule	273	Disobedience to quarantine rule
272	Adulteration of food or drink intended for sale	274	Adulteration of food or drink intended for sale
273	Sale of noxious food or drink	275	Sale of noxious food or drink
274	Adulteration of drugs	276	Adulteration of drugs
275	Sale of adulterated drugs	277	Sale of adulterated drugs
276	Sale of drug as a different drug or preparation	278	Sale of drug as a different drug or preparation

THE INDIAN PENAL CODE, 1860		THE BHARATIYA NYAYA SANHITA, 2023	
Section	Heading	Section	Heading
277	Fouling water of public spring or reservoir	279	Fouling water of public spring or reservoir
278	Making atmosphere noxious to health	280	Making atmosphere noxious to health
279	Rash driving or riding on a public way	281	Rash driving or riding on a public way
280	Rash navigation of vessel	282	Rash navigation of vessel
281	Exhibition of false light, mark or buoy	283	Exhibition of false light, mark or buoy
282	Conveying person by water for hire in unsafe or overloaded vessel	284	Conveying person by water for hire in unsafe or overloaded vessel
283	Danger or obstruction in public way or line of navigation	285	Danger or obstruction in public way or line of navigation
284	Negligent conduct with respect to poisonous substance	286	Negligent conduct with respect to poisonous substance
285	Negligent conduct with respect to fire or combustible matter	287	Negligent conduct with respect to fire or combustible matter
286	Negligent conduct with respect to explosive substance	288	Negligent conduct with respect to explosive substance
287	Negligent conduct with respect to machinery	289	Negligent conduct with respect to machinery
288	Negligent conduct with respect to pulling down or repairing buildings	290	Negligent conduct with respect to pulling down, repairing or constructing building, etc.
289	Negligent conduct with respect to animal	291	Negligent conduct with respect to animal
290	Punishment for public nuisance in cases not otherwise provided for	292	Punishment for public nuisance in cases not otherwise provided for
291	Continuance of nuisance after injunction to discontinue	293	Continuance of nuisance after injunction to discontinue
292	Sale, etc., of obscene books, etc.	294	Sale, etc., of obscene books, etc.
293	Sale, etc., of obscene objects to young person	295	Sale, etc., of obscene objects to child
294	Obscene acts and songs	296	Obscene acts and songs
294A	Keeping lottery office	297	Keeping lottery office
295	Injuring or defiling place of worship with inrent to insult religion of any class	298	Injuring or defiling place of worship with inrent to insult religion of any class
295A	Deliberate and malicious acts, intended to outrage religious feelings of any class by insulting its religion or religious beliefs	299	Deliberate and malicious acts, intended to outrage religious feelings of any class by insulting its religion or religious beliefs
296	Disturbing religious assembly	300	Disturbing religious assembly

THE INDIAN PENAL CODE, 1860		THE BHARATIYA NYAYA SANHITA, 2023	
Section	**Heading**	**Section**	**Heading**
297	Trespassing on burial places, etc.	301	Trespassing on burial places, etc.
298	Uttering words, etc., with deliberate intent to wound religious feelings of any person	302	Uttering words, etc., with deliberate intent to wound religious feelings of any person
378	Theft	303(1)	Theft
379	Punishment for theft	303(2)	
-	(No Provision)	304	Snatching (New Section)
380	Theft in a dwelling house, etc.	305	Theft in a dwelling house, or means of transportation or place of worship, etc.
381	Theft by clerk or servant of property in possession of master	306	Theft by clerk or servant of property in possession of master
382	Theft after preparation made for causing death, hurt or restraint in order to the committing of theft	307	Theft after preparation made for causing death, hurt or restraint in order to the committing of theft
383	Extortion	308(1)	Extortion
384	Punishment for extortion	308(2)	Punishment increases to 7 years
385	Putting person infear of injury in order to commit extortion	308(3)	
387	Putting person in fear of death or of grievous hurt, in order to commit extortion	308(4)	
386	Extortion by putting a person in fear of death or grievous hurt	308(5)	
389	Putting person in fear of accusation of offence, in order to commit extortion	306(6)	
388	Extortion by threat of accusation of an offence punishable with death or imprisonment for life, etc.	308(7)	
390	Robbery	309	Robbery
392	Punishment for robbery		
393	Attempt to commit robbery		
394	Voluntarily causing hurt in committing robbery		
391	Dacoity	310	Dacoity
395	Punishment for dacoity		
396	Dacoity with murder		
399	Making preparation to commit dacoity		
400	Assembling for purpose of committing dacoity		
402	Punishment for belonging to gang of dacoits		

THE INDIAN PENAL CODE, 1860		THE BHARATIYA NYAYA SANHITA, 2023	
Section	**Heading**	**Section**	**Heading**
397	Robbery, or dacoity, with attempt to cause death or grievous hurt	311	Robbery, or dacoity, with attempt to cause death or grievous hurt
398	Attempt to commit robbery or dacoity when armed with deadly weapon	312	Attempt to commit robbery or dacoity when armed with deadly weapon
401	Punishment for belongings to gang of thieves	313	Punishment for belonging to gang of robbers, dacoits, etc.
403	Dishonest misappropriation of property	314	Dishonest misappropriation of property
404	Dishonest misappropriation of property possessed by deceased person at the time of his death	315	Dishonest misappropriation of property possessed by deceased person at the time of his death
405	Criminal breach of trust	316(1)	Criminal breach of trust
406	Punishment for criminal breach of trust	316(2)	
407	Criminal breach of trust by carrier, etc.	316(3)	
408	Criminal breach of trust by clerk or servant	316(4)	
409	Criminal breach of trust by public servant, or by banker, merchant or agent	316(5)	
410	Stolen property	317(1)	Stolen property
411	Dishonestly receiving stolen property	317(2)	
412	Dishonestly receiving property stolen in the commission of a dacoity	317(3)	
413	Habitually dealing in stolen property	317(4)	
414	Assisting in concealment of stolen property	317(5)	
415	Cheating	318(1)	Cheating
417	Punishment for cheating	318(2)	
418	Cheating with knowledge that wrongful loss may ensue to person whose interest offender is bound to protect	318(3)	
420	Cheating and dishonestly inducing delivery of property	318(4)	
416	Cheating by personation	319(1)	Cheating by personation
419	Punishment for cheating by personation	319(2)	

THE INDIAN PENAL CODE, 1860		THE BHARATIYA NYAYA SANHITA, 2023	
Section	Heading	Section	Heading
421	Dishonest or fraudulent removal or concealment of property to prevent distribution among creditors	320	Dishonest or fraudulent removal or concealment of property to prevent distribution among creditors
422	Dishonestly or fraudulently preventing debt being available for creditors	321	Dishonestly or fraudulently preventing debt being available for creditors
423	Dishonest or fraudulent execution of deed of transfer containing false statement of consideration	322	Dishonest or fraudulent execution of deed of transfer containing false statement of consideration
424	Dishonest or fraudulent removal or concealment of property	323	Dishonest or fraudulent removal or concealment of property
425 426 440	Mischief Punishment for mischief Mischief committed after preparation made for causing death or hurt	324(1) 324(2) 324(6)	Mischief Punishment for mischief
428 429	Mischief by killing or maiming animal of the value of ten rupees Mischief by killing or maiming cattle, etc., of any value or any animal of the value of fifty rupees	325	Mischief by killing or maiming animal
430 431 432 433 434 435 436	Mischief by injury to works of irrigation or by wrongfully diverting water Mischief by injury to public road, bridge, river or channel Mischief by causing inundation or obstruction to public drainage attended with damage Mischief by destroying, moving or rendering less useful a light-house or sea-mark Mischief by destroying or moving, etc., a land-mark fixed by public authority Mischief by fire or explosive substance with intent to cause damage to amount of one hundred or (in case of agricultural produce) ten rupees Mischief by fire or explosive substance with intent to destroy house, etc.	326(a) 326(b) 326(c) 326(d) 326(e) 326(f) 326(g)	Mischief by injury, inundation, fire or explosive substance, etc.

THE INDIAN PENAL CODE, 1860		THE BHARATIYA NYAYA SANHITA, 2023	
Section	**Heading**	**Section**	**Heading**
437	Mischief with intent to destroy or make unsafe a decked vessel or one of twenty tons burden	327(1)	Mischief with intent to destroy or make unsafe a rail, aircraft, decked vessel or one of twenty tons burden
438	Punishment for the mischief described in section 437 committed by fire or explosive substance	327(2)	
439	Punishment for intentionally running vessel aground or ashore with intent to commit theft, etc.	328	Punishment for intentionally running vessel aground or ashore with intent to commit theft, etc.
441	Criminal trespass	329(1)	Criminal trespass and house trespass
442	House-trespass	329(2)	
447	Punishment for criminal trespass	329(3)	
448	Punishment for house-trespass	329(4)	
443	Lurking house-trespass	330(1)	House-trespass and house-breaking
445	House-breaking	330(2)	
453	Punishment for lurking house-trespass or house-breaking	331	Punishment for house-trespass or house-breaking
456	Punishment for lurking house trespass or house-breaking by night		
454	Lurking house-trespass or house-breaking in order to commit offence punishable with imprisonment		
457	Lurking house-trespass or house-breaking by night in order to commit offence punishable with imprisonment		
455	Lurking house-trespass or house-breaking after preparation for hurt, assault or wrongful restraint		
458	Lurking house-trespass or house-breaking by night after preparation for hurt, assault, or wrongful restraint		
459	Grievous hurt caused whilst committing lurking house-trespass or house-breaking		
460	All persons jointly concerned in lurking house-trespass or house breaking by night punishable where death or grievous hurt caused by one of them		

THE INDIAN PENAL CODE, 1860		THE BHARATIYA NYAYA SANHITA, 2023	
Section	Heading	Section	Heading
449	House-trespass in order to commit offence punishable with death	332(a)	House-trespass in order to commit offence
450	House-trespass in order to commit offence punishable with imprisonment for life	332(b)	
451	House-trespass in order to commit offence punishable with imprisonment	332(c)	
452	House-trespass after preparation for hurt, assault or wrongful restraint	333	House-trespass after preparation for hurt, assault or wrongful restraint
461	Dishonestly breaking open receptacle containing property	334(1)	Dishonestly breaking open receptacle containing property
462	Punishment for same offence when committed by person entrusted with custody	334(2)	
464	Making a false document	335	Making a false document
463	Forgery	336(1)	Forgery
465	Punishment for forgery	336(2)	
468	Forgery for purpose of cheating	336(3)	
469	Forgery for purpose of harming reputation	336(4)	
466	Forgery of record of Court or of public register, etc.	337	Forgery of record of Court or of public register, etc.
467	Forgery of valuable security, will, etc.	338	Forgery of valuable security, will, etc.
474	Having possession of document described in section 466 or section 467, knowing it to be forged and intending to use it as genuine	339	Having possession of document described in section 337 or section 338, knowing it to be forged and intending to use it as genuine
470	Forged document or electronic record	340	Forged document or electronic record and using it as genuine
471	Using as genuine a forged document or electronic record		
472	Making or possessing counterfeit seal, etc., with intent to commit forgery punishable under section 467	341(1)	Making or possessing counterfeit seal, etc., with intent to commit forgery punishable under section 338
473	Making or possessing counterfeit seal, etc., with intent to commit forgery punishable otherwise	342(2)	

THE INDIAN PENAL CODE, 1860		THE BHARATIYA NYAYA SANHITA, 2023	
Section	Heading	Section	Heading
475	Counterfeiting device or mark used for authenticating documents described in section 467 or possessing counterfeit marked material	342	Counterfeiting device or mark used for authenticating documents described in section 338 or possessing counterfeit marked material
476	Counterfeiting device or mark used for authenticating documents other than those described in section 467, or possessing counterfeit marked material		
477	Fraudulent cancellation, destination etc,. of will authority to adopt, or valuable security	343	Fraudulent cancellation, destination etc,. of will authority to adopt, or valuable security
477A	Falsification of accounts	344	Falsification of accounts
479	Property mark	345	Property Mark
481	Using a false property mark		
482	Punishment for using a false property mark		
489	Tampering with property mark with intent to cause injury	346	Tampering with property mark with intent to cause injury
483	Counterfeiting a property mark used by another	347	Counterfeiting a property mark
484	Counterfeiting a mark used by a public servant		
485	Making or possession of any instrument for counterfeiting a property mark	348	Making or possession of any instrument for counterfeiting a property mark
486	Selling goods marked with a counterfeit property mark	349	Selling goods marked with a counterfeit property mark
487	Making a false mark upon any receptacle containing goods	350(1)	Making a false mark upon any receptacle containing goods
488	Punishment for making use of any such false mark	350(2)	Same content as earlier
505	Criminal intimidation	351(1)	Criminal intimidation
506	Punishment for criminal intimidation If threat be to cause death or grievous hurt, etc.	351(2)	
507	Criminal intimidation by an anonymous communication	351(4)	

THE INDIAN PENAL CODE, 1860		THE BHARATIYA NYAYA SANHITA, 2023	
Section	Heading	Section	Heading
504	Intentional insult with intent to provoke breach of peace	352	Intentional insult with intent to provoke breach of peace
505	Statements conducing to public mischief	353	Statements conducing to public mischief
508	Act caused by inducing person to believe that he will be rendered an object of Divine displeasure	354	Act caused by inducing person to believe that he will be rendered an object of Divine displeasure
510	Misconduct in public by a drunken person	355	Misconduct in public by a drunken person
499 500 501 502	Defamation Punishment for defamation Printing or engraving matter known to be defamatory Sale of printed or engraved substance containing defamatory matter	356	Defamation
491	Breach of contract to attend on and supply wants of helpless savings	357	Breach of contract to attend on and supply wants of helpless person
-	(No Provision)	358	Repeal and savings (New Section)

❖ ❖ ❖

Chapter 1

THE BHARATIYA NYAYA SANHITA, 2023

INTRODUCTION

The Bharatiya Nyaya Sanhita, 2023 (hereinafter referred to as "BNS") is a criminal legislation which seeks to replace and thoroughly revise the erstwhile Indian Penal Code, 1860 (hereinafter referred to as "IPC").

By amending, repealing, and adding several sections, this Sanhita adopts a refined approach to criminal offences. The new law preserves the applicable provisions of the IPC while introducing some new offences. It eliminates offences that have been invalidated by the Supreme Court and increases penalties for several serious crimes. It also tackles modern challenges like terrorism and organized crime, differentiating between major and minor offenses and imposing strict penalties.

SCHEME OF THE SANHITA

- **Bhartiya Nyaya Sanhita (BNS): Act No. 45 of 2023**
  - **Date of Enactment:** December 25, 2023.
  - **Effective Date:** July 1, 2024 (with the exception of Section 106(2))
- **Preamble of the Sanhita**: Preamble of the Sanhita declares it to be an "An Act to consolidate and amend the provisions relating to offences and for matters connected therewith or incidental thereto."
- **Number of Sections/Chapters/Schedule:** The Sanhita comprises a total of **358** sections divided into **20** chapters. Further, 20 new offences have been added to the BNS, and 19 provisions of the IPC have been removed.
- **Scope of Application**
  - The Sanhita has both intra-territorial and extra-territorial operations.
  - According to **Section 1(3)**, every person shall be liable to punishment under this Sanhita and not otherwise for every act or omission contrary to the provisions thereof, of which he shall be guilty within India.
  - According to **Section 1(4)**, any person liable, by any law for the time being in force in India, to be tried for an offence committed beyond India shall be dealt with according to the provisions of this Sanhita for any act committed beyond India in the same manner as if such act had been committed within India.

NEED FOR INTRODUCING BHARATIYA NYAYA SANHITA, 2023

- The traditional criminal laws in India were originally crafted to serve British interests, with a primary focus on punishment rather than justice. It remained a relic of the pre-Independence British era, containing outdated provisions that no longer aligned with the evolving discourse on modern rights and inclusion. However, the recent reform of these laws through three key legislations marks a significant shift towards a legal framework that aligns with the evolving needs of society.
- This legislative progress sets India on a course towards a more equitable, accessible, and adaptable legal system. The reforms prioritize fair, timely, and evidence-based

trials, aiming to simplify the process of obtaining justice. These groundbreaking laws herald a future where justice is not only delivered but also inclusive and reflective of India's dynamic spirit.

- Unlike the IPC, which primarily focused on the perpetrator and defining punishments, the BNS places greater emphasis on the victims. It broadens the scope and inclusivity of offenses, particularly those against children and women, reflecting a shift towards a more victim-centered approach in the criminal justice system. The very name of the BNS underscores its objectives of fairness, inclusivity, and justice for all.

SOME MAJOR CHANGES INTRODUCED

- **Community Service as a Punishment**
  - As a new addition to the chapter on punishments, community service has been added as one of the punishments that may be given upon the conviction of an individual.
  - For offences such as attempting suicide to compel or restrain the exercise of lawful power, defamation, misconduct in public by a drunken person, and failure to appear at the specified place and time as required by a proclamation published under **sub-section (1) of section 84** of the BNS, 2023, community service can be awarded in addition to the prescribed punishment.
- **Commission of Offences through Electronic Means**
  - A new addition has been made in the form of **Section 2(39)** of the BNS which clearly states that all words or expressions with regards to technology and digital media in general, shall have the same meanings as those given in the Information Technology Act, 2002, as well as the Bhartiya Nagarik Suraksha Sanhita, 2023.
  - This will enable a much wider scope in terms of recognising various acts that fall under the ambit of an offence, thereby contributing to the detection and deterrence of crime. **Section 2(8)** of the BNS states that documents now include electronic and digital records.
- **Snatching as a Separate Offence**
  - **Section 304** of the BNS provides, for the first time, snatching as an offence distinct from theft. Snatching is a subset of theft wherein movable property is taken by force or quickness of action from a person.
  - Unlike theft, where the accused may employ deceitful means and take away property even without the knowledge of the person who owns it, snatching always involves the victim taking cognizance of the action at the time of commission itself, and it may even be accompanied with hurt or violence in order to give effect to the snatching.
  - The maximum punishment for snatching has also been set at three years instead of seven years for theft.
- **Offences Against Woman and Child:** Offences against woman and child which were scattered throughout in Indian Penal Code, 1860, have been consolidated under **Chapter V** titled "Of Offences Against Woman and Child Of Sexual Offences" of the Bharatiya Nyaya Sanhita, 2023. Offences against woman and child have been given precedence over other offences.
- **Organised Crime:** The new law introduces organized crime under **Section 111** of the BNS. This Section defines organized crime to include recognized offenses such as kidnapping and land grabbing, among others, when committed by or on behalf of a syndicate. Additionally, it outlines definitions for an organized crime syndicate, continuing unlawful activity, and economic offenses.
- **Petty Organised Crime:** BNS has also added Petty Organised Crime under **Section 112**, which states that whoever, being a member of a group or gang, either singly or

jointly, commits any act of theft, snatching, cheating, unauthorised selling of tickets, unauthorised betting or gambling, selling of public examination question papers or any other similar criminal act, is said to commit petty organised crime.

- **Terrorist Act**
  - A significant change resulting from the criminal law amendment is the introduction of the "Terrorist Act," which was previously absent from the IPC. **Section 113** of the BNS discusses Terrorist Acts, which are a new addition to the purview.
  - Mostly inspired by the provisions of the Unlawful Activities (Prevention) Act, 1967 (hereinafter referred to as the "UAPA"), Section 113 introduces fines, the limits of which are specifically mentioned, across various sub-sections, which are absent under the scheme of the UAPA.
- **Mob Lynching**
  - Mob lynching refers to the act of a mob killing an individual or group, usually due to perceived offenses or social prejudices, without any legal trial or due process. India did not have a specific central law that deals exclusively with mob lynching despite a rise in the incidents.
  - However, through an addition to the provision of murder, under **Section 103** of the BNS, any murder committed by a group of five or more people, specifically based on conditions like religion, caste or community, place of birth, personal belief, etc., is now distinctly punishable with death or life imprisonment with a fine, just like how a murder is punished.
- **Stringent Punishment for Hit-and-Run Cases:** The law also imposes severe penalties for hit-and-run incidents. If a driver causes a death through rash and negligent driving and then flees without reporting the incident to a police officer or a magistrate immediately, they face imprisonment for up to ten years and may also be subject to a fine.
- **Sexual Intercourse by Employing Deceitful means, etc: Section 69** introduces a novel provision, addressing sexual intercourse through deceitful means, or false promise of employment or promotion, or marrying by suppressing identity.

Removal of Certain Offences and Provisions

- **Removal of Adultery:** In conformity with a seminal decision of the Hon'ble Supreme Court of India in the case of **Joseph Shine v. Union of India,** which decriminalized the offence of adultery as given under **Section 497** of the IPC, the BNS completely removed the provision.
- **Non-Reproduction of Section 377 of the IPC**
  - In 2018, a landmark judgment of the Hon'ble Supreme Court of India that is **Navtej Singh Johar v. Union of India,** struck down the provision of **Section 377,** which punished acts of consensual sexual intercourse between adults.
  - The Hon'ble Court considered that the provision in question was a grave violation of Article 19(1)(a) of the Constitution, which guarantees all citizens a fundamental right to freedom of expression.
  - However, the remainder of the provision was kept in force, pertaining to bestiality, sodomy, etc., as they are separate offences within the same section, having no link with the sub-section in contention.
  - The BNS has completely removed all the provisions of **Section 377** of the IPC, even the ones that have not been expressly declared to be unconstitutional, as discussed above.
- **Removal of Sedition**
  - One of the most significant changes in the BNS is the removal of the colonial law of sedition, as was enshrined under **Section 124A** of the IPC.

- However, it must be noted that **Section 152** (Act endangering sovereignty, unity and integrity of India) of the BNS retains the essence of Section 124A which states that whoever, purposely or knowingly, by words, either spoken or written, or by signs, or by visible representation, or by electronic communication or by use of financial mean, or otherwise, excites or attempts to excite, secession or armed rebellion or subversive activities, or encourages feelings of separatist activities or endangers sovereignty or unity and integrity of India; or indulges in or commits any such act shall be punished with imprisonment for life or with imprisonment which may extend to seven years, and shall also be liable to fine.

- **Attempt to Commit Suicide Is No Longer an Offence:** Under Section 309 of the IPC, attempting to commit suicide was previously punishable. However, this provision has been entirely removed from the BNS. Instead, **Section 226** of the BNS addresses the act of attempting suicide to coerce or restrict the exercise of lawful authority, with penalties including simple imprisonment for up to one year, a fine, both, or community service.
- **Deleted Provisions:** Several other offences such as **Thug, Offences concerning Weights and measures** have been deleted.

Other Relevant Additions and Alterations

- **Use of Inclusive Language**
  - As a first, the BNS uses the term transgender under **Section 2(10),** under the definition of "gender", which was absent in the IPC.
  - In general, various provisions have been made gender neutral, such as the offence of voyeurism, having been defined and punished under **Section 77** of the BNS.
    - However, it must be noted that Section 77, along with other provisions, have incorporated the gender neutrality of the perpetrator, and not the victim. Therefore, for example, even though a woman may now be convicted for the offence of voyeurism, a man will never be able to complain about voyeuristic behavior, an area where the BNS could've legislated upon.
  - Similarly, a lot of offences, such as rape, have still been gendered, wherein only a woman can be a victim. This excludes transgenders from availing themselves of protection under various sexual offences, leaving their inclusion under Section 2(10) superficial.
    - However, it cannot be said that gender neutrality in the context of victims was not taken into consideration at all since, under **Section 96**, the BNS uses the word child, replacing the words minor girls in the erstwhile Section 366A of the IPC.
- **Alteration in Definitions:** Under IPC, there was no definition clause; instead there were interpretation clauses from **Sections 6 to 52A**. Under the new Act, these sections are grouped together and **Part II, Section 2** has definitions separately.
  - Various definitions have been altered to clarify certain intentions, such as in **Section 43** of the BNS, the word 'night' given under **Section 103** of the IPC has been replaced by the words 'after sunset and before sunrise'.
  - Further, under **Section 41** of the BNS, 'fire' has been expanded to include 'mischief by fire or any explosive substance'.
  - A new definition of "child" and transgender has been added to **Section 2 (3)** and **(10)** under the Sanhita. Aside from this, the meaning of "court" in **Section 2(5),** "document" in **Section 2(8),** which now includes electronic and digital records, "movable property" in **Section 2(21)**, and other terms have been changed.
- **Consolidation of Inchoate Offences:** All inchoate offences, namely conspiracy,

attempt, and abetment, have been incorporated under the same chapter. Under the IPC, they were given in various sections present in different Chapters of the Code.

- **Sexual Intercourse for False Promise of Marriage: Section 69** of the BNS is a relevant addition as it introduces an offence that was not present in the IPC. The offence of practicing deceit in order to effect sexual intercourse not amounting to rape has been considered a punishable offence under Section 69. Here, deceitful means are inclusive of false promises and inducements.
- **Rape**
  - Earlier it was defined under **Section 375** of the IPC, but it is now in **Section 63** of the BNS. The controversial exception for rape in a marriage, called Exception 2, is still in place. However, the age requirements have been changed. The wife must now be at least 18 years old in order to be able to agree for this exception, up from 15 years old.
  - Punishment for rape has been given under **Section 64** of BNS.
  - But, even after a lot of discussion, the rules against rape are still not gender-neutral. To this day, they still say that only women can be victims and only men can be offenders. The new Act talks about transgender people, but it doesn't say anything about them in the parts that talk about rape.
  - People who have sex with a woman while lying or promising to marry her can be fined and sent to prison for up to ten years under the new law (**Section 69**). This only applies if the person is not planning to keep the promise of marriage.
  - As of now, **Section 70** of the BNS provides punishment for gang rape has been changed.
- **Expansion of Provision of Gang Rape:** The provision of Section 376DA of the IPC that dealt with gang rape has been expanded and incorporated in the BNS in the form of Section 70(2), wherein a major change is the alteration of the words from 'under the age of sixteen to under the age of eighteen', thereby expanding the scope of the offence by bringing more cases under its purview.
- **Enhanced Punishment in case of Rash or Negligent Act:** While punishments for various offences have been significantly increased, one of the most notable changes is the enhancement of the punishment for causing death by a rash or negligent act. Previously covered under Section 304A IPC with a maximum sentence of two years, this offence now carries a 'penalty of up to five years' under **Section 106(1)** of the BNS.
- **Attempt to Murder:** Earlier attempt to murder under **Section 307** of IPC, has now, modified under **Section 109** of the BNS, anyone who commits an act with the intention or knowledge that, if it resulted in death, would constitute murder, faces imprisonment of up to ten years, along with a fine; if harm is inflicted, the punishment could include life imprisonment or the aforementioned penalties.
- **Making, Publishing or Circulating of False Information:** As a step towards curbing the spread of misinformation, the BNS also includes **Section 353**, which renders the making, publishing or circulating of false information backed with dishonest intention a punishable offence. Such a provision was not explicitly mentioned in the IPC, and it supplements the functioning of other laws dedicated to the same goal.
- **Forgery of Government Issued Documents:** Under **Section 337** of the BNS, which has incorporated the erstwhile offence of forgery of a document as given under Section 446 of the IPC, now the forgery of Government issued documents, such as the Aadhar Card, or the Voter Identity Card is also in the ambit, thereby expanding the scope of the offence.
- **Enhancement of Punishment in case of Mischief:** Mischief as an offence has been given specific pecuniary limits in **Sub-**

sections (4) and (5) of Section 324 of the BNS, wherein the amount of imprisonment increases as the value of the property destroyed or converted increases.

- **Gender Neutral Provisions**
  - The offence of kidnapping as envisaged in **Section 137** of the BNS has removed the distinction between the age of minor boys and girls for the purposes of kidnapping and now includes the words 'any child' which has been defined under 2(3) to mean 'any person below the age of eighteen years.' This has brought the kidnapping of boys aged between sixteen and eighteen into the ambit of the offence of kidnapping, which had been absent under Section 361 of the IPC.
  - **Section 76 and 77** of the BNS provides for gender neutral provision whoever causes an offence of assault or use of criminal force to woman with intent to disrobe or voyeurism is punishable under the respective sections. Earlier, in IPC, this offence was punishable for man only but now BNS makes it gender neutral.
  - **Section 141** provides for importation of girls or boys from foreign country. Whoever imports into India from any country outside India 'any girl under the age of twenty-one years or any boy under the age of eighteen years' with intent that girl or boy may be, or knowing it to be likely that girl or boy will be, forced or seduced to illicit intercourse with another person, shall be punishable under this Section.
- **Increment in Punishments:** Moreover, for 33 offences, the maximum sentence (i.e. imprisonment) for jail time has been increased, for 83 crimes, fines have been increased, and for 23 crimes, a mandatory minimum punishment has been put in place, 'Community Service' has been incorporated as a punitive measure for six minor offences.

COMPARATIVE CHART OF COMMON SECTIONS OF IPC AND BNS GENERALLY USED

Indian Penal Code, 1860 (IPC)	Title	Bharatiya Nyaya Sanhita, (2023)
Section 302	Punishment for murder	Section 103
Section 304B	Punishment for dowry death	Section 80
Section 379	Punishment for theft	Section 303
Section 376	Punishment for rape	Section 64
Section 420	Punishment for cheating	Section 318
Section 498A	Women subjected to cruelty by husband	Section 85
Section 120B	Punishment for criminal conspiracy	Section 61

❖❖❖

Chapter 2

GENERAL EXPLANATION

INTRODUCTION

The Bharatiya Nyaya Sanhita (BNS) 2023 includes Arrangement of Clauses, while the first chapter deals with **Preliminary Provisions (Section 1- Section 3).** The Section 8 to 52A of IPC are replaced by **Section 2 & 3 of BNS**. The sanhita includes definitions of "child" and "transgender" in **Section 2(3)** and **Section 2(10)**, which was not mentioned in the IPC 1862. In addition, the definition of "court" in **Section 2(5),** the definition of "document" in **Section 2(8)** (which now include electronic and digital records), the definition of "movable property" in **Section 2(21)**, and other definitions have become more constructive.

COMPARATIVE CHART OF THE BNS AND IPC		
Bharatiya Nyaya Sanhita, 2023 (BNS)	**Title**	**Indian Penal Code, 1860 (IPC)**
Section 1	Short title, commencement and application **EARLIER TITLE-** (Title and extent of operation of the Code)	Section 1
Section 1(3)	Short title, commencement and application **EARLIER TITLE- (**Punishment of offences committed within India)	Section 2
Section 1(4)	Short title, commencement and application **EARLIER TITLE-** (Punishment of offences committed beyond, but which by law may be tried within, India)	Section 3
Section 1(5)	Short title, commencement and application **EARLIER TITLE-** (Extension of Code to extra- territorial offences)	Section 4
Section 1(6)	Short title, commencement and application **EARLIER TITLE-** (Certain laws not to be affected by this Act)	Section 5
Section 2(1)	Act	Section 33
Section 2(2)	Animal	Section 47
Section 2(3)	Child (New section added)	
Section 2(4)	Counterfeit	Section 28
Section 2(5)	Court **EARLIER TITLE-** (Court of Justice)	Section 20
Section 2 (6)	Death	Section 46
Section 2 (7)	Dishonestly	Section 24
Section 2(8)	Document	Section 29

Section 2(9)	Fraudulently	Section 25
Section 2(10)	Gender	Section 8
Section 2(11)	Good faith	Section 52
Section 2(12)	Government	Section 17
Section 2(13)	Harbour	Section 52A
Section 2(14)	Injury	Section 44
Section 2(15)	Illegal and legally bound to do	Section 43
Section 2(16)	Judge	Section 19
Section 2(17)	Life	Section 45
Section 2(18)	Local law	Section 42
Section 2(19)	Man	Section 10
Section 2(20)	Month and year	Section 49
Section 2(21)	Movable property	Section 22
Section 2(22)	Number	Section 9
Section 2(23)	Oath	Section 51
Section 2(24)	Offence	Section 40
Section 2(25)	Omission	Section 33
Section 2(26)	Person	Section 11
Section 2(27)	Public	Section 12
Section 2 (28)	Public servant	Section 21
Section 2 (29)	Reason to believe	Section 26
Section 2(30)	Special law	Section 41
Section 2(31)	Valuable security	Section 30
Section 2(32)	Vessel	Section 48
Section 2(33)	Voluntarily	Section 39
Section 2(34)	Will	Section 31
Section 2(35)	Woman **EARLIER TITLE-** (Man, Woman)	Section 10
Section 2(36)	Wrongful gain	Section 23
Section 2(37)	Wrongful loss	Section 23
Section 2(38)	"Gaining wrongfully" "losing wrongfully"	Section 23
Section 2(39)	New sub-section added	
Section 3	General explanations **EARLIER TITLE-** (Property in possession of wife, clerk or servant)	Section 27
Section 3(1)	General explanations **EARLIER TITLE-** (Definitions in the Code to be understood subject to exceptions)	Section 6
Section 3(4)	General explanations **EARLIER TITLE-** (Words referring to acts include illegal omissions)	Section 32

Section 3(5)	General explanations **EARLIER TITLE-** (Acts done by several persons in furtherance of common intention)	Section 34
Section 3(6)	General explanations **EARLIER TITLE-** (When such an act is criminal by reason of its being done with criminal knowledge or intention)	Section 35
Section 3(7)	General explanations **EARLIER TITLE-** (Effect caused partly by act and partly by omission)	Section 36
Section 3(8)	General explanations **EARLIER TITLE-** (Co-operation by doing one of several acts constituting an offence)	Section 37
Section 3(9)	General explanations **EARLIER TITLE-** (Persons concerned in criminal act may be guilty of different offences)	Section 38

CHANGES IN BNS IN COMPARISON TO IPC

- **Section 1(4)** of BNS corresponding to Section 3 of IPC has been changed as follows:
  - The words "any Indian law" are replaced with **"any law for the time being in force in India"**
- **Section 1(5)** of BNS corresponding to Section 4 of IPC has been changed as follows:
  - The Explanation (b) to the Section 4 of the IPC has been omitted. Also, herein the word "Uganda" has been replaced with **"any place without and beyond India"** under the Illustration to the section.
  - A new definition of 'Child' is introduced in Section 2(3) of the BNS. It means a child below the age of 18 years.
- **Section 2(8)** of BNS corresponding to Section 29 of IPC has been changed as follows:
  - The words **"and includes electronic and digital record"** have been added.
- **Section 2(10)** of BNS corresponding to Section 8 of IPC has been changed as follows:
  - The word **"transgender"** is added to the definition of "gender" and The **"Explanation to Section 2 (10)"** of the BNS is a newly added provision
- **Section 2(20)** of BNS corresponding to Section 49 of IPC has been changed as follows:
  - The word "British calendar" has been **changed to "Gregorian calendar"**
- **Section 2(24)** of BNS corresponding to Section 40 of IPC has been changed as follows:
  - The general definition of offence which was construed through the words "the word "offence" denotes a thing made punishable by this Code" is changed to **"offence" means an act made punishable by this Sanhita"**
- **Section 2(28)** of BNS corresponding to Section 21 of IPC has been changed as follows:
  - The term "Military" has been changed to **"Army'**. The term **"juryman" is Omitted**. The words **"as defined in clause (31) of section 3 of the General Clauses Act, 1897"**are added for understanding the term "local authority". The words **"as defined in clause (31) of section 3 of the General Clauses Act, 1897"** are added for understanding the term "Government company"

GENERAL EXPLANATIONS

(Note: ***Sections 2(2), 2(5), 2(7), 2(8), 2(9), 2(10), 2(13), 2(16), 2(21), 2(26), 2(36), 2(37), 2(38)*** *of the BNS corresponds to* ***Sections 47, 20, 24, 29, 25, 8, 52A, 19, 22, 11, 23*** *of the IPC respectively*)

- **Animal**: **Section 2(2)** of BNS defines "Animal", means any living creature which does not include any human being.
- **Child: Section 2(3)** defines child as any person below the age of eighteen years. This Section is a newly added Section in BNS.
- **Court : Section 2(5)** of BNS defines Court. It means a Judge who is empowered by law to act judicially alone, or a body of Judges which is empowered by law to act judicially as a body, when such a Judge or body of Judges is acting judicially.
- **Dishonestly**: It is defined under **Section 2(7)** of BNS as anyone who engages in an action with the purpose of causing wrongful gain to one person or wrongful loss to another person is considered to be acting dishonestly.
  - It is crucial in this section that the accused has performed the crime with the deliberate goal of gaining anything unlawfully or causing harm to someone else.
- **Document: Section 2(8)** of BNS defines the term "document" as any content that is represented or described on a material using letters, figures, marks, or a combination of these methods. This definition also includes electronic and digital records that are intended or can be used as evidence of the content in question.
  - **Explanation 1** of this section meant that the method or material utilized to create the letters, figures, or marks, as well as the intended application of the evidence in a court, are not important.
  - For Examples:
    - A document is a written expression that outlines the conditions of a contract and can serve as evidence of the contract.
    - A cheque issued by a bank is a written instrument.
    - A power-of-attorney is a legal instrument.
    - A document refers to a map or plan that is designed to be utilized or has the potential to be used as proof.
    - A document is a written composition that provides guidance or instructions.
  - **Explanation 2** of this section explains that any information conveyed through letters, figures, or symbols, as defined by commercial or other customary practices, must be considered as conveyed by such letters, figures, or symbols as intended in this section, even if not explicitly stated.
- **Fraudulently**: **Section 2(9)** of BNS defines "Fraudulently" as Fraudulent conduct refers to actions performed with the specific intention to deceive and defraud, and not for any other purpose.
  - The term "intent to defraud" refers to the deliberate intention to deceive someone in a way that could result in their property loss as well as infringement of legal right. When something is presented in a way that is not genuine or accurate. The act of defrauding encompasses the violation of rights pertaining to property, life, and liberty.
- **Gender**: **Section 2(10)** provides that the pronoun "he" and its derivatives are used of any person, whether **male, female or transgender**.
  - Explanation.– "transgender" shall have the meaning assigned to it in clause (k) of **Section 2** of the Transgender Persons (Protection of Rights) Act, 2019

- **Harbour**: **Section 2(13)** provides that it includes supplying a person with shelter, food, drink, money, clothes, arms, ammunition or means of conveyance, or the assisting a person by any means, whether of the same kind as those enumerated in this clause or not, to evade apprehension.
- **Judge: Section 2(16)** of BNS defines Judge as an individual who hold an official designation as a judge, as well as those who are legally authorized to render a final judgment in any legal proceeding, whether it be civil or criminal. This includes judgments that are definitive, judgments that would become definitive if not appealed, and judgments that would become definitive if confirmed by another authority. It also includes individuals who are part of a group empowered by law to render such judgments.
- **Movable Property**: **Section 2(21)** defines Movable property as it includes property of every description, except land and things attached to the earth or permanently fastened to anything which is attached to the earth.
  - In the case of **Avtar Singh v. State,(1965),** it was established that electricity does not qualify as movable property.
- **Person: Section 2(26)** defines Person as it includes any corporate entity, regardless of its legal status whether incorporated or not, is considered a legal person. There are many points to keep in mind when we talk about a legal person:
  - An idol is considered a legal entity and is able to own property, thereby qualifying as a person under **Section 2(26)** held in **Jabbar v. State (1996)**.
  - An unborn child that has reached full development is considered a person.
  - Nagar Nigam is an entity that is not subject to jail but can be fined.
- **Wrongful Gain: Section 2(36)** defines wrongful gain as it means gain by unlawful means of property to which the person gaining is not legally entitled.
- **Wrongful Loss: Section 2(37)** defines wrongful loss as it means the loss by unlawful means of property to which the person losing it is legally entitled.
- **Gaining Wrongfully and Losing Wrongfully: Section 2(38)** defines Gaining wrongfully and Losing wrongfully as a person is said to gain wrongfully when such person retains wrongfully, as well as when such person acquires wrongfully. A person is said to lose wrongfully when such person is wrongfully kept out of any property, as well as when such person is wrongfully deprived of property.
  - **Wrongful** refers to the act of infringing against someone's legal rights without any justifiable reason.
  - **Unlawful** means refer to methods or actions that are not authorized or allowed by the law. Wrongful gains refer to the acquisition or retention of property or assets in an unlawful or unjust manner. This can occur through both wrongful acquisition and wrongful retention.
- **Transgender: Section 8** of IPC explicitly acknowledges only the male and female genders in its definition of "gender". The revised definition of "gender" in **Section 2(10)** of BNS now includes the recognition of "transgender" as well as the genders of "male" and "female". Gender [Section 2(10) of BNS]
- Transgender individuals are officially acknowledged as a distinct gender and their identity is clearly defined. **Section 2(10)** of the law explicitly includes transgender individuals and provides a definition for this term, which was not previously done in **Section 8** of the Indian Penal Code (IPC).
- The document is referred to as **Section 2(8)** of BNS or **Section 29** of IPC. According to **Section 2(8)** of BNS, the term "documents" include both electronic and digital records.

- **Judge** [defined in Section 2(16) of the BNS]. Section 19 of the Indian Penal Code (IPC), 1860, pertains to the definition of a "Judge". The definition of "Judge" in the old law is highly intricate.
- The definition of "Judge" encompasses not just persons who hold the official title of Judge, but also those who possess the power to issue final verdicts in any legal action, regardless of whether it is civil or criminal in nature. This concept includes those who have the authority to issue judgments that, if not challenged, would be regarded as final and conclusive. It also encompasses those who are part of a legally authorized group responsible for making such decisions.

DIFFERENCE BETWEEN IPC AND BNS

- IPC did not include a definition clause. The interpretation provisions were distributed among Sections 8 to 52A of the IPC.
- The definition of 'section' in section 50 of IPC has been eliminated by BNS because it is now a widely used term in numerous legislations and does not require any more explanation or clarification.
- The revised interpretation of the term 'child' can be found in section 2(3) of the BNS. Section 2(3) of BNS is a recently added clause. According to Section 2(3) of BNS, the term 'child' is defined as any individual who is under the age of 18 years.

JURISDICTION

- The Bharatiya Nyaya Sanhita (BNS) of 2023, similar to its predecessor, the Indian Penal Code (IPC), addresses two key aspects of jurisdiction in criminal matters: inter-territorial and extra-territorial jurisdiction.
- **Intra-Territorial and Extra-Territorial Jurisdictions**
  - As a general rule, enforcement of statutory law is always intra-territorial. No country will allow another country to enforce its laws within its territory. **Section 1** provides for intra territorial applicability of BNS, If any person commits the violation of BNS within the territory of India he shall be punishable under the sanhita.
  - Any person who commits the offence from outside India but effected upon the territory of India will also be said to have committed the offence within the territory of India because the effect of the offence will be directly upon the territory of India. Personal presence of the accused in India is not necessary at the time of commission of offence.

Case law

- **Mobarik Ali Ahmad v. State of Bombay, (1957)**
  - In this case, the Supreme Court held that the basis of jurisdiction under Section 2 of the Indian Penal Code is the place where the crime is committed. Corporal presence of the offender is immaterial.
  - The word 'every person' under this section means and includes citizens of India as well as non-citizens.
  - The Supreme Court clarified that the phrase 'every person' means all persons without limitation irrespective of nationality, allegiance, rank, caste, creed or color.
  - This section must be understood as comprehending every person without exception barring such as may be specifically exempted from criminal proceedings by virtue of Constitution or any other statutory provision.
- **Extra Territorial Jurisdiction**
  - The Bharatiya Nyaya Sanhita (BNS) of 2023 have extra-territorial operations. They may empower courts to exercise jurisdiction over citizens of the State even though they have committed the crime beyond the jurisdictional limits of the State concerned.

- **Clause 3 read with clause 4 of Section 1** deals with extraterritorial application of Bhartiya Nyaya Sanhita (BNS). When a person has committed a violation of the provisions of BNS outside the territory of India, but will be punishable under BNS. Provisions of these clauses extend the jurisdiction of courts in India over citizens of India beyond the territorial limits of India. Clause 3 provides that an act constituting an offence in India shall also be an offence when committed outside India.
- If any person, liable by any law for the time being in force in India, does an act in a foreign country which is not an offence in that country but is an offence in India, he may be prosecuted in India. This section gives the jurisdiction to Indian courts to try any person for offences committed beyond India, as though it had been committed in India. Following conditions are to be fulfilled:
  - Person should have committed an act outside India, which if committed in India would be punishable.
  - That person is liable under some Indian law to be tried in India for that offence.

- Clause 5 provides for extension of sanhita to extraterritorial offences. It provides that the provisions of this sanhita apply also to any offence committed by:
  - Any citizen of India in any place without and beyond India.
  - Any person on any ship or aircraft registered in India wherever it may be.
  - Any person in any place without and beyond India committing offence targeting a computer resource located in India.

Illustrative Scenarios

- **Scenario 1: Indian Citizen Abroad:** An Indian citizen commits fraud while residing in a foreign country. Under the BNS 2023, the individual can be prosecuted in India for the offense due to the extra-territorial jurisdiction provisions.
- **Scenario 2: Cybercrime**
  - **Impacting India:** A cyberattack originating from a foreign country targets Indian government websites. The BNS 2023 empowers Indian authorities to pursue legal action against the perpetrators, leveraging international cooperation mechanisms.
- **Scenario 3: Terrorism:** An act of terrorism plotted and executed abroad targets Indian nationals or interests. The BNS 2023 provides the legal framework to prosecute individuals involved in such acts, even if they are not physically present in India.

❖ ❖ ❖

Chapter 3

FUNDAMENTAL PRINCIPLES OF CRIMINAL LAW

INTRODUCTION

A crime or an offence can be described as an act which is prohibited by law and is so grave or serious in nature that it revolts against the moral sentiments of the society. Precisely speaking, the gravity or seriousness attached to an offence distinguishes it from a civil wrong and makes the offender liable for punishment. The criminal liability of an offender is adjudged on the touchstone of the legal principle which is embodied in the latin maxim "*actus non facit reum nisi mens sit rea*"; the maxim implies that an act of a person does not make him guilty unless he does that act with a guilty mind.

ACTUS NON FACIT REUM NISI MENS SIT REA

- The Latin maxim ***"actus non facit reum nisi mens sit rea"*** embodies the foundational principle of criminal law and literally means that "an act does not make one guilty unless the mind is also legally blameworthy". In other words, an act to be criminal must be done with a legally blameworthy or guilty mind.
- This maxim forms the very basis and foundation of criminal law and establishes both, a guilty act (*actus reus*) as well as a guilty mind (*mens rea*), as the necessary elements of a crime. It guards against wrongful punishment of an innocent person and ensures the establishment of a fair and effective criminal justice delivery system.
- Moreover, this maxim underscores the importance of mental state in determining culpability for criminal actions. In other words, it distinguishes a crime from civil injuries by making the guilty mind an essential ingredient of an offence.
- In view of the maxim, "*Mens Rea*" and "*Actus Reus*" are the two essential elements of a crime. Besides "*Mens Rea*" and "*Actus Reus*", reference to two other indispensable elements of a crime is also necessary; they are namely: First, a human being who is under legal obligation to act in a particular way and is also a fit subject for infliction of punishment and second, an injury to another human being or to the society at large.
- Therefore, the four essential elements of a crime are as under:
  - **Offender:** A human being who is under legal obligation to act in a particular way and is a fit subject for the infliction of the appropriate punishment by law.
  - **Mens Rea:** A legally blameworthy or guilty state of mind of the offender.
  - **Actus Reus:** An act or omission which is forbidden by law but is nevertheless done by the offender in furtherance of his mens rea.
  - **Injury:** An injury to another human being or to society at large by such an act of the offender. The injury means violation of a legal right and implies harm to another person or the society at large in body, mind, property or reputation.

Exceptions to the maxim *"Actus Non Facit Reum Nisi Mens Sit Rea"*

- **Absolute or Strict Liability Offences**: In certain offences, the law does not require proof of mens rea for criminal liability but punishes the offender on a mere commission or omission of the guilty act. These offences are referred to as the offences imposing absolute or strict criminal liability. These offences are generally regulatory in nature and emphasise on compliance rather than on intent (e.g., traffic violations, Statutory rape).
- **Public Welfare Offences**: These offences are the species of absolute/ strict liability offences and are primarily concerned with the protection of public health, safety, or welfare (e.g., The Prevention of Food Adulteration Act, 1954; The Essential Commodities Act, 1955, various Pollution Control laws etc.).

MENS REA

- *"Mens Rea"* represents the mental aspect of a crime. It is such mental state of the accused which is criminal in nature, i.e. prohibited by criminal law. It covers a wide range of mental conditions, the presence of which attach criminality to the act or omission of the offender.
- It is important to note that mens rea must coexist with *"Actus Reus"* which represents the physical element of a crime. Therefore, a mere criminal intention, not followed by a criminal act/ omission, does not constitute a crime.
- It is important to note that BNS does not use the word *"Mens Rea"* in any one of its provisions. However, the essence of *mens rea* is reflected in almost every offence of BNS in one or the other form.
- Depending upon the nature of a particular offence, BNS has incorporated the doctrine of *mens rea* in almost every offence by using the words such as "voluntarily", "intentionally", "knowingly", "with reason to believe", "dishonestly", "fraudulently", "maliciously", "intentional cooperation" etc. The aforesaid words invariably indicate the legally blameworthy mental condition which is an essential ingredient of a particular offence and is required to be present at the time of commission of such offence.
- **Intention**: The highest degree of *mens rea*, where the person aims to bring about a particular consequence. Intent is a subjective state of mind that must accompany the acts of certain crimes to constitute a violation.
- **Knowledge**: Awareness of certain facts or circumstances, leading to a conscious decision to act or refrain from acting. It is a person's state of mind towards existent facts that he has personally observed or whose existence has been transmitted to him by others whose veracity he has no cause to dispute.
- **Recklessness**: Conscious disregard of a substantial and unjustifiable risk. A person is said to be reckless when it comes to the consequences of his actions if he foresees the possibility of them happening but neither desires nor expects them to happen.
- **Negligence**: Failure to be aware of a substantial and unjustifiable risk where such failure constitutes a deviation from the standard of care that a reasonable person would observe.

Case Laws Illustrating *Mens Rea*

- **State of Maharashtra v. M.H. George (1965)**, in this case M.H. George was caught smuggling gold into India without declaring it to customs authorities. The Supreme Court held that mens rea was not a necessary ingredient in this case because the relevant statute imposed strict liability. The act of smuggling gold itself was sufficient for conviction, irrespective of the intent or knowledge.
- **Kartar Singh v. State of Punjab (1994)**, in this case Kartar Singh was involved in

acts of terrorism under the Terrorist and Disruptive Activities (Prevention) Act (TADA).The Supreme Court emphasised that mens rea is a fundamental principle of criminal jurisprudence. For conviction under TADA, it must be proved that the accused had the intent or knowledge that their actions would result in terrorist acts.

- **State of Haryana v. Rajender Singh (1996),** in this case Rajender Singh was accused of causing the death of a person by dangerous driving. The Supreme Court held that mens rea could be in the form of gross negligence. In this case, the accused's recklessness in driving constituted sufficient *mens rea* for a conviction of causing death by negligence.
- **Emperor v. Sardarkhan Jhaveri Khan (1927),** in this case the accused was involved in the illegal transport of opium. The Bombay High Court held that mens rea was an essential ingredient for conviction under the Opium Act. It had to be proven that the accused had knowledge or intent regarding the illegal nature of the act.

Significance of Mens Rea

- **Distinguished Levels of Culpability**: The principle of *mens rea* allows for proportionate punishment to the offender depending on the nature and degree of his state of mind.
- **Protection of Innocents**: It ensures that individuals who inadvertently commit an act without criminal intent are not wrongfully punished.
- **Moral Blameworthiness**: It reflects the moral blameworthiness of the accused, ensuring that punishment is justly meted out.

Principle of Mens Rea and Strict Liability

- It is a universally accepted legal principle that mens rea is an essential ingredient of offences. However, the principle of mens rea has certain exceptions. This necessarily implies that mens rea is not an essential ingredient of some offences and mere commission or omission of certain specified acts is made punishable in law.
- Statutes imposing strict or absolute criminal liability do not require *mens rea* as an essential element of crime and constitute the exception to the principle of mens rea.
- The principles of *mens rea* and strict liability form the bedrock of criminal law in India, each serving distinct purposes. *Mens rea* ensures that moral culpability is a cornerstone of criminal responsibility, aligning punishment with intent and awareness.
- In contrast, strict liability addresses specific regulatory and public welfare concerns, streamlining the prosecution process by eliminating the need to prove mens rea. Both principles are integral to maintaining a balance between individual rights and societal interests in the Indian legal system.

Characteristics of Strict/ Absolute Criminal Liability

- **No Need for *Mens Rea***: Strict or absolute criminal liability does not require proof of *mens rea*. The mere commission or omission of the *actus reus* (guilty act) is sufficient for criminal liability. Therefore, it can be concluded that strict liability prioritises public protection and regulatory compliance, often at the cost of individual intent.
- **Public Welfare Offences**: These are the offences in respect of which the principle of absolute/ strict criminal liability is utilised for the protection of public health, safety, or welfare (e.g., The Prevention of Food Adulteration Act, 1954; The Essential Commodities Act, 1955, various Pollution Control laws etc.).
- **Statutory Interpretation**: Often arises from specific statutes where the legislature has explicitly removed the requirement for mens rea.

Important Case Laws

- **State of Maharashtra v. M.H. George (1965)**
  - **Facts:** In this case, M.H. George was charged under the Customs Act for smuggling gold into India without declaring it to customs authorities.
  - The prosecution argued that George was in possession of uncustomed goods, which constituted a strict liability offence under the Customs Act.
  - **Legal Issue:** The primary legal issue was whether the offence under the Customs Act required proof of mens rea (a guilty mind) or if it was an offence of strict liability, where the act itself (possession of uncustomed goods) was sufficient for conviction.
  - **Court's Decision:** The Supreme Court of India held that the offence under the Customs Act was one of strict liability. The court reasoned that the language and purpose of the Customs Act indicated that Parliament intended to impose strict liability for certain offences related to customs duties and regulations.
    - **Strict Liability**: The court emphasised that strict liability offences do not require proof of mens rea. The focus is on the act itself (actus reus), such as possession of uncustomed goods, rather than the intent or knowledge of the accused.
    - **Legislative Intent**: The court interpreted the Customs Act to reflect Parliament's intention to impose strict liability for offences related to customs duties and regulations. This interpretation was based on the language and objectives of the statute.
    - **Public Policy**: The court considered the public policy behind customs regulations, emphasising the importance of compliance and deterrence in maintaining fiscal discipline and preventing smuggling activities.
- **Brend v. Wood (1946)**
  - The case involved a statutory offence where the defendant was charged under a regulation that made it an offence to have uncustomed goods (goods on which customs duty had not been paid) in his possession.
  - **Legal Issue:** The primary legal issue in *Brend v. Wood* was whether the statute under which the defendant was charged required proof of mens rea (guilty mind) or whether it imposed strict liability, meaning that the defendant could be convicted regardless of intent or knowledge.
  - **Court's Decision:**
    - **Presumption of *Mens Rea***: The court reaffirmed the general principle that mens rea is a fundamental component of criminal liability. It emphasised that for someone to be convicted of a criminal offence, it is generally necessary to prove that they had a guilty mind, unless the statute creating the offence explicitly states otherwise.
    - **Strict Liability**: The court acknowledged that certain statutes impose strict liability for regulatory or public welfare offences, where proving mens rea is not required. However, this should be clearly indicated by the wording of the statute or be necessary due to the nature of the offence.

- **Interpretation of Statutes**: When interpreting a statute, courts should look for explicit language or necessary implication that mens rea is not required. If the statute is silent or ambiguous, the presumption in favour of mens rea applies.
- The court had to decide if the statute implicitly required mens rea or if it intended to create an offence of strict liability.
- The court ultimately held that unless a statute explicitly or by necessary implication excludes mens rea, it is presumed that mens rea is required to establish criminal liability.

- **Nathulal v. State of Madhya Pradesh (1966)**
  - **Facts**: Nathulal was charged with selling food grains without a licence, believing he had a valid licence.
  - **Issue**: Whether mens rea was required for conviction under the Essential Commodities Act.
  - **Court's Decision:**The Supreme Court of India acquitted Nathulal, emphasising that mens rea was a necessary element of the offence. This case reflects the influence of principles similar to those in Brend v. Wood, affirming the need for mens rea in criminal liability unless explicitly excluded by statute.
- **Sherras v. De Rutzen (1895)**
  - **Facts:** In *Sherras v. De Rutzen*, the defendant, a publican (pub owner), was charged under a statute which made it an offence to serve alcohol to a police constable on duty.
  - The defendant served a drink to a police constable who was not wearing his armband, which indicated he was on duty. The defendant believed, reasonably, that the constable was off duty.
  - **Legal Issue:** The legal issue was whether the statute imposing the offence required proof of *mens rea* (a guilty mind) or if it was an offence of strict liability, meaning that the defendant could be convicted regardless of intent or knowledge.
  - **Court's Decision:** The court had to determine whether the offence under the statute required *mens rea* or if it was a strict liability offence. The court held that *mens rea* was required and that the defendant could not be convicted if he had a reasonable belief that the constable was off duty.
- **Sherras v. De Rutzen** is significant because it highlights the importance of mens rea in criminal law and establishes a strong presumption that mens rea is required for criminal liability unless a statute clearly indicates otherwise. This case serves as a leading authority on the interpretation of statutory offences and the necessity of mens rea in criminal law.
- **Subhash Shamrao Pachunde v. State of Maharashtra (2005)**
  - **Facts:** Subhash Shamrao Pachunde was charged under Section 138 of the Negotiable Instruments Act, 1881, for dishonour of a cheque.
  - The complainant alleged that a cheque issued by Pachunde was dishonoured due to insufficient funds. Pachunde contended that he had issued the cheque as a security and not for repayment of any debt.
  - **Legal Issue:** The main legal issue was whether Pachunde could be held criminally liable under Section 138 of the Negotiable Instruments Act, which imposes strict liability for dishonour of cheques due to insufficient funds.

- **Court's Decision:** The Supreme Court of India held that Section 138 of the Negotiable Instruments Act imposes strict liability on the drawer of a cheque in case of its dishonour due to insufficient funds or if it exceeds the amount arranged to be paid from that account. The court emphasised that under Section 138, the intent or knowledge of the drawer of the cheque about the insufficiency of funds is immaterial for establishing criminal liability.
  - **Strict Liability under Section 138**: The court clarified that Section 138 of the Negotiable Instruments Act is a strict liability offence.
  - **Legislative Intent**: The court interpreted Section 138 in line with its purpose to enhance the credibility of negotiable instruments in business transactions and ensure prompt payment.
  - **Public Interest**: The court underscored the public interest in ensuring the efficacy of cheques as instruments of payment and deterrence against their misuse, which justifies the imposition of strict liability.

ACTUS REUS

- *Actus reus* represents the physical aspect of a crime is a fundamental component of criminal liability, requiring the prosecution to demonstrate that the accused engaged in a conduct that constitutes a criminal offence. Through various landmark judgments, Indian courts have underscored the importance of actus reus, ensuring that only those who perform the requisite physical acts or omissions are held criminally responsible.
- *Actus reus*, or the "guilty act," is the physical component of a crime. It can be defined as such a result of human conduct which the law seeks to prevent and can arise due to illegal act or ommission of the offender.
- Generally, mere actus reus without mens rea does not constitute a crime. Rather, for a person to be convicted of a crime, the prosecution must prove beyond reasonable doubt that the accused committed the actus reus with the necessary mens rea (guilty mind).

Elements of *Actus Reus*

- **Conduct***:* The physical action or inaction (omission) by the accused.
- **Circumstances***:* The context or conditions under which the conduct occurred.
- **Consequences***:* The result or outcome of the conduct.

Case Laws Illustrating *Actus Reus*

- **Kartar Singh v. State of Punjab (1994 AIR 1733)**
  - **Facts**: Kartar Singh was involved in acts of terrorism.
  - **Issue**: Whether the physical acts committed by Kartar Singh constituted the actus reus of terrorism.
  - **Held**: The Supreme Court emphasised that the physical acts (e.g., planting bombs, carrying out attacks) performed by Kartar Singh constituted the actus reus of the offence. These acts, combined with the intent to cause terror, fulfilled the requirements for conviction under the Terrorist and Disruptive Activities (Prevention) Act (TADA).

- **Rupan Deol Bajaj v. KPS Gill (1996)**
  - **Facts**: KPS Gill, a senior police officer, was accused of outraging the modesty of Rupan Deol Bajaj by making unwelcome physical advances.
  - **Issue**: Whether Gill's actions constituted the actus reus of outraging modesty.
  - **Held**: The Supreme Court held that Gill's physical actions (e.g., slapping Bajaj on the posterior) constituted the actus reus of outraging the modesty of a woman. The physical act, coupled with the intent to outrage her modesty, was sufficient for conviction.
- **State of Andhra Pradesh v. Thummala Anjaneyulu (1997)**
  - **Facts**: Thummala Anjaneyulu was accused of causing death by rash and negligent driving.
  - **Issue**: Whether the actus reus of causing death by negligence was present.
  - **Held**: The Supreme Court held that the physical act of driving recklessly, which led to the death of a pedestrian, constituted the actus reus of causing death by negligence. The conduct (rash driving) and the consequence (death) fulfilled the actus reus requirements.

Significance of *Actus Reus*

- **Physical Manifestation of Crime**: *Actus reus* provides the tangible evidence of a crime, distinguishing mere thoughts from punishable actions.
- **Establishes Causation**: *Actus reus* helps in establishing a causal link between the accused's conduct and the criminal outcome.
- **Legal and Moral Responsibility**: It ensures that individuals are held accountable for their actions or omissions that result in harm.

SOME EXAMPLES OF MENS REA AND ACTUS REUS

- **Murder (Section 101 of BNS),** In murder following are the mens rea and actus reus
  - ***Mens Rea***: Intention to cause death or to cause such bodily injury that is likely to cause death.
  - ***Actus Reus:*** Causing death of a person.
- **Culpable Homicide (Section 100 of BNS),** In culpable homicide following are the mens rea and actus reus
  - ***Mens Rea:*** Intention to cause death or the knowledge that the act is likely to cause death.
  - ***Actus Reus:*** Causing death of a person by doing an act with such intention or knowledge.
- **Theft (Section 303 of BNS),** In theft following are the mens rea and actus reus:
  - ***Mens Rea:*** Dishonest intention to take property.
  - ***Actus Reus***: Moving a movable property out of the possession of another person without their consent.
- **Robbery (Section 309 of the BNS),** In robbery following are the mens rea and actus reus:
  - **Mens Rea**: Intent to commit theft with additional intent to cause fear or use force.
  - **Actus Reus**: Committing theft along with causing or attempting to cause harm, fear of harm, or wrongful restraint.

❖❖❖

Chapter 4

STAGES OF CRIME

INTRODUCTION

In criminal jurisprudence, the concept of the stages of crime refers to the sequential phases through which a criminal act progresses, from inception to completion. As per the **Bharatiya Nyaya Sanhita, 2023**, the stages of a criminal offence encompass various phases, from the initial thought or intention to commit the crime, through the actual execution of the offence, to the post-commission actions. These stages play a crucial role in determining an accused person's culpability and the appropriate legal consequences for their actions. Understanding these different stages assists in analysing both the *mens rea* (mental state which is culpable) and *actus reus* (physical act) of the accused, which are essential elements in establishing criminal liability.

STAGES OF CRIME

- There are four stages of Crime i.e., Intention, Preparation, Attempt and Actual Commission of the Offence.
- These stages collectively form the foundation of criminal liability and in determining guilt or innocence, assessing appropriate punishments, and ensuring justice within the framework of criminal law. Each stage is essential for both prosecution and defence in criminal proceedings.

Intention

- The intention is the first stage of any offence and is known as the mental or psycho stage. It is impossible to prove the mental state of man and the court cannot convict for what it can not know.
- In this stage, the offender decides the motive and decides his course or direction towards the offence. Law does not take notice of an intention, mere intention to commit an offence not followed by any act, cannot constitute an offence.
- The obvious reason for not prosecuting the accused at this stage is that it is very difficult for the prosecution to prove the guilty mind of a person.
- A intends to kill B but does nothing in the direction of reaching the target of killing B. A cannot be punished.
- In the case of **State of Maharashtra v. Mohd. Yakub (2011)**, the Supreme Court considered whether the accused had the intent to commit murder. The court emphasised that intent can be inferred from the evidence of the accused's actions and conduct. In this case, the accused's deliberate actions leading to the death of the victim were sufficient to establish intent for the offence.

Preparation

(**Note:** ***Section 149*** *of BNS corresponds to* ***Section 122*** *of IPC*)

(**Note:** ***Section 178*** *of BNS corresponds to* ***Sections 230, 231, 232, 246, 248, 255, 489A*** *of IPC respectively*)

(**Note:** ***Section 180*** *of BNS corresponds to* ***Sections 242, 243,252, 253, 259, 489C*** *of IPC respectively*)

(**Note:** ***Section 181*** *of BNS corresponds to* ***Sections 233, 234, 235, 256, 257, 489D*** *of IPC respectively*)

(**Note:** ***Section 310*** *of BNS corresponds to* ***Sections 391, 395, 399, 402*** *of IPC respectively*)

- It is the second stage of the crime. Preparation entails gathering all the materials needed to execute a planned criminal act. Since it can be challenging to demonstrate that all necessary preparations were made before the crime was committed, preparation is not illegal in and of itself. But in certain rare circumstances, even preparation might result in punishment.
- It means to arrange the necessary resources for the execution of the intentional criminal act. Intention and preparation alone are not enough to constitute a crime.
- For example, if A, after forming the intention to kill B, purchases a pistol and keeps it with him, it can be said to be preparation on his part.
- In **Ram Narain Poply v. CBI (2003)**, the Supreme Court held that preparation alone does not constitute an offence unless specified by law.
- **Preparation when Punishable**
  - Under **Section 149 of the BNS** Collecting arms, etc., with intention of waging war against the Government of India.
  - Under **Section 178, 181 of BNS** Counterfeiting coin, Government stamps, currency-notes or bank-notes.
  - Under **Section 180 of BNS, and Section 310 of BNS,** having counterfeit money, fraudulent documents, or fake weights and measurements, making plans to commit dacoity.
- The reason for not punishing the first two stages is that they are considered too remote to the completion of the intended crime. They are perceived as harmless acts.

Attempt

(**Note:** ***Sections 62*** *of BNS corresponds to* ***Section 511*** *of IPC*)

- An 'Attempt' is the third stage of crime. The first two stages generally are not punishable but once an act enters the third stage criminal liability arises. If the attempt is successful, the crime is committed.
- The term attempt means direct movement towards the commission of a crime after necessary preparations made to carry out an offence or it is an endeavour to commit crime. It is also called preliminary crime or inchoate crime.
- Attempt may broadly be defined as an intentional act done by a person in the direction of commission of a crime which failed in its object independent of the violation of the person doing it.
- **Section 62 of BNS** does provide punishment for attempting to commit a crime, where no express provision is made by BNS for the punishment of such attempt.
- For example, A makes an attempt to pick the pocket of Z by thrusting his hand into Z's pocket. A fails in the attempt as a consequence of Z's having nothing in his pocket. A is guilty of attempting to commit theft under Section 62.

Tests to Determine Whether the Act Amounts to Attempt

- **Proximity Test:** A connection between time and an action or an intention is called proximity. It is used in attempted cases that are in the third stage. The closeness of an action or intention to a time is what determines the concept of proximity. This idea is especially important when figuring out attempts, which is the third phase of a crime.
- It mainly focuses on whether an individual is "so near" to the outcome that there is a very high risk of success or "dangerously close" to completing the crime. Moreover, the act toward the commission of the offence need not be the penultimate act i.e., the act that comes first and leads to the crime. However, the action must be proximate to the desired outcome.

- In **State of Maharashtra v. Mohammed Yakub, (1980)**, it was held by supreme court that It should not be remotely leading towards the Commission of offence.The act of the accused is proximate if, though it is not the last act that he intended to do,is the last act that he was legally necessary for him to do, if the contemplated results is afterwards brought about without further conduct on his part.

- **Locus Paenitentiae (Time for Repentance):** The doctrine of '*Locus Poenitentiae*' says that when an act is such that there is ample time with the accused to choose whether to commit such crime or not; and it is within the control of that person.
- The intender may change his path or may fear the consequences, if the act is in control of the intended to not to commit the offence, then it is said to be mere preparation and not an attempt. Hence, it is not punishable under penal law.
  - In **Malkiat Singh v. State of Punjab (1970),** It was held by the supreme court that If the overt acts are such that they would be entirely harmless if the person changed his mind and did not proceed further, then that is the best indicator of whether a given set of acts constitutes an attempt or is merely preparation. If that were the case, it would just be preparation. However, in situations where the action taken would amount to an attempt to commit the offence if it weren't stopped by an unrelated causeway, it would be considered an offence of attempt.
- **Equivocality Test:** This test is a combination of the above two tests. This test requires the unequivocal intention through the act done which is considered to be fulfilled beyond a reasonable doubt that the end is towards the crime intended. The act must speak for itself.
  - To constitute an attempt the act must be such as to clearly and unequivocally indicate the intention to commit the offence.
- **Impossibility Test:** Since the act is impossible to perform, it cannot be tried and is therefore not guilty. Such actions as shooting a shadow, giving sugar to someone who believes it to be arsenic, killing a man through witchcraft, or cursing someone with the intent to harm them are not allowed under the law.
  - In these cases there is no probability of realising the accused's goal, but because what he does is not an act towards commission of that offence, but an act towards commission of something which cannot according to ordinary human experience result in hurt to another. His failure to cause hurt is due to his own act of omission.
- **Social Danger Test:** If the fact and circumstances of a case lead to the inference that the resultant consequences would have been grave, the crime of attempt is complete. In fact, it is the apprehension of social danger which the particular crime is calculated to excite, that determines the liability for an attempt.

Commission of Crime or Accomplishment

- The last stage in the commission of an offence is its successful completion. Committing the crime is the final step in the process. If the accused succeeds in his attempt, he commits a crime and will be guilty of it.
- If he fails, he will only be charged with attempting. If the crime is complete, the offender will be tried and punished as per the specific provisions provided in the Bharatiya Nyaya Sanhita.
- The case of **State of Maharashtra v. Mohd. Ajmal Amir Kasab (2012)**, deals with the 2008 Mumbai attacks where the accused, Kasab, was captured alive during the commission of terrorist acts. The court found him guilty of multiple offences, including murder and waging war against the nation, based on overwhelming evidence of his direct involvement in the execution of the attacks.

- For example, A fires at B with the intention to kill him, if B dies, A will be guilty of committing the offence of murder and if B is only injured, it will be a case of attempt to murder.

DIFFERENCES BETWEEN PREPARATION AND ATTEMPT		
Aspect	**Preparation**	**Attempt**
Definition	It involves actions taken towards making oneself ready or equipped to commit the offence, such as gathering tools, casing a location, or making arrangements, but without initiating the final act necessary to complete the crime itself.	Attempt signifies a direct and immediate step towards the commission of an offence. It involves actions that are proximate to the actual commission of the crime, demonstrating a clear intention to carry out the criminal act and taking substantial steps towards its completion.
Intent	In preparation, individuals engage in activities that demonstrate their readiness or intention to commit the offence in the future. This may involve planning, acquiring necessary items, or making logistical arrangements, but without the immediate intent to commit the crime at that moment.	Attempt requires a specific intent to commit a particular offence and involves actions that are beyond mere preparation. It signifies a direct effort towards the commission of the crime, where the accused takes steps that indicate a present and immediate danger of completing the offence if not prevented by external factors or intervention.
Criminal Liability	Preparation, in itself, is generally not punishable under BNS unless it falls under specific preparatory offences defined by law, such as preparing to wage war against the state.	Attempt is punishable under Section 62 of the BNS because it represents a critical stage where the actions of the accused pose a significant risk or immediate threat to public order or safety.
Stages of Crime	Preparation occurs in the preliminary stages of planning and readiness for the commission of a crime.	Attempt occurs when individuals have progressed beyond mere preparation and have taken steps that directly move towards the commission of the offence.
Example	An example of preparation could be an individual gathering tools, or making arrangements in advance for a burglary.	An attempt could involve an individual breaking into a building with the intent to steal, but being apprehended by security before any valuables are taken.
Punishment	Since preparation does not involve the immediate attempt to commit the offence, it is generally not punishable under BNS unless it falls under specific preparatory offences defined by law.	Attempt is punishable under IPC to deter individuals from progressing towards the commission of crimes.

OFFENCES

- In criminal law, offences can be categorised into two main types: choate and inchoate offences.
- Choate offences refer to completed or fully formed criminal acts that have been carried out to their intended completion.
- On the other hand, inchoate offences concern criminal actions that are initiated but remain incomplete.

Choate Offences

- Choate offences refer to the completed or fully executed criminal acts that have resulted in injury, harm, damage, or the intended outcome. In the choate offences, the elements of the offence are entirely present, and the perpetrator's intent is manifested through their actions.
- The key elements required to establish guilt in a choate offence include
  - ***Actus Reus***: The guilty act or physical conduct committed by the perpetrator. This could be an action or failure to act when there is a legal duty to act.
  - ***Mens Rea***: The criminal intent or mental state of the offender at the time of committing the crime. It includes degrees of intent, such as intentionally, knowingly, recklessly, or negligently.
  - **Concurrence:** The requirement that the guilty act and the criminal intent coincide, meaning the person intended to commit the act and then actually followed through with it.
- **Example:** If an individual successfully causes the death of another person, it is considered a choate offence since the act was carried out to its conclusion, that is, till the death of the person.

Inchoate Offences

(**Note:** ***Sections 109, 152*** *of BNS corresponds to* ***Sections 307, 124A*** *of IPC respectively*)

- Inchoate offences deal with actions that are incomplete or preparatory in nature, falling short of achieving the ultimate criminal objective. They represent an individual's intention to commit a crime without successfully executing it.
- Inchoate offences are incomplete offences as they only fulfil the mens rea aspect and not the Actus reus element of the crime. Thus, an attempt of an offence can be said to be an Inchoate offence.
- An attempt has not been defined directly in the Bharatiya Nyay Sanhiya, 2023. However, **Chapter IV** of the BNS mentions the punishment to attempt an offence with imprisonment or life imprisonment as the case may be.
- For instance, A, a person intends to kill B. He shoots at B but misses the target and hence the actual crime of murder or culpable murder doesn't take place. In such a case, A will be charged with the offence of Attempt to Murder under **Section 109** of the BNS.
- The **BNS** deals with the attempt majorly in three different ways which is as under:
  - Firstly, the attempt of the offence and its commission are simultaneously dealt with the common section and same punishment. For example, Sedition under **Section 152** of the BNS.
  - Secondly, they are treated as separate offences and thus are punished accordingly. For example, Attempt to Murder under **Section 109** of BNS, Attempt to Culpable Homicide under **Section 110** of BNS and Attempt to Suicide under **Section 226** of BNS.
  - Thirdly, remaining offences. This is provided in **Section 62** of the BNS, where it mentions the punishment of life imprisonment or simple imprisonment for committing such offence.

DIFFERENCE BETWEEN CHOATE AND INCHOATE OFFENCES

- When someone commits a choate offence, they may be charged with the crime and put on trial for the entire deed, which could result in jail time, fines, or probation.
- Inchoate offences, on the other hand, frequently result in less severe penalties than the completed crimes they involve, but they nevertheless have a significant impact on social order and public safety.
- Inchoate offences are given special consideration by courts and legal systems in order to avert potential harm and discourage criminal activity.

❖ ❖ ❖

Chapter 5

OFFENCES AGAINST PUBLIC TRANQUILITY

Offences against Public Tranquility under the Bharatiya Nayaya Sanhita (BNS) and Indian Penal Code (IPC) are critical to maintaining societal order and peace. The chapter addresses various crimes that disrupt the harmony and safety of the community, reflecting the legal system's commitment to protecting public peace and ensuring a stable social environment. The provisions herein encompass a range of activities, from rioting and affray to unlawful assemblies and the spreading of inflammatory messages. By outlining these offenses and their corresponding penalties, the BNS aims to deter actions that threaten public tranquility and to provide a legal framework for addressing disturbances that can undermine social cohesion.

COMPARATIVE CHART OF THE BNS AND IPC		
Bharatiya Nyaya Sanhita (BNS)	**Title**	**Indian Penal Code, 1860 (IPC)**
Section 3(5)	General explanation and expression **EARLIER TITLE**-(Act done by several persons in furtherance of common intention)	Section 34
Section 189(1)	Unlawful assembly	Section 141
Section 189(2)	Unlawful assembly **EARLIER TITLE**-(Being member of an unlawful assembly)	Section 142
Section 190	Every member of unlawful assembly guilty of offence committed in prosecution of common object	Section 149
RIOTING		
Section 191	Rioting	Section 146
Section 191	Rioting **EARLIER TITLE**-(Punishment for rioting)	Section 147
Section 191	Rioting **EARLIER TITLE**-(Rioting, armed with deadly Weapon)	Section 148
Section 192	Wantonly giving provocation with intent to cause riot—if rioting be committed; if not committed	Section 153
Section 193	Liability Of owner, occupier, etc., of land on which an unlawful assembly or riot takes place **EARLIER TITLE**-(Owner or occupier of land on which an unlawful assembly is held)	Section 154

Section 193	Liability Of owner, occupier, etc., of land on which an unlawful assembly or riot takes place **EARLIER TITLE**-(Liability of person for whose benefit riot is committed)	Section 155
Section 193	Liability Of owner, occupier, etc., of land on which an unlawful assembly or riot takes place **EARLIER TITLE**-(Liability of agent of owner or occupier for whose benefit riot is committed)	Section 156
	AFFRAY	
Section 194	Affray	Section 159
Section 194	Affray **EARLIER TITLE**-(Punishment for committing affray)	Section 160
Section 195	Assaulting or obstructing public servant when suppressing riot, etc	Section 152
	PROMOTING ENMITY BETWEEN DIFFERENT GROUPS	
Section 196	Promoting enmity between different groups on ground of religion, race, place of birth, residence, language, etc., and doing acts prejudicial to maintenance of harmony	Section 153A
Section 197	Imputations, assertions prejudicial to national Integration	Section 153B

CHANGES IN BNS IN COMPARISON TO IPC

- **Section 191(3)** of the BNS corresponding to **Section 148** in the IPC has changed as follows:
  - The punishment for imprisonment for rioting, armed with deadly weapons has been **changed to "five years" from "three years".**
- **Section 194** of the BNS corresponding to **Section 160** in the IPC has changed as follows:
  - The amount of fine is now changed to **"one thousand rupees" from "one hundred rupees".**
- **Section 195** of the BNS corresponding to **Section 152** in the IPC has changed as follows:
  - **It has been divided in two sub- sections wherein Section 195 (2) of the BNS deals with the "threaten or attempt" part of the concerned provision. Also,** the fine in section 195 given as fine **"which shall not be less than twenty-five thousand rupees".**
- **Section 196** of the BNS corresponding to **Section 153A** in the IPC has changed as follows:
  - Under new law **'electronic communication'** is also **added** as one of the modes of spreading disharmony etc.
- **Section 197** of the BNS corresponding to **Section 153B** in the IPC has changed as follows:
  - The words **"or through electronic communication"** are added under the sub-section (1) now. **Also, Section 197 (1) (d) of the BNS is added** which states as follows: (d) makes or publishes false or misleading information jeopardising the sovereignty, unity and integrity or security of India.

- The Bharatiya Nyaya Sanhita, 2023 (BNS) deals with the provision of joint and constructive liability under **Section 3(5) of Chapter I (Preliminary) and under Section 189–190 under Chapter XI (Offences against the Public Tranquility)** (The earlier Sections 34 of Chapter II (General Explanations) and Section 141 and 149 under Chapter VIII (Offences against the Public Tranquility) respectively. These provisions may be classified into:
  - A criminal act done in furtherance of common intention of all is covered under **Sections 3(5) of BNS.**
  - Where the offence is committed with the common object of an unlawful assembly is dealt under **Section 190** of the BNS.

ACT DONE BY SEVERAL PERSON IN FURTHERANCE OF COMMON INTENTION

(**Note:** ***Section 3(5) of the BNS*** *correspond to* ***Section 34 of the IPC***)

- According to the **Section 3(5) of BNS** when "a criminal act is done by several persons in furtherance of the common intention of all, each of such persons is liable for the act in the same manner as if it were done by him alone". This rule of criminal law is called joint and constructive criminal liability as it is implied by the law that the concerned persons are involved directly or indirectly in the crime.
- It means that if a crime is committed by one or more persons in furtherance of common intention, they will be held liable for the crime as if the crime was performed by them individually.
- This section recognises the principle of vicarious liability in the criminal jurisprudence. **Section 3(5)** of BNS does not create a distinct substantive offence.
- It is merely a rule of evidence and lays down the principle of joint liability.

Essential Ingredients

- The essence of liability under this section is simultaneous consensus of the minds of persons participating in the criminal action to bring about a particular result.
- The essential ingredients of **Section 3(5)** of BNS are as follows:
  - **Common Intention**: A prerequisite to invoke **Section 3(5)** of BNS is the presence of common intention. It refers to the mental element to commit the criminal act conjointly with another.
  - **Participation**: Actual participation (active or passive) in one form or the other in the commission of the offence is necessary.

Common Intention

- It must be shown that the criminal act complained against was done by the accused persons in the furtherance of the common intention of all, if this is shown, then liability for the crime may be imposed on any one of the persons in the same manner as if the act were done by him alone.
- The provision does not prescribe "the common intention of all" nor does it say "an intention common to all" but "in furtherance of common intention of all".
- In the absence of a common intention even if several persons simultaneously attack a man and each one of them by having his individual intention, namely, the intention to kill and each can individually inflict a separate fatal blow and yet none would have the common intention required by the Section. In a case like that each would be individually liable for whatever injury he caused but none could be vicariously convicted for the act of another.
- To convict the accused of an offence under this provision it should be proved that the criminal act was done in concert pursuant to a prearranged plan i.e. with prior meeting of minds.

SECTION 3(5) OF BNS
GENERAL EXPLANATIONS

When a criminal act is done by several persons in furtherance of the common intention of all, each of such persons is liable for that act in the same manner as if it were done by him alone.

Prior Meeting of Mind

- Common intention within the meaning of the section pre-supposes prior concert, which requires a pre-arranged plan of the accused participating in an offence.

Common Intention at the Spur of Moment

- Common intention can be formed at the spur of the moment. The pre arranged plan need not be elaborate, nor is a long interval of time required. It could arise and be formed suddenly. Such a pre-concert or pre-planning may develop on the spot or during the course of commission of the offence.
- The crucial test is that such a plan must precede the act constituting the offence (i.e. it must be anterior in point of time to the commission of the crime showing a prior concert).
- **Illustration:** Where during a fight a person calls the by-standers to help him kill a person and they join him; there is then necessary meeting of minds or formation of a pre-arranged plan though hastily formed and rudely conceived.
- In **Mehtab Singh v. State (1954)** it was held that the pre-arranged plan can come into existence the moment one person calls another for attacking a third person, even though the length of time between calling and the commission of the crime was only a few seconds and when both of them attack that third person, a common intention has come into existence before the attack is made.
- However, in **Sheoram Singh v. State of U.P. (1972)**, the Supreme Court held that common intention may develop suddenly during the course of an occurrence, but still unless there is cogent evidence and clear proof of such common intention, an accused cannot be vicariously held guilty under, **Section 34 of IPC (Section 3(5) of BNS)** . There is no rule that a common intention presupposes prior concert, which requires a prearranged plan of the accused participating in an offence.
  - Thus, it can be formed previously or in the course of occurrence and on the spur of the moment. The existence of a common intention is a question of fact in each case to be proved mainly as a matter of inference from the circumstances of the case.

Meaning of the Common Intention in Furtherance of all

- Under **Section 3(5) of BNS**, existence of common intention is not enough, the criminal act impugned to attract **Section 3(5) of BNS** must be committed in furtherance of the common intention.
- Whether an act is in furtherance of the common intention or not depends upon the common intention and the nature of the act. It is an incident of fact and not of law. Generally, the act done in furtherance of the common intention includes three types of acts:
  - The act which is directly intended in between all the confederates.
  - The act where the circumstances of the case leave no doubt to conclude that though the act was not directly intended in between them it was taken by all of them as included in the common intention.
  - The act which any one of the confederates commits in order to avoid or remove any obstruction or resistance put up in the way of the proper execution of the common intention.
    - In doing this type of the act the individual doer may cause a result not intended by any other of the confederates. Thus, only such acts

are not to be deemed to be the acts done in furtherance of the common intention as could not have taken place ordinarily in carrying out of the common intention.

- Common intention is different from the same intention in following manner:
  - It is now well settled that the common intention required by **Section 3(5) of BNS** is different from the same intention or similar intention. The persons having similar intention which is not the result of pre-concerted plan cannot be held guilty for the "criminal act" with the aid of **Section 3(5) of BNS.**
  - In **Dukhmochan Pandey v. State of Bihar (1998)** the distinction between common and similar intention came to be considered. The court noticed that intention could be formed previously or on the spot during the progress of a crime. Generally, such situations will involve a prearranged plan, which in turn presupposes a prior meeting of mind. But in a specific case, the intention may develop at the spur of the moment. Such common intention which developed at the spur of the moment is different from a similar intention actuated by a number of persons at the same time, and, therefore, the said distinction must be borne in mind which would be relevant in deciding whether **Section 34 of IPC (Section 3(5) of BNS)** will apply to all those who might have done some overt act on the spur of the moment.

Participation in Criminal Act

- Actual participation is a condition precedent to fasten liability under this provision.
- To participate means to take part, and part in an act may be taken by doing something which advances the common cause or which helps in the achievement of common cause.
- Participation can be through physical presence or without physical presence.

Participation Through Physical Presence

- The courts have emphatically and repeatedly stated that the essence of the provision is that the person must be physically present at the actual commission of the crime.
- In **S.R. Munupalli v. State (1955)**, it was observed that the emphasis in **Section 34 of IPC (Section 3(5) of BNS)** is on words "done by several persons", it is essential that they join in the actual doing of the act and not merely in planning its perpetration.

Participation without Physical Presence

- The actual physical participation in the crime is not always essential to fix liability.
- In **Desai v. State of Bombay (1960)**, the Supreme Court would appear to have modified the principle hitherto enunciated. Court observed, "A common intention-a meeting of minds to commit the crime invites the application of **Section 34 of IPC (Section 3(5) of BNS)**. But this participation need not in all cases be by physical presence." "In offences involving physical violence normally, presence at the scene of the offence, of the offenders sought to be rendered liable on the principle of joint liability may be necessary but such is not the case in respect of other offences, where the offence consists of diverse acts, which may be done at different times and places."

No Need of Overt Act

- In order to convict a person vicariously under **Section 3(5) of BNS,** it is unnecessary to prove that each and every one of them had indulged in overt acts. This is so because the acts of all the accused need not be the same or identical but must be actuated by the same common intention.
  - In **Rambilas Singh v. State of Bihar (1989)**, the Supreme Court observed: "It is true that in order to convict persons vicariously under **Section 34 of IPC (Section 3(5) of BNS)** or **Section 149 of IPC (section (190) of BNS)** it is not

necessary to prove that each and everyone of them had indulged in overt acts. Even so, there must be material to show that the overt act or acts of one or more of the accused was or were done in furtherance of the common intention of all the accused or in prosecution of the common object of the members of the unlawful assembly."

Case Laws

(Note: *Following cases deal with* ***Section 3(5) of the BNS,*** *ealier* ***Section 34 of the IPC*****)**

- **Tukaram v. State of Maharashtra (1979)**
  - **Facts:** The appellant and some others were accused of stealing some bundles of copper wire from the storehouse of a company. After stealing the bundles from the storehouse, they removed the bundles by a truck, which was stopped at the weighbridge where brokers to negotiate the sale of copper wire were present along with the appellant. There was, however, no evidence as to the presence of the appellant at the scene of occurrence. The appellant pleads innocence on the hopeful circumstances of absence of direct evidence connecting him and on the inconclusive probativeness of the sole circumstance found against him of the recovery of his statement to the police.
  - **VERDICT**: The Apex Court held that participation does not mean participation in actual doing or commission of a crime, if a person is directing the entire operation from some distance he would also be deemed to be participating in the crime and would be covered by **Section 34.**
- **Barendra Kumar Ghose v. King Emperor (1925)**
  - **Facts:** Several individuals were charged with committing a crime at a post office. According to the prosecution, the accused (Barendra Kumar Ghose), along with others, entered the post office armed with firearms, demanded money from the Postmaster, and fired shots that led to the Postmaster's death. The accused, however, provided a different account, claiming that only three people were involved and that he was not inside the post office and he did not shoot the Postmaster. He also contended that he was unaware of any plans to commit murder.
  - **Verdict:** Privy Council observed that **Section 34** deals with the doing of separate acts, similar or diverse by several persons, if all are done in furtherance of a common intention, each person is liable for the result of them all, as if he had done them himself.
    - The Council also discussed the difference between object and intention, in case the object is common, the intentions of the several members may differ and indeed may be similar only in respect that they are all unlawful.
    - The Council held that, "a criminal act" under **Section 34** means a unity of criminal behaviour, which results in punishment for acts done with other persons in furtherance of a common intention will be in the same manner, as if it were all done by the person alone.
- **Pandurang v. State of Hyderabad (1995)**
  - **Facts:** Five persons, including the three appellants, were prosecuted for the murder of one Ramchander with axes. Assailants ran away and absconded after attacking the deceased. Two eye-witnesses (deceased's sister-in-law and servant) narrated the whole incident substantially in the same version.
    - Nothing was known about what went on before the attack.
    - No evidence of prior meeting of minds so as to form common intention was found.
    - The assailants ran away but there is nothing to indicate that they ran away together.

- **Verdict:** The court in this case held that **Section 34** could not be attracted and each accused will be held liable for what he did.

- **Mahbub Shah v. Emperor (1945)**
  - **FACTS:** In the present case two persons (B & C) were cutting reeds from the land which did not belong to them. A (A's cousin) person came and asked them to hand over the reeds to him. 'C' tried to strike A's cousin with a lari and he shouted for help. 'A' and 'B' came for help armed with guns and 'A' shot at 'C' killing him. On these facts 'A' and 'B' were tried for murder under **Section 302 read with Section 34** of IPC.
  - **VERDICT:** The Privy Council held that 'A' and 'B' had the same intention to rescue A's cousin if needed be by guns but nothing on facts show that 'A' and 'B' had similar intention to kill 'C'. It was observed that the evidence fell short of proving that 'A' and 'B'had a premeditated concert to cause C's murder to rescue A's cousin.
    - It was further observed that **Section 34** lays down the concept of similar intention and not the common intention. Hence the court observed that similar intention could not be deduced from the facts of the present case and hence **Section 34** could not be attracted. The appellant was acquitted.

COMMON OBJECT OF AN UNLAWFUL ASSEMBLY UNDER BNS

(**Note:** *Section 189(1) of the BNS corresponds **to** Section 141 of the IPC*)

- **Section 189(1) of BNS** defines what constitutes an unlawful assembly. The code specifically forbids five or more persons to assemble and carry out acts forbidden by the provision.
- **Section 189(1) of BNS** provides for certain situations where an assembly becomes an unlawful assembly similarly **Section 189(2) of BNS** provides as to when a person is declared as a member of unlawful assembly.
- Just like joint liability, the "common object" is the *sine qua non* of this offence. Without such an object among members, there is no such assembly.
- **Section 190 of BNS** is a declaratory provision for the group liability of members of such an assembly, carrying out an act in the prosecution of a common object. To invoke **Section 190 of BNS** the assembly in contention must satisfy the criteria laid down in **Section 189(1) of BNS** of the code.

SECTION 189(1) OF BNS

Unlawful Assembly

An assembly of five or more persons is designated an "unlawful assembly", if the common object of the persons composing that assembly is:

(a) To overawe by criminal force, or show of criminal force, the Central Government or any State Government or Parliament or the Legislature of any State, or any public servant in the exercise of the lawful power of such public servant; or

(b) To resist the execution of any law, or of any legal process; or

(c) To commit any mischief or criminal trespass, or other offence; or

(d) By means of criminal force, or show of criminal force, to any person, to take or obtain possession of any property, or to deprive any person of the enjoyment of a right of way, or of the use of water or other incorporeal right of which he is in possession or enjoyment, or to enforce any right or supposed right; or

(e) By means of criminal force, or show of criminal force, to compel any person to do what he is not legally bound to do, or to omit to do what he is legally entitled to do.

Combined Analysis of Unlawful Assembly and Being Member of Unlawful Assembly

(**Note:** ***Section 190 of the BNS*** *corresponds to* ***Section 149 of the IPC***)

- **Principle of Vicarious Liability**: **Section 190** of BNS incorporates the principle of vicarious liability and holds a person liable for an offence, which he might not have actually committed or intended, by reason of his being a member of an unlawful assembly.
  - **Section 190** of BNS is an exception to the general principle of criminal law in the sense that a person can be convicted only on proof of his being a member of the unlawful assembly sharing the common object, notwithstanding as to whether he had actually participated in the commission of the crime or not.
  - Each and every member need not be necessarily involved in the overt acts. It is not necessary to prove by whom the particular injury was inflicted, if the accused are members of assembly.

> **SECTION 190 OF BNS**
>
> **Every Member of Unlawful Assembly Guilty of Offence Committed in Prosecution of Common Object:**
>
> If an offence is committed by any member of an unlawful assembly in prosecution of the common object of that assembly, or such as the members of that assembly knew to be likely to be committed in prosecution of that object, every person who, at the time of the committing of that offence, is a member of the same assembly, is guilty of that offence.

- **Membership of Unlawful Assembly**
  - Before recording a conviction under **Section 190** of BNS, , the essential ingredients of **Section 189(1) and 189(2)** of BNS must be established.
  - Offence must be committed by the member of such an unlawful assembly that commits the act.
- **Mere Presence is not Sufficient**
  - As far as presence under **Section 190 of BNS** is concerned, it is true that the mere presence of the accused is not sufficient to hold him guilty for sharing a common object as the prosecution has to further establish that they were not mere bystanders but in fact were sharing the common object.
  - It must be shown that he did something or omitted to do something which would make him a member of an unlawful assembly or unless the case falls under **Section 189(2) of BNS**
- **Five or more Persons**
  - A combined reading of **Section 189(1) and 190** of BNS reveals that if the assembly is of less than five persons, it will not be an unlawful assembly within the meaning of **Section 189(1) of BNS** and, therefore, cannot form the basis of conviction,
- **Common Object**
  - In fastening constructive liability, the importance of the common object is huge and it is on this basis alone that an accused is punished for the act of his associates. To establish that the accused was a member of an unlawful assembly, it must be shown either from his active participation or otherwise, that he shared the common object of the assembly.
  - The word 'object' means the purpose or design, and in order to make it 'common' it must be shared by all. A common object may be formed by express agreement after mutual consultation but that is by no means necessary. It may be formed at any stage by all or a few members of the assembly and the other members may just join and adopt it.
  - Common object is different from common intention and therefore it does not require a prior concert or pre planning among members of an unlawful assembly once formed common object need not continue to be the same. It may be modified or altered or abandoned at any stage.

- **In Prosecution of the Common Object**
  - The words "in prosecution of the common object have to be strictly construed." These words signify that the offence committed was immediately connected with the common object of the unlawful assembly, of which the accused were members.
  - The act must be such as to have been done with a view to accomplish the common object attributed to the members of the unlawful assembly.
  - There must be a nexus between the common object and the offence committed.
  - There must be proximity in relation to time and place between the members of the unlawful assembly and the criminal acts done by the members.
- **Knew to be Likely to be Committed in Prosecution of the Common Object**
  - **Section 190** of BNS applies not only to offences actually committed in pursuance of the common object, but even to offences which members of the assembly knew were likely to be committed.
  - In every case under **Section 190 of BNS** it is not necessary that the common object should directly be to commit a particular offence. It is sufficient that the particular result was such that the members of the assembly knew to be likely to be committed in prosecution of the common object.
  - This knowledge or state of mind must be shown to exist at the time of the offence, and not the knowledge acquired in the light of subsequent events. The use of the word "likely" implies something more than a possibility. A thing is likely to happen only when it will probably happen or may very well happen.
- **A Specific Overt act on the Part of the Accused is not Necessary:**
  - For the purpose of application of **Section 190** of BNS, the prosecution has to prove the presence and participation in an unlawful assembly.
  - The mere fact that no overt act has been attributed to the members of the unlawful assembly, disprove the charge under **Section 190 of BNS.**
  - In **Madan Singh v. State of Bihar (2004)**, the Court clarified that mere presence in an unlawful assembly cannot render a person liable unless there was a common object and he shared the same or was actuated by that common object and that object is one of those set out in **Section 189(1) of BNS**
    - Where common object of an unlawful assembly is not proved, the accused persons cannot be convicted with the help of **Section 190 of BNS**

Case Laws

(**Note:** *Following cases deal with **Section 189(1), 189(2), 190 of BNS**, earlier **Section 141, 142, 149 of IPC** respectively*)

- **Maina Singh v. State of Rajasthan (1976)**
  - **FACTS:** In this case the relations between deceased and accused/appellant were strained as the accused suspected that the deceased was passing on information about his smuggling activities. One day the accused along with four persons chased the deceased and fired at him. When the deceased fell down, the other accused persons went near him and gave 'gandasi' blows and the appellant/accused gave a blow or two with the butt end of his gun which broke and the broken pieces fell down. Ultimately, the deceased succumbed to his injuries on the spot, and the accused ran away.
  - **VERDICT**: In the present case the court held that there were only 5 named persons who were involved and apart from these 5 persons there was no evidence to show the involvement of another person. It was thus observed that in instances where the evidence does not point towards the involvement of any named or unnamed person, a single accused cannot be held liable under **Section 34 of IPC** or **Section 149** of the IPC.

- **Mizaji v. State of UP (1959)**
  - **FACTS**: There was a dispute between the two parties regarding a field. The five accused (appellants) came to the field armed with the different weapons. An altercation occurred between the two parties. One of the accused (Mizaji) fired, when he was asked so by his father and thus killed a member of the other party.
  - **VERDICT:** Supreme Court interpreted **Section 149 of IPC** which is related to common object i.e. where several people with the common intention to commit an offence and every person who at the time of committing that offence who is a member of the same assembly is guilty of that offence.

DISTINCTION BETWEEN COMMON INTENTION AND SIMILAR INTENTION UNDER BNS

- **Section 3(5)** of BNS enunciates a mere principle of liability, but creates no offence; **Section 190** of BNS is not merely a declaratory provision and it creates a distinct offence.
  - Thus, being a member of an unlawful assembly is by itself an offence.
- Under **Section 3(5)** of BNS two or more persons are required to be involved in the commission of the offence, whereas **Section 190** of BNS requires five or more persons of an unlawful assembly in the commission of an offence.
- **Section 3(5)** of BNS speaks of common intention whereas **Section 190** of BNS contemplates common object. The common object must be one of those specified in **Section 189(1)** of BNS whereas according to the strict language of **Section 3(5)** of BNS 'common intention' may be any intention whatsoever.
- **Section 3(5)** of BNS provides for 'common intention' which requires a preconcerted plan or agreement whereas. **Section 190** of BNS speaks about 'common object'.
- Some active participation is necessary under **Section 3(5)** of BNS but **Section 190** of BNS does not require it and the liability arises by reason of mere membership of the unlawful assembly with a common object.

RIOTING

(**Note:** ***Section 191 of the BNS*** *corresponds to* ***Section 146, 147 of the IPC***)

(**Note:** ***Section 191(3) of the BNS*** *corresponds to* ***Section 148 of the IPC***)

A riot is an unlawful assembly in a particular state of activity, accompanied by the use of force violence. It is only the use of force or violence that distinguishes noting from unlawful assembly

- **Section 191** defines the offence of rioting. It provides that whenever force or violence is used by an unlawful assembly, or by any member thereof, in prosecution of the common object of such assembly, every member of such assembly is guilty of the offence of rioting.
- **Ingredients**
  - (a) That the accused persons, being five or more in number formed an unlawful assembly
  - (b) They were animated by a common object
  - (c) That force or violence was used by the unlawful assembly or any members
  - (d) that such force or violence was used in prosecution of the common object.
- The word violence is not restricted to force used against persons only, but extends also force against inanimate objects. it is not necessary that the force or violence should be directed towards a particular person or particular property. Even the slightest use of force constitutes to frame the offence under rioting. To constituting rioting there should be actual use of force. The offence of rioting is independent of the effect of force.

For example, when a member of an unlawful assembly gives a blow to a person or throws a stone on a cow he is said to use the force even the harm caused is a slight one .Even, the inducement to moves also a force. If a person by his act makes an animals to move or if he stops the bus, he is said to use force and such case of unlawful assembly comes under this section.

- Resistance to the execution of an illegal warrant within reasonable bounds does not amount to rioting. For example, if a municipal commissioner with an illegal warrant comes to Demolish the building, then, the resistance to such a demolition will not amount to rioting.
- In a free fight there cannot be any formation of an unlawful assembly and common intention Each individual will be responsible for his individual acts. Because freefight is without premeditation.
- Actual force or violence must be used; a mere show of force is not sufficient. All members need not use force. The sanhita consequences will apply equally to all, if any of them uses force or violence. However, if the common object of an unlawful assembly is illegal, it is not rioting even if force is used by any member of that assembly." Similarly, use of force by persons in a sudden quarrel does not amount to rioting.
- **Section 191(2)** provides for **Punishment of Rioting**. According to this section, Whoever is guilty of rioting, shall be punished with imprisonment of either description for a term which may extend to two years, or with fine, or with both.

Punishment for Committing Riot with Deadly Weapon

- **Section 191(3)** provides that whoever is guilty of rioting, being armed with a deadly weapon or with anything which, used as a weapon of offence, is likely to cause death, shall be punished with imprisonment of either description for a term which may extend to five years, or with fine, or with both.
- **Section 191(3)** is an aggravated form of the offence of rioting mentioned in **Section 191(1)** and punished under **Section 191(3)** of the sanhita. It provides an enhanced punishment for a person who is armed with a deadly weapon while committing rioting. A mere fact that a person was carrying a deadly weapon while committing rioting makes him liable for the enhanced punishment as it converts 'rioting' (under 191(1) into an 'aggravated rioting' (under 191(3)).
- In the case of **Barendra v. State, (1978)**, the court held that an unlawful assembly that used force, if there, along with others, is only one member armed with a deadly weapon, he alone, and not other unarmed members of the assembly, will be liable under **Section 148** of IPC(now **Section 191(3)** of BNS). Rest of the members will be liable under **Section 148** (now **Section 191(1)** BNS).

Wantonly Giving Provocation with Intent to Cause Riot–If Rioting be Committed; If not Committed

(**Note:** ***Section 192 of the BNS*** *corresponds to* ***Section 153 of the IPC***)

- **Section 192** provides that whoever malignantly, or wantonly by doing anything which is illegal, gives provocation to any person intending or knowing it to be likely that such provocation will cause the offence of rioting to be committed, shall,
  - If the offence of rioting be committed in consequence of such provocation, be punished with imprisonment of either description for a term which may extend to one year, or with fine, or with both; and
  - If the offence of rioting be not committed, with imprisonment of either description for a term which may extend to six months, or with fine, or with both.

- Section 192 provides punishment for a person who, by doing an illegal act, maliciously or recklessly, gives provocation to another person to commit a riot. It brings within its ambit provocative words or acts that do not amount to instigation or abetment. The words "by doing an illegal act' connote that provisions of the section cannot be invoked unless the act done by a person was 'illegal' accompanied with his intent or knowledge that it would provoke others to commit a riot." However, it excludes from its mere chance provocation. To invoke **Section 192**, the provocation given must be likely to cause rioting.

Liability of Owner, Occupier, etc., of Land on Which an Unlawful Assembly or Riot Takes Place

(**Note:** ***Section 193(1), (2) and (3)*** *of the BNS corresponds to* ***Section 154, 155 and 156*** *of the IPC respectively*)

- **Section 193(1)** provides that whenever any unlawful assembly or riot takes place, the owner or occupier of the land upon which such unlawful assembly is held, or such riot is committed, and a person having or claiming an interest in such land, shall be punishable with fine not exceeding one thousand rupees, if he or his agent or manager, knowing that such offence is being or has been committed, or having reason to believe it is likely to be committed, do not give the earliest notice thereof in his or their power to the officer in charge at the nearest police station, and do not, in the case of his or their having reason to believe that it was about to be committed, use all lawful means in his or their power to prevent it and, in the event of its taking place, do not use all lawful means in his or their power to disperse or suppress the riot or unlawful assembly.
- **Section 193(2)** provides that whenever a riot is committed for the benefit or on behalf of any person who is the owner or occupier of any land respecting which such riot takes place or who claims any interest in such land, or in the subject of any dispute which gave rise to the riot, or who has accepted or derived any benefit therefrom, such person shall be punishable with fine, if he or his agent or manager, having reason to believe that such riot was likely to be committed or that the unlawful assembly by which such riot was committed was likely to be held, shall not respectively use all lawful means in his or their power to prevent such assembly or riot from taking place, and for suppressing and dispersing the same.
- **Section 193(3)** provides that whenever a riot is committed for the benefit or on behalf of any person who is the owner or occupier of any land respecting which such riot takes place, or who claims any interest in such land, or in the subject of any dispute which gave rise to the riot, or who has accepted or derived any benefit therefrom, the agent or manager of such person shall be punishable with fine, if such agent or manager, having reason to believe that such riot was likely to be committed, or that the unlawful assembly by which such riot was committed was likely to be held, shall not use all lawful means in his power to prevent such riot or assembly from taking place and for suppressing and dispersing the same.
- Sections 193 BNS deal with constructive liability of a person having interest in the land on which an unlawful assembly is held or a riot is committed and of a person for whose benefit such an assembly or riot is committed.
- Section 193 imposes criminal liability on an owner or occupier of land or a person having an interest in land for the failure of his servant or manager to give information

to the public authorities or to take adequate legal measures to stop the occurrence of an unlawful assembly or riot upon the land of such an owner or occupier. To be more precise, **Section 193** imposes liability on an owner or an occupier of the land on which an unlawful assembly or a riot has taken place for the following omissions of his servant or manager:

(i) Failure to give earliest notice to the public authorities about the unlawful assembly or riot;

(ii) Intentional failure to give notice of the unlawful assembly or riot which was about to be held or committed; and

(iii) Abstention from taking appropriate measures to suppress an unlawful assembly or riot. The owner's liability does not depend upon his knowledge of the riot or of the acts and intention of his servant or manager. He is punished for the taking place of an unlawful assembly or riot on his land.

- **Sections 193(2) and Section 193(3) Deals With the Liability of Persons for Whose Benefit a Riot is Committed**. The **Section 193(1)** deals with liability of the owner or an occupier of the land on which an unlawful assembly or a riot, who has derived benefits from such an assembly or riot and he or his agent, knowing or having reasons to believe that such assembly or riot is likely to take place, has failed to use lawful means within his reach to prevent, suppress or disperse it. While the **Section 193(2)** and **Section 193(3)** holds an agent or a manager of an occupier or an owner of the land on which a riot has taken place and from which such an owner or occupier has derived benefits responsible for his failure, having reasons to believe that such a riot is likely to take place, to resort to all lawful means within his power to prevent or suppress such a riot.

AFFRAY

(**Note:** ***Section 194*** *of the BNS corresponds to* ***Section 159*** *and* ***Section 160*** *of the IPC*)

The word 'affray' is derived from the French word "affraies" to terrify and in a legal sense it is taken for a public offence to the terror of the people.

- **Section 194(1)** lays down that when two or more persons, by fighting in a public place, disturb the public peace, they are said to commit an affray.

Punishment for Committing Affray

- **Section 194(2)** provides that whoever commits an affray, shall be punished with imprisonment of either description for a term which may extend to one month, or with fine which may extend to one thousand rupees, or with both.
- **Ingredients**
  (a) Two or more persons must fight
  (b) Fight must be in a public place
  (c) They must disturb the public place
- **Public Place**
  - Public place is a place where the public go, no matter whether they have a right to go or not.
    - **Example:** A railway station, a railway platform, a public urinal and a goods yard of a railway station are public places.
    - A private chabutra adjoining a public through fare, a railway station and platform at a time when no train is due, except a goods train are not public places
- There must be clear evidence of fighting in a public place and mere words do not constitute fighting for less any assault or breach of the peace.
- In the case of **C Subbarayudh v. State of Andhra Pradesh (1996)**, the Court held that if one person uses force and other person if he remains passive, in such a case there is no fighting and hence, no affray.

- Even a single person in a public place constitutes public. When two persons were fighting in a public and a third person defends himself, even in such cases the offence of affray is committed.

Assaulting or Obstructing Public Servant When Suppressing Riot, etc

(**Note:** ***Section 195*** *of the BNS corresponds to* ***Section 152 of the IPC***)

- **Section 195(1)** provides liability of a Person for Obstructing Suppression of Riot According to this section, Whoever assaults or obstructs any public servant or uses criminal force on any public servant in the discharge of his duty as such public servant in endeavouring to disperse an unlawful assembly, or to suppress a riot or affray, shall be punished with imprisonment of either description for a term which may extend to three years, or with fine which shall not be less than twenty-five thousand rupees, or with both.
- Whoever threatens to assault or attempts to obstruct any public servant or threatens or attempts to use criminal force to any public servant in the discharge of his duty as such public servant in endeavouring to disperse an unlawful assembly, or to suppress a riot or affray, shall be punished with imprisonment of either description for a term which may extend to one year, or with fine, or with both.
- **Section 195** stops a person from using force or threatening to use force against a public servant with a view to deterring him from dispersing an unlawful assembly or suppressing a riot or affray. It accordingly holds a person liable to an imprisonment for a term up to three years or with fine which shall not be less than twenty five thousand rupees, or with both, if he resists or attempts to resist a public servant in his endeavour to disperse an unlawful assembly or suppress a riot or affray.

AFFRAY, RIOT AND ASSAULT

- **Affray and Riot**
  - Affray cannot be committed in a private place but a riot can be.
  - An affray can be committed by two or more persons whereas a riot by five or more persons
- **Affray and Assault**
  - Affray can be committed only at public place whereas assault can be committed anywhere.
  - Affray is regarded as an offence against the public peace, whereas an assault is an offence against the person of an individual.

PROMOTING ENMITY BETWEEN GROUPS

Introduction

- The Constitution of India guarantees certain basic fundamental rights to its citizens. The most instrumental is the right to life, the right to equality and the right to freedom of speech and expression as provided under Article 21, Article 14 and Article 19 respectively. However, it is equally important that such rights are not misused by the citizens. For this particular reason, the legislation has various laws that not only act as safeguards to any potential misuse of these fundamental rights but also ensure harmony among different cultural and ethnic groups. BNS provides for various provisions in the form of restrictions or penalties. **Section 196 and 197** of the Sanhita (Earlier **Section 153A** and **Section 153B** IPC) strive to punish those who spread any form of religious enmity under the umbrella of the right to freedom of speech and expression.

Promoting Enmity Between Different Groups on Grounds of Religion, Race, Place of Birth, Residence, Language, etc., and Doing Acts Prejudicial to Maintenance of Harmony

(Note: *Section 196 of the BNS corresponds to Section 153A of the IPC*)

- **Section 196(1)** provides that whoever
  - (a) By words, either spoken or written, or by signs or by visible representations or through electronic communication or otherwise, promotes or attempts to promote, on grounds of religion, race, place of birth, residence, language, caste or community or any other ground whatsoever, disharmony or feelings of enmity, hatred or ill-will between different religious, racial, language or regional groups or castes or communities; or
  - (b) Commits any act which is prejudicial to the maintenance of harmony between different religious, racial, language or regional groups or castes or communities, and which disturbs or is likely to disturb the public tranquillity; or
  - (c) Organises any exercise, movement, drill or other similar activity intending that the participants in such activity shall use or be trained to use criminal force or violence or knowing it to be likely that the participants in such activity will use or be trained to use criminal force or violence, or participates in such activity intending to use or be trained to use criminal force or violence or knowing it to be likely that the participants in such activity will use or be trained to use criminal force or violence, against any religious, racial, language or regional group or caste or community and such activity for any reason whatsoever causes or is likely to cause fear or alarm or a feeling of insecurity amongst members of such religious, racial, language or regional group or caste or community,
    - shall be punished with imprisonment which may extend to three years, or with fine, or with both.

Punishment for Offence in Any Place of Worship or in Any Assembly Engaged in the Performance of Religious Worship or Religious Ceremonies

- **Section 196(2)** provides that whoever commits an offence specified in sub-section (1) in any place of worship or in any assembly engaged in the performance of religious worship or religious ceremonies, shall be punished with imprisonment which may extend to five years and shall also be liable to fine.

Essential Ingredients

- The essential ingredients of the sections can be enumerated as follows:
  - (1) Whoever by (a) words, either spoken or written; or (b) by signs; or (c) by visible representations; or(d) through electronic communication or(e) otherwise;
  - (2) Promotes or attempts to promote disharmony or feelings of enmity, hatred or ill-will;
  - (3) Between different religious, racial, language or regional groups or castes or communities;
  - (4) On grounds of religion, race, place of birth, residence, language, caste or community or any other ground; or
  - (5) The act may be prejudicial to the maintenance of harmony between different groups and which disturbs or is likely to disturb public tranquility or
  - (6) Organises any exercise, movement, drill or other similar activities in order to train for use of force or violence against any of the groups .

Scope of Section 196

- The section is not confined to the promotion of feelings of enmity on grounds of religion only. It takes in promotion of such feelings on other grounds such as race, place of birth, residence, language, caste or community. However, a fair and rational criticism of religious tenets, couched in temperate or restrained language, will not make the criticism fall within the ambit of the section.
- In the case of **Lalai Singh v. State of UP (1971)**, the Court held that it was perfectly legitimate to criticise hinduism for the doctrine of untouchability and the discriminatory caste practices followed by it, and the reprehensible treatment meted out to the castes considered lower in the caste hierarchy
  - However, it is equally important to note that it is not the mere language of the statement, but also the manner in which it is stated, that counts for examination of liability under the provision.
- In the case of **Azizul Haq Kausar Naqvi v. State of UP (1980)**, The Court held that where words spoken are couched in dignified temperate and mild language which are not such as would hurt the deepest religious convictions of any section of the people, then the act will not fall under the provision.
- In **Babu Rao Patel v. State (Delhi Administration) (1980)**, the accused had published an article in a newspaper that militant minorities thrive on communalism and specifically referred to Muslims generally as a 'basically violent community' apart from other aspersions to the Muslim community. The author had also criticised the naming of roads in Delhi after Mogul emperors, who according to the author, were lustful perverts, rapists and murderers.
  - The Supreme Court, after considering all the evidence in the case. held that the article, in the guise of political thesis or historical truth, actually promoted feelings of enmity, hatred and ill will between the Hindu and Muslim communities Therefore, the Court held the conviction of the accused by the trial court for offence under **Section 153A**, IPC(now **Section 196**) was held to be proper.

Imputations, Assertions Prejudicial to National Integration

(**Note:** ***Section 197 of the BNS*** *corresponds to* ***Section 153B of the IPC***)

- **Section 197(1)** provides that whoever, by words either spoken or written or by signs or by visible representations or through electronic communication or otherwise,
  - (a) Makes or publishes any imputation that any class of persons cannot, by reason of their being members of any religious, racial, language or regional group or caste or community, bear true faith and allegiance to the Constitution of India as by law established or uphold the sovereignty and integrity of India; or
  - (b) Asserts, counsels, advises, propagates or publishes that any class of persons shall, by reason of their being members of any religious, racial, language or regional group or caste or community, be denied, or deprived of their rights as citizens of India; or
  - (c) Makes or publishes any assertion, counsel, plea or appeal concerning the obligation of any class of persons, by reason of their being members of any religious, racial, language or regional group or caste or community, and such assertion, counsel, plea or appeal causes or is likely to cause disharmony or feelings of enmity or hatred or ill-will between such members and other persons; or

- (d) Makes or publishes false or misleading information, jeopardising the sovereignty, unity and integrity or security of India,
    - Shall be punished with imprisonment which may extend to three years, or with fine, or with both.

- **Section 197(2)** provides that whoever commits an offence specified in sub-section (1) in any place of worship or in any assembly engaged in the performance of religious worship or religious ceremonies, shall be punished with imprisonment which may extend to five years and shall also be liable to fine.
- In the context of increased communal and caste tensions erupting in different parts of the country, which threatened not just the peaceful relations between and amongst different communities and groups of people, but also the integrity of the country itself.
- "Electronic communication" is added as one of the methods of disseminating designated activities under **Section 197** of the BNS and false or misleading information making or publishing that endangers India's sovereignty, unity, integrity, or security is also covered by **Section 197(1)(d)** of the BNS.
- **Essential Ingredients of Section 197 of BNS**
  - The signs, remarks, or statements must incite hatred, animosity, and discord among various linguistic, racial, and religious groups.
  - Two or more communities must be the source of the purported animosity. According to Section 197 of BNS, merely mentioning the other group is insufficient to warrant punishment.
  - *Mens rea* is required, meaning that the perpetrator must have intended to sow discord and hatred among various social groupings and communities.
  - Spoken or written, the remarks must be grave and must offend the group's or community's strong religious beliefs.

❖❖❖

Chapter 6

PUNISHMENTS

INTRODUCTION

Punishment is the penalty on someone as a result of their wrongdoing. It is awarded to the offenders with the aim to prevent them from committing crimes. The object of law is to protect the society and deter the criminals, the same can be achieved by imposing appropriate punishment. The types of punishment that can be awarded in a criminal trial are provided under **Section 4** of the Bharatiya Nyayan Sanhita, 2023 (BNS) (**Section 53** of the Indian Penal Code, 1860).

COMPARATIVE CHART OF THE BNS AND IPC

Bharatiya Nyaya Sanhita, 2023 (BNS)	TITLE	Indian Penal Code, 1860 (IPC)
Section 4	Punishment	Section 53
Section 5	Commutation of sentence **EARLIER TITLE:** (Commutation of Sentence of death)	Section 54
	EARLIER TITLE: (Commutation of Sentence of imprisonment of life)	Section 55
Section 8	Amount of fine, liability in default of payment of fine, etc. **EARLIER TITLE:** (Amount of fine)	Section 63
	EARLIER TITLE: (Sentence of imprisonment for non-payment of fine)	Section 64
	EARLIER TITLE: (Limit to imprisonment for non-payment of fine, when imprisonment and fine awardable)	Section 65
	EARLIER TITLE: (Description of imprisonment for non-payment of fine)	Section 66
	EARLIER TITLE: (Imprisonment for non-payment of fine when offence punishable with fine only	Section 67
Section 11	Solitary Confinement	Section 73
Section 12	Limit of Solitary Confinement	Section 74
Section 13	Enhanced punishment for certain offences after previous conviction	Section 75

CHANGES IN BNS IN COMPARISON TO IPC

- **Section 4** of the BNS is the corresponding of Section 53 of IPC, it has been modified as follows:
  - **Community Service** has been included as a form of punishment. Although the BNS does not define community service, **Section 23** of the Bharatiya Nagarik Suraksha Sanhita (BNSS) explains it as "work that the court may require a convict to perform as a punishment, which benefits the community and for which the individual shall not receive any compensation."

THEORIES OF PUNISHMENT

Theories of Punishment is that area of study which helps us to understand the jurisprudential and logical reasoning behind punishing a criminal. The following theories are important to be discussed:

- **Retributive Theory:** When an offender breaks the law, justice requires that they suffer in return, and that the response to a crime is proportional to the offence.
  - Proportionality requires that the level of punishment be related to the severity of the offending behaviour. However, this does not mean that the punishment has to be equivalent to the crime. A retributive system must punish severe crimes more harshly than minor crimes.
  - The severity of crime can be determined in multiple ways. Severity can be determined by the amount of harm, unfair advantage or the moral imbalance that the crime caused.
  - An eye for an eye, tooth for a tooth is associated with the retributive theory.
- **Deterrent Theory:** Deterrence is based on the idea that the threat of punishment will deter people from committing crime and reduce the probability and/or level of offending in society. Criminal deterrence theory has two possible applications:
  - The first is that punishments imposed on individual offenders will deter or prevent that particular offender from committing further crimes.
  - The second is public knowledge, that certain offences will be punished has a generalised deterrent effect which prevents others from committing crime.
- **Preventive Theory:** Preventive theory of punishment seeks to prevent prospective crimes by disabling the criminals. Main object of the preventive theory is transforming the criminal, either permanently or temporarily:
  - By creating the fear of punishment.
  - By disabling the criminal permanently or temporarily from committing any other crime.
- **Reformative Theory:** Reformative theory considers punishment to be curative more than to be deterrent. According to this theory, crime is like a disease which cannot be cured by killing; rather it can be cured with medicine with the help of the process of reformation.
  - There has been an increasing emphasis in the reformation and rehabilitation of the offender as a useful and self-reliant member of the society without subjecting him to the deleterious effect of jail life.
  - The Probation of Offenders Act, 1958 derives its jurisprudential essence from the Reformative Theory of Punishment.
  - In the case of **Musakhan v. State of Maharashtra (1976)**, the Hon'ble Supreme Court propounded that the Probation of Offenders Act is a social legislation which is meant to reform offenders so as to prevent them from becoming hardened criminals by providing an educative and reformative treatment to them by the Government.

TYPES OF PUNISHMENT

Punishments under Indian criminal law are outlined in **Section 4** of BNS (Section 53 of IPC). The BNS specifies various types of punishments for different offences, aiming to serve multiple purposes such as deterrence, retribution, reformation, and prevention. The detailed overview of the types of punishments and their implications under Indian criminal law is provided hereunder.

Death Penalty or Capital Punishment

- **Section 4(a)** of BNS provides the 'Death Penalty' as a form of punishment.
- The death penalty is the most severe form of punishment and is awarded for the most heinous crimes.
  - **Applicability**: Reserved for crimes such as murder, terrorism, and certain cases of rape resulting in death or persistent vegetative state.
  - **Constitutional Validity**: The constitutional validity of the death penalty in India has been a subject of extensive legal debate. The Supreme Court of India has addressed the issue multiple times, balancing the need for justice with the constitutional guarantee of life and liberty. Following judgments and Constitutional provisions are necessary to be understood in this regard:
- **Article 21 of the Constitution**: **Article 21** guarantees the right to life and personal liberty, stating that no person shall be deprived of life or personal liberty except according to the procedure established by law. This article has been central to the debate on the death penalty.
- **Jagmohan Singh v. State of U.P. (1973):** The Supreme Court, in a unanimous decision, upheld the constitutional validity of the death penalty. The following are the key points of the judgment:
  - (i) **Regarding Article 21:** The Court held that the right to life is not absolute and can be deprived by "procedure established by law." The death penalty, as prescribed by law, does not violate Article 21 as long as it is imposed following due legal procedure.
  - (ii) **Regarding Article 14:** The Court rejected the argument that the death penalty is arbitrary and violates the right to equality. It noted that judicial discretion in sentencing is guided by established principles, and the imposition of the death penalty is not left to the whim of judges.
  - (iii) **Regarding Article 19:** The Court found no merit in the argument that the death penalty infringes on the freedoms guaranteed under Article 19. It reasoned that the death penalty is imposed as a consequence of a person's actions, which have already been determined to be outside the bounds of law.
- **Bachan Singh v. State of Punjab (1980)**: This landmark judgment upheld the constitutional validity of the death penalty but laid down the "rarest of rare" doctrine. The Court held that the death penalty should only be imposed in the "rarest of rare" cases where the alternative option is unquestionably foreclosed. This principle guides Indian courts in deciding whether to impose the death penalty.
- **Machhi Singh v. State of Punjab (1983)**: This case further elaborated on the "rarest of rare" doctrine, setting out specific criteria for courts to consider when deciding whether a case falls under this category. These criteria include the manner of commission of the murder, the motive for the murder, the anti-social or abhorrent nature of the crime, and the magnitude of the crime.
- **Mithu v. State of Punjab (1983)**: The Supreme Court struck down **Section 303** of the Indian Penal Code (Section 104 of BNS), which mandated the death penalty

for offenders already serving a life sentence. The Court held that such mandatory death sentences were unconstitutional, as they violated **Article 21** by not allowing for judicial discretion.

REVIVAL OF SECTION 303 OF IPC

- **Section 303** of the Indian Penal Code, which mandates the death sentence for a person who commits murder while undergoing imprisonment for life was struck down by the Supreme Court in Mithu v. State of Punjab (1983) since it violated Article 14 and 21 of the Constitution of India.
- In the new penal code i.e. The Bharatiya Nyaya Sanhita 2023 (BNS), the old Section 303 is replaced with **Section 104** as: "Whoever, being under sentence of imprisonment for life, commits murder, shall be punished with death or with imprisonment for life, which shall mean the remainder of that person's natural life."

Arguments Against the Death Penalty

- **Human Rights**: It has been time and again submitted that infliction of the death penalty is incompatible with the right to life and is difficult to reconcile with the right to live free of torture. Universal Declaration of Human Rights under **Article 3** states that "Everyone has the right to life, liberty and security of person." The death penalty, by its very nature, directly contradicts this right.
- **Irreversibility**: The possibility of wrongful convictions and the irreversible nature of the death penalty are significant concerns.
- **International Perspective**: Many countries have abolished the death penalty, and there is increasing global pressure on India to do the same.

Life Imprisonment

- **Section 4(b)** of BNS provides 'Imprisonment for Life' as a form of punishment.
- The convict is imprisoned for the remainder of their natural life, though they may be eligible for parole or commutation under certain conditions. Commutation of life sentence is provided under **Section 5** of BNS (Section 55 of IPC).
  - **Applicability**: Common for crimes such as murder, kidnapping for ransom and drug trafficking.

Judicial Precedents

- **Gopal Vinayak Godse v. State of Maharashtra (1961)**: The Supreme Court of India clarified that life imprisonment means imprisonment for the convict's entire life unless the sentence is commuted or remitted by the government.
- **Rattan Lal v. State of Punjab (1964)**: The Supreme Court held that life imprisonment is not the same as imprisonment for a fixed term, such as 14 or 20 years. Life imprisonment lasts for the convict's entire life.
- **Swamy Shraddananda v. State of Karnataka (2008)**: In this case, the Supreme Court introduced the concept of "life imprisonment without remission" as an alternative to the death penalty in cases where the crime was considered heinous but did not warrant the death penalty. This judgment empowered courts to sentence convicts to life imprisonment without the possibility of remission or early release.

Imprisonment

- **Section 4(c)** of BNS mentions 'Imprisonment' of following description:
  - **Simple Imprisonment**: The convict is confined to prison without hard labour. It is generally prescribed for less severe offences where the objective is to punish without imposing physical hardship.
  - **Rigorous Imprisonment**: The convict is required to perform hard labour. Prescribed for more serious offences where the law intends to impose both the deprivation of liberty and physical hardship.

- The courts have the discretion to decide whether a convict should be sentenced to simple or rigorous imprisonment, depending on the nature and severity of the crime, the circumstances of the case, and the provisions of the BNS.
- In some cases, the court may convert rigorous imprisonment to simple imprisonment based on factors like the convict's health, age, or other humanitarian grounds.

Forfeiture of Property

- **Section 4(d)** of BNS provides 'Forfeiture of Property' as a form of punishment.
- It involves the loss of ownership rights over property as a consequence of committing certain offences. The property forfeited typically becomes the property of the state. This form of punishment is intended to penalise the offender economically, in addition to other forms of punishment such as imprisonment or fines.
- **Applicability**: Used in cases of crimes like corruption (Prevention of Corruption Act), smuggling, and certain anti-terrorism laws.
    - Example: **Section 154** of BNS (Section 126 of IPC) - **Committing depredation on territories of foreign State at peace with Government of India**: Whoever commits depredation, or makes preparations to commit depredation, on the territories of any foreign State at peace with the Government of India, shall be punished with imprisonment of either description for a term which may extend to seven years, and shall also be liable to fine and to forfeiture of any property used or intended to be used in committing such depredation, or acquired by such depredation.

Fine

- **Section 4(e)** of BNS provides 'Fine' as a form of punishment.
- Under the Bharatiya Nyaya Sanhita, 2023, fine is a monetary penalty imposed on an offender as a form of punishment. Fine can be imposed either as the sole punishment or in conjunction with other forms of punishment, such as imprisonment.

Provisions of the BNS Related to Fines

- The BNS contains numerous provisions where fines are prescribed either as a part of the sentence or as an alternative to imprisonment.
- Some provisions relating to fine are described below:
    - **Section 8(1) of BNS (Section 63 of IPC)** states that where no sum is specified as the maximum fine, the amount of the fine that can be imposed is unlimited, but it should not be excessive.
    - **Section 8(2) of BNS (Section 64 of IPC)** provides that when an offender is sentenced to a fine and is unable to pay it, they may be sentenced to imprisonment in default of payment.
    - **Section 8(3) of BNS (Section 65 of IPC)** limits the term of imprisonment imposed in default of payment of a fine. This imprisonment cannot exceed one-fourth of the maximum term of imprisonment provided for the offence.
- The court has the discretion to decide the amount of the fine, considering factors like the nature of the offence, the offender's financial capacity, and the need to prevent undue hardship.
- If the offender fails to pay the fine, they may be subjected to imprisonment in default. The term of such imprisonment is specified by the court and must comply with the limits set out in **Section 8(4) and 8(5)** of BNS (Sections 64 and 65 of the IPC).

Community Service

- **Section 4(f)** of BNS provides 'Community Service' as a form of punishment.
- This is a new punishment added in the Sanhita. Community service is a Court ordered penalty that requires an offender to perform unpaid work for the benefit of

the community. It's typically used for non-violent, minor offences as an alternative to incarceration.

- **Example:** Cleaning parks and public spaces, assisting with social welfare programs, working on environmental projects, volunteering at educational institutions or non-profit organisations.
- **Objectives:**
  - **Rehabilitation:** Community service aims to rehabilitate offenders by providing them with an opportunity to learn new skills, contribute positively to society, and make amends for their wrongdoing.
  - **Restorative Justice:** It promotes the concept of restorative justice by focusing on repairing the harm caused to the community by the offender's actions.
  - **Reduced Incarceration Costs:** Community service can be a cost-effective alternative to incarceration, freeing up space in prisons and reducing the financial burden on the justice system.

Solitary Confinement

(**Notes:** ***Section 11, 12, 13*** *of the BNS corresponds to* ***Section 73, 74, 75*** *of the IPC, respectively*)

- Solitary confinement isolates prisoners from seeing or communicating with other inmates. It may or may not involve hard labour.
- The concept of solitary confinement finds its place under **Section 11** of BNS (Section 73 of IPC). When someone is sentenced to rigorous imprisonment, the court can order them to spend some time in solitary confinement. This solitary confinement cannot exceed a total of 3 months. The duration is determined by the length of the sentence:
  - **Less than 6 months:** Solitary confinement is limited to **1 month** maximum.
  - **6 months to 1 year:** Solitary confinement cannot exceed **2 months** total.
  - **Over 1 year:** Solitary confinement is capped at a maximum of **3 months.**
- In **Kishore Singh v. State of Rajasthan,** the court clarified that solitary confinement means complete isolation from other prisoners and the outside world.

Limit of Solitary Confinement

- **Section 12** of BNS (Section 74 of IPC) provides for Limit of Solitary Confinement:
  - Solitary confinement can only be imposed for a maximum of 14 days at a time with an interval between the period of solitary confinement of not less duration than such period.
  - For sentences longer than 3 months, solitary confinement is limited to a maximum of 7 days per month with an interval between the period of solitary confinement of not less duration than such period.

Enhanced Punishment

- **Section 13** of the **Bharatiya Nyaya Sanhita, 2023 (Section 75 of IPC)** provides for enhanced punishment.
- It mentions whoever, having been convicted by a Court in India, of an offence punishable under **Chapter X or Chapter XVII** of BNS with imprisonment of either description for a term of three years or upwards, shall be guilty of any offence punishable under either of those Chapters with like imprisonment for the like term, shall be subject for every such subsequent offence to imprisonment for life, or to imprisonment of either description for a term which may extend to ten years.

❖❖❖

Chapter 7

GENERAL EXCEPTIONS

INTRODUCTION

- The general rule is that a person is presumed to know the nature and consequences of the act that he does and is, therefore, responsible for it in law. However, there are various kinds of acts done under the circumstances mentioned in **Chapter III**, comprising **Section 14 to 44 of the Bharatiya Nyaya Sanhita, 2023** (Earlier, **Section 76 to 106** of Indian Penal Code, 1860) which do not amount to an offence under this Sanhita. In other words, these provisions operate as clauses of non-culpabality and an act covered thereunder does not attract criminal liability for its doer.
- It is important to note that Chapter III is titled as "General Exceptions" which indicates that these exceptions are applicable to all the offences under Sanhita and not merely to certain specific offences.
- General Exceptions can be classified into the following two categories:
  - **Excusable Exceptions**: Where there is lack of *mens rea* on the part of the person committing the offence either by reason of mistake of fact, or by reason of the act being done accidentally, or by reason of infancy, insanity, etc. These exceptions are provided under **Sections 14, 17, 18, 20, 21, 22, 23, 24** of BNS.
  - **Justifiable Exceptions:** Where the circumstances under which the act is committed provide legal justification like the act is done in the exercise of the right of private defence. These exceptions are provided under **Sections 15, 16, 19, 25, 26, 27, 30, 31, 32, 33** of BNS.
- In case of general exceptions the Burden of Proof is reversed. As a general rule, the burden of proof is on the prosecution to prove the guilt of the accused whereas in case of general exceptions the burden of proof lies on the accused that his case lies in the general exceptions.
  - **Section 108 of the Bharatiya Sakshaya Adhiniyam, 2023** provides that if an accused person claims the benefit of exceptions, the burden of proving his plea that his case falls under the general exception lies upon the accused.

COMPARATIVE CHART OF THE BNS AND IPC

Bharatiya Nyaya Sanhita, 2023	Title	Indian Penal Code, 1860
Section 14	Act done by a person bound, or by mistake of fact believing himself bound, by law	Section 76
Section 15	Act of Judge when acting judicially	Section 77
Section 16	Act done pursuant to the judgment or order of Court	Section 78
Section 17	Act done by a person justified, or by mistake of fact believing himself justified, by law	Section 79
Section 18	Accident in doing a lawful act	Section 80

Bharatiya Nyaya Sanhita, 2023	Title	Indian Penal Code, 1860
Section 19	Act likely to cause harm, but done without criminal intent, and to prevent other harm	Section 81
Section 20	Act of a child under seven years of age	Section 82
Section 21	Act of a child above seven and under twelve of immature understanding	Section 83
Section 22	Act of a person of unsound mind	Section 84
Section 23	Act of a person incapable of judgment by reason of intoxication caused against his will	Section 85
Section 24	Offence requiring a particular intent or knowledge committed by one who is intoxicated	Section 86
Section 25	Act not intended and not known to be likely to cause death or grievous hurt, done by consent	Section 87
Section 26	Act not intended to cause death, done by consent in good faith for person's benefit	Section 88
Section 27	Act done in good faith for benefit of child or insane person, by or by consent of guardian	Section 89
Section 28	Consent known to be given under fear or misconception	Section 90
Section 29	Exclusion of acts which are offences independently of harm cause	Section 91
Section 30	Act done in good faith for benefit of a person without consent	Section 92
Section 31	Communication made in good faith	Section 93
Section 32	Act to which a person is compelled by threats	Section 94
Section 33	Act causing slight harm	Section 95

CHANGES IN BNS IN COMPARISON TO IPC

- **Section 78** of IPC uses **"Court of Justice,"** while **Section 16** of the BNS simply uses **"Court."**
- **Section 19** of BNS simplifies the terminology by omitting **"steam"** from the illustrations, using **"vessel"** in general. **Section 81** of IPC includes **"steam vessel,"** which is more specific. Both sections otherwise convey the same principle regarding actions taken in good faith to prevent greater harm.
- **Section 27** of BNS replaces **"insane person"** with **"person of unsound mind"** and includes the term **"lawful charge"** for clarity. **Section 89 of IPC** used the term ***"insane person"*** which has a more general connotation.

MISTAKE OF FACT

- Mistake of fact as a general exception has been dealt with under Sections 14 and 17 of BNS. Section 14 provides that nothing is an offence which is done by a person who is, or who by reason of a mistake of fact and not by reason of mistake of law, in good faith, believes himself to be bound by law to do it.
  - **Illustration**: A soldier following orders to disperse a mob or an officer arresting some people under the mistaken belief that they are the perpetrators of crime. He has committed no offence due to the operations of this provision.
- It is to be remembered that 'mistake of law' is no defence, but mistake of fact can be a defence. *Ignorantia facit excusat, Ignorantia*

juris non excusat which means Ignorance of fact is excusable, but ignorance of law is not excusable.

- In **R. v. Prince (1875)**, "taking an unmarried girl under the age of 16 years out of possession and against the will of her father was held not to be a good defence to an indictment for abduction because the accused intended to do and did a wrongful or immoral act and not an innocent act".
- According to **Section 17** of BNS, nothing is an offence which is done by any person who is justified by law, or who by reason of a mistake of fact and not by reason of a mistake of law in good faith, believes himself to be justified by law, in doing it.
- **Illustration:** A sees Z commit what appears to be murder. He in good faith seizes Z, to hand him over to the police. A has committed no offence, though it may turn out that Z was acting in self-defence.

DISTINCTION BETWEEN SECTION 14 AND SECTION 17 OF THE BHARATIYA NYAYA SANHITA, 2023

- Under **Section 14**, a person is bound by law but in Section 17 he is justified by law in doing an act. In other words, the distinction is between a real or supposed legal obligation/compulsion and a real or supposed legal justification in doing the particular act. However, under both the sections, there is a bona fide intention to advance the law (mens rea is absent in both).
- Where A mistook in good faith another's umbrella to be his own and took the defence that at the time of taking the umbrella he was intoxicated and erroneously believed that the umbrella was his own, the defence is tenable under **Section 14**. Where A shoots at B (A's inmate) who enters his room at night under circumstances which make A to believe in good faith that B is a burglar, it was held that A will not be liable for shooting B and will be entitled to claim defence of justifiable mistake under **Section 17**.

JUDICIAL ACTS

- **Sections 15 and 16** of BNS deal with the general exception of judicial acts.
- **Section 15** deals with the act of a Judge as a defence to criminal liability and provides that nothing is an offence which is done by a Judge when acting judicially in the exercise of any power which is, or which in good faith he believes to be, given to him by law.
- For instance, by virtue of the protection given to judges by Section 15 of BNS, a judge who punishes a person with death penalty is not liable for the murder of that person.
- **Section 16** of BNS deals with the acts done pursuant to judgment or order of Court. Section 16 provides that nothing which is done in pursuance of, or which is warranted by the judgment or order of, a Court; if done whilst such judgment or order remains in force, is an offence. The protection given by Section 16 is applicable notwithstanding that Court may have had no jurisdiction to pass such judgment or order, provided the person doing the act in good faith believes that the Court had such jurisdiction.
- For instance, an officer of the court who arrests a person in pursuance of court's order does not incur any criminal liability and has committed no offence.

ACCIDENT IN DOING A LAWFUL ACT

- **Section 18** of BNS provides that nothing is an offence which is done by accident or misfortune, and without any criminal intention or knowledge in the doing of a lawful act in a lawful manner by lawful means and with proper care and caution.
  - **Illustration:** A is at work with a hatchet; the head flies off and kills a man who is standing by. Here, if there was no want of proper caution on the part of A, his act is excusable and not an offence.
- When the act is done due to want of proper care and caution then the same cannot be termed as an accident.

- Section 18 of BNS is corollary to the latin maxim *Actus Reus Non-Facit Reum Nisi Mens Sit Rea* which means an act doesn't render a man guilty of a crime unless his mind is guilty.
- In the case of **Tunda v. State (1950)**, it was observed by the Court that when an act is done without criminal intention or knowledge, it will come under **Section 80** of the IPC (now Section 18 of the BNS).
  - In this case, the accused Tunda and the deceased were friends who were interested in wrestling and were engaged in a wrestling bout. While wrestling, the deceased got injured on his head and it resulted in his death.
  - In this case, Allahabad High Court observed that the injury that caused death was the result of an accident and there was no foul play on part of the accused. In addition to that, the court held that there was an implied consent of the deceased in taking any risk in the wake of wrestling. Therefore, the accused was entitled to get benefits under both **Section 80 and 87** of the Indian Penal Code, 1860 (Now **Section 18 and 25** of BNS).
- In the case of **Jageshwar vs. Emperor (1924)**, it was observed that when an act is is not lawful and is not done in lawful manner by lawful means, it will not come under **Section 80** of the Indian Penal Code, 1860 (Now **Section 18** of BNS). In this case, the accused was hitting the victim but he accidentally hit his wife who was carrying an infant child. No sooner did the blow hit the head of the child and it resulted in his death. The Court held that the accused will not be entitled to the benefits of **Section 80** of IPC. It's because even though the death of the child was by accident, the act was not lawful.

NECESSITY

- The general exception of necessity is based on a legal principle that allows individuals to act in a manner that would normally be illegal or unethical but is permissible for protecting a greater good or for preventing a greater harm.
- This general exception is based on the idea that in certain situations, the need to prevent greater harm or protect a greater good can justify actions that might otherwise be considered unlawful or immoral.
- As per **Section 19** of the BNS, Nothing is an offence merely by reason of its being done with the knowledge that it is likely to cause harm, if it be done without any criminal intention to cause harm, and in good faith for the purpose of preventing or avoiding other harm to person or property.
  - However, the risk of doing such an act will be weighed against the nature and need of each situation
- The Explanation appended to Section 19 very clearly provides that it is a question of fact in such a case whether the harm to be prevented or avoided was of such a nature and so imminent so as to justify or excuse the risk of doing the act with the knowledge that it was likely to cause harm.
  - **Illustrations:**
  - A, in a great fire, pulls down houses in order to prevent the conflagration from spreading. He does this with the intention in good faith of saving human life or property. Here, if it be found that the harm to be prevented was of such a nature and so imminent as to excuse A's act, A is not guilty of the offence.
  - A Captain of a ship turned the direction of the ship of 100 people in order to save their lives, but harming the life of 30 people of a small boat, without any intention or negligence or fault on his part. He will not be liable because necessity is a condition in which a person causes small harm to avoid greater harm.

Conditions for Defence

- **Urgent Threat:** An urgent threat is the first requirement for the defence of necessity. There must be a serious and immediate threat, and the only way to avert the harm short of breaking the law must exist. There could be a financial, psychological, or material risk.
    - In the case of **State of Maharashtra v. Mohd. Ajmal Mohammad Amir Kasab & Ors. (2012)**, the SC recognized the defence of necessity and held that the existence of an imminent threat is a necessary condition for the defence to apply. In this case, Kasab was one of the terrorists who attacked Mumbai in 2008. He argued that he had no choice but to participate in the attack as he was threatened by his handlers. The Court rejected his defence as there was no imminent threat to his life or the life of his family.
- **Proportionality:** The second requirement is proportionality. The benefit of not breaking the law must exceed the cost of doing so. The defence will not be accepted if breaking the law will cause more harm than it will prevent. The defence can only be applied in situations where there is a genuine and immediate threat to life, limb or property.
    - In the case of the **State of Uttar Pradesh v. Sanjay Kumar (2012)**, the Supreme Court held that the defence of necessity can only be invoked if the harm prevented is greater than the harm caused by breaking the law. In this case, the accused had stolen a motorcycle in order to take his pregnant wife to the hospital. The court held that the defence of necessity could not be applied as the harm caused by the theft of the motorcycle was greater than the harm prevented.
- **No Other Feasible Option**: The accused must not have any other reasonable way to prevent the harm, there must be no other feasible option.
    - In the case of **State of Maharashtra v. Dr. Praful B. Desai (2003)**, the Supreme Court held that the defence of necessity can only be applied if there was no other reasonable choice available to the accused. In this case, the accused had performed a surgery without the consent of the patient in order to save the patient's life. The court held that the defence of necessity could be applied as there was no other reasonable choice available to the accused to save the patient's life.

Exceptions to Doctrine of Necessity

- In the case of **Regina v. Dudley and Stephens (1884 England)**, the two accused persons, namely Thomas Dudley and Edwin Stephens, and a cabin boy named Richard Parker were cast adrift in a boat without food and water due to a shipwreck. Later, on the eighteenth day, when the three of them had been without food and water for several days, Dudley proposed to Stephen that one should be put to death to save the rest. Accordingly, they decided that it would be better to kill Parker so that they could save their own lives. On the twentieth day, both Dudley and Stephens killed Parker and fed on his flesh for four days. Later, a vessel rescued them and they were charged with committing the murder of Richard Parker.
    - It was held by the Court that killing an innocent person in order to save one's own life does not justify murder even though it was committed under the extreme necessity of hunger. Subsequently, the defendants were sentenced to death, however, it was later reduced to six months imprisonment.
- In the case of **United States v. Holmes (1842)**, an American vessel by the name 'William Brown' containing 65 passengers and 17 crew members hit an iceberg and sank rapidly. As a result, the longboat was cast

adrift in the stormy sea. In order to prevent the boat from being sunk, the members of the crew threw some of the passengers overboard. Later, when a case came up for the trial of one of the crew members, the Court held that such situations of necessity may be considered a defence against the charge of criminal homicide. However, the Court stated that those who are sacrificed must be fairly selected depending on the group of people present.

ACT OF CHILD

- As per **Section 20** of the BNS, nothing is an offence which is done by a child under seven years of age.
  - The reason for this exemption is that children below the age of seven years cannot understand the difference between right and wrong. The law aims to protect them by granting complete immunity from criminal prosecution, trial, and conviction.
  - A child under the age of seven is *doli incapax* means 'incapable of wrongdoing' and therefore receives absolute immunity.
  - It is believed that a child under the age of seven cannot distinguish between right and wrong. He does not have the mental capacity to understand the nature and consequences of his actions.
- **Section 21** of the BNS provides partial immunity from criminal liability to children who are above 7 and below 12 years of age. According to this section:
  - If a child is above 7 and below 12 years old, and
  - If it is proven that the child has not yet reached a sufficient level of maturity to understand the nature and consequences of his actions on that particular occasion
  - Then, any act committed by that child will not be considered an offence.
- **Section 21** applies not only to offences under the BNS but also extends its protection to offences under local and special laws.
- **Section 21** assumes that a child over 7 years old but under 12 is *doli capax*, i.e able to commit crimes according to his or her maturity level. However, this is a hypothesis that can be refuted. That can be disproved by leading evidence to the contrary.
  - In the case of **Ulla Mahapatra v. The King (1950)**, a boy above eleven and below twelve years of age picked up his knife and advanced towards another. He threatened the other by saying that he would cut him into bits and did actually what he said. It was held that he was having sufficient maturity of understanding, because he did what he intended.
  - In the case of **Abdul Satar v. The Crown (1949)**, two accused both under the age of twelve, broke through the locks of two stores and walked inside with the purpose to steal. They used the defence of a lack of maturity. The Court ruled that the accused's behaviour of opening the shop's locks demonstrates his maturity level.
  - Beyond the age of 12 years, there is no immunity from criminal liability, even if the offender is a person of under-developed understanding.
  - All the juveniles in conflict with law are now governed by the Juvenile Justice (Care and Protection of Children) Act, 2015. The perusal of JJ Act makes it clear that it is not giving any punishment to juveniles but at the same time it is not exonerating the juveniles from criminal liability. It would appear that something akin to immunity is provided to delinquent juveniles under this Act.

DIFFERENCE BETWEEN SECTION 20 AND 21 OF THE BNS

- **Section 20** provides complete immunity from criminal liability to the children below the age of 7 years whereas **Section 21** provides partial immunity from criminal liability to children who are above 7 and below 12 years of age.
- A child under the age of seven is 'doli incapax' meaning 'incapable of wrongdoing' and therefore receives absolute immunity whereas **Section 21** assumes that a child over 7 years old but under 12 is doli capax, i.e able to commit crimes according to his or her maturity level.

UNSOUNDNESS OF MIND

- **Section 22 of BNS** deals with the general exception of unsoundness of mind. The unsoundness of mind dealt under Section 22 of BNS basically presupposes a state in which the accused is incapable of knowing the nature of his act, or that what he is doing is either wrong or contrary to law.
  - In different contexts, the word "madness" has a different meaning and defines different levels of mental disorders. Any person suffering from mental illness is not exempt from criminal liability "*ipso facto*".
- Compos mentis means a composed mind. Non compos mentis means not having control or composure over one's mind. A person suffering from unsoundness of mind is Non compos mentis i.e. 'not of sound mind'. Unsoundness of mind may be temporary such as in case of lunatics, permanent (idiocy), natural or supervening, by birth or by illness, e.g. Schizophrenics, and sometimes also by extreme consumption of, or addiction to alcohol or drugs.
- The law as contained under **Section 22** is based on following maxims:
  - **Furious Furor Sub Puniter:** A mad man is punished by his madness only.
  - **Furious Nulle Voluntas Est:** There is no free will of the madman.
- **Section 22** applies where a person, as a result of mental disease or defect, lacks substantial capacity to know or appreciate either that the conduct was against the law or that it was against commonly accepted moral principles, or both.
  - **For Example:** A person may kill a child under an insane delusion that he is saving him from sin and sending him to heaven. Here he is incapable of knowing by reason of insanity that he is doing what is morally as well as legally wrong.
- In **Dayabhai Thakkar v. State of Gujarat, (1964)**, the SC held that whenever a plea of legal insanity is set up, the Court has to consider whether at the time of commission of the offence, the accused was suffering from unsoundness of mind or not. The crucial point of time for ascertaining the state of mind of the accused is the material time when the offence takes place.
- In **Queen-Empress v. Kader Nasyer (1896),** the court held that unsoundness of mind which 'materially impairs' the cognitive faculties of the mind forms a ground of exemption from criminal responsibility. On the other hand, the court in **Lakshmi v. State (1958)**, required complete extinguishment of the ability to know the nature or consequences of one's acts. In other words, varying degrees of incapacity have been held sufficient.
- The phrase "incapable of knowing" makes it clear that the burden of proof is with the accused to demonstrate that his mental illness prevented him from understanding the consequences of his acts.
- What a person knows and what they are capable of knowing are two very different things. It doesn't matter if he was aware of the nature of his activities, what is protected by **Section 22** is an organic or inherent

incapacity, not a false belief that may have been the product of distorted potentiality. This incapacity might result from a sudden episode of insanity or delusion, a halted mental development, or another medically recognised cause.

- In the case of **Lakshmi v. State (1958)**, the Court observed "A person might believe so many things. His convictions won't be able to keep him safe once it is discovered that he is capable of discriminating between good and wrong. He assumes the risk that he will be held accountable by the law for the action that came from him if his potentialities cause him to come to the incorrect judgment. The case that the law defends is one in which a man has fully lost the ability to discern between good and wrong, as well as between lawful and illegal. A man cannot be heard to beg to be protected where such light is proven to be flickering, on the grounds that he was deceived by his own faulty intuition, or by whatever fancy illusion that had been tormenting him and which he had mistaken for truth. We mostly derive our beliefs from the faculty of intuition. However, our understanding of the nature of knowledge and its substance originate from our ability to reason and think. If the faculties of cognition and reason are discovered to be intact and brilliant, it will not help a man to claim that, at the pivotal time, he was obscured by an encroaching cloud of intuition that was throwing its thick, shadowy shadows over them".
- Indian law relating to unsoundness of mind is based on the **McNaughten's Case**. Following propositions can be derived from this case:
    - Every man is presumed to be sane and to possess sufficient degree of reason until the contrary is proved to the satisfaction of the court.
    - To establish the defence of insanity it must be clearly proved that at the time of committing the act the accused was labouring in defect of reason (inability to think rationally and pertains to incapacity to reason).
    - If the accused was conscious that the act which ought not be done or it was contrary to law then he would be punishable.
- The following propositions regarding burden of proof in the context of the plea of insanity have been laid down by the Supreme Court in the case of **T.N. Lakshmaiah v. State of Karnataka (2002).**
    - The prosecution must prove beyond reasonable doubt that the accused had committed the offence with the requisite mens rea and the burden of proving that always rests on the prosecution from the beginning to the end of the trial.
    - There is a rebuttable presumption that the accused was not insane, when he committed the crime, in the sense laid down by **Section 22** of the BNS. The accused may rebut it by placing before the court all the relevant evidence oral, documentary or circumstantial, but the burden of proof upon him is no higher than that rests upon party to civil proceedings i.e. on a preponderance of probabilities.
    - Even if the accused was not able to establish conclusively that he was insane at the time he committed the offence, the evidence placed before the court by the accused or by the prosecution may raise a reasonable doubt in the mind of the court as regards one or more of the ingredients of the offence, including mens rea of the accused and in that case the court would be entitled to acquit the accused on the ground that the general burden of proof resting on the prosecution was not discharged.

LEGAL INSANITY DIFFERENT FROM MEDICAL INSANITY

- Every person suffering from mental disease cannot be allowed to avoid responsibility for a crime by invoking the plea of insanity. A person whose cognitive faculties are so impaired as to make it impossible for him to know the nature of his act or that what he was doing was wrong or contrary to law, is exempted from criminal responsibility and comes within the purview of legal insanity.
- Legal insanity means incapability of a person to understand the nature or consequences of his actions at the time of the commission of the offence. Medical insanity deals with a person's behavior and conduct at all times. A person subject to fits of insanity will be termed as medically insane. Mere abnormalities of mind, partial delusion, irresistible impulses or compulsive behavior of psychopaths all constitute instances of medical insanity.
- The difference is dealt in the leading case, **Surendra Mishra v. State of Jharkhand (2011)**, in this case it was held that the person held for criminal liability has to prove legal insanity, not medical insanity if he intends to benefit under Section 84 of **IPC** (Now **Section 22**, BNS). Even if the evidence says that the accused is in mental disturbance, in the absence of specific proof from the doctor or the nature of the mental disturbance, this would not prove the accused was mentally unfit or insane at the time of the incident.
- In the recent case, **Tufan @ Tofan v. State of Madhya Pradesh, (2022)**, the Madhya Pradesh High Court, Gwalior Bench, recently elucidated the difference between the term 'Legal Insanity' and 'Medical Insanity' in the context of Section 84 of IPC (Now, Section 22 of the BNS). The Court opined that in order to bring a case within the ambit of this provision , the accused has to prove that they were suffering from Legal Insanity.
- "Any person, who is suffering from any kind of mental weakness is called "medical insanity," however "legal insanity" means, a person suffering from mental illness should also have a loss of reasoning power. Furthermore, the legal insanity must be at the time of incident. In other words, it can be said that in order to attract legal insanity, a person should be incapable of knowing the nature of the act, or he is doing what is either wrong or contrary to law. Thus, mere abnormality of mind or compulsive behavior is not sufficient to take benefit of Section 84 of IPC (Now, Section 22 of the BNS)".

INTOXICATION

- A person's act committed under the influence of intoxicants may not reflect his real character as intoxication impairs perception, reasoning and the ability to foresee consequences.
  - Such a person is exempted by the **Section 23 and 24** of the BNS from criminal liability but only under prescribed situations.
- **Section 23** of BNS provides that nothing is an offence which is done by a person:
  - Who at the time of doing it, is, by reason of intoxication,
  - Incapable of knowing the nature of the act, or
  - That he is doing what is either wrong, or contrary to law, provided that the thing which intoxicated him was administered involuntarily without his will or knowledge.
- **For Example:** 'A' drank alcohol given by a friend thinking it to be a cold drink. He became intoxicated and hit a person while driving his car back home. He will not be liable as alcohol was administered to him without his will and knowledge.
- Voluntary toxication is punishable under **Section 24** of the BNS. There is a Latin term,

"*Qui pecat ebrius luat sobrius.*" It means "let him who sins when drunk, be punished when he is sober". If a man chooses to get drunk, it is a voluntary act. That voluntary species of madness from which it is the party's power to abstain must be answered for. An offence committed because of voluntary drunkenness has no excuse in law.

- **Section 24** applies to cases where an act done is not an offence unless done with a particular intent:
  - A person who does the act in a state of intoxication, shall be liable to be dealt with as if he had the same knowledge as he would have had if he had not been intoxicated.
  - Unless the thing which intoxicated him was administered to him without his knowledge or against his will.
- **Section 24** says that a person voluntarily intoxicated will be deemed to have the same knowledge as he would have had if he had not been intoxicated.
  - **For Example:** A person intoxicated, stabs another person under influence of alcohol which was administered to him in the party against his knowledge or will, he will not be liable. But if that person had stabbed that person under voluntary intoxication, then he would be liable.
- In **Basudev v. The State of Pepsu (1956)**, it was held that "so far as knowledge is concerned the court must attribute to the intoxicated man the same knowledge as if he was quite sober but so far as intent or intention is concerned, the court must gather it from the attending general circumstances of the case paying due regard to the degree of intoxication". There is no such observation in the judgment

TEST OF DRUNKENNESS

In **Director of Public Prosecutor v. Beard, (1920),** a prisoner ravished a 13 years old girl and raped her. He put his hand on her mouth to prevent her from screaming and his thumb was pressing on her neck. Due to suffocation, she died. He claimed drunkenness. The Court held that he was guilty of murder and sentenced him to the death penalty, saying that the defence of drunkenness prevails only when it is reasonable to believe that the accused did not know what he was doing or whether it was right or wrong. House of Lords laid down the three test regarding drunkenness:

- Evidence of drunkenness which renders the accused incapable of forming a specific intent essential to constitute a crime should be taken into consideration with other facts.
- Insanity, whether produced by drunkenness or otherwise is a defence to the crime charged.
- Evidence of drunkenness falling short of a proved incapacity in the accused to form the intent necessary to constitute a crime, and merely establishing that his mind was affected by drink so that he more readily gave way to some violent passion, does not rebut presumption that a man intends that natural consequence of his acts.

- **Suraj Jagannath Jadhav v. State of Maharashtra (2020)**, in this case, the appellant/accused Suraj Jagannath Jadav who was intoxicated started abusing and assaulting his wife and poured kerosene on her body, who was around 18 to 20 weeks pregnant. When she was trying to run out of the house to save herself and attempting to open the latch of the door, the accused came from behind and threw a lighted match stick on her and set her ablaze. Suraj Jaganath Jadav was convicted of an offence punishable by **Section 302** of IPC in the trial court due to which he filed an appeal in the High Court of Bombay.

- It was held that the intention of the accused to cause death was clear and the defence of pouring water on the deceased appeared to be an attempt to hide this guilt.
- The accused failed in proving that he was in a highly inebriated condition and he lost all the senses. Inebriation can be defined as an act done by a person where his power of thinking becomes blurred and he is unaware of its consequences. In this case, the accused was in his complete senses and was very well aware of the consequences of his act. Thus, the accused will be liable under **Section 302** of IPC.

- **Mohd. Anwar v. State (NCT of Delhi) (2020)**, Supreme Court held that in order to successfully establish the defence of unsoundness of mind under **Section 84** of IPC, (Now, **Section 22** of the BNS) accused must show preponderance of probabilities that s/he suffered from a serious mental disease which would effect individual's ability to distinguish right and wrong. It must also be established that the accused was afflicted by such disability particularly at the time of commission of crime and that but for such impairment, crime would not have been committed.

CONSENT

- Consent means "to agree upon the same thing in the same sense." It is said to be given when a person agrees upon a thing being done with his own will and not because of any fear, force or misconception. The element of consent excuses offences against the human body and property.
- **Sections 25 to Section 28** of the BNS lays down that if certain acts are committed with the victim's consent, they will not be considered an offence, and the offender will not be held liable for the same.
- The general exception of consent is based on the legal maxim *volenti non fit injuria* which means harm caused with the consent cannot be considered as an injury and it does not amount to an offence.

Act Not Intended and Not Known to Be Likely to Cause Death or Grievous Hurt, Done by Consent

- **Section 25** states that nothing which is not intended to cause death, or grievous hurt, and which is not known by the doer to be likely to cause death or grievous hurt, is an offence by reason of any harm which it may cause, or be intended by the doer to cause, to any person, above eighteen years of age, who has given consent, whether express or implied, to suffer that harm; or by reason of any harm which it may be known by the doer to be likely to cause to any such person who has consented to take the risk of that harm.
- **Illustration:** A and E agreed to fence each other for enjoyment. This agreement implies the consent of each other to suffer harm which, in the course of such fencing, may be caused without foul play and if A while playing fairly hurts E, then A, has committed no offence.
- In **Poonai Fattemah v. Emp. (1869)**, the accused who professed to be a snake charmer, induced the deceased to believe him that he had the power to protect him from any harm caused by the snake bite. The deceased believed him and got bitten by the snake and died. The defence of consent was rejected.

Act Not Intended to Cause Death, Done by Consent in Good Faith for Person's Benefit

- **Section 26** states nothing which is not intended to cause death is an offence by reason:
  - Of any harm which it may cause, or
  - Be intended by the doer to cause, or
  - Be known by the doer to be likely to cause,
  - To any person for whose benefit it is done in good faith,

- Who has given a consent, whether expressed or implied to suffer that harm, or to take the risk of that harm.

- In **R.P Dhanda v. Bhurelal (1986)**, the appellant, a medical doctor, performed an eye operation for cataract with patient's consent. The operation resulted in the loss of eyesight. The doctor was protected under this defence as he acted in good faith.

Act Done in Good Faith for Benefit of Child or Person of Unsound Mind

- **Section 27** states that nothing which is done in good faith for the benefit of a person:
  - Under twelve years of age, or
  - Of unsound mind, or
  - By consent, either express or implied, of the guardian or other person having lawful charge of that person,
  - Is an offence by reason of any harm which it may cause, or be intended by the doer to cause or be known by the doer to be likely to cause to that person.

PROVISO TO SECTION 27

This exception shall not extend to:

(a) The intentional causing of death, or to the attempting to cause death.

(b) The doing of anything which the person doing it knows to be likely to cause death, for any purpose other than the preventing of death or grievous hurt, or the curing of any grievous disease or infirmity.

(c) The voluntary causing of grievous hurt, or to the attempting to cause grievous hurt, unless it be for the purpose of preventing death or grievous hurt, or the curing of any grievous disease or infirmity.

(d) The abetment of any offence, to the committing of which offence it would not extend.

Consent Known to be Given Under Fear or Misconception

- **Section 28** lays down following situations under which the consent given by a person is not considered as a valid consent:
  - **Person Giving Consent under the Fear of Injury:** Under criminal law, consent obtained by threat and violence would not be a valid consent. **For example**, Z threatened A with a knife to sign his property paper in favour of X, Z's son. Here the consent was given under fear of injury.
  - **Person Giving Consent under the Misconception of Facts:** If consent is obtained under a misconception of facts, then it will have no value in the eyes of law. **For example**, a woman had consensual sexual intercourse with a doctor on the belief that he was making a medical examination of her. The doctor would be held guilty as he made her believe that he was doing a medical examination of her.
  - **Consent Given by Insane Person:** People who are of unsound mind, or in an intoxicated state of mind are to understand the nature and consequences of their acts and therefore, incapable to give their consent. **For example**, A, in a heavily drunken state, signed his property paper in favour of the liquor shop owner just to get one more liquor bottle. In the eyes of the law, his consent has no value.
  - **Consent Given by Child:** Consent given by a child under the age of 12 years has no value in the eyes of law. In this case, the consent will be given by the child's guardians or person in charge of him.

- In **Jakir Ali v. State of Assam (2007)**, it was proved beyond doubt that the accused had sexual intercourse with the victim on a false promise of marriage. The Guwahati High Court held that submission of the body by a woman under fear or misconception of fact cannot be construed as consent and so conviction of the accused under **Sections 376 and 417** of the Indian Penal Code, 1860 was proper.

- **Section 28** of the BNS talks about what does not amount to consent. It describes consent in a negative term. It states, a consent given by a person under the fear of injury, or under a misconception of facts, or by reason of unsoundness of mind, intoxication, or a child under the age of 12 years (unless the contrary appears from the context), who is incapable to understand the nature and consequences of the consented act, is no consent.

Exclusion of Acts Which are Offences Independently of Harm Caused

- **Section 29** deals with exclusion of acts which are offences independently of harm caused and provides that the exceptions in **Sections 25, 26 and 27** do not extend to acts which are offences independently of any harm which they may cause, or be intended to cause or be known to be likely to cause, to the person giving the consent, or on whose behalf the consent is given.
- **Illustration**: Causing miscarriage (unless caused in good faith for the purpose of saving the life of the woman) is an offence independently of any harm which it may cause or be intended to cause to the woman. Therefore, it is not an offence "by reason of such harm"; and the consent of the woman or of her guardian to the causing of such miscarriage does not justify the act.

Act Done in Good Faith for Benefit of a Person without Consent

- **Section 30** states that nothing is an offence by reason of any harm which it may causes to a person for whose benefit it is done in good faith, even without that person's consent, if the circumstances are such that it is impossible for that person to signify consent, or if that person is incapable of giving consent, and has no guardian or other person in lawful charge of him from whom it is possible to obtain consent in time for the thing to be done with benefit.
  - Provided that this exception shall not extend to:
    - The intentional causing of death, or the attempting to cause death.
    - The doing of anything which the person doing it knows to be likely to cause death, for any purpose other than the preventing of death or grievous hurt, or the curing of any grievous disease or infirmity.
    - The voluntary causing of hurt, or to the attempting to cause hurt, for any purpose other than the preventing of death or hurt.
    - The abetment of any offence, to the committing of which offence it would not extend.

Communication Made in Good Faith

- **Section 31** provides that no communication made in good faith is an offence by reason of any harm to the person to whom it is made, if it is made for the benefit of that person.
- **Illustration:** A doctor in good faith tells the wife that her husband has cancer and his life is in danger. The wife died of shock after hearing this. The doctor will not be liable because he communicated this news in good faith.

Act to Which a Person is Compelled by Threats

- An act to which a person is compelled by threats to do it is included as a general exception under **Section 32** of BNS. Section 32 provides that except murder, and offences against the state punishable with death, nothing is an offence which is done by a person compelled to do it under threats, which, at the time of doing it, reasonably causes the apprehension that instant death to that person will otherwise be the consequence.

- **Proviso to Section 32** states that the person should not on his own accord, or from a reasonable apprehension of harm to himself short of instant death, place himself in the situation by which he became subject to such constraints.
- **Explanation 1** states A person who, of his own accord, or by reason of a threat of being beaten, joins a gang of dacoits, knowing their character, is not entitled to the benefit of this exception, on the ground of his having been compelled by his associates to do anything that is an offence by law.
- Further, **Explanation 2** states that A person seized by a gang of dacoits, and forced, by threat of instant death, to do a thing which is an offence by law; for example, a smith compelled to take his tools and to force the door of a house for the dacoits to enter and plunder it, is entitled to the benefit of this exception.

Act Causing Slight Harm

- An act of causing slight harm is included as a general exception under **Section 33** of BNS. Nothing is an offence by reason that it causes, or that it is intended to cause, or that it is known to be likely to cause, any harm if that harm is so slight that no person of ordinary sense and temper would complain of such harm.
- This section is based on maxim *De Minimis Non Curat Lex* which means the law does not take account of trifling matters.
- In **Mrs. Veeda Menezes v. Yusuf Khan and Anr (1966)**, during the course of exchange of high tempers and abusive words between appellant's husband and the respondent, the latter threw a file of papers at the former which hit the appellant causing a scratch on the elbow. The Supreme Court held that the harm caused was slight and hence held the accused not guilty.

❖❖❖

Chapter 8

RIGHT OF PRIVATE DEFENCE

INTRODUCTION

- The general rule is that a person is presumed to know the nature and consequences of the act that he does and is, therefore, responsible for it law. However, there are various kinds of acts done under the circumstances mentioned in **Chapter III** from **Section 14 to 44 of the Bharatiya Nyaya Sanhita, 2023** (Earlier, **Section 76 to 106** of Indian Penal Code, 1860) which will not amount to offences under this Sanhita. In other words, these acts (exceptions) are exempted from the category of offences under the Bharatiya Nyaya Sanhita, 2023.
- The present chapter deals with the Right of Private Defence provided under **Section 34-44** of BNS. This right comes under the category of Justifiable Exceptions.
- This right is rooted in the principle of self-preservation, acknowledging that in certain circumstances, individuals may be compelled to act in their defense without waiting for law enforcement authorities to intervene. The BNS outlines the extent and limitations of this right, ensuring that while individuals can defend themselves, their actions must be proportionate to the threat faced and must not exceed the boundaries of necessary force.
- **Section 108 of the Bharatiya Sakshaya Adhiniyam, 2023** provides that if an accused person claims the benefit of exceptions, the burden of proving his plea that his case falls under the general exception lies upon the accused.

COMPARATIVE CHART OF THE BNS AND IPC		
Bharatiya Nyaya Sanhita, 2023 (BNS)	**Title**	**Indian Penal Code, 1860 (IPC)**
Section 34	Things done in private defence	Section 96
Section 35	Right of private defence of body and of property	Section 97
Section 36	Right of private defence against the act of a person of unsound mind, etc.	Section 98
Section 37	Acts against which there is no right of private defence	Section 99
Section 38	When the right of private defence of the body extends to causing death	Section 100
Section 39	When such right extends to causing any harm other than death	Section 101
Section 40	Commencement and continuance of the right of private defence of body	Section 102
Section 41	When the right of private defence of property extends to causing death	Section 103

Section 42	When such right extends to causing any harm other than death	Section 104
Section 43	Commencement and continuance of the right of private defence of property	Section 105
Section 44	Right of private defence against deadly assault when there is risk of harm to innocent person	Section 106

CHANGES IN BNS IN COMPARISON TO IPC

- **Section 41** of the BNS corresponds to **Section 103** in the IPC has changed as follows:
  - The words "House-breaking by night" are changed to **"house-breaking after sun set and before sunrise"**and The words "Mischief by fire" are changed to **"mischief by fire or any explosive substance"**.
- **Section 43** of the BNS corresponds to **Section 105** in the IPC has changed as follows:
  - The words "House-breaking by night" are changed to **"house-breaking after sunset and before sunrise"**

Things Done in Private Defence

(**Note:** ***Section 34*** *of the BNS corresponds to* ***Section 96*** *of the IPC*)

- **Section 34** provides that nothing is an offence which is done in the exercise of the right of private defence.
- Right of private defence has been clearly incorporated in the BNS with a purposive scheme in mind and cannot be said to be an offence in return; rather it must proceed in the presence of a reasonable apprehension of harm to person or property.
- The reasonable apprehension can only be justified if the accused had an honest belief that there is danger and that such belief is reasonably warranted by the conduct of the aggressor and the surrounding circumstances.
- In **Sukumaran v. State (2019),** the Supreme Court held that a mere reasonable apprehension is enough to put the right of self defence into operation. It is not necessary that there should be actual commission of the offence.
- The right of private defence under **Section 34** is not exhaustive. It is actually extended by the succeeding provisions of the BNS with varying degrees of circumstances.
- In the case of **V. Subramani v. State of Tamil Nadu (2005),** Supreme Court held that the right of self defence has to be pleaded and proved by the accused.

Right of Private Defence of Body and of Property

(**Note:** ***Section 35*** *of the BNS corresponds to* ***Section 97*** *of the IPC*)

- Every person has a right, subject to the restrictions contained in **Section 37,** to defend:
  - His own body, and the body of any other person, against any offence affecting the human body;
  - The property, whether movable or immovable, of himself or of any other person, against any act which is an offence falling under the definition of:
    - Theft, robbery, mischief or criminal trespass, or
    - Which is an attempt to commit theft, robbery, mischief or criminal trespass.
- **Section 35** provided that the right is available against an offence (affecting human body or property, in certain cases) and can be exercised by a person either by himself or by any other person on his behalf.
- In **Shankar Balu Patil v. State of Maharashtra (2007),** Supreme Court held that the nature of right of private defence is purely preventive and not offensive.

Right of Private Defence Against Act of a Person of Unsound Mind

(**Note:** *Section 36 of the BNS corresponds to Section 98 of the IPC*)

- **Section 36** of BNS mentions when an act, which would otherwise be a certain offence, is not that offence, by reason of the youth, the want of maturity of understanding, the unsoundness of mind or the intoxication of the person doing that act, or by reason of any misconception on the part of that person, every person has the same right of private defence against that act which he would have if the act were that offence.
  - Z, a person of unsound mind, attempts to kill A; Z is guilty of no offence. But A has the same right of private defence which he would have if Z were sane.

Acts Against Which There Is No Right of Private Defence

(**Note:** *Section 37 of the BNS corresponds to Section 99 of the IPC*)

- **Section 37** of the BNS states that there is no right of private defence against acts:
  - By a public servant acting in good faith under the colour of his office
  - Which does not reasonably cause the apprehension of death or of grievous hurt, if done, or attempted to be done, by direction of public servant acting in good faith under colour of his office, though that act may not be strictly justifiable by law.
  - In which there is time to have recourse to protection of the public authorities.
- **Extent to Which the right may be Exercised:** The right of private defence in no case should extend to the inflicting of more harm than it is necessary to inflict for the purpose of defence.
- **Explanations 1 and 2 to Section 37** provides that a person is not deprived of the right of private defence against an act of a public servant unless he knows of or has reason to believe that the attacker is a public servant or is acting under the direction of a public servant.
- Thus, the right of private defence of body/property can be exercised against a public servant only in the following three cases:
  - When the act of the public servant reasonably causes apprehension of death/grievous hurt.
  - When the public servant does not act in good faith under the colour of his office.
  - When the person exercising the right does not know or have any reason to believe that the attacker is a public servant or is acting under the direction of a public servant.
- In **Amjad Khan v. State (1952),** during a riot, a mob of Hindus was on the rampage. When the mob started attacking the appellant's shop, the appellant fired, which caused death and injuries to some persons. The court held that the appellant had no time to recourse to the public authorities, and there was a reasonable apprehension of death or grievous hurt to the appellant.
- In the case of the **State of U.P. v. Niyamat (1987),** the court held that there is a marked difference between the acts which are wholly illegal and the acts which may not be strictly justifiable by law (or irregular acts).
  - Where the police had illegally arrested a person, and police but a with a view to rescuing that person launched attack on the only after a constable had fired at them, it was held that the villagers had acted in exercise of right of private defence as the act of firing shots caused reasonable apprehension of death/grievous hurt in their minds.
  - On the other hand, if a police officer, acting bona fide under colour of his office, arrests a person without authority, the person so arrested has no right of self defence against the police officer.

- There is no right of defence in cases in which there is time to have recourse to the protection of public authorities. However, this does not mean that a person must run away to have recourse to the protection of public authorities when he is attacked, instead of protecting himself.
- **Section 37** also lays down the extent to which the right may be observed. The measure of self-defence must always be proportionate to the quantum of force used by the attacker and which it is necessary to repel. The extent of force which may be used depends upon the circumstances of each case. The nature of the attack, the danger apprehended, the imminence of danger and the real necessity of inflicting harm by retaliation for the purpose of self-defence, are some of the important factors to be considered in deciding whether the right of defence has been exceeded.
- In **Dominic Varkey v. State of Kerala (1971),** the Supreme Court broadly stated, the right of private defence rests on three ideas:
  - **Firstly,** that there must be no more harm inflicted than is necessary for the purpose of defence.
  - **Secondly**, that there must be reasonable apprehension of danger to the body from the attempt or threat to commit some offence.
  - **Thirdly**, that the right does not commence until there is a reasonable apprehension.
  - In short, the right of self-defence is not available to a person who resorts to retaliation for past injury but to him who is suddenly confronted with the immediate necessity of averting an impending danger not of his creation.

Right of Private Defence of Body

(**Note:** ***Sections 38, 39*** *of the BNS corresponds to* ***Sections 100, 101*** *of the IPC respectively*)

- According to **Section 38,** the right of private defence of the body extends (subject to the restrictions mentioned in **Section 37**) to the voluntary causing of death or of any other harm to the assailant in cases where:
  - Such an assault may reasonably cause the apprehension that death will otherwise be the consequence of such assault;
  - Such an assault may reasonably cause the apprehension that grievous hurt will otherwise be the consequence of such assault;
  - Such an assault with the intention of committing rape;
  - Such an assault with the intention of gratifying unnatural lust;
  - Such an assault with the intention of kidnapping or abduction;
  - Such an assault with the intention of wrongfully confining a person under circumstances which may reasonably cause him to apprehend that he will be unable to have recourse to the public authorities for release;
  - An act of throwing or administering acid or an attempt to throw or administer acid which may reasonably cause the apprehension that grievous hurt will otherwise be the consequence of such act.
- Four under mentioned cardinal conditions must exist before the benefit of private defence is extended to causing death :
  - The accused must be free from fault in bringing about the encounter,
  - There must be an impending peril to life or of bodily harm as provided under, either real or so apparent as to create honest belief of an existing necessity,

- There must be no safe or reasonable mode of escape by retreat,
- There must have been a necessity for taking life.

- The term 'reasonable' implies what any common man in that situation would apprehend. No man is permitted to make use of this right in situations where danger or threat is only probable or likely or where one's fears are founded upon 'probabilities' or 'possibilities.' The apprehension must be reasonable and not fanciful. Self-created fears of a hypersensitive man do not permit the use of this right.
- **Nand Kishore Lal v. Emperor (1924),** accused Sikhs abducted a Muslim woman and converted her to Sikhism, a situation arose where the woman's relatives demanded her return almost a year later. Despite the woman's express unwillingness to rejoin her Muslim husband, her relatives attempted to take her by force. In response, the accused resisted and one of them caused the death of the woman's assailants while defending her. The court held that the accused had the right to defend the woman against her assailants, and this right extended to causing death under relevant legal provisions. The actions of the accused in causing the death of the assailants were deemed lawful, and they were not held to have committed any offence in this context.
- In the **State of U.P. v. Ram Swarup (1974),** after a dispute between the deceased and one Ganga Ram, the latter came with his three sons one of them being Ram Swarup, armed with dangerous weapons. The deceased, taken by surprise, attempted to rush before he could retreat, Ram Swarup shot him dead at point-blank range, the defence version was that a scuffle had taken place between the deceased and Ganga Ram and that Ganga Ram was assaulted with lathis by the servants of the deceased. The question arose as to whether Ram Swarup had a right of private defence and if so, whether he had not exceeded the same.
- The Supreme Court observed that the right of self-defence is a right of defence and not of retribution. It is available in the face of imminent peril to those who act in good faith. The Court held that appellant had no right of private defence as evidenced by the facts and circumstances of the case:
  - Considering the nature of injuries received by Ganga Ram (as per medical evidence he had four contusions on his person and all those injuries were simple in nature), it is impossible to hold that there could be a reasonable apprehension as to death/grievous hurt under **Section 100** of IPC **(**Now **Section 38** of BNS**)**.
  - More harm than necessary was inflicted for the purpose of self-defence.
  - The right of private defence ends with necessity for it. Ram Swarup had fired at the deceased from a close range when the latter was fleeing in fear of his life, thus the act of Ram Swarup was deliberate.
- **Mohinder Pal Jolly v. State of Punjab (1979)**, in a scenario where workers of a factory were throwing brickbats from outside the gates, prompting the factory owner to use his revolver and cause the death of a worker, the court ruled that the relevant legal provision did not protect the factory owner in this instance. Therefore, the factory owner was not shielded by the law in this situation.
- Further, **Section 39** is corollary to **Section 38.** It provides that if any of the circumstances enumerated under **Section 38** does not exist the right of private defence of the body does not extend to causing the death of the attacker but the person who defends is entitled, subject to the restrictions of **Section 37**, to voluntarily cause to him any other harm other than death.

Right of Private Defence of Property

(**Note:** ***Section 41, 42*** *of the BNS corresponds to* ***Section 103, 104*** *of the IPC*)

- **Section 41** provides the Acts against which the right of private defence of property can be exercised (subject to the restrictions mentioned in **Section 37**). Every person has the right to defend the property (whether movable or immovable) of himself or of any other person against:
  - Robbery
  - House-breaking after sunset and before sunrise
  - Mischief by fire or any explosive substance committed on any building, tent or vessel, which building, tent or vessel is used as a human dwelling, or as a place for the custody of property
  - Theft, mischief or house-trespass, under such circumstances as may reasonably cause apprehension that death or grievous hurt will be the consequence, if such right of private defence is not exercised.
- **For Example:** A enters by night a house, which he is legally entitled to enter. Z, in good faith, taking A for a house-breaker, attacks A. Here Z, by attacking A under this misconception, commits no offence. But A has the same right of private defence against Z, which he would have if Z were not acting under this misconception.
- In **Kurrim Bux v. Queen-Empress (1865):** A, finding a thief entering into a house in the middle of night through an entrance in the side wall, seized him while invading his body and held him with his face down to the ground to prevent his further entrance and thereby caused his death by suffocation. At the trial, A pleads the right of private defence. It was held that the right of private defence was a good justification. It is not the intention of the law that the right to defend property is available only when the thief has already affected entry, for property may be protected by attacking the thief inside the house as much as by preventing his entry into it.
- In **Puran Singh v. State of Punjab (1975)**, the Apex Court discussed the nature of possession which may entitle a trespasser to exercise the right of private defence of property. In this case, the appellants had taken forcible possession of the land in dispute a month before the occurrence and had grown wheat crops on it and the complainant party (armed with guns, axes, etc.) tried to re-enter the land and destroy the crops grown by the appellants. It was held that for a trespasser to be entitled to exercise the right of private defence of property, he must be in actual physical possession of the property over sufficiently long period and the possession must be to the knowledge (express or implied) of the owner or without any attempt of concealment and which contains an element of ***animus possidendi*** (intent to possess). Further, the Court observed that in the following circumstances right of private defence can be exercised :
  - There is no sufficient time for recourse to the public authorities.
  - There must be a reasonable apprehension of death or grievous hurt to the person or danger to the property concerned.
  - More harm than necessary should not have been caused.
- **Jassa Singh v. State of Haryana (2002),** the Supreme Court clarified that the right of private defence concerning property does not include the right to cause the death of a person who commits acts of trespass on open land. According to the court, only house trespass committed under circumstances that could reasonably lead to death or grievous harm is specifically listed as an offence under **Section 103** of IPC (Now, **Section 41** of the BNS) regarding the right of private defence.

- The process of dispossession of the true owner by the trespasser must be complete and final and must be acquiesced in by the true owner. One of the usual tests to determine the quality of settled possession in the case of cultivable land, would be whether or not the trespasser after having taken possession had grown any crop. If so, then even the true owner has no right to destroy the crop grown by the trespasser and take forcible possession, to which case the trespasser will have a right of private defence.
- Further, **Section 42** is corollary to Section **41.** It provides that where the offence of theft, mischief or criminal trespass has been committed or attempted but the description are different from those enumerated in **Section 41**, the right of private defence of property extends only up to the extent to voluntarily causing any other harm than death.

Commencement and Continuation of Right of Private Defence

(**Note:** *Section 40, 43 of the BNS corresponds to Section 102, 105 of the IPC respectively*)

- **Section 40** provides that the right to private defence of the body commences as soon as reasonable apprehension of danger to the body arises and continues as long as such apprehension of danger to the body continues.
- **Section 43** provides that the right of private defence of property commences as soon as the reasonable apprehension of danger to the property commences.
    - The right continues in the case of theft:
        - Offender has affected his retreat with the property, or
        - Assistance of the public authority is obtained, or
        - Property is recovered
    - In the case of robbery, so long as the offender causes or attempts to cause to any person death or hurt or wrongful restraint or instant fear of that.
    - In the case of criminal trespass, mischief and house breaking as long as the aforesaid offences continue.
- Thus, the right of private defence of the property commences and continues as long as the danger lasts. The extent to which the exercise of the right will be justified will depend, not on the actual danger, but on whether there was reasonable apprehension of such danger.
- **Burden of Proof:** According to **Section 108** of Bharatiya Sakshaya Adhiniyam, 2023 (earlier **Section 105** of the Indian Evidence Act, 1872), the burden of proving the exception is on the person who benefits from it (i.e. on the accused). It is well settled that even if an accused does not plead self-defence, it is open to the Court to consider such a plea if the same arises from the material on record.
- In **Deo Narain v. State of U.P. (1973),** the accused was in possession of a plot of land. The complainant party went to that plot with an aggressive design to disturb the possession of the accused by unlawful use of force. A clash followed in which one member of the complainant party was killed by a spear injury caused by Deo Narain. It was proved that Deo Narain had received head injuries before he had inflicted injury on the member of the complainant party. The Court finds the use of a knife in self-defence in excess of the right of private defence. The appellant exceeded his right of private defence by using his spear with greater force than was necessary, and by giving a dangerous blow with considerable force with a spear on the chest of the deceased though he had only. The High Court convicted the appellant of an offence under **Section 304** of the IPC (Now **Section 105** of BNS) and sentenced him to rigorous imprisonment for five years.

- The Supreme Court observed: "According to **Section 102**, the right of private defence of body commences as soon as a reasonable apprehension of danger to the body arises from an attempt or threat to commit the offence though the offence may not have been committed, and such right continues so long as such apprehension of danger to the body continues". The threat, however, must reasonably give rise to the present and imminent danger and not remote or distant. This right rests on the general principle that where crime is endeavoured to be committed by force, it is lawful to repel that force in self-defence. To say that the appellant could only claim the right to use force after he had sustained a serious injury by an aggressive wrongful assault is a complete misunderstanding of the law embodied in the above section. The Supreme Court however, allowed the appeal and the appellant was acquitted. The Court held in such moments of excitement on disturbed mental equilibrium, it is somewhat difficult to expect parties facing grave aggression to coolly weigh, as if in golden scales, and calmly determine with a composed mind as to what precise kind and severity of blow would be legally sufficient for effectively meeting the unlawful aggression. Therefore, the appellant has not exceeded the right of private defence.
- In **Kishan v. State of M.P. (1974),** an altercation occurred between the accused and one Bucha. The accused left the place, and after sometime returned with his friends and started beating Bucha. Bucha picked up a khutai lying nearby and gave three blows with it on the head of one of the friends of the accused, who became unconscious. Thereafter, the accused (Kishan) and his friends caught hold of Bucha, Kishan snatched the khutai from the hand of Bucha and gave some blows on his head which led to his death. It was argued that Kishan had acted in exercise of the right of self-defence. The Lower Court held that when the appellant (Kishan) snatched Khutai from Bucha and struck blows on his head, he was acting in the exercise of the right of self-defence. Bucha was held to be an aggressor. The High Court, however, held that the appellants had come prepared to beat the accused and so they were the aggressors. Bucha was fully justified in defending himself.
    - The Supreme Court, agreeing with the High Court, held that the right of private defence was not available as Kishan and his friends had taken the law into their own hands. When Bucha had given the khutai blows, he was acting in exercise of right of self-defence and, therefore, Bucha was not the aggressor and, in fact, it was the accused and his friends who were the aggressors and that consequently the right of self-defence was not available to the accused. The Apex Court observed that the right of private defence can be claimed by a person who is attacked by another, and not by the one who goes to beat others. Under the guise of exercising this right, a person cannot shield his aggressive designs. Further, there cannot be private defence against private defence.
- In **James Martin v. State of Kerala (2004),** the question related to the exercise of the 'right of private defence' by the accused during a skirmish and altercation between bandh activists and the accused. The accused took the stand that the firing resulting in the death of two bandh activists and sustaining of grievous injuries to several others occurred when their house and other buildings, situated in a common compound, and movable properties kept therein were set on fire by an angry mob of bandh activists when the accused failed to heed their unlawful demand to close down the flour mill which was operated on that day. The Trial Court and the High Court held that the accused exceeded the right of

private defence and when two persons have lost lives, it cannot be said that the act done by the accused was within the permissible limits.

- The Court, in the present case, further observed: The number of injuries is not always a safe criterion for determining who the aggressor was. It cannot be stated as a universal rule that whenever the injuries are on the body of the accused persons, a presumption must necessarily be raised that the accused persons had caused injuries in exercise of the right of private defence.
- On appeal to the Supreme Court, the court held that the acts by the appellant were within reasonable limits and had a right to exercise private defence.

Right of Private Defence Against Deadly Assault when there is Risk of Harm to Innocent Person

(**Note:** ***Section 44*** *of the BNS corresponds to* ***Section 106*** *of the IPC*)

- **Section 44** of BNS provides that if in the exercise of the right of private defence against an assault which reasonably causes the apprehension of death, the defender is so situated that he cannot effectively exercise that right without risk of harm to an innocent person, his right of private defence extends to the running of that risk.
- **Illustration**: If A is attacked by mob which attempts to a murder him and he cannot effectually exercise his right of private defence without firing on the mob, and he cannot fire without risk of harming young children who are mingled with the mob, A commits no offence if by so firing he harms the children.

Circumstances in which there is no Right of Private Defence

- The right of private defence does not mean an unlimited right. The right of private defence is not available in the following situations:
  - The aggressor cannot claim the right to private defence; an aggressor himself creates a danger to his own life.
  - There cannot be private defence against private defence.
  - There is no right of private defence under the Act against any act which is not in itself an offence under it.

❖❖❖

Chapter 9

ABETMENT

INTRODUCTION

Section 45 to 60 of Chapter IV of Bharatiya Nyaya Sanhita, 2023 (BNS) (Earlier, Chapter V from Section 107 to 120 of the IPC) deals with Abetment. This penalises abetment as abetment leads to crime and many crimes would be impossible but for support and encouragement received from others who, though not actively cooperating with the criminal, still prepare his ground and facilitate his work. Indeed, it is seldom that a criminal acts without accomplices. He does not feel the same confidence as when he has friends to consult, advise and assist him in his corrupt plan.

COMPARATIVE CHART OF THE BNS AND IPC

Bharatiya Nyaya Sanhita, 2023 (BNS)	Title	Indian Penal Code,1860 (IPC)
Section 3(5)	General Explanations	Section 34
Section 45	Abetment of a thing	Section 107
Section 46	Abettor	Section 108
Section 47	Abetment in India of offences outside India	Section 108A
Section 48	Abetment outside India for offence in India (Newly added provision)	-
Section 49	Punishment of abetment if the act abetted is committed in consequence and where no express provision is made for the punishment	Section 109
Section 50	Punishment of abetment if person abetted does not act with a different intention from that of abettor	Section 110
Section 51	Liability of abettor when one act abetted and different act done	Section 111
Section 52	Abettor when liable to cumulative punishment for act abetted and for act done.	Section 112
Section 53	Liability of abettor for an effect caused by the act affected different from that intended by abettor	Section 113
Section 54	Abettor present when offences committed	Section 114
Section 55	Abetment of offence punishable with death or imprisonment for life	Section 115
Section 56	Abetment of offence punishable with imprisonment	Section 116

Section 57	Abetting Commission of offence by the public or by More than 10 Persons	Section 117
Section 58	Concealing design to commit offence punishable with death or imprisonment for life	Section 118
Section 59	Public servant concealing design to commit offence which it is his duty to prevent	Section 119
Section 60	Concealing design to commit offence punishable with imprisonment	Section 120

CHANGES IN BNS IN COMPARISONS TO IPC

- **Section 57** of the BNS corresponding to **Section 117** of the IPC has been changed as follows:
  - Change in punishment **"punished with imprisonment of either description for a term which may extend to seven years and with fine"**
- **Section 58 and 59** of BNS corresponding to Sections 118 and 119 of the IPC respectively, has been modified as follows:
  - The expression **'or by the use of encryption or any other information hiding tool'** has been added in the new provision.

ABETMENT

- Abetment under simple terms, refers to the instigation of someone to commit a crime by another person. However, this does not cover the entire meaning and the elements of the crime, by which the Courts decide the act to be abetment. To prove it to be abetment, certain criteria need to have happened a certain way.
- In the case of **Sanju v. State of Madhya Pradesh (2002)**, Hon'ble Supreme court defined 'abet' as meaning to aid, to assist or to give aid, to command, to procure, or to counsel, to countenance, to encourage, or encourage or to set another one to commit. The definition of 'abet' as laid down, makes it clear that abetment only occurs when there are at least two persons involved, which further directs us towards the arrangement and operation of the act.
- In usual parlance, a person is held to be liable only if he or she has personally committed a crime. Detouring from the usual concept, the concept of Abetment says that he who has helped the criminal or provided him with any assistance in any form can also be held to be liable.
- In the case of **Rajat Prasad v. C.B.I**, it was held that for an act to be considered as abetment, it is necessary for the abettor to have criminal intent. The fact of the need to have a culpable mental state was emphasised here, to give rise to abetment.
- Bharatiya Nyaya Sanhita, 2023 deals with the provisions related to abetment in detail which are discussed as follows.

Abetment of a Thing

(**Note:** ***Section 45*** *of the BNS correspond to* ***Section 107*** *of the IPC*)

- According to **Section 45** a person abets the doing of a thing, who:
  - Instigates any person to do that thing; or
  - Engages with one more other person or persons in any conspiracy for the doing of that thing, if an act or illegal omission takes place in pursuance of that conspiracy, and in order to the doing of that thing; or
  - Intentionally aids, by any act or illegal omission, the doing of that thing.
- **Explanation 1 of Section 45** provides that a person who, by wilful misrepresentation, or by wilful concealment of a material fact which he is bound to disclose, voluntarily causes or procures, or attempts to cause

or procure, a thing to be done, is said to instigate the doing that thing.

- **Illustration:** A, a public officer, is authorized by a warrant from a Court of Justice to apprehend Z. B, knowing that fact and also that C is not Z, wilfully represents to A that C is Z, and thereby intentionally causes A to apprehend C. Here, B abets by instigation the apprehension of C.

- **Explanation 2 of Section 45** provides that whoever, either prior to or at the time of the commission of an act, does anything in order to facilitate the commission of that act, and thereby facilitates the commission thereof, is said to aid the doing of that act.

ABETMENT IN GENERAL

- When an offence is committed and several persons take part in the commission of it, each person contributes in a manner and degree different from the others to the doing of the criminal act.
- The act may be done by the hands of one person while another is present or is close at hand ready to afford help, or the actual doer may be a guilty agent acting under the orders of an absent person, and besides these participators, there may be other persons who contribute indirectly to the commission of the offence by advice, suggestion, conspiracy or aid.
- Abetment under Sanhita involves the active complicity on the part of the abettor, at a point of time prior to the actual commission of the offence; and it is the essence of the crime of abetment that the abettor should substantially assist the principal culprit towards the commission of the offence. Here, the abettor gets or procures the acts by means of guilty agents. The agent being urged forward by a person who will not himself act, but who procures or instigates another to put in execution his criminal intention.

Modes of Abetment

Abetment by Instigation:

- Instigation basically means suggesting, encouraging or inciting a person to do or abstain from doing something. Instigation may take place either directly or indirectly, by written or oral words, or even by gestures and hints.
- In abetment by instigation, there has to be some active involvement of the abettor towards the preparatory phase of the crime.
- **Explanation 1** of **Section 45** throws some light on what instigation may mean in this context. It says that instigation may generally happen even by:
  (a) Wilful misrepresentation; or
  (b) Wilful concealment of a material fact which a person is bound to disclose.
- **For Example**: A court directs Amit, a police officer, to arrest Raj under an arrest warrant. Brijesh informs Amit that Chandan is Raj despite knowing that he is not. Under this misrepresentation, Amit ends up arresting Chandan instead of Raj. In this case, Brijesh is guilty of abetting Amit in wrongfully apprehending Chandan.

Abetment by Conspiracy

- Conspiracy basically means an agreement between two or more persons to commit an unlawful act. Merely intending to commit an offence is not sufficient for this purpose. Thus, the conspirators must actively agree and prepare themselves to commit that offence, it becomes a conspiracy. Furthermore, the act which the conspirators conspire to commit itself must be illegal or punishable.
  - **For example,** in dowry death cases, the in-laws of the victim are often guilty of abetment by conspiracy. They may do so by constantly taunting, torturing or instigating the victim. Even suicides may take place in this manner through abetment by conspiracy.

- **If an Act or Illegal Omission Takes Place:** This means that there must be something more than a mere plotting to amount to an abetment under this clause. There must be some act or illegal omission in pursuance of that conspiracy.
- For an offence of abetment to be accomplished via conspiracy a mere combination of persons or agreement is not enough; an act or illegal omission must take place in pursuance of that conspiracy, and amount to a distinct offence for each distinct offence abetted by conspiracy.
- **Abetment by Intentional Aiding:** The third manner in which abetment may take place is by intentionally aiding the offender in committing that offence. This generally happens when the abettor facilitates the crime or helps in committing it. The intention to aid the offender is very important.
- In the case of **Jamuna Singh v. State of Bihar (1967),** the Supreme Court considered the issue of Jamuna Singh, accused of instigating another person to set fire to the hut of another, thereby committing an offence under **Section 436** read with **section 109**, IPC (Now, **Section 326(g)** read with **Section 49** of the BNS). However, the hut was set on fire not by the person instigated but another.
  - The Patna High Court had acquitted Jodha Singh, the person who allegedly set fire to the hut. In considering the challenge to the continued conviction of the appellant as the main person himself had been acquitted.
  - Further, the Supreme Court, after a detailed consideration of the case law, held that, it is not necessary for the offence of abetment that the act abetted must be committed. It is only in the case of a person abetting an offence by intentionally aiding another to commit that offence that the charge of abetment against him would to expect to fail, when the person alleged to have committed the offence is acquitted of that offence.
    - It was also held that, it was not desirable to hold that an abettor cannot be punished if the person actually committing the offence is acquitted.
    - The Court further said that the abettor's guilt depends upon the nature of the offence abetted and the manner of abetment and not upon the commission of the abetted offences. The court clearly pointed out that the offence of abetment is complete when the alleged abettor has instigated another or engaged with another in a conspiracy to commit the offence.
- **Abetment by Illegal Omission:** Criminal liability for abetment by illegal omission depends on legal provisions and obligations.
  - For abetment to be proven, it must be shown that the accused intentionally aided the offence through non-interference.
  - **For Example**: A police officer's duty is to prevent crime; if aware of a crime and does not prevent it, he will be liable for abetment.

DISTINCTION BETWEEN ABETMENT AND COMMON INTENTION

Basis	Abetment	Common Intention
Definition	**Section 45** deals with the concept of abetment, where an individual instigates, conspires, or intentionally aids in committing a crime.	**Section 3(5)** pertains to acts done by multiple persons with a common intention, holding each person liable as if they had committed the crime alone.
Nature of Involvement	Involvement under **Section 45** is through instigation, conspiracy, or providing intentional aid to the principal offender.	Involvement under **Section 3(5)** requires actual participation in the commission of the criminal act with a shared common intention.

Basis	Abetment	Common Intention
Presence at Crime Scene	The abettor under **Section 45** does not need to be physically present at the scene of the crime to be held liable.	For **Section 3(5)** to apply, individuals must be present and actively participate in the criminal act.
Common Intention	Common intention is not a prerequisite under **Section 45**; the focus is on the act of abetment itself.	A shared common intention among all participants is essential under **Section 3(5)** for establishing collective liability.
Liability	The liability under **Section 45** is based on the individual's role in encouraging, conspiring, or aiding the crime.	Under **Section 3(5)**, each participant is held equally responsible for the entire crime due to their shared common intention and participation.

DISTINCTION BETWEEN THE ABETMENT (SECTION 45 OF BNS) AND THE OFFENCE OF CRIMINAL CONSPIRACY (SECTION 61 OF BNS)

- **Provision under BNS**
  - **Abetment: Section 45** of the BNS (107 of the IPC).
  - **Criminal Conspiracy: Section 61** of BNS (Section 120A of the IPC)
- **Parties Involved**
  - **Abetment:** It usually has two parties, the abettor (one who abets) and the principal offender (one who commits an offence).
  - **Criminal Conspiracy:** It has at least two parties known as conspirators.
- **Methods**
  - **Abetment:** It can be committed via various methods including conspiracy, instigation, and intentional aid.
  - **Criminal Conspiracy:** It is one of the methods of abetment.
- **Elements**
  - **Abetment:** It requires three essential elements, instigation, active participation, and the intention to facilitate the commission of crime.
  - **Criminal Conspiracy:** It has two essential elements, an agreement between 2 or more persons and an intention to commit a crime.
- **Agreement**
  - **Abetment:** No prior agreement is required between the abettor and the principal offender. The abettor can assist before, during, or after the crime.
  - **Criminal Conspiracy:** It requires an agreement (either explicit or implicit) between two or more individuals to commit a crime.
- **Nature of Offence**
  - **Abetment:** It is not a substantive offence on its own as it requires instigating, aiding, or conspiring to commit the offence.
  - **Criminal Conspiracy:** It is a substantive offence which means a mere agreement to commit an offence is punishable even though the same is not committed.
- **Case Law**
  - **Noor Mohammad Momin v. State of Maharashtra, (1970)**, this case shows the difference between criminal conspiracy and abetment to conspiracy. Criminal conspiracy has a wider jurisdiction than abetment by a conspiracy. An individual is guilty of conspiracy with the mere agreement between a group of people to commit an offence.

Abettor

(**Note:** ***Section 46*** *of the BNS correspond to* ***Section 108*** *of the IPC*)

- Abetment under the BNS involves active complicity on the part of the abettor at a point of time prior to the actual commission of that offence, and it is of the essence of the crime of abetment that the abettor should substantially assist the principal culprit towards the commission of the offence.
- The definition of an Abettor is provided under **Section 46** of the BNS. According to this **Section 46,** A person abets an offence, who:
  - Abets either the commission of an offence, or
  - The commission of an act which would be an offence, if committed by a person capable by law of committing an offence with the same intention or knowledge as that of the abettor.
- The exclusive scope and clear interpretation of the term Abettor is mentioned in 5 explanations of **Section 46** which includes:
  - **Abetment of Illegal Omission***:* **Explanation 1 of Section 46** provides that the abetment of the illegal omission of an act may amount to an offence although the abettor may not himself be bound to do that act.
  - **The Effect of Abetment is Immaterial: Explanation 2 of Section 46** provides that to constitute the offence of abetment it is not necessary that the act abetted should be committed, or that the effect requisite to constitute the offence should be caused.
    - **Illustrations**

      (a) A instigates B to murder C. B refuses to do so. A is guilty of abetting B to commit murder.

      (b) A instigates B to murder D. B in pursuance of the instigation stabs D. D recovers from the wound. A is guilty of instigating B to commit murder.
  - **A Person Abetted Need not Necessarily be Capable of Committing the Offence***:* **Explanation 3 of Section 46** provides that it is not necessary that the person abetted should be capable by law of committing an offence, or that he should have the same guilty intention or knowledge as that of the abettor, or any guilty intention or knowledge.
    - **Illustration:** A, with a guilty intention, abets a child or a person of unsound mind to commit an act which would be an offence, if committed by a person capable by law of committing an offence, and having the same intention as A. Here A, whether the act be committed or not, is guilty of abetting an offence.
  - **Abetment of Abetment is an Offence: Explanation 4 of Section 46** provides that the abetment of an offence being an offence, the abetment of such an abetment is also an offence.
    - **Illustration:** A instigates B to instigate C to murder Z. B accordingly instigates C to murder Z, and C commits that offence in consequence of B's instigation. B is liable to be punished for his offence with the punishment for murder; and, as A instigated B to commit the offence, A is also liable to the same punishment.
  - **Engagement in the Conspiracy on Account of which the Offence is Committed is Enough to make him Liable as an Abettor: Explanation 5 of Section 46** provides that it is not necessary to the commission of the offence of abetment by conspiracy that the abettor should concert the offence with the person who commits it. It is sufficient if he engages in the conspiracy in pursuance of which the offence is committed.

- **For Example:** Ram makes a plan with Mohan to kill Raju. It was decided that Ram will give the poison. Mohan explains the plan to Ravi who arranges the poison and delivers it to Mohan. Ram gave the poison and Raju died as a consequence. Here, Ravi has committed the offence although he did not conspire with Ram he engaged himself in the conspiracy to kill Raju.

- **Section 46** of BNS states that a person who abets either the commission of a crime or commission of an act that would be an offence is called an abettor.
- Five propositions in **Section 46** are as follows:
  - The subsiding of an act's illegal omission or failure may amount to an offence, even though the abettor may not be bound to that act. If a public servant is guilty of illegal action or if a private person instigates him and he abets the offence, it makes the public servant guilty.
  - To constitute abetment, it is not necessary for the act to have been committed. The crime of abetment depends upon the intention of the offender who abets and not upon the actual actions done by the abetted. Abetment is considered complete upon instigation, even if:
    - The act abetted isn't carried out,
    - The person abetted refuses to act,
    - The intended result doesn't occur,
    - The means used are physically incapable of causing the desired effect
  - The third provision is that the person doesn't need to be capable by law of committing an offence or crying or having the same intentions or knowledge as the abettor. Abetment is a significant offence, irrespective of the criminal intent or knowledge to be the same as that of abettor; just mere instigation to commit a criminal offence is necessary, either capable by law or not.
  - When the abetment of an offence is a crime, the abetment of such an abetment is also a crime.
    - In this case,the substantive abetment must be the abetment of an offence. It is not necessary that such offences should be committed.
  - To constitute the offence of abetment by conspiracy, it is not necessary that the abettor is sure of a concert offence with the person who commits it. It is enough if the person engages in the conspiracy in pursuance.
- As any prudent man would understand what is stated above as abetment if a person instigates another person to conduct a specific thing, one might also consider the chances of the person abetted doing the wrong action, even though he was abetted for conducting a different action.
- In simpler words, it can be said that the act abetted was one, however the act conducted by the person abetted was different. In such a case, the abettor would be held liable for the act which was executed by the person abetted, as an act done by himself as the act executed even though was different was a consequence or a pursuit of the conspiracy due to the instigation made by the abettor for the action thought of, to be executed by the person abetted.

Abetment in India of Offences Committed Outside India

(**Note:** ***Section 47*** *of the BNS correspond to* ***Section 108A*** *of the IPC*)

- **Section 47** of BNS provides that a person abets an offence within the meaning of this Sanhita who, in India, abets the commission of any act without and beyond India which would constitute an offence if committed in India.
- **Illustration**: A, in India, instigates B, a foreigner in country X, to commit a murder in that country, A is guilty of abetting murder.

- **Section 108A** was added in the Penal Code in 1898 (Now, Section 47 of the BNS) with a view to overrule a decision of the Bombay High Court in the case of **Queen Empress v. Ganapatrao Ramachandra, (1984)** in which it was held that the abetment in India by an Indian citizen of an offence committed in a foreign country was not punishable under the Code. The Section 108A states that a person would be guilty of an abetment, if he abets the commission of an act outside India, which if done in India, would constitute an offence.
- But, under BNS the new provision has been added under **Section 48** as abetment outside India for offence Committed in India.

Abetment Outside India for Offence Committed in India

- **Section 48** of BNS provides that a person abets an offence within the meaning of this Sanhita who, without and beyond India, abets the commission of any act in India which would constitute an offence if committed in India.
- **Illustration**: A, in country X, instigates B, to commit a murder in India, A is guilty of abetting murder.
- Under **Section 47**, a person who abets an offence outside India is not punishable unless an offence committed in India whereas **Section 48** provides that a person who abets an offence without and beyond India is said to commit an offence in India.
- Abetment by a person outside India has been made an offence under **Section 48** to allow prosecution of persons located in foreign countries.
- **Section 48** of the BNS has extended jurisdiction to criminalise abetment outside India, broadening the scope of legal enforcement.

PUNISHMENTS FOR ABETMENT

Punishment of Abetment if Act Abetted is Committed in Consequence and Where No Express Provision is made for its Punishment

(**Note:** ***Section 49*** *of the BNS corresponds to* ***Section 109*** *of the IPC*)

- **Section 49** provides whoever abets any offence shall, if the act abetted is committed in consequence of the abetment, and no express provision is made by this Sanhita for the punishment of such abetment,
  - Be punished with the punishment provided for the offence.
- **Explanation of the Section 49** provides that an act or offence is said to be committed in consequence of abetment, when it is committed in consequence of the instigation, or in pursuance of the conspiracy, or with the aid which constitutes the abetment
- **Illustrations**: A instigates B to give false evidence. B, in consequence of the instigation, commits that offence. A is guilty of abetting that offence, and is liable to the same punishment as B.

Punishment of Abetment if Where Person Abetted does act with Different Intention from that of Abettor

(**Note:** ***Section 50*** *of the BNS corresponds to* ***Section 110*** *of the IPC*)

- **Section 50** provides that whoever abets the commission of an offence shall, if the person abetted does the act with a different intention or knowledge from that of the abettor, be punished with
  - Punishment provided for the offence which would have been committed if the act had been done with the intention or knowledge of the abettor and with no other.

Liability of Abettor When One Act Abetted and Different Act Done

(**Note:** *Section 51 of the BNS corresponds to Section 111 of the IPC*)

- **Section 51** provides that when an act is abetted and a different act is done, the abettor is liable for the act done, in the same manner and to the same extent as if he had directly abetted it:
  - Provided that the act done was a probable consequence of the abetment, and was committed under the influence of the instigation, or with the aid or in pursuance of the conspiracy which constituted the abetment.
- **Illustration:** A instigates a child to put poison into the food of Z, and gives him poison for that purpose. The child, in consequence of the instigation, by mistake puts the poison into the food of Y, which is by the side of that of Z. Here, if the child was acting under the influence of A's instigation, and the act done was under the circumstances a probable consequence of the abetment, A is liable in the same manner and to the same extent as if he had instigated the child to put the poison into the food of Y.

Abettor when Liable to Cumulative Punishment for Act Abetted and for Act Done

(**Note:** *Section 52 of the BNS corresponds to Section 112 of the IPC*)

- **Section 52** provides if the act for which the abettor is liable under **Section 51** is committed in addition to the act abetted, and constitute a distinct offence.
  - The abettor is liable to punishment for each of the offences.
- **Illustration**: A instigates B to resist by force a distress made by a public servant. B, in consequence, resists that distress. In offering the resistance, B voluntarily causes grievous hurt to the officer executing the distress. As B has committed both the offence of resisting the distress, and the offence of voluntarily causing grievous hurt, B is liable to punishment for both these offences; and, if A knew that B was likely voluntarily to cause grievous hurt in resisting the distress, A will also be liable to punishment for each of the offences.

Liability of Abettor for an Effect Caused by Act Abetted Different from that Intended by Abettor

(**Note:** *Section 53 of the BNS corresponds to Section 113 of the IPC*)

- **Section 53** provides that when an act is abetted with the intention on the part of the abettor of causing a particular effect, and an act for which the abettor is liable in consequence of the abetment, causes a different effect from that intended by the abettor, the abettor is liable for the effect caused, in the same manner and to the same extent as if he had abetted the act with the intention of causing that effect, provided he knew that the act abetted was likely to cause that effect.
- **Illustration:** A instigates B to cause grievous hurt to Z. B, in consequence of the instigation, causes grievous hurt to Z. Z dies in consequence. Here, if A knew that the grievous hurt abetted was likely to cause death, A is liable to be punished with the punishment provided for murder.

Abettor Present when Offence is Committed

(**Note:** *Section 54 of the BNS corresponds to Section 114 of the IPC*)

- **Section 54** provides that whenever any person, who is absent would be liable to be punished as an abettor, is present when the act or offence for which he would be punishable in consequence of the abetment is committed,
  - He shall be deemed to have committed such an act or offence.

Abetment of Offence Punishable with Death or Imprisonment for Life

(**Note:** ***Section 55*** *of the BNS corresponds to* ***Section 115*** *of the IPC*)

- **Section 55** lays down whoever abets the commission of an offence punishable with death or imprisonment for life, shall, if that offence be not committed, and no express provision is made under this Sanhita for the punishment of such abetment,
  - Be punished with imprisonment of either description for a term which may extend to seven years, and shall also be liable to fine; and
  - If any act for which the abettor is liable in consequence of the abetment, and which causes hurt to any person, is done, the abettor shall be liable to imprisonment of either description for a term which may extend to fourteen years, and shall also be liable to fine.

Abetment of Offence Punishable with Imprisonment

(**Note:** ***Section 56*** *of the BNS corresponds to* ***Section 116*** *of the IPC*)

Section 56 provides that whoever abets an offence punishable with imprisonment shall, if that offence be not committed in consequence of the abetment, and no express provision is made under this Sanhita for the punishment of such abetment,

- Be punished with imprisonment of any description provided for that offence for a term which may extend to one-fourth part of the longest term provided for that offence; or with such fine as is provided for that offence, or with both;
- And if the abettor or the person abetted is a public servant, whose duty it is to prevent the commission of such offence, the abettor shall be punished with imprisonment of any description provided for that offence, for a term which may extend to one-half of the longest term provided for that offence, or with such fine as is provided for the offence, or with both.

Abetting Commission of Offence by Public or by More than Ten Persons

(**Note:** ***Section 57*** *of the BNS corresponds to* ***Section 117*** *of the IPC*)

Section 57 provides that whoever abets the commission of an offence by the public generally or by any number or class of persons exceeding ten, shall be punished with:

- Imprisonment of either description for a term which may extend to seven years and
- With fine.

Concealing Design to Commit Offence Punishable with Death or Imprisonment for life

(**Note:** ***Sections 58*** *of BNS corresponds to* ***Sections 118*** *of the IPC*)

Section 58 provides that whoever intending to facilitate or knowing it to be likely that he will thereby facilitate the commission of an offence punishable with death or imprisonment for life, voluntarily conceals by any act or omission, or by the use of encryption or any other information hiding tool, the existence of a design to commit such offence or makes any representation which he knows to be false respecting such design shall:

- **Offence Committed:** Be punished with imprisonment of either description for a term which may extend to seven years; or
- **Offence not Committed:** With imprisonment of either description, for term which may extend to three years, and shall also be liable to fine.

Public Servant Concealing Design to Commit Offence which it is his Duty to Prevent

(**Note:** ***Sections 59*** *of BNS corresponds to* ***Sections 119*** *of the IPC*)

Section 59 provides that whoever, being a public servant, intending to facilitate or knowing it to be likely that he will thereby facilitate the commission of an offence which it is his duty as such public servant to prevent, voluntarily conceals, by any act or omission or by the use of encryption or any other information hiding tool, the existence of a design to commit such offence, or makes any representation which he knows to be false respecting such design shall:

- **Offence Committed:** Be punished with imprisonment of any description provided for the offence, for a term which may extend to one-half of the longest term of such imprisonment, or with such fine as is provided for that offence, or with both; or
- **Offence Punishable with Death:** If the offence be punishable with death or imprisonment for life,with imprisonment of either description for a term which may extend to ten years.
- **Offence not Committed:** Shall be punished with imprisonment of any description provided for the offence for a term which may extend to one-fourth part of the longest term of such imprisonment or with such fine as is provided for the offence, or with both.

Concealing Design to Commit Offence Punishable with Imprisonment

(**Note:** ***Sections 60*** *of BNS corresponds to* ***Sections 120*** *of the IPC*)

Section 60 provides that whoever, intending to facilitate or knowing it to be likely that he will thereby facilitate the commission of an offence punishable with imprisonment, voluntarily conceals, by any act or illegal omission, the existence of a design to commit such offence, or makes any representation which he knows to be false respecting such design shall:

- **Offence Committed:** Be punished with imprisonment of the description provided for the offence, for a term which may extend to one-fourth; and
- **Offence not Committed:** To one-eighth, of the longest term of such imprisonment, or with such fine as is provided for the offence, or with both.

Case Laws

- In **Pramod Shriram Telgote v. State of Maharashtra, (2018)**, it was held that "clear mens rea to commit the offence is a sine qua non for conviction under **Section 306** IPC".
- In **Channu v. State of Chattisgarh, (2017)**, it was held that "merely because wife committed suicide in matrimonial house, husband and in-laws can't be charged for abetment to suicide."
- In **Gurucharan Singh v. State of Punjab, (2016)**, it was held that "in order to convict a person for abetment of suicide, there has to be a clear mens rea to commit an offence."

❖❖❖

Chapter 10

CRIMINAL CONSPIRACY

INTRODUCTION

The Indian Penal Code, 1860 recognized the gravity of acts done under a conspiracy and the same has been incorporated in the Bharatiya Nyaya Sanhita, 2023, understanding that the collective intent and planning behind criminal activities pose a substantial threat to public order and safety.

The concept of criminal conspiracy has evolved through judicial interpretations, shaping a comprehensive framework that addresses various aspects of conduct under conspiracy. Indian courts have elucidated the elements necessary to establish a conspiracy, such as the existence of an agreement, the intention to commit an offence, and the involvement of two or more persons.

The provision of Criminal Conspiracy is dealt under **Chapter IV, Section 61** of Bharatiya Nyaya Sanhita, 2023 (BNS). Earlier, the Indian Penal Code incorporated it under **Sections 120A and 120B under Chapter VA.**

COMPARATIVE CHART OF THE BNS AND IPC		
Bharatiya Nyaya Sanhita, 2023 (BNS)	**Title**	**Indian Penal Code, 1860 (IPC)**
Section 61(1)	Criminal Conspiracy	Section 120A
Section 61(2)	Punishment for Criminal Conspiracy	Section 120B

CRIMINAL CONSPIRACY

(**Note:** ***Section 61(1)*** *of the BNS corresponds to* ***Section 120A*** *of the IPC*)

- **Section 61(1) of BNS** mentions when two or more persons agree with the common object to do, or cause to be done:
    - (a) An illegal act; or
    - (b) An act which is not illegal by illegal means, such an agreement is designated a criminal conspiracy.
- **Proviso 1 to Section 61(1)** provided that no agreement except an agreement to commit an offence shall amount to a criminal conspiracy unless some act besides the agreement is done by one or more parties to such agreement in pursuance thereof.
- **Explanation to Section 61(1)** provides that it is immaterial whether the illegal act is the ultimate object of such agreement, or is merely incidental to that object.
- **Illegal Means:** Agreement to do an act which even though lawful but by unlawful means constitute conspiracy. The end does not justify the means for instance agreement to steal some food articles from a shop of wealthy businessmen to distribute that food to hungry and starving children is not justifiable.

Punishment for Criminal Conspiracy

(**Note:** ***Section 61(2)*** *of the BNS corresponds to* ***Section 120B*** *of the IPC*)

- Punishment for Criminal Conspiracy is mentioned under **Section 61(2),** whoever is a party to a criminal conspiracy:

- (a) To commit an offence punishable with death, imprisonment for life or rigorous imprisonment for a term of two years or upwards, shall, where no express provision is made in this Sanhita for the punishment of such a conspiracy, be punished in the same manner as if he had abetted such an offence.
- (b) Other than a criminal conspiracy to commit an offence punishable as aforesaid shall be punished withimprisonment of either description for a term not exceeding six months, or with fine or with both.

Essentials of Criminal Conspiracy

- **Agreement**: An agreement between two or more persons to commit an illegal act, or an act that is not illegal but is done illegally, is the first and most crucial element of a criminal conspiracy. The agreement needs to be made prior to the crime being committed and between two or more persons.
- **Intention**: The intention to commit the crime is the second component of criminal conspiracy. The parties to the agreement must share a common object to commit the illegal act. The intent must be to commit the crime, not simply to discuss it.
- **Act:** An act in furtherance of the agreement to commit an offence is the third element of criminal conspiracy. This act can be anything that aids in the commission of the crime, such as the purchase of weapons, the gathering of information about the victim, or the planning of the crime's details.
- **Criminality**: The act must be illegal, according to the fourth element of criminal conspiracy. The agreement must be to commit a legally punishable offence. If the act is legal but the means by which it is carried out are illegal, it can still be considered criminal conspiracy.
- **Parties**: The final element of criminal conspiracy is that two or more people must be involved in the agreement. If the act is carried out by a single person, it does not constitute criminal conspiracy.
- **Actus reus:** The *actus reus* in a conspiracy is the agreement to execute the illegal conduct, not the execution of it. It is not enough that two or more persons pursued the same unlawful object at the same time or in the same place; it is necessary to show a meeting of minds, a consensus to give effect to an unlawful purpose. It is not, however, necessary that each conspirator should have been in communication with every other.

Case Laws

- In **Rajender v. State (NCT of Delhi), (2019)**, Supreme Court observed that following three essentials must be proved to establish the charge of criminal conspiracy:
  - There must be a criminal object;
  - There must be a plan or scheme embodying means to accomplish that;
  - There must be an agreement between two or more persons to cooperate for its accomplishment.
- In another case, **Yogesh alias Sachin Jagdish Joshi v. State of Maharashtra, (2008)**, the Supreme Court held that to constitute an offence of conspiracy meeting the mind of two or more persons is *sine qua non.* Conspiracy can be inferred from surrounding circumstances as direct proof is difficult to find.

Proof of Conspiracy

- The offence of criminal conspiracy can be proved by either direct or circumstantial evidence.
- Because a conspiracy is typically created in a discreet and quiet setting, it is nearly impossible to provide any concrete proof regarding the criminal conspiracy's formation date, members, purpose, or intended course of action.
- It was believed that agreement or meeting of minds is one of the main pieces of evidence to prove the conspiracy under this section

and also it is one of the hardest one to prove because as we know the fact that the offender by himself does not agree to a fact that he is involved with someone.

- It is only a matter of circumstances that one can prove that there is a meeting of minds or an agreement between those two. Hence, criminal conspiracy is based on circumstantial evidence as in most cases there is no direct evidence to prove the same.

Husband and Wife in Law of Conspiracy

- Under English Law, if a man and his wife are the only parties to a conspiracy they cannot be inducted for conspiracy because legally they are deemed to be one person.
- Under Indian Law, husband and wife are considered as a single entity, but under civil conspiracy, they are considered as two and can be charged with conspiracy.

Things Said or Done by Conspirators in Reference to Common Design

(**Note:** ***Section 8*** *of the BSA corresponds to* ***Section 10*** *of the IEA*)

- Pertaining to the realm of criminal conspiracy under Bharatiya Nyaya Sanhita, 2023, Bharatiya Sakshya Adhiniyam, 2023 (BSA) plays a crucial role.
  - Particularly, **Section 8** of BSA serves as a critical legal instrument in dealing with criminal conspiracy cases.
- **Section 8** of BSA says where there is reasonable ground to believe that two or more persons have conspired together to commit an offence or an actionable wrong, anything said, done or written by any one of such persons in reference to their common intention, after the time when such intention was first entertained by any one of them, is a relevant fact as against each of the persons believed to be so conspiring, as well for the purpose of proving the existence of the conspiracy as for the purpose of showing that any such person was a party to it.

SECTION 8 OF BSA, ILLUSTRATION

- Reasonable ground exists for believing that A has joined in a conspiracy to wage war against the State.
- The facts that B procured arms in Europe for the purpose of conspiracy, C collected money in Calcutta for a like object, D persuaded persons to join the conspiracy in Bombay, E published writings advocating the object in view at Agra, and the contents of letter written by H giving an account of conspiracy, are each relevant, both to prove the existence of conspiracy, and to prove A's complicity in it, although he may have been ignorant of all of them, and although the persons by whom they were done were strangers to him, and although they may have taken place before he joined the conspiracy or after he left it.

- The underlying principle on which **Section 8** of BSA is based is the principle of agency which means, if two or more persons conspire together to commit an offence, each is regarded as being the agent of the other and each conspirator is liable for what is done by his fellow conspirator.
- **Section 8** further provides a prima facie evidence affording a reasonable ground to believe that two or more persons have entered into a conspiracy.
  - The acts statements of a conspirator can only be used to establish the existence of a conspiracy and the involvement of a specific individual in it. It cannot be used to support the opposite party or demonstrate that the subject in question was not involved in the plot.
- In **Sardar Sardul Singh v. State of Maharashtra, (1965)** it was stated that anything said, done or written may be proved against a conspirator who joined after or left before such thing was said, done or written.
- One unique aspect of the rule is that anything said, written, or done by any member of

the conspiracy can be used as evidence against the other members, even if it is done without their knowledge or in their absence. The only requirement is that the act must mention their common intention.

- **Test of Prima Facie Conspiracy:** Only a prima facie case of conspiracy has to be made out to bring **Section 8 of BSA** into operation.
- In **Kehar Singh v. Delhi Admn (1980)** where, the fact that two accused, one of whom actually caused death, were seen together before the event isolating themselves on a rooftop and making every possible effort to conceal their conversation from the family members, was held to be enough prima facie proof of conspiracy so as to punish one for the action of the other.
- **Section 8 of BSA** has a potential to rope in the innocent with the guilty, and to rope in people who have genuinely abandoned and regretted.
- **Section 8 of BSA** is nevertheless considered a "necessary evil" as:
  - **Section 8 of BSA** has been deliberately enacted in order to make such acts/ statements of a co-conspirator admissible against the whole body of conspirators, because of the nature of the crime.
  - A conspiracy is planned in secret and carried out covertly. Consequently, unless there is a common thread uniting all of the accused, it is obviously not possible for the prosecution to link each isolated act or statement of one accused with the acts or statements of the others.
  - **Relevancy of Statement as Evidence**: Only those statements are relevant which are made during the time conspiracy exists.
    - In **Mirza Akbar v. Emperor (1940),** the wife and her paramour were prosecuted for murder and conspiracy to murder her husband and hired a sharpshooter. The main evidence against the wife and her paramour was the letters exchanged between them in which they expressed deep love and affection towards each other. During the trial for conspiracy to murder her husband, the wife had made certain statements implicating paramour. The Privy Council finally held that the statements are not consistent with a conspiracy because they were made after attaining the object, therefore they are not admissible as evidence, but they do not vitiate the proceedings.

Criminal Conspiracy Creates Joint Liability

- Under the provision of Criminal Conspiracy all those who are members of criminal conspiracy are liable for punishment as if they had abetted the offence which they had agreed to commit.
- Whether or not these offences that were thus agreed to be committed have actually been committed is not relevant to the creation of the offence.
- If the criminal act is committed, they step into the area of the specific offence and become liable for punishment under the relevant Section.
- For example, if A and B conspire to murder C, and later they murder C, they would each be liable to be convicted under **Section 103 of BNS** (Section 302 of the IPC) read with **Section 61 of BNS.** But if their agreement to murder C does not make any progress and the plot is discovered, this agreement or plot itself becomes a substantive offence punishable under **Section 61 of BNS** and each one of them will be liable as if he had abetted the offence of murder.
- Criminal conspiracy, thus, creates a joint liability of the persons who enter into an agreement to commit an illegal act and each one of them is liable to the same extent as another.

Common Intention to Commit Crime and Conspiracy

- There is not much substantial difference between conspiracy as defined in **Section 61 of BNS** and acting on a common intention, as contemplated in **Section 3(5) of BNS** (Section 34 of the IPC).
- While in the former, the gist of the offence is bare engagement and association to break the law even though the illegal act does not follow, the gist of the offence under **Section 3(5) of BNS** is the commission of a criminal act in furtherance of a common intention of all the offenders, which means that there should be unity of criminal behaviour resulting something, for which an individual would be punishable, if it were all done by himself alone.

Can a Company be Prosecuted for Criminal Conspiracy

- A corporation is virtually in the same position as an individual and may be convicted of common law as well as statutory offence, including those requiring mens rea.
- The criminal liability of a corporation would arise when an offence is committed in relation to the business of the corporation by a person or a body of persons in control of its affairs.
- In these situations, it would be important to confirm that the person or group of people has such a strong degree of control over the corporation that it can be said that the corporation acts and thinks through the person or group of people.

❖❖❖

Chapter 11

OFFENCES AGAINST WOMAN AND CHILDREN

OFFENCES AGAINST WOMAN

In the 20th century, significant strides were made globally to advance the rights and freedoms of individuals. However, despite these advancements, there remains a pressing need to safeguard the modesty of women in India. The country has a rich legal framework designed to protect women from various forms of violence and exploitation, including domestic violence, criminal force, rape, assault, molestation, and sexual harassment. These laws represent crucial steps toward ensuring the safety and dignity of women.

Offences against Woman and Children are dealt under **Chapter V** from **Sections 63 to 99** of the Bharatiya Nyaya Sanhita, 2023 (BNS). The offences are consolidated under one chapter and categorised as follows:

- Sexual Offences
- Criminal Force And Assault Against Women
- Offence Relating To Marriage
- Causing Miscarriage
- Offences Against Child

SEXUAL OFFENCES

- **Chapter V** of Bharatiya Nyaya Sanhita, 2023 (BNS) comprising **Sections 63 to 73** deals with sexual offences. These offences are dealt as under:
  - Rape (Defined under **Section 63** and punishable under **Section 64**).
  - Punishment for Certain aggravated forms of rape (**Section 65**) .
  - Punishment for Causing death of the victim or resulting in persistent vegetative state of the victim (**Section 66**).
  - The Sexual intercourse by husband upon his wife during separation (**Section 67**).
  - Sexual intercourse by a person in authority (**Section 68**).
  - Sexual intercourse by employing deceitful means, etc (**Section 69**).
  - Gang Rape (**Section 70**).
  - Punishment for repeat offenders (**Section 71**).
  - Disclosure of identity of victim of certain offences (**Section 72**).
  - Printing or publishing of any matter relating to Court proceedings without permission (**Section 73**)
- The earlier Penal Code i.e., the Indian Penal Code, 1860 dealt with the sexual offences under **Sections 375 - 376E**.

COMPARATIVE CHART OF THE BNS AND IPC

Bharatiya Nyaya Sanhita, 2023 (BNS)	Title	Indian Penal Code, 1860 (IPC)
Section 63	Rape	Section 375
Section 64	Punishment for Rape	Section 376
Section 65	Punishment for rape in certain cases	Section 376(3)

Bharatiya Nyaya Sanhita, 2023 (BNS)	Title	Indian Penal Code, 1860 (IPC)
Section 65(2)	Punishment for rape in certain cases **EARLIER TITLE-**(Punishment for rape on woman under 12 years of age)	Section 376AB
Section 66	Punishment for causing death or resulting in persistent vegetative state of the victim	Section 376A
Section 67	Sexual intercourse by husband upon his wife during separation	Section 376B
Section 68	Sexual intercourse by a person in authority	Section 376C
Section 69	Sexual intercourse by employing deceitful means	Newly added
Section 70	Gang Rape	Section 376D
	Punishment for gang rape on woman under sixteen years age	Section 376DA
	Punishment for gang rape on woman under twelve years age	Section 376DB
Section 71	Punishment for repeat offenders	Section 376E
Section 72	Disclosure of identity of victim of certain offences, etc.	Section 228A
Section 73	Printing or publishing of any matter relating to Court proceeding without permission	Section 228A(3)

CHANGES IN BNS IN COMPARISON TO IPC

- **Section 63** of the BNS corresponds to **Section 375** of IPC, has changed as follows:
  - The word "fifteen years" has been changed to "**eighteen years**" under the Section 63 Exception 2 of the BNS.
- **Section 64** of the BNS corresponds to **Section 376** of IPC, has changed as follows:
  - The word "military" has been changed to "army" in Explanation (a) to the Section 64 (2)
- **Section 70(2)** of the BNS corresponds to **Section 376 DA** of IPC, has changed as follows:
  - The word "sixteen years" has been changed to "eighteen years" under the Section 70(2) and the death penalty also added as punishment under section 70(2).
- **Section 72** of the BNS corresponds to **Section 228A** of IPC has changed as follows:
  - The word "minor" has been changed to "child"

RAPE

(**Note:** ***Section 63*** *of the BNS corresponds to* ***Section 375*** *of the IPC*)

The offence of rape has been defined under **Section 63** of BNS. As per the definition, a person is said to commit the offence of rape if he does any one of the four acts specified in **Section 63** under any one of the seven circumstances enumerated therein.

- A person is guilty of committing the offence of rape if he does any one of the following four acts, namely:
  - **Penetration:** If he penetrates his penis, to any extent, into the vagina, mouth, urethra or anus of a woman or makes her do so with him or any other person.
  - **Insertion:** If he inserts, to any extent, any object or a part of the body, not being the penis, into the vagina, the urethra or anus of a woman or makes her to do so with him or any other person.
  - **Manipulation**: If he manipulates any part of the body of a woman so as to cause penetration into the vagina, urethra, anus

or any part of the body of such woman or makes her to do so with him or any other person.

  - **Application:** If he applies his mouth to the vagina, anus, urethra of a woman or makes her do so with him or any other person.

- The aforesaid four acts must be done under any one of the following seven circumstances, namely:
  - Against the will of the woman
  - Without the consent of the woman
  - With the consent of the woman, when her consent has been obtained by putting her or any person in whom she is interested, in fear of death or of hurt.
  - With her consent, when the man knows that he is not her husband and that her consent is given because she believes that he is another man to whom she is or believes herself to be lawfully married.
  - With her consent when, at the time of giving such consent, by reason of unsoundness of mind or intoxication or the administration by him personally or through another of any stupefying or unwholesome substance, she is unable to understand the nature and consequences of that to which she gives consent.
  - With or without her consent, when she is under eighteen years of age.
  - When she is unable to communicate consent.

Rape Committed on a Woman "Against her Will" & "Without her Consent"

- Key differences between the terminologies used "Against her Will" & "Without her Consent"can be enumerated as follows:
  - The expressions "against her will" & "without her consent" appear to be synonyms and may also overlap in certain cases. However, there is a fine distinction between "an act done against the will' and "an act done without the consent" of a person.
  - In the words of Sir Hari Singh Gaur, the word "will" implies the faculty of reasoning power of mind which determines whether to do an act or not. On the other hand, "consent" means an intelligent, positive concurrence of the "will". Therefore, every act done "without will" is "without consent" but every act done "without consent" is not "without will".
  - In the decision of **State of U.P. v. Chhoteylal, (2011)**, Hon'ble Apex Court has observed that the expression "against her will" would ordinarily mean that the intercourse was done by a man with a woman despite her resistance and opposition. On the other hand, the expression "without her consent" would comprehend an act of reason accompanied by deliberation.
  - Likewise, in the case of **State of H.P. v. Mango Ram, (2000)** Hon'ble Apex Court has held that for the purposes of the offence of rape, consent requires voluntary participation not only after the exercise of intelligence based on the knowledge of the significance and moral quality of the act but also after having fully exercised the choice between the resistance and assent.
    - To absolve a person from criminal liability of rape, consent must be completely free in nature and must not be covered by clauses (iii) to (vii) of **Section 63** of BNS. In other words, a consent covered under clauses (iii) to (vii) of **Section 63** is no consent in the eyes of law.

MEANING/ DEFINITION OF CERTAIN WORDS UNDER SECTION 63

- For the purposes of **Section 63**, "vagina" also includes labia majora.
- Consent means an unequivocal voluntary agreement when the woman, by words, gestures or any form of verbal or non-verbal communication, communicates willingness to participate in the specific sexual act. However, a woman who does not physically resist to the act of penetration shall not by the reason only of that fact, be regarded as consenting to the sexual activity.

Exceptions of Rape

As per the provisions of **Section 63,** the offence of rape has two exceptions:

- A medical procedure or intervention does not constitute rape.
- Sexual intercourse or sexual acts by a man with his own wife, the wife not being under eighteen years of age, is not rape.

Punishment for Rape

(**Note:** ***Section 64*** *of the BNS corresponds to* ***Section 376(1) & (2)*** *of the IPC*)

Section 64 of BNS lays down the punishment for the offence of rape. **Section 64(1)** lays down the punishment for the offence of rape simpliciter. **Section 64(2)** lays down the punishment for certain aggravated forms of rape.

- **Punishment for Rape Simpliciter:** In view of **Section 64(1),** a person who commits the offence of rape is punishable with rigorous imprisonment of ten years which may extend to life imprisonment and is also liable to fine.
- **Punishment for Aggravated Forms of Rape:** In view of the provisions of **Section 64(2):**
  - **Rape by Police Officer:** A police officer shall be punished with rigorous imprisonment of ten years, which may extend to life imprisonment (which shall mean imprisonment for the remainder of that person's natural life) and shall also be liable to fine if he commits rape:
    - Within the limits of the police station to which he is appointed.
    - In the premises of any station house.
    - On a woman in his custody or in the custody of a police officer subordinate to him.
  - **Rape by Public Servant:** A public servant shall be punished with rigorous imprisonment of ten years, which may extend to life imprisonment (which shall mean imprisonment for the remainder of that person's natural life, and shall also be liable to fine if he commits rape on a woman in his custody or in the custody of a public servant subordinate to him.
  - **Rape by Member of the Armed Forces:** A member of the armed forces depolyed in an area by the Central/ State Governemnt shall be punished with rigorous imprisonment of ten years, which may extend to life imprisonment (which shall mean imprisonment for the remainder of that person's natural life, and shall also be liable to fine if he commits rape in such area.
  - **Rape by Person on Management/ Staff of Jail, Remand Home etc.:** A person on the management or on the staff of a jail, remand home or other place of custody established by/ under law or of a women's or children's institution shall be punished with rigorous imprisonment of ten years, which may extend to life imprisonment (which shall mean imprisonment for the remainder of that person's natural life, and shall also be liable to fine if he commits rape on any inmate of such jail, remand home, place or institution.

- **Rape by Person on Management/ Staff of Hospital:** A person being on the management or on the staff of a hospital shall be punished with rigorous imprisonment of ten years, which may extend to life imprisonment (which shall mean imprisonment for the remainder of that person's natural life), and shall also be liable to fine if he commits rape on a woman in that hospital.
- **Rape by Relative, Guardian or other Person in Position of Trust:** A person being a relative, guardian or teacher of, or a person in a position of trust or authority towards the woman shall be punished with rigorous imprisonment of ten years, which may extend to life imprisonment (which shall mean imprisonment for the remainder of that person's natural life), and shall also be liable to fine if he commits rape on such woman.
- **Rape During Communal or Sectarian Violence:** A person shall be punished with rigorous imprisonment of ten years, which may extend to life imprisonment (which shall mean imprisonment for the remainder of that person's natural life), and shall also be liable to fine if he commits rape during communal or sectarian violence.
- **Rape on a Woman Knowing her to be Pregnant:** A person shall be punished with rigorous imprisonment of ten years, which may extend to life imprisonment (which shall mean imprisonment for the remainder of that person's natural life), and shall also be liable to fine if he commits rape on a woman knowing her to be pregnant
- **Rape on a Woman Incapable of Giving Consent:** A person shall be punished with rigorous imprisonment of ten years, which may extend to life imprisonment (which shall mean imprisonment for the remainder of that person's natural life), and shall also be liable to fine if he commits rape, on a woman incapable of giving consent
- **Rape by a Person having Control or Dominance over a Woman:** A person being in a position of control or dominance over a woman shall be punished with rigorous imprisonment of ten years, which may extend to life imprisonment (which shall mean imprisonment for the remainder of that person's natural life), and shall also be liable to fine if he commits rape on such woman
- **Rape on a Woman Suffering from Disability:** A person shall be punished with rigorous imprisonment of ten years, which may extend to life imprisonment (which shall mean imprisonment for the remainder of that person's natural life, and shall also be liable to fine if he commits rape on a woman suffering from mental or physical disability.
- **Causing Grievous Bodily hurt etc. while Committing Rape:** A person shall be punished with rigorous imprisonment of ten years, which may extend to life imprisonment (which shall mean imprisonment for the remainder of that person's natural life), and shall also be liable to fine if he causes grievous bodily harm or maims or disfigures or endangers the life of a woman while committing rape.
- **Rape Committed Repeatedly on the Same Woman:** A person shall be punished with rigorous imprisonment of ten years, which may extend to life imprisonment (which shall mean imprisonment for the remainder of that person's natural life), and shall also be liable to fine if he commits rape repeatedly on the same woman.

DEFINITION OF CERTAIN WORDS UNDER SECTION 64

For the purposes of Section 64:

(a) "Armed forces" means the naval, army and air forces and includes any member of the Armed Forces constituted under any law, including the paramilitary forces and any auxiliary forces that are under the control of the Central Government or the State Government.

(b) "Hospital" means the precincts of the hospital and includes the precincts of any institution for the reception and treatment of persons during convalescence or of persons requiring medical attention or rehabilitation.

(c) "Police Officer" has the same meaning as assigned to the expression "police" under the Police Act, 1861.

(d) "Women's or Children's Institution" means an institution, whether called an orphanage or a home for neglected women or children or a widow's home or an institution called by any other name, which is established and maintained for the reception and care of women or children.

Rape on Woman Under Sixteen Years of Age

(**Note: Section 65(1)** of the BNS corresponds to **Section 376(3)** of the IPC)

- **Section 65(1)** of BNS inter alia lays down the punishment for the offence of rape committed on a woman under sixteen years of age. In view of the provisions of **Section 65(1)**:
  - A person who commits rape on a woman under sixteen years of age shall be punished with rigorous imprisonment for a term which shall not be less than twenty years, but which may extend to imprisonment for life, which shall mean imprisonment for the remainder of that person's natural life, and shall also be liable to fine:
- The fine imposed on the accused shall be just and reasonable to meet the medical expenses and rehabilitation of the victim.
- The fine imposed on the accused shall be paid to the victim.

Rape on Woman Under Twelve Years of Age

(**Note:** ***Section 65(2)*** *of the BNS corresponds to* ***Section 376AB*** *of the IPC*)

- **Section 65(2)** of BNS inter alia lays down the punishment for the offence of rape committed on a woman under twelve years of age. In view of the provisions of **Section 65(2)**:
  - A person who commits rape on a woman under twelve years of age shall be punished with rigorous imprisonment for a term which shall not be less than twenty years, but which may extend to imprisonment for life, which shall mean imprisonment for the remainder of that person's natural life, and with fine or with death.
  - The fine imposed shall be just and reasonable to meet the medical expenses and rehabilitation of the victim.
  - The fine imposed shall be paid to the victim.

Causing Death or Resulting in Persistent Vegetative State of Victim

(**Note:** ***Section 66*** *of the BNS corresponds to* ***Section 376A*** *of the IPC*)

- **Section 66** of BNS inter alia provides punishment for causing death or resulting in persistent vegetative state of a rape-victim.
- **Essential Elements:** Following are the essentials of the provision laid down under **Section 66**:
  - The accused must have committed the offence of rape punishable under **Section 64(1) or 64(2)**.
  - In the course of such commission, he must have inflicted an injury which caused the death of the woman or caused the woman to be in a persistent vegetative state.

- If both the aforesaid two conditions are fulfilled, the accused is liable to be punished with:
    - Rigorous imprisonment for a term which shall not be less than twenty years, but which may extend to imprisonment for life, which shall mean imprisonment for the remainder of that person's natural life, or
    - Death.

Sexual Intercourse by Husband upon his Wife During Separation

(**Note:** ***Section 67*** *of the BNS corresponds to* ***Section 376B*** *of the IPC*)

- **Section 67** of BNS inter alia provides punishment for sexual intercourse by husband upon his wife during the period of separation.
- **Essential Elements and Punishment:** Following are the essentials of the provision laid down under **Section 67**:
    - The wife of the accused must be living separately either under a decree of separation or otherwise.
    - The accused must have non-consensual sexual intercourse with his wife during the period of separation. The phrase "sexual intercourse" under **Section 67** means any of the acts mentioned in **Section 63(a)-(d)** of the BNS.
    - If the aforesaid conditions are satisfied, the accused is liable to be punished with imprisonment of either description for a term which shall not be less than two years but which may extend to seven years, and is also liable to fine.

Sexual Intercourse by a Person in Authority

(**Note:** ***Section 68*** *of the BNS corresponds to* ***Section 376C*** *of the IPC*)

- BNS also contains provisions to prevent abuse of power by persons in authority. **Section 68** of BNS is one of such provisions which punishes the persons who are in positions of authority and who exploit their positions to induce or seduce women for sexual intercourse.
- **Essential Elements:** Following are the essentials of the offence dealt with under **Section 68** of BNS:
    - The accused must be a person falling under any one of the following categories, namely:
        - A person in a position of authority or in a fiduciary relationship with the victim.
        - A public servant.
        - A superintendent or manager of a jail, remand home or other place of custody established by or under any law, or a women's or children's institution. "Superintendent", in relation to a jail, remand home or other place of custody or a women's or children's institution, includes a person holding any other office in such jail, remand home, place or institution by virtue of which such person can exercise any authority or control over its inmates.
        - A person on the management of a hospital or being on the staff of a hospital. The expressions "hospital" and "women's or children's institution" respectively have the same meanings as in Section 64(b)-(d) of BNS.
- The accused must abuse such position or fiduciary relationship to induce or seduce a woman to have sexual intercourse with him. The expression "sexual intercourse" means any of the acts mentioned in **Section 63(a) to (d)** of BNS.
- The woman (victim) must either be in the custody of the accused or under his charge or present in the premises.
- The sexual intercourse must not amount to the offence of rape.
- If all the aforesaid conditions are fulfilled, the accused shall be punished with rigorous imprisonment of either description for a term which shall not be less than five years, but which may extend to ten years, and shall also be liable to fine.

Sexual Intercourse by Employing Deceitful Means

- **Section 69** of BNS punishes sexual intercourse by employing deceitful means. Section 69 is a new provision and has been introduced to prevent sexual exploitation of women at the hands of fraudulent persons.
- **Essential Elements and Punishment:** Following are the **essentials** of the offence dealt with under **Section 69** of BNS:
  - The offender must have sexual intercourse with a woman by deceitful means, or by making a promise to marry her without any intention of fulfilling the same. Under the section, "deceitful means" has been defined to include inducement for/ false promise of employment, promotion, or of marrying by suppressing identity.
  - The sexual intercourse must not amount to the offence of rape.
  - If the aforesaid conditions are satisfied, the accused shall be punished with imprisonment of either description for a term which may extend to ten years and shall also be liable to fine.
  - This Section is newly introduced in the BNS.

Gang Rape

(**Note:** *Section 70(1) of the BNS corresponds to Section 376D of the IPC*)

Section 70 of BNS inter alia defines the offence of Gang rape and provides punishment therefor.

Essentials & Punishment of Gang Rape

- In view of the provisions of **Section 70(1),** the offence of gang rape is committed where a woman is raped by one or more persons by constituting a group or by acting in furtherance of a common intention.
- **Section 70(1)** incorporates the doctrine of constructive/ joint liability in relation to the offence of gang rape and fastens criminality on each of the persons who committed the rape by constituting a group or by acting in furtherance of common intention. Accordingly, each of the persons who commit the offence of gang rape is punishable with rigorous imprisonment for a term which shall not be less than twenty years but which may extend to imprisonment for life which shall mean imprisonment for the remainder of that person's natural life and with fine.
- The fine imposed under **Section 70(1)** must be just and reasonable to meet the medical expenses and rehabilitation of the victim and is required to be paid to the victim.

Punishment of Aggravated Form of Gang Rape

(**Note:** *Section 70(2) of the BNS corresponds to Section 376 DA & 376DB of the IPC*)

- An aggravated form of gang rape i.e. gang rape with a woman under eighteen years of age is punishable under **Section 70(2)** of BNS.
- If the offence of gang rape is committed upon a woman under 18 years of age, each of the accused persons who committed the offence is liable to punished with:
  - Imprisonment for life, which shall mean imprisonment for the remainder of that person's natural life and with fine, or
  - With Death.
- The fine imposed under **Section 70(1)** must be just and reasonable to meet the medical expenses and rehabilitation of the victim and is required to be paid to the victim.

Repeat Offenders

(**Note:** *Section 71 of the BNS corresponds to Section 376E of the IPC*)

- Under the provisions of BNS, repeat offenders of sexual offences have been dealt with and strictly. **Section 71** of BNS prescribes very stringent punishment, which may also be the sentence of death, for such offenders.

- In view of the provisions of **Section 71**, a person who has been previously convicted of an offence punishable under **Section 64, 65 66 or 70** of BNS and is subsequently convicted of an offence punishable under any of the said sections shall be punished:
  - With imprisonment for life which shall mean imprisonment for the remainder of that person's natural life, or
  - With Death.

Disclosure of Identity of Victim

(**Note:** ***Section 72*** *of the BNS corresponds to* ***Section 228A (1) & (2)*** *of the IPC*)

- In order to safeguard the privacy of women who are victims of sexual offences, **Section 72** of BNS punishes the disclosure of identity of such victims under certain circumstances. **Section 72(1)** lays down the punishment for such disclosure and **Section 72(2)** specifies various exceptions in respect thereof.
- **Essential Ingredients:** The offence of identity-disclosure of the victims (of certain sexual offences) has the following essential ingredients:
  - The accused must print or publish the name or any matter which may make known the identity of the victim, i.e., the woman against whom an offence punishable under **Section 64, 65, 66, 67, 68, 69, 70 or 71** is alleged or found to have been committed (called the of such offences).
  - The printing or publication as aforesaid must not be covered under any one of the exceptions provided under **Section 72(2)** of BNS.
  - If the above-said conditions are fulfilled, the offender is liable to be punished with imprisonment of either description for a term which may extend to two years and is also liable to fine.
- **Exceptions**: In view of the provisions of **Section 70(2)**, the following printing or publication constitute exceptions of the provisions of **Section 70(1)**, i.e., these printing or publication of name or any matter may make known the identity of the victim if such printing or publication but are nevertheless exempted from criminal liability:
  - A printing or publication by or under the order in writing of the officer-in-charge of the police station or the police officer making the investigation into such offence acting in good faith for the purposes of such investigation.
  - A printing or publication by or with the written authorisation of the victim.
  - A printing or publication by or with the written authorisation of the next of kin of the victim where the victim is dead or a child or of unsound mind.
  - However, such authorisation shall only be given by the next of kin to the chairman or the secretary (by whatever name called) of any recognised welfare institution or organisation.
  - A "recognised welfare institution or organisation", for the purposes of **Section 72(2)**, means a social welfare institution or organisation by the Central or State Government on that behalf.

Printing or Publishing Without Permission the Matters Relating to Court Proceedings

(**Note:** ***Section 73*** *of the BNS corresponds to* ***Section 228A (3)*** *of the IPC*)

- In order to maintain the sanctity of judicial/court proceedings and to safeguard the privacy of victims of sexual offences, **Section 73** of BNS punishes the person who unauthorisedly print or publish any matter relating to court proceedings.
- **Essential Ingredients and Punishment:**
  - The offender must print or publish a matter in relation to the proceeding before a Court.

- The printing or publication as aforesaid must be without the permission of the Court before whom the proceeding is pending.
- The proceeding must be with respect to an offence referred to in **Section 72** of BNS.
- If all the aforesaid conditions are satisfied, the offender shall be punished with imprisonment of either description for a term which may extend to two years and shall also be liable to fine.

- **Exception:** The printing or publication of the judgment of any High Court or the Supreme Court does not amount to an offence within the meaning of **Section 73** of BNS.

CRIMINAL FORCE AND ASSAULT AGAINST WOMEN

- In the new criminal law that is Bharatiya Nyaya Sanhita, 2023 (BNS), the offences related to women have been consolidated in a single chapter. **Chapter V** from **Section 74 to 79** of the BNS deals with the 'Criminal Force and Assault against women'.

COMPARATIVE CHART OF THE BNS AND IPC

Bharatiya Nyaya Sanhita, 2023 (BNS)	Title	Indian Penal Code, 1860 (IPC)
Section 74	Assault or use of criminal force on a woman with intent to outrage her modesty	Section 354
Section 75	Sexual Harassment	Section 354A
Section 76	Assault or use of Criminal force to women with intent to disrobe	Section 354B
Section 77	Voyeurism	Section 354C
Section 78	Stalking	Section 354D
Section 79	Word, Gesture, or act intended to insult modesty of woman	Section 509

CHANGES IN BNS IN COMPARISON TO IPC

Sections 76 and 77 of BNS corresponding to **Sections 354B and 354C** respectively, have been changed as follows:

- The expression **'whoever'** is used instead of 'man' in **Sections 76 and 77** of the BNS.
- This change has been brought to make these offences gender neutral.

Outraging Modesty of Woman

(**Notes:** ***Section 74*** *of the BNS corresponds to* ***Section 354*** *of the IPC*)

- **Section 74** deals with assault or use of criminal force to woman with intent to outrage her modesty. **Section 74** states that whoever:
  - Assaults or uses criminal force on any woman,
  - With the intention to outrage the modesty of women or knowing that the act will most likely outrage their modesty.
- **Punishment for Outraging the Modesty of a Woman:** The person will be punished with imprisonment for a term that shall not be less than one year but may extend to five years and will also be liable to a fine.
- **Essentials of Section 74 of the BNS:**
  - **Presence of Assault or Criminal Force:** **Section 129** of the BNS (Section 350 of IPC) deals with criminal force, and **Section 130** of the BNS (Section 351 of the IPC) deals with assault. The essential

ingredient is the presence of intention and knowledge in criminal force and assault.

- Criminal force states that anyone who uses force intending to cause any harm, injury, fear, or annoyance to any person without his permission, knowing that it will create fear and cause harm is called criminal force.
- **For Example:** 'A' encouraged 'B' to throw a stone at 'C' with the intention of creating fear and causing harm to 'C'. 'A' is guilty of using criminal force on 'C'.
- Assault states that any person who makes any gesture or any action with the knowledge that it will make the other person apprehend the meaning of the gesture is to harm, injure or create fear is said to have committed an assault. Assault is said to take place when the opposite party from the gesture of the person comprehends the danger.
- **For Example:** 'X' with the intention to create fear in the mind of 'Y' went towards him with a knife in his hand. 'X' has committed an assault against 'Y'.

- **Assault Must be on a Woman:** The victim of assault needs to be a woman, as it deals with crimes against women.
- **Presence of Intention and Knowledge:** The intention is the main factor on the basis of which an accused is either convicted or acquitted. The presence of knowledge is also equally important for committing the act. On that basis, the charges are weighed, and the punishment is given accordingly.
- **Outraging the Modesty of a Woman:** The definition of modesty is not given in the BNS. The meaning of modesty for a woman is determined by various judgements of the Apex Court.
  - In **Raju Pandurang Mahale v. State of Maharashtra (2004)**, the Supreme Court concluded that the essence of the woman's modesty was her sex. The Apex Court in its judgement defined 'modesty' in the same manner as it is given in the Oxford Dictionary in relation to a woman since the word 'modesty' has not been defined in the Indian Penal Code.
  - **State of H.P. v. Mango Ram (2000)**, the Supreme Court held that forcefully pulling a woman's clothes amounts to an assault with intent to outrage modesty under **Section 354** of IPC (**Section 74** of BNS).

Sexual Harassment

(**Notes:** ***Section 75*** *of the BNS corresponds to* ***Section 354A*** *of the IPC*)

- Sexual Harassment has been defined under **Section 75** of the BNS. The section is divided into three sub-clauses. The first sub-clause lists down the acts that are considered to be sexual harassment, whereas the second and third sub-clauses mention the respective punishments prescribed for the offence.
- **Section 75(1)** provides that a man committing any of the following acts shall be guilty of the offence of sexual harassment:
  - Physical contact and advances involving unwelcome and explicit sexual overtures; or
  - A demand or request for sexual favours; or
  - Showing pornography against the will of a woman; or
  - Making sexually coloured remarks.
- **Punishment for Sexual Harassment: Section 75(2)** provides that any man who commits the offence specified in clause (i) or clause (ii) or clause (iii) of **Section 75(1)** shall be punished with rigorous imprisonment for a term which may extend to three years, or with fine, or with both.
- Further, **Section 75(3)** provides that any man who commits the offence specified

in **clause (iv) of Section 75(1)** shall be punished with imprisonment of either description for a term which may extend to one year, or with fine, or with both.

- An offence under **Section 75** BNS is cognizable, bailable and can be tried by any magistrate. The offence is not listed under compoundable offences under **Section 359** of the BNSS (Section 320 of CrPC). Thus, cases of sexual harassment cannot be compounded by the parties.

Case Laws

- In the case of **State of Punjab v. Major Singh (1967),** the offender interfered with the epithelial duct of a seven-and-a-half-month-old female child, which led to an injury in the vagina of the infant. The accused was held guilty under **Section 354** of the Indian Penal Code (Section 74 of BNS). It was observed that there is no age limit, no measure of understanding of the abusive act and that the consciousness of a female is not essential to constitute the offence. The criminal intention and knowledge of the offender are at the crux of the matter. The provision of **Section 354** would be applicable when a reasonable man believes that the act he is committing is sufficient to tarnish the modesty of the victim. The court further stated that the act of removing a woman's saree coupled with a request for sexual intercourse would be an outrage to the modesty of a woman.
- **Vishaka v. State of Rajasthan (1997)**, it is though not directly linked to **Section 354** IPC (Section 74 of BNS), this landmark case addressed the issue of sexual harassment in the workplace. The Supreme Court laid down guidelines for preventing and redressing instances of sexual harassment (Vishaka Guidelines), which later led to the enactment of the Sexual Harassment of Women at Workplace (Prevention, Prohibition, and Redressal) Act in 2013.

DIFFERENCE BETWEEN SECTION 74 AND 75 OF THE BNS

- **Section 74** and **Section 75** both penalise sexual offences against women. **Section 74** deals with the offence of using assault or criminal force on a woman with the intention of outraging her modesty. It provides a punishment of imprisonment for a minimum term of one year and maximum term of five years, along with fine. On the other hand, **Section 75,** as discussed above, criminalises sexual harassment.
- From the face of it, they sound similar and also seem to have similar usage. But if examined closely, there is a difference in their language and intention. Looking closer into the phrasing of both Sections, we can point out this one major difference between the two:
  - **Section 74** focuses on the "act," which is essentially a physical act. The criminal intention plays a major role in determining whether such a "physical act" is an offence. Moreover, the use of force is also highlighted in this section.
  - **Section 75**, on the other hand, includes non-physical acts as well. For example, demand for sexual favours, showing pornography, and making sexually coloured remarks have also been made to constitute an offence under this section. Unlike **Section** 74, acts of sexual harassment can be committed without the application of force.

Assault or Use of Criminal Force to Women With Intent to Disrobe

(Notes: ***Section 76*** *of the BNS corresponds to* ***Section 354B*** *of the IPC*)

- **Section 76** whoever :
  - Assaults or uses criminal force to any woman or
  - Abets such act with the intention of disrobing or compelling her to be naked,
  - shall be deemed to have committed the offence defined in this section.

- **Punishment:** A person who commits this offence, shall be punished with imprisonment of either description for a term which shall not be less than three years but which may extend to seven years, and shall also be liable to fine.

Voyeurism

(**Notes:** ***Section 77*** *of the BNS corresponds to* ***Section 354C*** *of the IPC*)

- **Section 77** provides that whoever watches, or captures the image of a woman engaging in a private act in circumstances where she would usually have the expectation of not being observed either by the perpetrator or by any other person at the behest of the perpetrator or disseminates such image shall be:
  - Punished on first conviction with imprisonment of either description for a term which shall not be less than one year, but which may extend to three years, and shall also be liable to fine, and be punished.
  - On a second or subsequent conviction, with imprisonment of either description for a term which shall not be less than three years, but which may extend to seven years, and shall also be liable to fine.
- **Explanation 1** provides that for the purposes of this section, "private act" includes an act of watching carried out in a place which, in the circumstances, would reasonably be expected to provide privacy and where the victim's genitals, posterior or breasts are exposed or covered only in underwear; or the victim is using a lavatory; or the victim is doing a sexual act that is not of a kind ordinarily done in public.
- **Explanation 2** provides that where the victim consents to the capture of the images or any act, but not to their dissemination to third persons and where such image or act is disseminated, such dissemination shall be considered an offence under this section.
- This section punishes a man who captures images of a woman or intentionally watches her doing a private act. Nevertheless, if a woman consents to have her photos taken or allows for any activity but does not consent to disseminate the same to any third party, and where such image or act is disseminated by any other person, he shall be liable under the BNS.
- An offence under **Section 77** is cognizable and bailable at the first conviction but cognizable and non-bailable at the second or subsequent conviction.

Stalking

(**Notes:** ***Section 78*** *of the BNS corresponds to* ***Section 354D*** *of the IPC*)

- Stalking refers to a form of harassment that involves repeated and persistent intent to cause fear or harm to the person who is being followed. It can be in any form, be it physical or online.
- **Section 78 (1)** provides that any man who:
  - (i) Follows a woman and contacts, or attempts to contact such woman to foster personal interaction repeatedly despite a clear indication of disinterest by such woman; or
  - (ii) Monitors the use by a woman of the internet, e-mail or any other form of electronic communication, commits the offence of stalking:
- Provided that such conduct shall not amount to stalking if the man who pursued it proves that:
  - (i) It was pursued for the purpose of preventing or detecting crime and the man accused of stalking had been entrusted with the responsibility of prevention and detection of crime by the State; or
  - (ii) It was pursued under any law or to comply with any condition or requirement imposed by any person under any law; or
  - (iii) In the particular circumstances such conduct was reasonable and justified.

- **Punishment: Section 78(2)** provides that whoever commits the offence of stalking shall be punished on
  - First conviction with imprisonment of either description for a term which may extend to three years, and shall also be liable to fine; and
  - Second or subsequent conviction, with imprisonment of either description for a term which may extend to five years, and shall also be liable to fine.

Word, Gesture, or act Intended to Insult Modesty of Woman

(**Notes:** ***Section 79*** *of the BNS corresponds to* ***Section 509*** *of the IPC*)

- **Section 79** provides that whoever, intending to insult the modesty of any woman:
  - Utters any words,
  - Makes any sound or gesture, or
  - Exhibits any object in any form,
  - Intending that such word or sound shall be heard, or
  - Such gesture or object shall be seen, by such woman, or intrudes upon the privacy of such woman.
    - Shall be punished with simple imprisonment for a term which may extend to three years, and also with fine.

Case Laws

- In the case of **Rupan Deol Bajaj v. Kanwar Pal Singh Gill (1995)**, the accused hit the back of a lady at a public gathering. The petitioner was an I.A.S. officer who lodged an F.I.R. against the accused. The learned Chief Judicial Magistrate of Chandigarh held the accused guilty under **Section 354 and Section 509** of the IPC (Section 74 and 79 of BNS respectively). The Supreme Court referred to the Oxford Dictionary to find the meaning of the word 'modesty'. It was observed that the behaviour of the offender outraged the decency of the woman. This case is also known as the "butt-slapping case" in the media.
- In the recent case of the **State of Maharashtra v. Rovena Aadnya Amit Bhosle (2020)**, it was held that women could also be held guilty of outraging the modesty of women. The accused was a woman who assaulted her neighbour by tearing her nightdress in the passage of the building in front of several people. The victim was left completely naked and was beaten with a shoe. The metropolitan magistrate of the Mumbai Court held the accused guilty under **Section 354** of the IPC as being gender neutral. She was convicted and sentenced to one year of rigorous imprisonment for outraging another woman's modesty. As she was the mother of three, the youngest being only one and a half years old, she was awarded the minimum punishment stated under **Section 354** of the Indian Penal Code.

OFFENCES RELATING TO MARRIAGE

- Marriage, as a social institution, holds a significant place in Indian society, carrying both cultural and legal implications. Over the years, the legal framework governing marriage and related offences has evolved to protect individuals from exploitation, abuse, and injustices within marital relationships.
- The BNS laid the foundation for addressing various offences related to marriage, including dowry deaths, bigamy, deceitful marriages, and cruelty. These provisions aimed to uphold the sanctity of marriage and ensure the well-being and rights of individuals involved.
- However, societal changes and the increasing awareness of gender-based violence have highlighted the need for more robust and comprehensive legal protections. In response to these evolving needs, the Bharatiya Nyaya Sanhita (BNS) 2023 has been introduced to replace the IPC. **Chapter V** from **Section 80 to 87** of the BNS deals with the 'Offences related to Marriage.

COMPARATIVE CHART OF THE BNS AND IPC		
Bharatiya Nyaya Sanhita, 2023 (BNS)	Title	Indian Penal Code, 1860 (IPC)
Section 80	Dowry death	Section 304B
Section 81	Cohabitation caused by man deceitfully inducing belief of lawful marriage	Section 493
Section 82 (1)	Marrying again during the lifetime of the husband or wife	Section 494
Section 82 (2)	Marrying again during life time of husband or wife, concealment of former marriage	Section 495
Section 83	Marriage ceremony fraudulently gone through without lawful marriage	Section 496
Section 84	Enticing or taking away or detaining with criminal intent a married woman	Section 498
Section 85	Husband or relative of husband of a woman subjecting her to cruelty	Section 498A
Section 86	Cruelty defined	Explanation of Section 498A

Dowry Death

(**Note:** ***Section 80*** *of the BNS corresponds to* ***Section 304B*** *of the IPC*)

- **Section 80 (1)** provides that where the death of a woman is caused by any burns or bodily injury or occurs otherwise than under normal circumstances within seven years of her marriage and it is shown that soon before her death she was subjected to cruelty or harassment by her husband or any relative of her husband for, or in connection with, any demand for dowry, such death shall be called "dowry death", and such husband or relative shall be deemed to have caused her death.
- **Explanation:** For the purposes of this subsection, "dowry" shall have the same meaning as in **Section 2** of the Dowry Prohibition Act, 1961.
- **Section 80** of BNS imposes a statutory obligation on a court to presume that the accused committed the dowry death when the prosecution proves that:
  - (i) Death of his wife had occurred otherwise than under normal circumstances within seven years of her marriage and
  - (ii) Soon before her death she was subjected to cruelty or harassment by her husband or his relatives in connection with demand for dowry.
- The main component of **Section 80** is that the death of the woman should not only be under the circumstances specified in the section, but should also be the consequence of demands for dowry.
- **Punishment of Dowry Death: Section 80(2)** lays down the punishment of offence. According to this section, whoever commits dowry death shall be punished with imprisonment for a term which shall not be less than seven years but which may extend to imprisonment for life.
- **Essential Ingredients**
  - The death of a woman should be caused by burns or bodily injury or otherwise than under normal circumstances.
  - Such a death should have occurred within seven years of her marriage.

- She must have been subjected to cruelty or harassment by her husband or by any relative of her husband.
- Such cruelty or harassment should be for, or in connection with, the demand for dowry; and
- Such cruelty or harassment is shown to have been meted the woman soon before her death.

MEANING OF THE TERM DOWRY

As per the explanation to **Section 80**, the term dowry shall have the same meaning as in **Section 2 of Dowry Prohibition Act, 1961.**

Section 2 sub-section 1 of Dowry Prohibition Act, 1961 defines the dowry as follows:

- Any property or valuable security given or agreed to be given either directly or indirectly:
  - By one party to a marriage to another party to the marriage, or
  - By parents of either party to a marriage or by any other person, to either party to the marriage or to any other person at or before or any time after the marriage in connection. with the marriage of the said parties, but does not include dower or mehar in the case of persons to whom the Muslim Personal Law applies.

- **Section 80** does not explain the term 'cruelty'. However, **Section 85** explains as to what amounts to 'cruelty'.

Case Laws

(**Note:** ***Section 80, Section 85, Section 108*** *of the BNS corresponds to* ***Section 304B, Section 498A, Section 306*** *of the IPC respectively*)

- In **Shanti v. State of Haryana (1991),** the Supreme Court held that **Section 304B** of IPC and **Section 498 A** of IPC are not mutually exclusive and the meaning of 'cruelty' given in explanation to **Section 498A**, having regard to the common background to **Section 304B** and **Section 498A**, can be applied to **Section 304B**.
- In the case of **Kaliyaperumal v. State of Tamil Nadu (2004)**, the Court held that the explanation of cruelty as given in **Section 498A** can be relied on for the purposes of **Section 304B** as well.
- In the case of **Nunna Venkateswarlu v. State of Andhra Pradesh, (1996)** the Andhra Pradesh High Court convicted a person under **Section 498A** of IPC and **Section 306** IPC instead of **Section 304B** IPC, on the ground that the term used in the Section is "given or agreed to be given". As such where the accused continuously tortured and harassed his wife to sell five acres of land gifted to her by her father at the time of marriage and to give the sale proceeds to the accused, the Court held that for the purposes of dowry there has to be a prior agreement between the parties which is not there in the present case. However the judgment of Andhra pradesh may not be good law in view of the judgment of SC in **Himachal Pradesh v. Nikku Ram.**
- The Hon'ble Supreme Court in the case of **Himachal Pradesh v. Nikku Ram, (1995),** held that a demand made after marriage could also be a part of the consideration because an implied agreement has to be read to give property or valuable securities, even if asked after the marriage as a part of consideration for the marriage.

PRESUMPTION AS TO DOWRY DEATH

(**Note:** ***Section 118*** *of the BSA corresponds to* ***Section 113B*** *of the IEA*)

- **Section 118** of the BSA provides for presumption as to dowry death.
- According to **Section 118,** when the question is whether a person has committed the dowry death of a woman and it is shown that soon before her death, such woman had been subjected by such person to cruelty or harassment for, or in connection with, any demand for dowry,
  - The Court shall presume that such person had caused the dowry death.

- **Explanation:** It provides that for the purposes of this section, "dowry death" shall have the same meaning as in **Section 80** of the Bharatiya Nyaya Sanhita, 2023.
- This presumption will arise only when the prosecution has established the basic element of demand for dowry. The initial burden lies on the prosecution to prove the ingredients of **Section 80** of the BNS, including the fact that soon before her death, she had been subjected by the accused persons to cruelty or harassment for, or in connection with, any demand for dowry.
- If the prosecution succeeds in discharging this initial burden, then positively the provisions of **Section 118** of the BSA come into play and can be pressed into service for drawing the presumption against the accused person that he has caused dowry death. "The presumption, therefore, needs to be invoked by having regard to the proximity of the cruelty or harassment and death of the victim." It cannot be invoked merely because the alleged death occurred within seven years of her marriage.
- Once the statutory requisites are established, a court is bound by law to invoke the presumption as **Section 80** of BNS and **Section 118** of BSA uses the words **" shall presume"** and it is on the accused to rebut the presumption. If he fails, the court is bound to act upon it.
- In the recent case of **State of Karnataka v. MN Basavaraja and others, (2024)**, The Supreme Court recently decided that testimonies from family members of the deceased in dowry death cases should not be dismissed simply because they are considered interested witnesses. The bench pointed out that a woman facing harassment over dowry is likely to confide in her immediate family, making their testimony crucial for bringing the culprits to justice.

Deceitful Marriage or Fraudulent Marriage

(**Note:** ***Section 81*** *of the BNS corresponds to* ***Section 493*** *of the IPC*)

- **Section 81** that states about cohabitation caused by man deceitfully inducing belief of lawful marriage provides that every man who by deceit causes any woman who is not lawfully married to him to believe that she is lawfully married to him and to cohabit or have sexual intercourse with him in that belief is said to commit offence under this section.
- Deceitful marriage involves a man causing a woman to believe falsely that she is lawfully married to him, leading her to cohabit or engage in sexual intercourse under that false belief.
- This offence is non-cognizable and non-bailable. This act of deception is specifically addressed under **Section 81** of the BNS.
- For example, John, tells Mary that he has legally divorced his first wife and marries Mary in a ceremonial but non-legal manner. Mary, believing she is legally married, lives with John and has sexual relations with him. This constitutes deceitful marriage as defined under **Section 81**.

Essentials of Deceitful Marriage

- **Deceit:** The man must have used deceit, meaning a false statement or representation, to convince the woman of a lawful marriage.
- In **Ram Chandra Bhagat v. The State of Jharkhand, (2013)**, deceit was defined as "a false statement of fact made by a person knowingly or recklessly with the intent that it shall be acted upon, thereby causing injury."
- **Belief of Lawful Marriage:** The woman must believe that she is lawfully married to the man.
- **Cohabitation or Sexual Intercourse:** The woman, under the false belief of lawful marriage, cohabits with or engages in sexual intercourse with the man.

- If a man forges marriage documents to convince a woman that they are married, leading her to live with him as his wife, it meets these essentials.

- In **Subhransu Shekhar Somant Ray v. State of Orissa, (2002)**, the prosecutrix testified that she initially resisted sexual relations with the accused. However, when he applied vermilion to her hair parting, proclaimed her as his wife, and promised to acknowledge her publicly after securing a job, she consented to intercourse.
  - This testimony was deemed sufficient to establish an offence under **Section 81** of BNS (Section 493 of IPC), which addresses cohabitation caused by a man deceitfully inducing a belief of lawful marriage.
- **Punishment for Deceitful Marriage:** The person shall be punished with imprisonment of either description for a term which may extend to ten years, and shall also be liable to fine.
- **For Example:** Raj deceives Sita into believing they are lawfully married by forging a marriage certificate and conducting a fake ceremony. Sita, convinced of the marriage's authenticity, cohabits and engages in a marital relationship with Raj. It is later revealed that Raj is already married, making his marriage to Sita void.

Bigamy

(**Note:** *Section 82 of the BNS corresponds to Section 494 & 495 of the IPC*)

- **Section 82** mentions marrying again during the lifetime of husband or wife.
- Bigamy is the act of entering into a marriage with one person while still legally married to another.
- A legal or *de facto* separation of the couple does not alter their marital status as married persons. In the case of a person in the process of divorcing his or her spouse, that person is taken to be legally married until such time as the divorce becomes final or absolute under the law of the relevant jurisdiction.
- Bigamy laws do not apply to couples in a *de facto* or cohabitation relationship or that enter such relationships when one is legally married. If the prior marriage is for any reason void, the couple is not married, and hence each party is free to marry another without falling foul of the bigamy laws.
- **Section 82** of the BNS makes the bigamy a punishable offence.
- **Section 82(1)** provides that whoever, having a husband or wife living, marries in any case in which such marriage is void by reason of its taking place during the life of such husband or wife, shall be punished with:
  - Imprisonment of either description for a term which may extend to seven years, and shall also be liable to fine.
- **Exception**
  - **Court Declaration of Void Marriage:** Bigamy laws do not apply if the first marriage has been declared void by a court of competent jurisdiction.
  - **Seven Years Absence:** If a spouse has been continually absent for seven years and has not been heard of as being alive within that time, the other party may contract a subsequent marriage.
    - However, they must inform the new spouse of the true facts before marriage.
    - Example: If Priya's husband Rahul disappears without a trace for seven years and she remarries, informing her new husband of the situation, she would not be guilty of bigamy under **Section 82.**
  - Bigamy laws apply to all individuals in India except Muslim males, who are allowed multiple wives under Muslim Personal Law.
  - In **Radhika Sameena v. SHO Habeeb Nagar Police Station (1996)**, it was held that a Muslim male, married under the Special Marriage Act, 1954, faces **Section**

82 of BNS (Section 494 IPC) charges for subsequent marriage under Muslim Law. Since the first marriage was under the Special Marriage Act, its provisions apply, rendering the second marriage void.

- **Section 82(2)** provides that whoever commits the offence under **sub-section (1)** having concealed from the person with whom the subsequent marriage is contracted, the fact of the former marriage, shall be punished with:
  - Imprisonment of either description for a term which may extend to ten years, and shall also be liable to fine.

Essentials of Bigamy

- **Existence of First Valid Marriage:** There must be a valid and subsisting first marriage at the time of entering into the second marriage.
- **Subsequent Marriage During Subsistence of First Marriage:** The second marriage must take place while the first marriage is still legally valid and subsisting.
- **Knowledge of Invalidity:** The accused must know or have reason to believe that the second marriage is void due to the existence of the first marriage.
- In **Satya Devi v. Khem Chand (2013)**, the wife accused her husband of bigamy and cruelty. Due to her inability to prove the validity of her marriage, the second marriage was upheld as valid, resulting in the dismissal of her case.

Effect of Conversion to Other Religions

Conversion means converting oneself from one religion to another. After the enactment of the Hindu Marriage Act (1955), it was shown that many Hindu husbands converted to Islam and married again as per Muslim personal law to exonerate themselves from the criminal liability of bigamy, as the offence of bigamy does not apply to a Muslim marriage. The matter came before the Supreme Court for the first time in the case of **Sarla Mudgal v. Union of India (1995)**.

- In the above case the questions before the Supreme Court were:
  - Can Hindus who have married under the law of Hinduism be married again under the law of Islam?
  - What will be the authenticity of such a marriage?
  - Does the converted husband commit the offence under **Section 494** of the IPC (**Section 82** of BNS)?
- **The Supreme Court answered:**
  - A marriage celebrated under Hindu law cannot automatically be dissolved by converting to another religion. Where a marriage takes place under Hindu law, the parties acquire certain rights by the marriage itself. Such as the wife's right to be maintained by the husband, having an equal share in the husband's property, etc. These rights will not be dissolved just because the husband converted to another religion. If he wants to end his liability, he has to divorce his wife as per Hindu law.
  - On the question of the validity of such marriage, the Court said, in the case of a Hindu husband who marries a second time after converting to Islam, the marriage is void because it occurs during the lifetime of his first wife.
  - In this situation, parties who have been married under the Hindu Marriage Act continue to be married according to Hindu law even if their husband embraces Islam to seek another wife.
  - As for the applicability of **Section 494** IPC, the Court ruled that the second marriage is void since it takes place during the lifetime of the first wife, making the accused liable for bigamy.
- Another landmark judgment is **Lily Thomas v. Union of India, (2000)**, the petitioner challenged the decision of the Supreme Court given in **Sarla Mudgal v. Union of India (1995)**. According to him, the decision violated the right to life and liberty,

as well as rights to freedom of religion protected by **Articles 20, 21, 25 and 26** of the Constitution.

- The Supreme Court affirmed its decision on Sarla Mudgal and held that the second marriage solemnised by a Hindu during the subsistence of the first marriage is an offence punishable under penal law.
- The Constitution guarantees that every individual has not only the right to believe in the religion of his choice but also the right to express his beliefs and ideas in a manner that does not infringe on someone else's religious freedom and personal rights. According to the court, when a Hindu husband contracted a second marriage after converting, he was not doing so out of conscience but to achieve his ulterior motives. According to **Article 25** of the Constitution, these rights are guaranteed without encroaching on similar rights of others.
- The Court further said it is not possible for the husband or wife to end the marital bonds already established as a result of a valid Hindu marriage by converting to another religion. Therefore, during the lifetime of the first marriage, another marriage cannot be performed, even under any other personal law. If such a marriage were to take place, the person would be subject to prosecution under **Section 494** of IPC.

Marriage Ceremony Fraudulently gone through without Lawful Marriage

(**Note:** ***Section 83*** *of the BNS corresponds to* ***Section 496*** *of the IPC*)

- **Section 83** provides that whoever, dishonestly or with a fraudulent intention, goes through the ceremony of being married, knowing that he is not thereby lawfully married, shall be punished with:
  - Imprisonment of either description for a term which may extend to seven years, and shall also be liable to fine.
- For example, Raj, already married, knowingly enters into a marriage ceremony with Maya, concealing his existing marital status from her and intending to deceive her into believing they are lawfully married. This constitutes fraudulent marriage under **Section 83**.
- In **Ram Chandra Bhagat v. State of Jharkhand (2013)**, the Court considered whether a man's promise to marry a woman, followed by cohabitation for nine years, constituted inducement to believe in marriage.
  - The Court ruled that the promise did not induce a genuine belief in marriage, and therefore, the man was not held liable.
- **Exception:** If the accused genuinely believes the marriage to be legally binding without any fraudulent intent or awareness of its invalidity, they cannot be held liable under **Section 83.**

Enticing or Taking away or Detaining with Criminal Intent a Married Woman

(**Note:** ***Section 84*** *of the BNS corresponds to* ***Section 498*** *of the IPC*)

- **Section 84** provides that whoever takes or entices away any woman who is and whom he knows or has reason to believe to be the wife of any other man, with intent that she may have illicit intercourse with any person, or conceals or detains with that intent any such woman, shall be punished with
  - Imprisonment of either description for a term which may extend to two years, or with fine, or with both.
- In **Emperor v. Madan Gopal (1912)**, the accused was convicted under **Section 498 IPC** (now **Section 84** in BNS) for enticing Musammat Kharag Kumari, assumed to be the complainant's wife. Despite the accused's claims of no evidence of enticement or proof of a valid marriage, the courts upheld the conviction.

- The court ruled that unless proven otherwise, marriages are presumed valid under the law, even with caste differences, and the accused failed to rebut this presumption.
- This case affirmed that **IPC Section 498 (now Section 84 in BNS)** applies only to marriages legally recognized.

CRUELTY TO MARRIED WOMEN

(Note: ***Section 85** & **86** of the BNS corresponds to **Section 498A** and Explanation to **Section 498A** of the IPC, respectively*)

Husband or Relative of The Husband of a Woman Subjecting her to Cruelty

- **Section 85** - Husband or relative of the husband of a woman subjecting her to cruelty - It provides that whoever, being the husband or the relative of the husband of a woman, subjects such woman to cruelty shall be punished under this provision.
- **Section 86 'Cruelty'** defined.
- For the purposes of **Section 85**, "cruelty" means:
  - (a) Any wilful conduct which is of such a nature as is likely to drive the woman to commit suicide or to cause grave injury or danger to life, limb or health (whether mental or physical) of the woman; or
  - (b) Harassment of the woman where such harassment is with a view to coercing her or any person related to her to meet any unlawful demand for any property or valuable security or is on account of failure by her or any person related to her to meet such demand.
- Cruelty, as defined under **Section 86** and elaborated in **Section 85** of the BNS, encompasses various forms of abusive conduct towards a woman by her husband or his relatives.
- It includes acts that endanger her life, limb, or mental health, or harass her with the intention of coercing her or her relatives into meeting unlawful demands.
- The term "cruelty" includes any willful conduct likely to drive the woman to commit suicide, cause grave injury, or endanger her life, limb, or health, whether mental or physical.
- It also encompasses harassment with the intent of coercing her or her relatives to meet unlawful demands for property or valuable security or as retaliation for failing to meet such demands.
- **Sarla Prabhakar v. State of Maharashtra (1990)**, highlighted the scope and definition of cruelty, focusing on protecting women from both mental and physical harassment in their matrimonial homes.
- It broadens the definition to include not only physical harm but also psychological and emotional harm, reflecting contemporary understanding of abuse in marital relationships.
- On January 31, 2009, Chief Justice of India, Justice K. G. Balakrishnan, speaking to India's National Commission for Women, emphasized that **Section 498A** of the IPC **(Section 85 & 86** of BNS**)** was frequently "misused" and often wrongly implicated relatives not directly involved in matrimonial disputes.
- In **Arnesh Kumar v. State of Bihar (2014)**, the Supreme Court of India addressed the misuse of **Section 85** (Section 498A IPC), noting innocent family members were unfairly implicated without evidence.
- The Court stressed on police conducting diligent investigations to prevent undue harassment during arrests.

Essential Ingredients

- **Wilful Conduct Likely to Cause Harm:** The term "cruelty" includes any wilful conduct that is likely to drive the woman to commit suicide, cause grave injury, or endanger her life, limb, or mental health **(Section 86(a))**.

- **Harassment with Coercive Intent:** It also encompasses harassment aimed at coercing the woman or her relatives to meet unlawful demands for property or valuable security **(Section 86(b)).**

Punishment

- **Imprisonment**
  - The accused shall be liable to imprisonment for a term which may extend to three years.
  - This imprisonment can vary depending on the severity and nature of the cruelty inflicted upon the woman.
- **Fine**
  - In addition to imprisonment, the accused shall also be liable to pay a fine.
  - The amount of the fine is discretionary and may be determined by the Court based on the circumstances of the case.
- In **Arun Vyas v. Anita Vyas (1999),** the Supreme Court recognized cruelty as a continuing offence under the BNS, meaning each instance of cruelty restarts the limitation period for filing a complaint.
  - This interpretation is crucial in ensuring that victims can seek justice even if the abuse spans a long period.
- In **Smt. Raj Rani v. Delhi Administration (2000)**, Raj Rani was convicted under **Section 498A IPC** (Now, Sections 85 and 86 in BNS) based on a suicide note left by her sister-in-law, Veena.
  - The trial court sentenced her to 5 years imprisonment.
  - On appeal, the Delhi High Court found no concrete evidence of cruelty as defined under **Section 498A IPC** in the suicide note, leading to her acquittal by the Supreme Court.
- **Reema Aggarwal v. Anupam (2004),** This case broadened the application of **Section 498A of the IPC (Section 85 & 86 of BNS)** to include women in second marriages, thereby ensuring that protections against cruelty extend to all women, regardless of the legitimacy of their marital status.

Kidnapping, Abducting or Inducing a Woman to Compel her Marriage, Compelled, to Marry any Person Against her Will, or in Order that etc.

(**Note:** *Section 87 of the BNS corresponds to Section 366 of the IPC*)

- **Section 87** provides that whoever kidnaps or abducts any woman with intent that she may be compelled, or knowing it to be likely that she will be compelled, to marry any person against her will, or in order that she may be forced or seduced to illicit intercourse, or knowing it to be likely that she will be forced or seduced to illicit intercourse, shall be punished with:
  - Imprisonment of either description for a term which may extend to ten years, and shall also be liable to fine; and
- Whoever, by means of criminal intimidation as defined in this Sanhita or of abuse of authority or any other method of compulsion,
  - Induces any woman to go from any place with intent that she may be, or knowing that it is likely that she will be,
  - Forced or seduced to illicit intercourse with another person shall also be punishable as aforesaid.
- Where a woman has no intention of marriage or lawful intercourse when kidnapped, this section applies.
- The section requires:
  - Kidnapping or abduction of any woman.
  - Such kidnapping or abducting must be:
    - With intent that she may be compelled or knowing it to be likely that she will be compelled to marry any person against her will; or
    - In order that she may be forced or seduced to illicit intercourse, or knowing it to be likely that she will be forced or seduced to illicit intercourse.
  - Mere submission without resistance cannot tantamount to consent.

CAUSING MISCARRIAGE

- Miscarriage is the premature expulsion of the child or foetus from the mother's womb at any period of pregnancy before the term of gestation is completed.
- According to medical science, miscarriage is defined as losing one's pregnancy before the 20th week, and when the pregnancy is deliberately eliminated it is known as abortion.
- But coming to the Bharatiya Nyaya Sanhita miscarriage is interpreted as the premature expulsion of a baby or foetus from the womb of the mother at any period of pregnancy before the gestation period is completed. No distinction is made between miscarriage and abortion in the BNS.
- **Chapter V** from **Section 88 to 92** of the BNS deals with the 'Causing Miscarriage'.

COMPARATIVE CHART OF THE BNS AND IPC

Bharatiya Nyaya Sanhita, 2023 (BNS)	Title	Indian Penal Code, 1860 (IPC)
Section 88	Causing miscarriage	Section 312
Section 89	Causing miscarriage without women's consent	Section 313
Section 90	Death caused by act done with intent to cause miscarriage	Section 314
Section 91	Act done with intent to prevent child being born alive or to cause it to die after birth	Section 315
Section 92	Causing death of quick unborn child by act amounting to culpable homicide	Section 316

Causing Miscarriage

(**Note:** ***Section 88*** *of the BNS corresponds to* ***Section 312*** *of the IPC*)

- According to **Section 88** of BNS whoever voluntarily causes a woman with child to miscarry shall, if such miscarriage be not caused in good faith for the purpose of saving the life of the woman, be punished with imprisonment of either description for a term which may extend to three years, or with fine, or with both; and, if the woman be quick with child, shall be punished with imprisonment of either description for a term which may extend to seven years, and shall also be liable to fine.
- A woman who causes herself to miscarry, is within the meaning of this section.
- In **Rajesh Kumar v. State of Chhattisgarh (2024),** the Chhattisgarh High Court recently held that a person cannot be convicted for the offence of causing a miscarriage if the child in the mother's womb is full-grown or if there is no expulsion of the foetus from the womb before gestation is over.
- Miscarriage involves the expulsion of a child from the womb before gestation is over, the Court explained, while acquitting a doctor in a case where the foetus of a deceased woman was found "safe and dead" in her womb.
- **Death in Attempt to Terminate Pregnancy**
  - In the case of **Akhil Kumar v. State of M.P.**, a lady who had an unnatural pregnancy for 24 weeks was given an injection to end it, but the next day she passed away without experiencing a miscarriage.
    - According to **section 511 of IPC** (Section 62 of BNS) and **section 312 of IPC** (Section 88 of BNS), the doctor was deemed to have intentionally caused a miscarriage because it is assumed that he is aware of the potential side effects of the medication.

- In order to provide for safe abortions, termination of certain pregnancies by registered medical practitioners has been legalised with the enactment of **The Medical Termination of Pregnancy Act, 1971 (MTP Act)**.
    - The Act provides for termination of pregnancy by registered medical practitioner where its continuance would involve a risk to life of pregnant women and grave injury to her physical and mental health or were there is substantial risk that if the child was born that would suffer from such physical or mental abnormalities as to be seriously handicapped.
    - If it is alleged that the pregnancy was caused by rape or that a contraceptive method was ineffective used by a married women or her husband it would be presumed to constitute a grave injury to the mental health of the pregnant women.
    - Good faith by itself is not enough. It has to be good faith for the purpose of saving the life of the mother or the child and not otherwise.
    - In **Suchita Srivastava v. Chandigarh Administration (2009)** Court examined **Section 3 of the MTP Act**, emphasising a woman's right to consent to termination under **Article 21** guarantees of liberty, stating that forced termination violates her reproductive choice.
        - Reproductive rights, including privacy, dignity, and the option to carry a pregnancy to full term, were underscored as essential human rights. Regarding mental retardation, the Court differentiated it from mental illness under the MTP Act, affirming the requirement of a mentally retarded person's own consent for termination. It made clear that loosening this requirement would unfairly limit women's access to reproductive healthcare.
        - The Court balanced women's right to bodily autonomy with state interests in protecting potential life, noting the MTP Act's provisions as reasonable restrictions. It cited international agreements on rights of mentally retarded persons to support personal autonomy. Disagreeing with the High Court's approach, it applied a 'best interests' test, ruling against the termination due to risks and emotional impact on the Appellant.
        - In the case of **Surender Chauhan v. State of M.P. (2000)**, the conviction under this section was held valid, where death of the woman was caused by the accused while causing abortion when he was not legally competent to terminate the pregnancy of the deceased. The person who had taken the woman to that 'Doctor' with intent to cause her miscarriage was also held guilty of the offence.

Causing Miscarriage without Woman's Consent

(**Note:** ***Section 89*** *of the BNS corresponds to* ***Section 313*** *of the IPC*)

- In **Section 89 of BNS** provides that whoever commits the offence defined in the last preceding section without the consent of the woman, whether the woman is quick with child or not,
    - Shall be punished with imprisonment for life or with imprisonment of either description for a term which may extend to ten years, and also shall be liable to fine.
- Under **Section 89** of BNS the act should have been done without the consent of the woman. Under it the person procuring the abortion is alone punished but under **Section 88** of BNS such person as well as the woman who causes herself to miscarry are both punished.
- **Example**: A woman named Priya was five months pregnant. Her husband, Rajesh, did not want the child and forcibly took her to

a clinic where he coerced the doctor into performing an abortion without Priya's consent. Priya was against the abortion, but Rajesh threatened her, and despite her refusal, the procedure was carried out. This would fall under **Section 89** of BNS.

- In the case of **Tulsi Devi v. State of U.P.**, a woman was convicted under **Section 313 of IPC** (Section 89 of BNS) for kicking a pregnant woman and causing a miscarriage.
- In the case of **Pranab Kanti Das v. State of West Bengal,** a doctor was charged under **Section 313 of IPC** (Section 89 of BNS) for administering a pill to his pregnant wife, resulting in a miscarriage.
- In the case of **Moidenkutty Haji v. Kunhikoya,** a comparison of **Section 312 of IPC** (Section 88 of BNS) **and Section 313 of IPC** (Section 89 of BNS) is made, showing that the punishment under **Section 312 of IPC** (Section 88 of BNS) is for a shorter period of time than under **Section 313 of IPC** (Section 89 of BNS) and that in **Section 312 of IPC** (Section 88 of BNS) the woman herself is also subject to punishment in addition to the person who caused the miscarriage.

Death Caused by Act Done with Intent to Cause Miscarriage

(**Note:** ***Section 90*** *of the BNS corresponds to* ***Section 314*** *of the IPC*)

- Under **Section 90** of BNS, whoever, with intent to cause the miscarriage of a woman with child, does any act which causes the death of such woman, shall be punished with imprisonment of either description for a term which may extend to ten years, and shall also be liable to fine.
  - If Act Done without Women's Consent
    - If the act is done without the consent of the woman, shall be punished either with imprisonment for life, or with the punishment above-mentioned.
    - The knowledge that the act is likely to result in death is not necessary for the offender to commit this crime.
    - This section provides for the case where death occurs in causing miscarriage. The act of the accused must have been done with intent to cause the miscarriage of a woman with child.
- In case of **State Represented by P.P. of High Court v. Dr. Joaquim Antonio D'Silva (1999)**, the Supreme Court addressed a case under **Section 314 IPC** (Section 90 of BNS),
  - Where a miscarriage was conducted with the consent of a separated married woman. The respondent discouraged postmortem after her death, issued a false death certificate citing low blood pressure and jaundice, and denied involvement in the termination of pregnancy. Despite lacking authorization, he performed the procedure at an unauthorised clinic.
    - Considering these factors, the Court sentenced him to 3 years rigorous imprisonment and a Rs. 50,000 fine under **Section 314** part two I.P.C. (**Section 90 of BNS**), with six months' simple imprisonment for default. The fine was designated as compensation for the deceased's father upon recovery.

Act Done With Intent to Prevent Child Being Born Alive or to Cause it to Die After Birth

(**Note:** ***Section 91*** *of the BNS correspond to* ***Section 315*** *of the IPC*)

- According to **Section 91 of BNS** whoever before the birth of any child does any act with the intention of thereby preventing that child from being born alive or causing it to die after its birth, and does by such act prevent that child from being born alive, or causes it to die after its birth, shall if such act be not caused in good faith for the purpose of saving the life of the mother, be punished with imprisonment or either description for a term which may extend to ten years, or with fine, or with both.

- Any act done with the intention here mentioned which results in the destruction of the child's life, whether before or after its birth, is made punishable.
- Intention is one of the major ingredients of **Section 91 of BNS.**

Causing Death of Quick Unborn Child by Act Amounting to Culpable Homicide

(**Note:** ***Section 92*** *of the BNS correspond to* ***Section 316*** *of the IPC*)

- According to **Section 92** of BNS, whoever does any act under such circumstances, that if he thereby caused death he would be guilty of culpable homicide, and does by such act cause the death of a quick unborn child, shall be punished with
  - Imprisonment of either description for a term which may extend to ten years, and shall also be liable to fine.
- **Illustration:** A, knowing that he is likely to cause the death of a pregnant woman does an act which, if it caused the death of the woman, would amount to culpable homicide. The woman is injured, but does not die; but the death of an unborn quick child with which she is pregnant is thereby caused. A is guilty of the offence defined in this section.
- This section punishes offences against children in the womb where the pregnancy has advanced beyond the stage of quickening and where the death is caused after the quickening and before the birth of the child.
- Any act or omission of such a nature and done under such circumstances as would amount to the offence of culpable homicide, if the sufferer were a living person, will, if done to a quick unborn child whose death is caused by it, constitute the offence here punished.
- Unless the mother is the target of the act intentionally or knowingly which brings it within the purview of **Section 100 of BNS**, it cannot constitute an offence under this section merely because the death of a quick unborn child has resulted from an act against the mother.

OFFENCES AGAINST CHILDREN

Children all over the world are considered among the most vulnerable & innocent victims of crimes committed in society. The Bharatiya Nyaya Sanhita, 2023 (BNS) recognises the various offences committed against children and penalises their commission under **Section 93 to 99 of chapter V.**

COMPARATIVE CHART OF THE BNS AND IPC

Bharatiya Nyaya Sanhita(BNS)	Title	Indian Penal Code, 1860 (IPC)
Section 93	Exposure and abandonment of a child under twelve years, by a parent or person having care of it.	Section 317
Section 94	Concealment of birth by secret disposal of dead body	Section 318
Section 95	Hiring, employer or engaging a child to commit an offence **(Newly added section)**	-
Section 96	Procuration of child **EARLIER TITLE -** (Procuration of minor girl)	Section 366A
Section 97	Kidnapping or abducting child under ten years of age with intent to steal from its person.	Section 369
Section 98	Selling children for purposes of prostitution, etc.	Section 372
Section 99	Buying a child for purposes of prostitution, etc. **EARLIER TITLE-**(Buying minors for purposes of prostitution, etc.)	Section 373

CHANGES IN BNS IN COMPARISON TO IPC

- **Section 96** of the BNS corresponds to **Section 366A** in the IPC has changed as follows:
  - The words "any minor girl under the age of eighteen years" are changed to **"any child"**
- **Section 98** of the BNS corresponds to **Section 372** in the IPC has changed as follows:
  - The words "any person under the age of eighteen years" are changed to **"any child"**
- **Section 99** of the BNS corresponds to **Section 373** in the IPC has changed as follows:
  - The word "minor" has been changed to "child". There has been a change in respect to the term of imprisonment as **"punished with imprisonment of either description for a term which shall not be less than seven years but which may extend to fourteen years"**

Exposure and Abandonment of Child Under 12 Years of Age by Parent or Person Having care of it

(**Note:** ***Section 93*** *of the BNS corresponds to* ***Section 317*** *of the IPC*)

- **Section 93** provides whoever being the father or mother of a child under the age of twelve years, or having the care of such child, shall expose or leave such child in any place with the intention of wholly abandoning such child,
  - Shall be punished with imprisonment of either description for a term which may extend to seven years, or with fine, or with both.
- **Explanation**: This section is not intended to prevent the trial of the offender for murder or culpable homicide, as the case may be, if the child dies in consequence of the exposure.

Essential Ingredients

- **Child to be Under Twelve Years**: This Section is meant to protect the interests of children below twelve years of age, because they are not in a position to protect themselves. The primary responsibility is cast on the parents and adults, who may have the custody of the child to bring up with child and to provide adequate care for the child of tender age.
  - It applies equally to legitimate and illegitimate children.
- **Responsibility is on Both Father and Mother or person having care of such Child**: As far as **Section 93** is concerned, the provision makes both the father and mother equally duty bound to care for the child. The section makes no difference between children born in wedlock or outside the wedlock.
- Apart from the parents, the Section also makes persons under whose care the child is placed, equally liable. Thus, day care centers, creches, orphanages, etc., are all covered by this provision.
- The words **"expose or leave"** mean leaving the child in danger, neglecting the child and not giving the child adequate protection from natural elements like cold, heat and other hazards.
- The phrase **"to abandon child"** in its ordinary usage means something more than leaving the child behind. It means leaving the child without protection.
- The word **"leave"** must be read along with or read *ejusdem generis* with expose. It does not mean merely temporarily and physically leaving the child, it should be with intention to leave it to its fate.
- **Explanation** provides that when the exposure and abandonment of the child under twelve years of age, results in its death, then the father, mother or person in whose care the child have been left in, will be liable for murder or culpable homicide, however, such death of the child should be as a consequence of the exposure.

Concealment of Birth by Secret Disposal of Dead Body

(Note: *Section 94 of the BNS corresponds to Section 318 of the IPC*)

- **Section 94** provides that whoever, by secretly burying or otherwise disposing of the dead body of a child whether such child die before or after or during its birth, intentionally conceals or endeavours to conceal the birth of such child, shall be
  - Punished with imprisonment of either description for a term which may extend to two years, or with fine, or with both.

Essential Ingredients

- **Secret Disposal of Bodies of Children**: In India, we have the registration of Births and Deaths Act, 1969, which makes it compulsory on the part of every person to register every birth and death with the local authorities. One of the main principles behind this section is to detect and if possible, prevent infanticide.
- **Dead Body of Child:** The body of the child may be secretly buried or otherwise disposed of, meaning cremated, thrown into rivers, wells, or left in forest for wild beasts to eat. The word 'body' indicates that the foetus must have developed in the mother's womb into a human shape.
- **Conceals or Endeavours to Conceal Birth:** The secret disposal of the body of the child is to conceal or endeavours to conceal the birth.
- In the case of **Lilawati v. State of Punjab (1982)**: The court held that when the birth of the child took place in a hospital and was attended to by nurses and for at least 24 hours, the birth of the child was known to a number of persons; it was held that there was no concealment of birth in this case.

Hiring, Employer or Engaging a Child to Commit an Offence

- **Section 95** is a newly added section under the BNS, there was no such provision in the IPC.
- **Section 95** provides that whoever hires, employs or engages any child to commit an offence shall be:
  - Punished with imprisonment of either description which shall not be less than three years but which may extend to ten years, and with fine; and
  - If the offence be committed shall also be punished with the punishment provided for that offence as if the offence has been committed by such person himself.
- **Explanation:** Hiring, employing, engaging or using a child for sexual exploitation or pornography is covered within the meaning of this section.

Procuration of Child

(Note: *Section 96 of the BNS corresponds to Section 366A of the IPC*)

- **Section 96** provides that whoever, by any means whatsoever, induces any child to go from any place or to do any act with intent that such child may be, or knowing that it is likely that such child will be, forced or seduced to illicit intercourse with another person shall be
  - Punishable with imprisonment which may extend to ten years, and shall also be liable to fine.
- **Section 96** punishes a person who makes a child move from any place with intent to force or seduce her for illicit intercourse with another person.
- The term **'illicit intercourse'** used in these provisions means sexual intercourse between a man and woman who are not "husband and wife." And the word **'seduced'**

(to illicit intercourse) means inducing or enticing or tempting a child to submit to illicit intercourse not only for the first time but also at any time or on any occasion.

- For convicting a person under **Section 96**, it is essential to establish that he has induced a child to go from any place with the intent (or knowledge) that child would be forced or seduced to illicit intercourse with someone other than himself.
- In the case of **Jinish lal Sah v. State of Bihar (2003)**, the Court held that in the absence of any proof disclosing coercion or inducement by the accused, he deserves acquittal of charges under **Section 366A** (Now, **Section 96** BNS).

Kidnapping or Abducting Child under Ten Years of Age with Intent to Steal from its Person

(**Note:** ***Section 97*** *of the BNS corresponds to* ***Section 369*** *of the IPC*)

- **Section 97** lays down that whoever kidnaps or abducts any child under the age of ten years:
  - With the intention of taking dishonestly any movable property from the person of such child,
  - Shall be punished with imprisonment of either description for a term which may extend to seven years, and shall also be liable to fine
- **Section 97** as evident from its phraseology, provides punishment for kidnapping or abducting a child with the intention of taking movable property from the person of such child. The kidnapper or abductor may be ordered to undergo simple or rigorous imprisonment for a term up to seven years and may be ordered to pay a fine.

Selling Child for Purposes of Prostitution, etc.

(**Note:** ***Section 98*** *of the BNS corresponds to* ***Section 372*** *of the IPC*)

- **Section 98** provides that whoever sells, lets to hire, or otherwise disposes of any child
  - With intent that such child shall at any age be employed or used for the purpose of
  - Prostitution or illicit intercourse with any person or for any unlawful and immoral purpose, or knowing it to be likely that such child will at any age be employed or used for any such purpose,
  - Shall be punished with imprisonment of either description for a term which may extend to ten years, and shall also be liable to fine.
- **Explanation 1**: When a female under the age of eighteen years is sold, let for hire, or otherwise disposed of to a prostitute or to any person who keeps or manages a brothel, the person so disposing of such female shall, until the contrary is proved, be presumed to have disposed of her with the intent that she shall be used for the purpose of prostitution.
- **Explanation 2**: For the purposes of this section "illicit intercourse" means sexual intercourse between persons not united by marriage or by any union or tie which, though not amounting to a marriage, is recognised by the personal law or custom of the community to which they belong or, where they belong to different communities, of both such communities, as constituting between them a quasi-marital relation

Essential Ingredients

- A person selling, lending, or disposing of any other person.
- The person who is being subjected to sale, lent or disposal is a minor child.
- Such selling, lending, or disposing of has been done with an intention to force that child into prostitution, illicit intercourse, or any unlawful or immoral purpose.
- In the case of **Santosh Santra @ Bachu v. State of West Bengal (1983)**, the court held that for invoking the provisions of

Section 372 of IPC(now, Section 98 of BNS), the prosecution is required to prove that the accused has sold or let to hire a child with intent of knowledge that the person would be used for either of the purposes mentioned therein.

- **Explanation 1 of Section 98** lays down shall presumption. When a female under the age of eighteen years is sold, let for hire, or otherwise disposed of to a prostitute or to any person who keeps or manages a brothel then it shall be presumed that disposed of such a child with the intent that she shall be used for the purpose of prostitution unless contrary is proved.

Buying Child for Purposes of Prostitution, etc.

(**Note:** *Section 99 of the BNS corresponds to Section 373 of the IPC*)

- **Section 99** provides that whoever buys, hires or otherwise obtains possession of any child:
  - With intent that such child shall at any age be employed or used for the purpose of prostitution or illicit intercourse with any person or for any unlawful and immoral purpose, or knowing it to be likely that such child will at any age be employed or used for any such purpose.
  - Shall be punished with imprisonment of either description for a term which shall not be less than seven years but which may extend to fourteen years, and shall also be liable to fine.
- **Explanation 1**: Any prostitute or any person keeping or managing a brothel, who buys, hires or otherwise obtains possession of a female under the age of eighteen years shall, until the contrary is proved, be presumed to have obtained possession of such female with the intent that she shall be used for the purpose of prostitution.
- **Explanation 2**: "Illicit intercourse" has the same meaning as in **Section 98.**
- Section 98 provides punishment for selling a child of either sex for the purpose of prostitution, illicit intercourse or for any other immoral purpose, while **Section 99** provides punishment for a person who buys such a child.
- Such person may be of either sex, married or unmarried or leading an immoral life the offence is complete the moment there is sale or letting to hire a child with the intention specified in **Section 98.**
- **Section 99**, as stated earlier, makes a person criminally responsible for buying hiring, or obtaining possession of a child for the purposes specified.
- **Explanation 1 of Section 99** lays down shall presumption. It states that Any prostitute or any person keeping or managing a brothel buys, hires or otherwise obtains possession of a female under the age of eighteen years then it shall be presumed that possession of such a child with the intent that she shall be used for the purpose of prostitution unless contrary is proved.

❖❖❖

Chapter 12

OFFENCES AFFECTING HUMAN BODY

INTRODUCTION

Chapter VI of Bhartiya Nyay Sanhita, 2023 (BNS) comprising **Sections 100- 146** deals with the offences affecting the human body. **Sections 100-112** of the BNS deal with offences affecting human life; these offences are as under:

- Culpable homicide simpliciter (As provided under **Section 100** and punishable under **Section 105**)
- Murder (As provided under **Section 101** and punishable under **Section 103**)
- Culpable Homicide not amounting to murder (As Covered by Exceptions I- V of **Section 101** and punishable under **Section 105**)
- Culpable homicide by causing death of a person other than the person whose death was intended (As provided under **Section 102**).
- Murder by Life Convict (As provided under **Section 104**).
- Causing death by negligence (As provided under **Section 106**)
- Abetment of suicide of child or person of unsound mind (As provided under **Section 107**)
- Abetment of suicide (As provided under **Section 108**)
- Attempt to murder (As provided under **Section 109**)
- Attempt to commit culpable homicide (As provided under **Section 110**)
- Organised Crime (As provided and punishable under **Section 111**)
- Petty Organised Crime (As provided and punishable under **Section 112**)
- Terrorist Act (As provided and punishable under **Section 113**)

The earlier Penal Code i.e., the Indian Penal Code, 1860 dealt with the offences affecting life under Chapter XVI from Sections 299-311.

COMPARATIVE CHART OF THE BNS AND IPC

Bharatiya Nyaya Sanhita, 2023 (BNS)	Title	Indian Penal Code, 1860 (IPC)
Section 100	Culpable Homicide	Section 299
Section 101	Murder	Section 300
Section 102	Culpable Homicide by causing death of a person other than the person whose death was intended	Section 301
Section 103	Punishment for Murder	Section 302
Section 104	Punishment for Murder by Life Convict	Section 303
Section 105	Punishment for Culpable Homicide Not amounting to Murder (Changed)	Section 304

Section 106	Causing Death by negligence	Section 304A
Section 107	Abetment of suicide by child or person of unsound mind **EARLIER TITLE:** (Abetment of suicide by child or Insane person)	Section 305
Section 108	Abetment of suicide	Section 306
Section 109	Attempt to Murder (Changed)	Section 307
Section 110	Attempt to commit culpable homicide	Section 308
Section 111	Organised Crime (Newly added section)	
Section 112	Petty Organised Crime (Newly added section)	
Section 113	Terrorist Act (Newly added section)	

CHANGES IN BNS IN COMPARISON TO IPC

- **Section 101** of the BNS corresponds to **Section 300** in the IPC has changed as follows:
  - The words **"if the act by which the death is caused"** are added in each clause to the Section 101 of the BNS and The words "The above exception is subject to the following provisos" are changed to **"Provided that the provocation is not"** under Exception 1 to the Section 101 of the BNS.
- **Section 103** of the BNS corresponds to **Section 302** in the IPC has changed as follows:
  - **A new sub-section has been added** which relates to mob lynching under Section 103 sub-section (2).
- **Section 104** of the BNS corresponds to **Section 303** in the IPC has changed as follows:
  - The punishment of **"imprisonment for life"** has now been added to the provision.
- **Section 105** of the BNS corresponds to **Section 304** in the IPC has changed as follows:
  - The punishment has been changed under Section 105 of the BNS as follows: **"Imprisonment of either description for a term which shall not be less than five years but which may extend to ten years"** and **"Imprisonment of either description for a term which may extend to ten years and with fine"**
- **Section 106** of the BNS corresponds to **Section 304A** in the IPC has changed as follows:
  - **Enhanced Punishment** extending **up to 5 years** and shall also be liable to fine
  - **Liability for registered medical practitioner** has been added.
  - A new subsection has been added in the form of **Section 106 (2)** which deals with hit and run case.
- **Section 107** of the BNS corresponds to **Section 305** in the IPC has changed as follows:
  - In the title, the words "insane person" have been changed to "**unsound mind**"
- **Section 109** of the BNS corresponds to **Section 307** in the IPC has changed as follows:
  - The Punishment of **"imprisonment of life"** is added for attempt to murder by life-convicts under **Section 109(2)**.

CULPABLE HOMICIDE

(**Note:** ***Section 100*** *of the BNS corresponds to* ***Section 299*** *of the IPC*)

Homicide literally means killing of a human being by another human being; Culpable denotes such killing which is made punishable by law.

- **Section 100** of BNS defines the offence of Culpable Homicide.
- As per **Section 100**, a person is guilty of the offence of Culpable Homicide when he causes death of a human being by doing an act:
  - With the intention of causing death, or
  - With the intention of causing such bodily injury as is likely to cause death, or
  - With the knowledge that he is likely by such act to cause death.

Essential Elements of Culpable Homicide

According to the definition provided by **Section 100** of BNS, the offence of Culpable Homicide has the following essential ingredients:

- **Causing of Death by the Accused:** A person is guilty of the offence of culpable homicide only when he "causes" death of a human being by doing an act. In other words, the death must be caused as a direct result of the act done by the accused. **Explanation 1 to 3 of Section 100,** enumerate the circumstances wherein the presence or absence of certain factors in causing death does not affect the culpability of the accused person.
  - **Explanation 1 of Section 100** provides that a person who causes bodily injury to another who is laboring under a disorder, disease or bodily infirmity, and thereby accelerates the death of that other, shall be deemed to have caused his death.
  - **Explanation 2 of Section 100** provides that where death is caused by bodily injury, the person who causes such bodily injury shall be deemed to have caused the death, although by resorting to proper remedies and skilful treatment the death might have been prevented.
  - **Explanation 3 of Section 100** provides that the causing of the death of a child in the mother's womb is not homicide. But it may amount to culpable homicide to cause the death of a living child, if any part of that child has been brought forth, though the child may not have breathed or been completely born.
    - However, it is an equally settled principle of law that death should be the proximate causal consequence of the act of the accused. In the celebrated case of **Moti Singh v. State of Uttar Pradesh (1964)**, Hon'ble Apex Court has held that the relation between death and its primary cause should not be too remote in nature.
- **Guilty Intention or Knowledge:** For the offence of culpable homicide, guilty intention or knowledge of the accused is the requisite form of mens rea and is one of the essential ingredients.
  - Intention signifies the desire or manifestation of a person to achieve a certain objective. Intention, for the offence of culpable homicide, means an intention:
    - To cause death, or
    - To cause a bodily injury likely to cause death.

ILLUSTRATIONS (A) AND (B) OF SECTION 100

Illustrations (a) and (b) of **Section 100** present a situations of culpable homicide committed with requisite intention.

- **Illustration (a):** A lays sticks and turf over a pit, with the intention of thereby causing death, or with the knowledge that death is likely to be thereby caused. Z, believing the ground to be firm, treads on it, falls in and is killed. A has committed the offence of culpable homicide.
- **Illustration (b):** A knows Z to be behind a bush. B does not know it. A, intending to cause, or knowing it to be likely to cause Z's death, induces B to fire at the bush. B fires and kills Z. Here B may be guilty of no offence; but A has committed the offence of culpable homicide.

- Knowledge means consciousness or awareness of a person. In law, it signifies an awareness with regard to consequences of one's acts. Knowledge, for the offence of culpable homicide, means the knowledge of the accused that he is likely by his act to cause the death of a human being.

ILLUSTRATION (C) OF SECTION 100

- **Illustration (c) of Section 100** presents a suitable example of culpable homicide done with requisite guilty knowledge. This illustration also clarifies that death caused inadvertently by the accused while doing an unlawful act without intending to kill or cause death by doing an act which the accused knew was likely to cause death will not amount to the offence of culpable homicide.
- **Illustration (c):** A, by shooting at a fowl with intent to kill and steal it, kills B, who is behind a bush; A not knowing that he was there. Here, although A was doing an unlawful act, he was not guilty of culpable homicide, as he did not intend to kill B, or to cause death by doing an act that he knew was likely to cause death.

Punishment for Culpable Homicide

(**Note:** ***Section 105*** *of the BNS corresponds to* ***Section 304*** *of the IPC*)

The offences of culpable homicide as covered under **Section 100** and of culpable homicide not amounting to murder as covered under the five exceptions of **Section 101** are both punishable under Section 105 of BNS. In view of the provisions of **Section 105**:

- The offence of culpable homicide covered by 2nd part of Section 100 (i.e., death caused by doing an act with the intention of causing such bodily injury as is likely to cause death) is punishable with:
  - Life imprisonment and with fine, or
  - Imprisonment of either description for a term which shall not be less than five years but which may extend to ten years and with fine.
- The offence of culpable homicide covered by 3rd part of Section 100 (i.e., death caused by doing an act with the knowledge that it is likely to cause death) is punishable with imprisonment of either description for a term which may extend to ten years and with fine.

MURDER

(**Note:** ***Section 101*** *of the BNS corresponds to* ***Section 300*** *of the IPC*)

BNS incorporates the entire statutory scheme of the IPC with regard to the definition and concept of the offences of culpable homicide and murder. Under the statutory scheme of BNS, the offence of murder has been defined in reference to the offence of culpable homicide.

- **Section 101** of BNS, containing four clauses and five exceptions, defines the offence of murder and and incorporates each and every essential of the offence of murder as defined earlier in **Section 300** of the IPC.
- **Section 101** provides that except in the cases enumerated in the **Exceptions 1- 5** of the provision, culpable homicide is murder:
  - (a) If the act by which the death is caused is done with the intention of causing death; or
  - (b) If the act by which the death is caused is done with the intention of causing such bodily injury as the offender knows to be likely to cause the death of the person to whom the harm is caused; or
  - (c) If the act by which the death is caused is done with the intention of causing bodily injury to any person and the bodily injury intended to be inflicted is sufficient in the ordinary course of nature to cause death; or
  - (d) If the person committing the act by which the death is caused, knows that it is so imminently dangerous that it must, in all probability, cause death, or such bodily injury as is likely to cause death, and commits such act without any excuse for incurring the risk of causing death or such injury as aforesaid.

Inter-relation between Culpable Homicide and Murder

- It is clear from the phraseology of Section 101 that murder is an aggravated form of culpable homicide; it is a culpable homicide with certain additional characteristics. In other words, Culpable Homicide is the genus of which Muder is the species. Accordingly, every murder is culpable homicide but every culpable homicide is not murder.
- In the leading case of **State of Andhra Pradesh v. R Punnayya, (1977)**, Hon'ble Apex Court has observed that "In the scheme of the Penal Code, 'culpable homicide' is genus and 'murder' its species. All 'murder' is 'culpable homicide' but not vice-versa. Speaking generally, 'culpable homicide' sans 'special characteristics of murder', is 'culpable homicide not amounting to murder'.
- Therefore, an offence of culpable homicide amounts to the offence of murder only when it fulfills the specific statutory requirements as laid down in Clauses (a)-(d) of Section 101.
- However, if an act falls within Clauses (a)-(d) of Section 101 but is simultaneously covered by any one of the five exceptions laid down thereunder, it does not become the offence of murder but is reduced to the offence of culpable homicide not amounting to murder.

Culpable Homicide and Muder: Clause-wise Comparison

The clauses of **Section 100** and those of **Section 101** are overlapping in nature and therefore, clause-wise comparison is necessary to clearly understand the two provisions.

- **Section 100- Clause (a) and Section 101- Clause (a)**
  - **Section 100- Clause (a)** of BNS provides that a person is guilty of the offence of culpable homicide if he causes death (of a human being) by doing an act with the intention of causing death.
  - **Section 101- Clause (a)** provides that culpable homicide is murder if the act by which the death is caused is done with the intention of causing death.
  - In the case of **Reg. v. Govinda (1876)**, **Melvill J** of Hon'ble Bombay High Court exhaustively brought out the distinction between the offences of culpable homicide and murder as defined respectively under Section 299 and 300 of the IPC; the distinction is invariably applicable to the present provisions of BNS.
  - It has been held in the case of **Reg. v. Govinda** that Section 299- Clause (a) and Section 300- Clause- (1) show that where there is an intention to kill, the offence is always murder.
  - Therefore, an act falling under Section Section 100 (a) would automatically fall within Section 101 (a) of BNS and would always be the offence of murder.
  - **Illustration (a) of Section 101** : A shoots Z with the intention of killing him. Z dies in consequence. A commits murder
- **Section 100- Clause (b) and Section 101- Clause (b)**
  - **Section 100- Clause (b)** of BNS provides that a person is guilty of the offence of culpable homicide if he causes death (of a human being) by doing an act with the intention of causing such bodily injury likely to cause death.
  - **Section 101- Clause (b)** provides that culpable homicide is murder if the act by which the death is caused is done with the intention of causing such bodily injury as the offender knows to be likely to cause the death of the person to whom the harm is caused.
  - The primary distinction between Section 100- Clause (b) and Section 101- clause (b) lies in the phrase "bodily injury as the offender knows to be likely to cause the death of the person to whom the harm is caused" used in Section 101- Clause (b).

It postulates the specific knowledge on the part of the offender that the person harmed is likely to die by the harm caused by him. However, no such knowledge is required under Section 100- Clause (b). Therefore, the offence is murder if the offender has special knowledge that due to a peculiar health condition or situation, the victim (deceased) is likely to be killed by an injury which would not ordinarily cause death.

- **Illustration (b) of Section 101** further clarifies this legal position:
  - A, knowing that Z is laboring under such a disease that a blow is likely to cause his death, strikes him with the intention of causing bodily injury. Z dies in consequence of the blow. A is guilty of murder, although the blow might not have been sufficient in the ordinary course of nature to cause the death of a person in a sound state of health.
  - But if A, not knowing that Z is laboring under any disease, gives him such a blow as would not in the ordinary course of nature kill a person in a sound state of health, here A, although he may intend to cause bodily injury, is not guilty of murder, if he did not intend to cause death, or such bodily injury as in the ordinary course of nature would cause death.

- **Section 100- Clause (b) and Section 101- Clause (c)**
  - **Section 100- Clause (b)** of BNS provides that a person is guilty of the offence of culpable homicide if he causes death (of a human being) by doing an act with the intention of causing such bodily injury likely to cause death.
  - **Section 101- Clause (c)** provides that culpable homicide is murder if the act by which the death is caused is done with the intention of causing bodily injury to any person and the bodily injury intended to be inflicted is sufficient in the ordinary course of nature to cause death.
  - In the case of **Reg. v. Govinda, (1876)** the distinction between Section 299- Clause (b) and Section 300- Clause (3) of the IPC (which is equally applicable to Section 100- Clause (b) and Section 101- Clause (c) of BNS) in the following terms:
    - "The offence is culpable homicide, if the bodily injury intended to be inflicted is likely to cause death; it is murder, if such injury is sufficient in the, ordinary course of nature to cause death. The distinction is fine, but appreciable... It is a question of degree of probability. Practically, I think, it will generally resolve itself into a consideration of the nature of the weapon used. A blow from the fist or a stick on a vital part may be likely to cause death; a wound from a sword in a vital part is sufficient in the ordinary course of nature to cause death."

- Furthermore, in the leading decision of **Virsa Singh v. State of Punjab (1958)**, Hon'ble Apex Court has held that the following facts must be proved to a case under Section 300, 3rdly of the IPC which invariably applies to Section 101- Clause (c) of the BNS.
  - **First**, it must establish, quite objectively, that a bodily injury is present.
  - **Secondly,** the nature of the injury must be proved; These are purely objective investigations.
  - **Thirdly,** it must be proved that there was an intention to inflict that particular bodily injury, that is to say, that it was not accidental or unintentional, or that some other kind of injury was intended.
  - **Fourthly,** once these three elements are proved to be present, the enquiry proceeds further, it must be proved that the injury of the type just described made

up of the three elements set out above is sufficient to cause death in the ordinary course of nature. This part of the enquiry is purely objective and inferential and has nothing to do with the intention of the offender.

- Once these four elements are established by the prosecution, the offence becomes murder under thirdly of Section 300 and it doesn't matter that: there was no intention to cause death; there was no intention even to cause an injury of a kind that is sufficient to cause death in the ordinary course of nature; there is no knowledge that an act of that kind will be likely to cause death.

- **Section 100- Clause (c) and Section 101- Clause (d)**
  - **Section 100- Clause (c)** of BNS (corresponding to Section 299- Clause (c) of the IPC) provides that a person is guilty of the offence of culpable homicide if he causes death (of a human being) by doing an act with the knowledge that he is likely by such act to cause death.
  - **Section 101- Clause (d)** (corresponding to Section 300- Clause 4 of the IPC) provides that culpable homicide is murder if the person committing the act by which the death is caused, knows that it is so imminently dangerous that it must, in all probability, cause death, or such bodily injury as is likely to cause death, and commits such act without any excuse for incurring the risk of causing death or such injury as aforesaid.
  - The distinction between the two provisions relates to the degree of knowledge of the accused regarding the consequences of his acts. In **Reg. v. Govinda, (1876)** Hon'ble Court has held that Section 299- Clause (c) and Section 300- Clause (4) are intended to apply (but are not limited) to cases in which there is no intention to cause death or bodily injury, nevertheless death has ensued. Furious driving, firing at a mark near a public road, would be cases of this description. Whether the offence is culpable homicide or murder, depends upon the degree of risk to human life. If death is a likely result, it is culpable homicide; if it is the most probable result, it is murder.
  - **Illustration (c) of Section 100 and illustration (d) of Section 101** further clarify the aforesaid distinction.

ILLUSTRATION (C) OF SECTION 100 AND ILLUSTRATION (D) OF SECTION 101

- **Illustration (c) of Section 100:** A knows Z to be behind a bush. B does not know it. A, intending to cause, or knowing it to be likely to cause Z's death, induces B to fire at the bush. B fires and kills Z. Here B may be guilty of no offence; but A has committed the offence of culpable homicide.
- **Illustration (d) of Section 101:** A without any excuse fires a loaded cannon into a crowd of persons and kills one of them. A is guilty of murder, although he may not have had a premeditated design to kill any particular individual.

Punishment for Murder and its Aggravated Forms

(**Note:** ***Section 103,104*** *of the BNS correspond to* ***Section 302, 303*** *of the IPC respectively*)

- **Punishment for Murder: Section 103** inter alia lays down the punishment for murder. In view of the provisions of **Section 103(1),** the offence of murder is punishable with death or life imprisonment and with fine.
- **Punishment for Mob Lynching:** Section 103(2) is a new provision of BNS which punishes the offence of mob lynching. Section 103(2) inter alia creates legal fiction with regard to criminal liability of the offenders of mob lynching and provides that when a group of five or more persons acting in concert commits murder on the

ground of race, caste or community, sex, place of birth, language, personal belief or any other similar ground each member of such group shall be punished with death or with imprisonment for life, and shall also be liable to fine.

- **Punishment for Murder by Life Convict: Section 104** of BNS deals with the punishment for the offence of murder committed by a life-convict and provides that if a person, being under sentence of life imprisonment for life, commits murder, he shall be punished with death or with life imprisonment which shall mean the remainder of that person's natural life.

CULPABLE HOMICIDE NOT AMOUNTING TO MURDER

Apart from enumerating the circumstances under which culpable homicide becomes murder, **Section 101** of BNS also enumerates certain exceptions under which an act of the accused ceases to be the offence of murder.

- If an act which falls within **Clauses (a)- (d) of Section 101** and is also covered by any one of the five exceptions laid down thereunder, it is no more an offence of murder but is reduced to the offence of culpable homicide not amounting to murder.
- The five exceptions of Section 101 are partial defences, i.e. they do not absolve the accused completely but only reduce his criminal liability from the offence of murder to that of culpable homicide not amounting to murder.
- The five exceptions to the offence of Murder are partial defences to the as enumerated under Section 101 are as under:
    - **Exception 1:** Grave and Sudden Provocation
    - **Exception 2:** Exceeding the Right to Private Defence
    - **Exception 3:** Act of Public Servant
    - **Exception 4:** Death caused in sudden fight
    - **Exception 5:** Death caused by consent

Exception 1: Grave and Sudden Provocation

Exception 1 to Section 101 of BNS lays down that the offence of murder will be reduced to "culpable homicide not amounting to murder, if murder is committed by the accused due to the provocation given to him by the accused".

Essential Ingredients

- The deceased must have given provocation to the accused.
- The provocation must be grave as well as sudden in nature. Grave nature of the provocation implies that it must be serious enough to unsettle the mind of the accused and to lead the accused to lose his power of self-control. Likewise, the sudden nature of the provocation implies that it must not leave time to the accused to cool down or to regain control over himself.
- By reason of the aforesaid grave and sudden provocation, the offender must have been deprived of the power of self-control.
- While being so deprived of his power of self control, the accused should have caused the death of the person who gave the provocation or the death of any other person by mistake or accident.
- **Illustrations (a) & (b)** appended to Exception 1 further clarify this legal position.

ILLUSTRATIONS (A) & (B) APPENDED TO EXCEPTION 1

Illustration (a): A, under the influence of passion excited by a provocation given by Z, intentionally kills Y, Z's child. This is murder, in as much as the provocation was not given by the child, and the death of the child was not caused by accident or misfortune in doing an act caused by the provocation.

Illustration (b): Y gives grave and sudden provocation to A. A, on this provocation, fires a pistol at Y, neither intending nor knowing himself to be likely to kill Z, who is near him, but out of sight. A kills Z. Here A has not committed murder, but merely culpable homicide.

Exceptions to Grave and Sudden Provocation

The Exception of grave and sudden provocation is itself subject to the following three exceptions:

- It must not be sought or voluntarily provoked by the offender as an excuse for killing or doing harm to any person.
  - **Illustration (f):** Z strikes B. B is by this provocation excited to violent rage. A, a bystander, intending to take advantage of B's rage, and to cause him to kill Z, puts a knife into B's hand for that purpose. B kills Z with the knife. Here B may have committed only culpable homicide, but A is guilty of murder.
- It must not be given by anything done in obedience to the law, or by a public servant in the lawful exercise of the powers of such public servant.
  - **Illustration (c):** A is lawfully arrested by Z, a bailiff. A is excited to sudden and violent passion by the arrest, and kills Z. This is murder, in as much as the provocation was given by a thing done by a public servant in the exercise of his powers.
- It must not be given by anything done in the lawful exercise of the right of private defence.
  - **Illustration (e):** A attempts to pull Z's nose. Z, in the exercise of the right of private defence, lays hold of A to prevent him from doing so. A is moved to sudden and violent passion in consequence, and kills Z. This is murder, in as much as the provocation was given by a thing done in the exercise of the right of private defence.

TEST OF GRAVE AND SUDDEN PROVOCATION

- The provocation contemplated by Exception 1 of Section must be grave as well as sudden in nature. Therefore, the accused would not get the benefit of Exception 1 if the provocation is grave but not sudden or sudden but not grave. The Explanation of Exception 1 to Section 101 of BNS provides that whether the provocation was grave and sudden enough to prevent the offence from amounting to murder is a question of fact.
- The law regarding grave and sudden provocation as an exception to the offence of murder (governed earlier by Exception 1 to Section 300 of the IPC and completely applicable to the present provision) has been crystallized by Hon'ble Apex Court in the celebrated case of **K M Nanavati v. State of Maharashtra (1962)**, wherein it was held as under:
  - The test of "grave and sudden" provocation is whether a reasonable man, belonging to the same class of society as the accused, placed in the situation in which the accused was placed would be so provoked as to lose his self-control.
  - In India, words and gestures may also, under certain circumstances, cause grave and sudden provocation to an accused so as to bring his act within the first Exception to s. 300 of the Indian Penal Code.
  - The mental background created by the previous act of the victim may be taken into consideration in ascertaining whether the subsequent act caused grave and sudden provocation for committing the offence.
  - The fatal blow should be clearly traced to the influence of passion arising from that provocation and not after the passion had cooled down by lapse of time, or otherwise giving room and scope for premeditation and calculation.

Exception 2: Exceeding the Right to Private Defence

Exception 2 to Section 101 of BNS lays down that the offence of murder will be reduced to "culpable homicide not amounting to murder, if murder is committed by the accused because he exceeded his right to private defence".

Essential Ingredients

- The accused must have the right to private defence of body or property against the deceased.
- In the exercise of the right to private defence, he should exceed the power given to him by law and cause death of the deceased.
- The death must be caused without premeditation and without any intention of doing more harm than is necessary for the purpose of such defence. In other words, it is only when the accused exceeds his right to private defence unintentionally that the offence of murder committed by him will be mitigated to the offence of culpable homicide not amounting to murder.
- The illustration appended to the Exception 2 further clarifies the provision.
  - **Illustration:** Z attempts to horsewhip A, not in such a manner as to cause grievous hurt to A. A draws out a pistol. Z persists in the assault. A, believing in good faith that he can by no other means prevent himself from being horsewhipped, shoots Z dead. A has not committed murder, but only culpable homicide.

Exception 3: Acts of Public Servant

Exception 3 to Section 101 of BNS lays down that the offence of murder will be reduced to "culpable homicide not amounting to murder, if murder is committed by a public servant under certain circumstances enumerated thereunder".

Essential Ingredients

- The offence of murder must be committed by a public servant or by a person aiding a public servant.
- The accused should exceed the powers given to him by law while acting for the advancement of public justice.
- Death should be caused by the accused as a result of an act done by him in good faith which he believes to be lawful and necessary for the due discharge of his duty.
- The act in question must also be done and without ill-will towards the deceased.

Exception 4: Death Caused in Sudden Fight

Exception 4 to Section 101 of BNS lays down that the offence of murder will be reduced to "culpable homicide not amounting to murder, if murder is caused in a sudden fight".

Essential Ingredients

- The offence of murder must be committed without premeditation.
- It must be committed in a sudden fight in the heat of passion upon a sudden quarrel. In view of the Explanation appended to Exception 4, it is immaterial which party offers the provocation for the offence or commits the first assault.
- The accused must not have taken undue advantage or acted in a cruel or unusual manner.

Exception 5: Death Caused by Consent

- **Exception 5 to Section 101** of BNS lays down that the offence of murder will be reduced to "culpable homicide not amounting to murder when the person whose death is caused is above the age of eighteen years and suffers death or takes the risk of death with his own consent.
- The illustration appended to Exception 5 further clarifies that, for the applicability of this exception, the deceased must be of the age of majority.
  - **Illustration:** A, by instigation, voluntarily causes Z, a child to commit suicide. Here, on account of Z's youth, he was incapable of giving consent to his own death; A has therefore abetted murder.

Punishment for Culpable Homicide Not Amounting to Murder

As stated earlier, the offences of culpable homicide covered under **Section 100** and of culpable homicide not amounting to murder covered under the five exceptions of **Section 101** are both punishable under **Section 105** of BNS. In view of the provisions of **Section 105:**

- The offence of culpable homicide not amounting to murder covered simultaneously by **Clause (a) of Section 101** (i.e., an act done with the intention of causing death) and **Exceptions 1 to 5 of Section 101** provided in the section is punishable with:
  - Life imprisonment and with fine, or
  - Imprisonment of either description for a term which shall not be less than five years but which may extend to ten years and with fine.
- The offence of culpable homicide not amounting to murder covered simultaneously by **Clauses (b) or (c) of Section 101** (i.e. an act done with the intention of causing such bodily injury as is likely to cause death) and **Exceptions 1 to 5 of Section 101** provided in the section is punishable with:
  - Life imprisonment and with fine, or
  - Imprisonment of either description for a term which shall not be less than five years but which may extend to ten years and with fine.
- The offence of culpable homicide not amounting to murder covered simultaneously by **Clauses (d) of Section 101** (i.e. an act done with the knowledge that it is likely to cause death) and **Exceptions 1 to 5 of Section 101** provided in the section is punishable with imprisonment of either description for a term which may extend to ten years and with fine.

CULPABLE HOMICIDE BY CAUSING DEATH OF A PERSON OTHER THAN THE PERSON WHOSE DEATH WAS INTENDED

(**Note:** ***Section 102*** *of the BNS corresponds to* ***Section 301*** *of the IPC*)

- **Section 102** of BNS deals with Culpable Homicide by causing death of a person other than the person whose death was intended.
- **Section 102** gives statutory recognition to the **Doctrine of Transfer of Malice.**
- Following are the essential ingredients of Section 102:
  - The offender does an act which he intends or knows to be likely to cause death.
  - By doing such act, the offender commits culpable homicide and causes the death of a person whose death he neither intended nor knew himself to be likely to cause.
  - If both the aforesaid two conditions are satisfied, the offender shall be liable to be dealt with in the same manner as if he had caused the death of the person whose death he intended or knew himself to be likely to cause.
- In the case of **Public Prosecutor v. Moorthy (1912),** it has been very categorically reiterated and held that there will be no difference in criminal liability of the accused when the act done with guilty intention or knowledge does not cause death of the person aimed at but causes death of some other person whose death was neither intended nor known to be likely to be caused.
- In the leading case of **Shankarlal Kachrabhai & Others v. State Of Gujarat, (1965),** Hon'ble Apex Court has explained the provisions of Section 301 of IPC (corresponding to Section 102 of BNS) by means of an an illustration and held as under:

"This section deals with a different situation. It embodies what the English authors describe as the doctrine of transfer of malice or the transmigration of motive. Under the section if A intends to kill B, but kills C whose death he neither intends nor knows himself to be likely to cause, the intention to kill C is by law attributed to him. If A aims his shot at B, but it misses B either because B moves out of the range of the shot or because the shot misses the mark and hits some other person C, whether within sight or out of sight, under **Section 301**, A is deemed to have hit C with the intention to kill him. What is to be noticed is that to invoke **Section 301** of the Indian Penal Code A shall not have any intention to cause the death or the knowledge that he is likely to cause the death of C."

CAUSING DEATH BY NEGLIGENCE

(**Note:** ***Section 106*** *of the BNS corresponds to* ***Section 304A*** *of the IPC*)

Section 106 lays down the offence of causing death by negligence and provides punishments in respect thereof.

- **Section 106(1)** declares that, whoever causes death of any person by doing any rash or negligent act not amounting to culpable homicide is liable to be punished with imprisonment of either description for a term which may extend to five years, and is also liable to fine.
- **Section 106(1) of BNS corresponds to Section 304A** of IPC which provided the maximum imprisonment of two years in cases of death caused by rash or negligent acts. However, Section 106(1) has enhanced the maximum imprisonment from two years to five years which reflects a strict legislative approach in dealing with cases of death caused by rash or negligent act.

DIFFERENCE BETWEEN CRIMINAL RASHNESS AND NEGLIGENCE

Section 106 of BNS punishes death caused by rash and negligent acts. However, there is a substantial difference between criminal rashness and negligence.

- A person is said to be rash when he acts with utter indifference to the consequences of his acts and which he hopes may not take place.
- Criminal negligence is the omission to do something which a person of reasonable prudence, guided by those considerations which ordinarily regulate human behavior, would do or doing something which a prudent and reasonable person would not do.

- **Provisions for Medical Practitioners**
  - **Section 106(1)** also introduces new provision for medical practitioners and provides that if such rash or negligent act as aforesaid is done by a registered medical practitioner while performing a medical procedure, he shall be punished with imprisonment of either description for a term which may extend to two years and shall also be liable to fine.
  - In view of the **Explanation of Section 106(1)**, a "registered medical practitioner" for the purposes of the provision and lays down that a , ha"registered medical practitioner" means a medical practitioner who possesses any medical qualification recognised under the National Medical Commission Act, 2019 and whose name has been entered in the National Medical Register or a State Medical Register under that Act.
- **Provisions with Regard to Hit and Run Cases**
  - **Section 106(2)** introduces new provisions dealing with hit and run cases and provides stringent punishment for such cases.
  - Section 106(2) provides that whoever:

- **Causes death** of any person by rash and negligent driving of vehicle not amounting to culpable homicide, and
- **Escapes** without reporting it to a police officer or a Magistrate soon after the incident shall be punished with maximum imprisonment of ten years, and shall also be liable to fine.

- Hit and Run is defined under **Section 161(1) (b)** of the **Motor Vehicles Act, 1988** as, ""hit and run motor accident" means an accident arising out of the use of a motor vehicle or motor vehicles the identity whereof cannot be ascertained in spite of reasonable efforts for the purpose"
- However, if the driver reports the incident immediately after the accident, they will be charged under Section 106(1) instead of Section 106(2). Section 106(1) provides for a punishment of up to five years for causing death by any rash or negligent act not amounting to culpable homicide.
- It is pertinent to note that under the repealed Indian Penal Code, 1860 the maximum punishment for causing death by negligence extended to 2 years.
- **Note:** Due to the widespread protest across the nation against the stringent punishment prescribed by the newly introduced Section, the Home Ministry in its press release has stayed the enforcement of **Section 106(2)** of BNS. The provisions of BNS, except the provision of sub-section (2) of **Section 106** and entry relating to **Section 106(2)** of BNS in the first schedule of BNSS have come into force from 1st of July, 2024.

ABETMENT OF SUICIDE OF CHILD OR PERSON OF UNSOUND MIND

(**Note:** ***Section 107*** *of the BNS corresponds to* ***Section 305*** *of the IPC*)

Section 107 of BNS deals with the offence of abetment of suicide of child or insane person and provides punishment therefore.

- **Section 107** declares that if any child, any person of unsound mind, any delirious person or any person in a state of intoxication, commits suicide, whoever abets the commission of such suicide, shall be punished with death or imprisonment for life, or maximum imprisonment of ten years, and shall also be liable to fine.
- Accordingly, conditions must be fulfilled for the applicability of **Section 107** of BNS:
  - A person must have committed suicide. A liability under **Section 107** would not arise if a peron has made an attempt to commit suicide.
  - Such person must be a child, a person of unsound mind, a delirious person or a person in a state of intoxication. **Section 107** has no application in cases where any other person commits suicide.
  - The accused must have abetted the suicide of such person. The act of the accused must conform to the definition of abetment as provided under **Section 45** of BNS, i.e. the accused must instigate, conspire or intentionally aid the suicide of the victim.
- The offence under **Section 107** is an aggravated form of the offence dealt with under **Section 108** of BNS. Therefore, all the ingredients of **Section 108** must also be fulfilled in respect of **Section 107** of BNS.

Abetment of Suicide

(**Note:** ***Section 108*** *of the BNS corresponds to* ***Section 306*** *of the IPC*)

Section 108 of BNS deals with the offence of abetment of suicide and provides provides punishment therefor.

- **Section 108** declares that if any person commits suicide, whoever abets the commission of such suicide, shall be punished with imprisonment of either description for a term which may extend to ten years, and shall also be liable to fine.

- For the applicability of **Section 108**, it is essential that a person must have committed suicide. A liability under section 108 would not arise, if a peron has made an attempt to commit suicide.
- Moreover, the Act of the accused must conform to the definition of abetment as provided under **Section 45 of BNS**, i.e. the accused must instigate, conspire or intentionally aid the suicide of the victim.
- In the leading case of **Gangula M. Reddy v. State of A.P., (2010)**, Hon'ble Apex Court has held as under:

  "Abetment involves a mental process of instigating a person or intentionally aiding a person in doing of a thing. Without a positive act on the part of the accused to instigate or aid in committing suicide, conviction cannot be sustained... in order to convict a person u/s 306 IPC there has to be a clear mens rea to commit the offence.

  It also requires an active act or direct act which led the deceased to commit suicide seeing no option and this act must have been intended to push the deceased into such a position that he committed suicide."

ATTEMPT TO MURDER

(**Note:** ***Section 109*** *of the BNS corresponds to* ***Section 307*** *of the IPC*)

- **Section 109** of BNS deals with the offence of Attempt to Murder and provides punishment therefor.
- **Essential Ingredients:** In view of the provisions of **Section 109(1)**, following are the essential ingredients of the offence of attempt to murder:
  - **Intention or Knowledge:** The act in question must be done by the accused with such intention or knowledge and under such circumstances that death be caused by that act, he would be guilty of the offence of murder. In other words, the accused must have the intention or knowledge to commit the offence of murder. **Illustrations (a) & (b)** of **Section 109** inter alia clarify the provision with regard to the offence of attempt to murder committed with guilty intention.
    - **Illustration (a):** A shoots at Z with intention to kill him, under such circumstances that, if death ensued, A would be guilty of murder. A is liable to punishment under this section.
    - **Illustration (b):** A, with the intention of causing the death of a child of tender years, exposes it in a desert place. A has committed the offence defined by this section, though the death of the child does not ensue.
  - In view of the provisions of Section 109 read together with Section 101 of BNS, the accused must have the:
    - Intention to cause death, or
    - Intention to cause such bodily injury which the offender knows to be likely to cause death, or
    - Intention to cause such bodily injury which is sufficient in the ordinary course of nature to cause death, or
    - Knowledge that the act done by him is so imminently dangerous that it must in all probability cause death or cause such bodily injury as is likely to cause death.
- **Overt Act**
  - The accused must actually try or make an attempt to commit the offence of murder by doing an overt act.
  - The overt act must not amount to mere preparation which essentially consists of devising necessary measures for commission of the offence of murder. Rather, it must be a direct movement towards the commission of offence after the preparations are made.
  - In the leading case of **Malkiat Singh vs. State of Punjab, (1970)**, Hon'ble Apex Court has held that the test for determining

whether the act of the accused constituted an attempt or preparation is whether the overt acts already done are such that if the offender changes his mind and does not proceed further in its progress, the acts already done would be completely harmless.

- **Illustrations (c) & (d)** of Section 109 inter alia clarify the distinction between preparation and attempt to commit the offence of murder.

ILLUSTRATIONS (C) & (D) OF SECTION 109

- **Illustration (c):** A, intending to murder Z, buys a gun and loads it. A has not yet committed the offence. A fires the gun at Z. He has committed the offence defined in this section, and, if by such firing he wounds Z, he is liable to the punishment provided by the latter part of sub-section (1).
- **Illustration (d):** A, intending to murder Z by poison, purchases poison and mixes the same with food which remains in A's keeping; A has not yet committed the offence defined in this section. A places the food on Z's table or delivers it to Z's servants to place it on Z's table. A has committed the offence defined in this section.

- However, the Act in question need not be penultimate but only proximate in nature. In the leading case of **Om Prakash v. State of Punjab, (1961)**, Hon'ble Apex Court has reiterated and held that for the offence of attempt to murder, the act towards the commission of murder need not be a single act. The act done must not also be the last or penultimate act done for committing the offence of murder.
- Subsequently, elaborating upon the scope of Section 307 of IPC (corresponding to Section 109 of BNS), Hon'ble Apex Court, in the leading case of **State of Maharashtra v. Balram Bama Patil, (1983)**, has held that, "... To justify a conviction under this section it is not essential that bodily injury capable of causing death should have been inflicted. An attempt in order to be criminal need not be the penultimate act. It is sufficient in law, if there is present an intent coupled with some overt act in execution thereof."

Punishments

- In view of the provisions of **Section 109(1)**, the offence of attempt to murder simpliciter is punishable with imprisonment of either description for a term which may extend to ten years, and fine.
- In view of the provisions of **Section 109(1)**, if hurt is caused to any person while committing the offence of attempt to murder, the offender is liable either to imprisonment for life, or to such punishment as mentioned hereinbefore.
- In view of the provisions of **Section 109(2)**, when any person offending under Section 109(1) is under the sentence of life imprisonment and if hurt is caused by him, he may be punished with death or with life imprisonment which shall mean the remainder of his natural life.

ATTEMPT TO COMMIT CULPABLE HOMICIDE

(**Note:** ***Section 110*** *of the BNS corresponds to* ***Section 308*** *of the IPC*)

- **Section 110** of BNS deals with the offence of attempt to commit culpable homicide and provides punishment therefor.
- **Sections 109** and **110** of BNS deal with cognate offences; these provisions have been expressed in similar language and therefore, should be interpreted in similar manner.
- **Essential Ingredients:** In view of the provisions of **Section 110**, following are the essential ingredients of the offence of attempt to commit culpable homicide not amounting to murder:

- Intention or Knowledge: The act in question must be done by the accused with such intention or knowledge and under such circumstances that if death be caused by that act, he would be guilty of culpable homicide not amounting to murder. In other words, the accused must have the intention or knowledge of to commit the offence of culpable homicide not amounting to murder.
  - The illustration of **Section 110** inter alia clarifies the provision in cases where the offence of "attempt to commit culpable homicide" is committed with guilty intention.
  - **Illustration:** A, on grave and sudden provocation, fires a pistol at Z, under such circumstances that if he thereby caused death, he would be guilty of culpable homicide not amounting to murder. A has committed the offence defined in this section.

- **Overt Act**
  - The accused must actually try or make an attempt to commit the offence of culpable homicide not amounting to murder by doing an overt act.
  - The overt act must not amount to mere preparation which essentially consists of devising necessary measures for commission of the offence of murder. Rather, it must be a direct movement towards the commission of offence after the preparations are made.
  - For the offence of attempt to commit culpable homicide not amounting to murder, the act towards the commission of murder need not be a single act but may consist of a series of acts. The act done must not also be the last or penultimate act done for committing the offence of culpable homicide.

Punishments

In view of the provisions of **Section 110 of BNS:**

- The offence of attempt to commit culpable homicide not amounting to murder is punishable with imprisonment of either description for a term which may extend to three years, or with fine, or with both.
- If hurt is caused to any person during the commission of such offence, it shall be punishable with imprisonment of either description for a term which may extend to seven years, or with fine, or with both.

ORGANISED CRIME

- **Section 111** of BNS has introduced the offence of "Organised Crime" with the objective of curbing unlawful activities carried out by syndicates which pose a serious threat to law and order of the state.
- **Organised Crime: Section 111(1)** defines the offence of "organised crime". In view of the definition, any continuing unlawful activity shall constitute the offence of "organised crime" if it is committed:
  - By any person or a group of persons acting in concert, singly or jointly, either as a member of an organised crime syndicate or on behalf of such syndicate,
  - By use of violence, threat of violence, intimidation, coercion, or by any other unlawful means,
  - To obtain direct or indirect material benefit including a financial benefit.
- **Continuing Unlawful Activity:** The **Explanation** of Section 111(1) defines "continuing unlawful activity". In view of the definition, a "**continuing unlawful activity**" has the following essential ingredients:
  - It must be an activity prohibited by law which is a cognizable offence punishable with imprisonment of three years or more.
  - It must have been undertaken by any person, either singly or jointly, as a member of an organised crime syndicate or on behalf of such syndicate.
  - In respect of the aforesaid offence, more than one charge-sheets must have been

filed before a competent Court within the preceding period of ten years and that Court must have cognizance of such offence and includes economic offence.

- Moreover, a continuing unlawful activity includes the certain other offences irrespective of whether or not it is a cognizable offence punishable with imprisonment of three years more, whether or not in respect of it more than one charge-sheets has been filed before a competent Court within the preceding period of ten years and whether or not that Court has its cognizance.
- These offences are as under:
  - Economic offence
  - Kidnapping
  - Robbery
  - Vehicle theft
  - Extortion
  - Land grabbing
  - Contract killing
  - Economic offence
  - Cyber-crimes
  - Trafficking of persons, drugs, weapons or illicit goods or services
  - Human trafficking for prostitution or ransom.
- The **Explanation** of **Section 111(1)** also defines **"organised crime syndicate"**. In view of the definition, "organised crime syndicate" means a group of two or more persons who,acting either singly or jointly, as a syndicate or gang indulge in any continuing unlawful activity.
- The **Explanation** of **Section 111(1)** also defines **"economic offence".** In view of the definition, "economic offence" includes:
  - Criminal breach of trust
  - Forgery
  - Counterfeiting of currency-notes, bank-notes and Government stamps
  - Hawala transaction
  - Mass-marketing fraud
  - Running any scheme to defraud several persons
  - Doing any act in any manner with a view to defraud any bank or financial institution or any other institution or organization for obtaining monetary benefits in any form.

Punishments for Organised Crime

- **Section 111(2)** lays down the punishment for the offence of organised crime:
  - **Section 111(2)(a)** provides that whoever commits organised crime shall, if such offence has resulted in the death of any person, be punished with death or imprisonment for life, and shall also be liable to fine which shall not be less than ten lakh rupees.
  - **Section 111(2)(b)** provides that whoever commits organised crime shall, in any other case, be punished with imprisonment for a term which shall not be less than five years but which may extend to imprisonment for life, and shall also be liable to fine which shall not be less than five lakh rupees.
- **Punishment for Attempt, Abetment or Conspiracy: Section 111(3)** provides that whoever abets, attempts, conspires or knowingly facilitates the commission of an organised crime, or otherwise engages in any act preparatory to an organised crime, shall be punished with imprisonment for a term which shall not be less than five years but which may extend to imprisonment for life, and shall also be liable to fine which shall not be less than five lakh rupees.
- **Punishment for being Member of Organised Crime: Section 111(4)** provides that any person who is a member of an organised crime syndicate shall be punished with imprisonment for a term which shall not be less than five years but which may extend to imprisonment for life, and shall also be liable to fine which shall not be less than five lakh rupees.

- **Punishment for Harboring or Concealing the Offender: Section 111(5)** provides that whoever, intentionally, harbours or conceals any person who has committed the offence of an organised crime shall be punished with imprisonment for a term which shall not be less than three years but which may extend to imprisonment for life, and shall also be liable to fine which shall not be less than five lakh rupees
  - The **Proviso of Section 111(5)** makes the provision inapplicable to any case in which the harbor or concealment is by the spouse of the offender.
- **Punishment for Possession of Property: Sections 111(6) and 111(7)** lay down the punishment in respect of possession of property.
  - **Section 111(6)** provides that whoever possesses any property derived or obtained from the commission of an organised crime or proceeds of any organised crime or which has been acquired through the organised crime, shall be punishable with imprisonment for a term which shall not be less than three years but which may extend to imprisonment for life and shall also be liable to fine which shall not be less than two lakh rupees.
  - **Section 111(7)** provides that if any person on behalf of a member of an organised crime syndicate is, or at any time has been in possession of movable or immovable property which he cannot satisfactorily account for, shall be punishable with imprisonment for a term which shall not be less than three years but which may extend to imprisonment for ten years and shall also be liable to fine which shall not be less than one lakh rupees.

PETTY ORGANISED CRIME

- **Section 112** of BNS has introduced the offence of " Petty Organised Crime" with the objective of curbing unlawful activities carried out by syndicates which are less serious in nature but nevertheless pose a serious threat to law and order machinery of the state.
- **Section 112(1)** provides that a person is said to commit petty organised crime who, being a member of a group or gang, either singly or jointly, commits any act of:
  - Theft,
  - Snatching,
  - Cheating,
  - Unauthorised selling of tickets,
  - Unauthorised betting or gambling,
  - Selling of public examination question papers or any other similar criminal act.
- **Theft: Explanation** of Section 112(1) lays down an inclusive definition of "theft" for the purposes of the provision. As per the definition, "theft" includes:
  - Trick theft,
  - Theft from vehicle, dwellinghouse or business premises, cargo theft, pick pocketing,
  - Theft through card skimming, shoplifting and
  - Theft of Automated Teller Machine (ATM).
- **Punishment: Section 111(2)** lays down the punishment for petty organised crime and provides that the offence of petty organised crime is punishable with imprisonment for a term which shall not be less than one year but which may extend to seven years, and is liable to fine.

TERRORIST ACT

Section 113 of BNS is a pioneer provision as it has defined and introduced the offense of terrorism in the general penal law of the land. **Section 113(1)** lays down a very comprehensive definition of the offence of "terrorist attack". In view of the definition, a the offence of "terrorist attack" is said to be committed by any one of the following persons who:

- A person who does any act with the intent to threaten or likely to threaten the unity, integrity, sovereignty, security, or economic security of India, or with the intent to strike terror or likely to strike terror in the people or any section of the people in India or in any foreign country:
  - (a) by using bombs, dynamite or other explosive substance or inflammable substance or firearms or other lethal weapons or poisonous or noxious gases or other chemicals or by any other substance (whether biological, radioactive, nuclear or otherwise) of a hazardous nature or by any other means of whatever nature to cause or likely to cause:
    - (i) death of, or injury to, any person or persons; or
    - (ii) loss of, or damage to, or destruction of, property; or
    - (iii) disruption of any supplies or services essential to the life of the community inIndia or in any foreign country; or
    - (iv) damage to, the monetary stability ofIndia by way of production or smuggling or circulation of counterfeit Indian paper currency, coin or of any other material; or
    - (v) damage or destruction of any property inIndia or in a foreign country used or intended to be used for the defence ofIndia or in connection with any other purposes of the Government of India, any State Government or any of their agencies.
  - (b) A person who overawes by means of criminal force or the show of criminal force or attempts to do so or causes death of any public functionary or attempts to cause death of any public functionary.
  - (c) A person who detains, kidnaps or abducts any person and threatening to kill or injure such person or does any other act in order to compel the Government of India, any State Government or the Government of a foreign country or an international or inter-governmental organization or any other person to do or abstain from doing any act.
- **Public Functionary:** The Explanation of **Section 113(1)** defines the phrase "public functionary". In view of the definition, "public functionary" means the constitutional authorities or any other functionary notified in the Official Gazette by the Central Government as public functionary.
- **Counterfeit Indian Currency:** The Explanation of Section 113(1) also defines the phrase "counterfeit Indian currency". In view of the definition, "counterfeit Indian currency" means the counterfeit currency as may be declared after examination by an authorised or notified forensic authority that such currency imitates or compromises with the key security features ofIndian currency.
- **The Explanation of Section 113** declares that the officer not below the rank of Superintendent of Police shall decide whether to register the case under Section 113 or under the Unlawful Activities (Prevention) Act, 1967.

Punishment for Terrorist Attack

- **Section 113(2)** lays down the punishment for terrorist act:
  - **Section 113(2)(a)** provides that whoever commits a terrorist act shall, if such offence has resulted in the death of any person, be punished with death or imprisonment for life, and shall also be liable to fine.
  - **Section 113(2)(b)** provides that whoever commits a terrorist act shall, in any other case, be punished with imprisonment for a term which shall not be less than five years but which may extend to imprisonment for life, and shall also be liable to fine.

- **Punishment for Conspiracy, Abetment, Attempt etc.: Section 113(3)** provides that whoever conspires or attempts to commit, or advocates, abets, advises or incites, directly or knowingly facilitates the commission of a terrorist act or any act preparatory to the commission of a terrorist act, shall be punished with imprisonment for a term which shall not be less than five years but which may extend to imprisonment for life, and shall also be liable to fine.
- **Punishment for Organizing Camps etc.: Section 113(4)** provides that whoever organises or causes to be organised any camp or camps for imparting training in terrorist act, or recruits or causes to be recruited any person or persons for commission of a terrorist act, shall be punished with imprisonment for a term which shall not be less than five years but which may extend to imprisonment for life, and shall also be liable to fine.
- **Punishment for Being Member of an Organisation Involved in Terrorist Attack: Section 113(5)** provides that any person who is a member of an organisation which is involved in a terrorist act shall be punished with imprisonment for a term which may extend to imprisonment for life, and shall also be liable to fine.
- **Punishment for Harbouring or Concealing the Terrorist: Section 113(6)** provides that whoever voluntarily harbours or conceals, or attempts to harbour or conceal any person knowing that such person has committed a terrorist act shall be punished with imprisonment for a term which shall not be less than three years but which may extend to imprisonment for life, and shall also be liable to fine:
  - The **Proviso of Section 113(6)** makes the provision inapplicable to any case in which the harbor or concealment is by the spouse of the offender.
- **Punishment for Possessing Proceeds of Terrorist Acts: Section 113(7)** provides that whoever knowingly possesses any property derived or obtained from commission of any terrorist act or acquired through the commission of any terrorist act shall be punished with imprisonment for a term which may extend to imprisonment for life, and shall also be liable to fine.

❖❖❖

Chapter 13

OTHER OFFENCES AGAINST HUMAN BODY

HURT & GRIEVOUS HURT

Hurt and grievous hurt are offences that impact the human body, thereby infringing upon an individual's rights under **Articles 19 and 21** of the Indian Constitution. Hurt is a genus, while grievous hurt is a specific type within that category. **Sections 114-125** of the BNS (Earlier, Section 319-338 of the IPC) address various forms of hurt, grievous hurt, and their aggravated forms.

COMPARATIVE CHART OF THE BNS AND IPC

Bharatiya Nyaya Sanhita, 2023(BNS)	Title	Indian Penal Code, 1860 (IPC)
Section 114	Hurt	Section 319
Section 115	Voluntarily causing hurt	Section 321
	EARLIER TITLE- (Punishment for voluntarily causing hurt)	Section 323
Section 116	Grievous hurt	Section 320
Section 117	Voluntarily causing grievous hurt	Section 322
	EARLIER TITLE- (Punishment for voluntarily causing grevious hurt)	Section 325
Section 118	Voluntarily causing hurt or grievous hurt by dangerous weapons or means	Section 324
	EARLIER TITLE- (Voluntarily causing hurt by dangerous weapons or means)	Section 326
Section 119	Voluntarily causing hurt or grievous hurt to extort property, or to constrain to an illegal to an act	Section 327
	EARLIER TITLE- (Voluntarily causing hurt to extort property, or to constrain to an illegal to an act)	Section 329
Section 120	Voluntarily causing hurt or grievous hurt to extort confession, or to compel restoration of property	Section 330
	EARLIER TITLE- (Voluntarily causing hurt to extort confession, or to compel restoration of property)	Section 331

Section 121	Voluntarily causing hurt or grievous hurt to deter public servant from his duty	Section 332
	EARLIER TITLE- (Voluntarily causing hurt to deter public servant from his duty)	Section 333
Section 122	Voluntarily causing hurt or grievous hurt on provocation	Section 334
	EARLIER TITLE- (Voluntarily causing hurt on provocation)	Section 335
Section 123	Causing hurt by means of poison, etc., with intent to commit an offence	Section 328
Section 124	Voluntarily causing grievous hurt by use of acid, etc.	Section 326A
	EARLIER TITLE- (Voluntarily throwing or attempting to throw acid)	Section 326B
Section 125	Act endangering life or personal safety of others	Section 336
	EARLIER TITLE- (Causing hurt by act endangering life or personal safety of others)	Section 337
	EARLIER TITLE- (Causing grievous hurt by act endangering life or personal safety of others)	Section 338

CHANGES IN BNS IN COMPARISON TO IPC

- **Section 115(2)** of the BNS, corresponding to Section 323 of the IPC, has been changed as follows:
  - The fine has been increased which may extend to **ten thousand rupees.**
- **Section 116** of the BNS, corresponding to Section 320 of the IPC, has been changed as follows:
  - The threshold period of suffering has been reduced from **twenty days to fifteen days.**
- **Section 117** of the BNS, corresponding to Sections 322 and 325 of the IPC, has introduced the following changes:
  - **Section 117(3)** is a newly added provision which provides, "Whoever commits an offence under sub-section (1) and in the course of such commission causes any hurt to a person which causes that person to be in permanent disability or in persistent vegetative state, shall be punished with rigorous imprisonment for a term which shall not be less than ten years but which may extend to imprisonment for life, which shall mean imprisonment for the remainder of that person's natural life".
  - **Section 117(4)** is a newly added provision which provides, "When a group of five or more persons acting in concert, causes grievous hurt to a person on the ground of his race, caste or community, sex, place of birth, language, personal belief or any other similar ground, each member of such group shall be guilty of the offence of causing

grievous hurt, and shall be punished with imprisonment of either description for a term which may extend to seven years, and shall also be liable to fine".

- **Section 118(1)** of the BNS, corresponding to Section 324 of the IPC, has been changed as follows:
  - Increased the fine which may extend to **twenty thousand rupees.**
- **Section 118(2)** of the BNS, corresponding to Section 326 of the IPC, has been changed as follows:
  - The **mandatory minimum imprisonment for one year** has been added.
- **Section 119(2), 120(2)** of the BNS, corresponding to Section 329, 331 of the IPC, have been changed as follows:
  - Added the words "any purpose referred to in sub-section (1)".
- **Section 121(1)** of the BNS, corresponding to Section 332 of the IPC, has been changed as follows:
  - Increased the imprisonment from **three to five years**.
- **Section 121(2)** of the BNS, corresponding to Section 333 of the IPC, has been changed as follows:
  - Added the mandatory **minimum imprisonment of one year**.
- **Section 122(1)** of the BNS, corresponding to Section 334 of the IPC, has been changed as follows:
  - Increased the fine from five **hundred to five thousand rupees**.
- **Section 122(1)** of the BNS, corresponding to Section 335 of the IPC, has been changed as follows:
  - Increased the imprisonment from **four to five years** and the fine from **two thousand to ten thousand rupees**.
- **Section 124(1)** of the BNS, corresponding to Section 326A of the IPC, has added the words **"causes a person to be in a permanent vegetative state"**.
- **Section 124(2)** of the BNS, corresponding to Section 326B of the IPC, has added the words "permanent vegetative state".
- **Section 125** of the BNS, corresponding to Section 336 of the IPC, has increased the fine from rupees **two hundred and fifty to two thousand five hundred rupees**.
- **Section 125(a)** of the BNS, corresponding to Section 337 of the IPC, has increased the fine from from **five hundred to five thousand rupees**.
- **Section 125(b)** of the BNS, corresponding to Section 338 of the IPC, has increased the imprisonment from **two years to three years** and fine from **one thousand to ten thousand rupees**.

HURT

(**Note:** ***Section 114*** *of the BNS corresponds to* ***Section 319*** *of the IPC.*)

- **Section 114** defines hurt as "whoever causes bodily pain, disease or infirmity to any person is said to cause hurt". In other words, hurt is caused when the act of a person causes bodily pain, disease or infirmity to another person. To cause hurt, direct physical contact is not necessary.
- The phrase "bodily pain" signifies that, in order to constitute hurt, the pain must be physical and not mental in nature. However, the section only requires the causing of bodily pain; severity of such pain is no criteria to determine as to whether or not hurt has been caused.

- Causing a disease means communicating a disease to another person. Likewise, infirmity denotes an unhealthy state of body and means inability of an organ to function properly.

Voluntarily Causing Hurt

(**Note:** ***Section 115*** *of the BNS corresponds to* ***Section 321, 323*** *of the IPC.*)

Section 115 of BNS defines the offence of voluntarily causing hurt and provides punishment therefor. It must be noted that, under the statutory scheme of BNS (earlier, the IPC), causing hurt is not an offence but voluntarily causing hurt is an offence.

Essential Ingredients of Voluntarily Causing Hurt

Section 115(1) defines the offence of voluntarily causing hurt; the essential ingredients of the offence are as under:

- **Guilty Intention or Knowledge:** The offender must do an act with the intention of causing hurt to a person or with the knowledge that he is likely thereby to cause hurt to a person. The extent of injury caused by the offender is not relevant to determine as to whether the offender has voluntarily caused hurt to a person. Rather, the requisite intention or knowledge of the offender is the key factor for determining his liability for the offence.
- **Causing Hurt in Consequence:** The phrase "does thereby cause hurt to any person" signifies that the offender must actually cause hurt to a person in consequence of his aforesaid act. Therefore, if the offender does an act with guilty intention or knowledge but no hurt is caused by his act, he cannot be held guilty for the offence of voluntarily causing hurt.
- **Punishment for Voluntarily Causing Hurt: Section 115(2)** lays down the punishment for the offence of voluntarily causing hurt and provides that a person who voluntarily causes hurt is liable to be punished with imprisonment of either description for a term which may extend to one year, or with fine which may extend to ten thousand rupees, or with both.
- However, the above-said punishment is not applicable in the cases covered by **Section 122(1)** of BNS. **Section 122(1)** deals with voluntarily causing hurt on grave and sudden provocation.

GRIEVOUS HURT

(**Note:** ***Section 116*** *of the BNS corresponds to* ***Section 320*** *of the IPC.*)

- **Section 116** of BNS defines Grievous Hurt. In view of the definition, grievous hurt is also a hurt having certain aggravated characteristics. Hurt is the genus of which grievous hurt is the species. In fact, a hurt cannot be termed as a grievous hurt unless it comes specifically within the injuries specified under Section 116.
- Only the following kinds of hurt are designated as "grievous" hurt:
  - Emasculation
  - Permanent privation of the sight of either eye
  - Permanent privation of the hearing of either ear
  - Privation of any member or joint
  - Destruction or permanent impairing of the powers of any member or joint
  - Permanent disfiguration of the head or face
  - Fracture or dislocation of a bone or tooth
  - Any hurt which endangers life or which causes the sufferer to be during the space of fifteen days in severe bodily pain, or unable to follow his ordinary pursuits.

Voluntarily Causing Grievous Hurt

(**Note:** ***Section 117*** *of the BNS corresponds to* ***Section 322, 325*** *of the IPC.*)

Section 117 of BNS defines the offence of voluntarily causing hurt and provides punishment thereof.

Essential Ingredients of Voluntarily Causing Grievous Hurt

Section 117(1) defines the offence of voluntarily causing grievous hurt. A person is said to voluntarily cause grievous hurt when he voluntarily causes hurt and the following two condition are also satisfied, namely:

- **Guilty Intention or Knowledge:** The offender must intend to cause grievous hurt or must know that he is likely to cause grievous hurt.
- **Causing Grievous Hurt in Consequence:** The offender must actually cause grievous hurt to a person in consequence of his aforesaid act. The Explanation of **Section 117(1)** categorically states that a person cannot be liable to voluntarily cause grievous hurt except when he both causes grievous hurt and intends or knows himself to be likely to cause grievous hurt. However, a person will be liable for the offence of voluntarily causing grievous hurt if he intends or knows himself to be likely to cause grievous hurt of one kind but he actually causes grievous hurt of another kind.
- The **illustration** of **Section 117(1)** further clarifies this legal position.
  - **Illustration:** A, intending or knowing himself to be likely permanently to disfigure Z's face, gives Z a blow which does not permanently disfigure Z's face, but which causes Z to suffer severe bodily pain for the space of fifteen days. A has voluntarily caused grievous hurt.
- **Punishment for Voluntarily Causing Grievous Hurt : Section 117(2)** lays down the punishment for the offence of voluntarily causing grievous hurt and provides that a person who voluntarily causes grievous hurt is liable to be punished with imprisonment of either description for a term which may extend to seven years, and is also liable to fine.
- However, the above-said punishment is not applicable in the cases covered by **Section 122(2)** of BNS. **Section 122(1)** deals with voluntarily causing grievous hurt on grave and sudden provocation.

NEWLY ADDED OFFENCES IN SECTION 117

Permanent Disability or Persistent Vegetative State

Section 117(3) is a new provision of BNS and inter alia punishes a person for causing permanent disability or persistent vegetative state of another person.

- The offender must have voluntarily caused grievous hurt to a person (hereinafter; the victim).
- In the course of such commission, the offender must have caused such hurt to the victim which causes him to be in permanent disability or in persistent vegetative state.
- If the aforesaid conditions are satisfied, the offender is liable to be punished with rigorous imprisonment for a term which shall not be less than ten years but which may extend to imprisonment for life, which shall mean imprisonment for the remainder of that person's natural life.

Grievous Hurt by Mob Lynching

Section 117(4) is also a new provision of BNS which, inter alia, prescribes punishment for voluntarily causing grievous by mob lynching:

- Grievous Hurt must have been caused by a group of five or more persons acting in concert with each other.
- Grievous Hurt must have been caused by such group on the ground of his race, caste or community, sex, place of birth, language, personal belief or any other similar ground,
- If the aforesaid conditions are satisfied, Section 117(4) imposes joint and constructive liability on each member of such group for causing grievous hurt. Each member of such a group is liable to be punished with imprisonment of either description for a term which may extend to seven years, and shall also be liable to fine.

VOLUNTARILY CAUSING HURT AND GRIEVOUS HURT BY DANGEROUS WEAPONS OR MEANS

(**Note:** ***Section 118*** *of the BNS corresponds to* ***Section 324, 326*** *of the IPC.*)

Voluntarily Causing Hurt by Dangerous Weapons or Means

Section 118(1) deals with the offence of voluntarily causing hurt by dangerous weapons or means and prescribes punishment in respect thereof.

Essentials and Punishment

- The offender must have committed the offence of voluntarily causing hurt.
- The offence of voluntarily causing hurt must have been caused by the accused by any one of the following means:
  - By means of an instrument for shooting, stabbing or cutting.
  - By any instrument which, used as a weapon, is likely to cause death.
  - By means of fire or heated substance.
  - By means of poison
  - By means of corrosive substance
  - By means of an explosive substance
  - By means of a substance which is deleterious for the human body to inhale, swallow, or to receive into the blood.
  - By means of any animal.
- If the above-said conditions are satisfied, the offender is liable to be punished with imprisonment of either description for a term which may extend to three years, or with fine which may extend to twenty thousand rupees, or with both.
- The punishment laid down under **Section 118(1)** does not apply to the cases covered by **Section 122(1)** of BNS. **Section 122(1)** deals with voluntarily causing hurt on grave and sudden provocation.

Voluntarily Causing Grievous Hurt by Dangerous Weapons or Means

- **Section 118(2)** deals with the offences of voluntarily causing grievous hurt by dangerous weapons or means and prescribes punishment in respect thereof.

Essentials and Punishment

- The offender must have committed the offence of voluntarily causing grievous hurt.
- The offence of voluntarily causing hurt must have been caused by the accused by any one of the means referred to under **Section 118(1)** of BNS.
- If the above-said conditions are satisfied, the offender is liable to be punished with life imprisonment, or with imprisonment of either description for a term which shall not be less than one year but which may extend to ten years, and is also liable to fine.
- The punishment laid down under **Section 118(2)** does not apply to the cases covered by **Section 122(2)** of BNS. **Section 122(2)** deals with voluntarily causing grievous hurt on grave and sudden provocation.

VOLUNTARILY CAUSING HURT OR GRIEVOUS HURT TO EXTORT PROPERTY OR TO CONSTRAINT TO AN ILLEGAL ACT

(**Note:** ***Section 119*** *of the BNS corresponds to* ***Section 327, 329*** *of the IPC.*)

Voluntarily Causing Hurt to Extort Property or to Constraint to an Illegal Act

Section 119(1) deals with the offence of voluntarily causing hurt to extort property, or to constrain to an illegal act.

Essentials and Punishment

- The offender must have committed the offence of voluntarily causing hurt.
- The offence of voluntarily causing hurt must have been caused for any one the following purposes:

- For the purpose of the purpose of extorting a property or valuable security from the sufferer or from any person interested in the sufferer, any property or valuable
- For the purpose of constraining the sufferer or any person interested in such sufferer to do anything which is illegal or which may facilitate the commission of an offence.

- If the above-said conditions are satisfied, the offender is liable to be punished with life be punished with imprisonment of either description for a term which may extend to ten years, and is also liable to fine.

Voluntarily Causing Grievous Hurt to Extort Property or to Constraint to an Illegal Act

Section 119(2) deals with the offence of voluntarily causing grievous hurt to extort property, or to constrain to an illegal act.

Essentials and Punishment

- The offender must have committed the offence of voluntarily causing grievous hurt.
- The offence of voluntarily causing grievous hurt must have been caused for any one of the purposes referred to under Section 119(1) of BNS.
- If the above-said conditions are satisfied, the offender is liable to be punished with life imprisonment, or imprisonment of either description for a term which may extend to ten years, and is also liable to fine.

VOLUNTARILY CAUSING HURT OR GRIEVOUS HURT TO EXTORT CONFESSION ETC.

(**Note:** *Section 120 of the BNS corresponds to Section 330, 331 of the IPC.*)

Voluntarily Causing Hurt to Extort Confession

- **Section 120(1)** deals with the offence of voluntarily causing hurt to extort confession, or to compel restoration of property.

Essentials and Punishment

- The offender must have committed the offence of voluntarily causing hurt to a person.
- The offence of voluntarily causing hurt must have been caused for any one the following purposes:
  - For the purpose of extorting a confession from the sufferer or from any person interested in the sufferer. **Illustration (a)** of **Section 120(1)** further clarifies this provision.
    - **Illustration (a):** A, a police officer, tortures Z in order to induce Z to confess that he committed a crime. A is guilty of an offence under this section.
  - For the purpose of extorting information which may lead to the detection of an offence or misconduct from the sufferer or from any person interested in the sufferer. **Illustration (b)** of Section 120(1) further clarifies this provision.
    - **Illustration (b):** A, a police officer, tortures B to induce him to point out where certain stolen property is deposited. A is guilty of an offence under this section.
  - For the purpose of constraining the sufferer or any person interested in the sufferer to restore or to cause the restoration of any property or valuable security.

    Illustration (c) of **Section 120(1)** further clarifies this provision.
    - **Illustration (c):** A, a revenue officer, tortures Z in order to compel him to pay certain arrears of revenue due from Z. A is guilty of an offence under this section.
  - For the purpose of constraining the sufferer or any person interested in the sufferer to satisfy any claim or demand

- For the purpose of constraining the sufferer or any person interested in the sufferer to give information which may lead to the restoration of any property or valuable security, shall be punished

- If the above-said conditions are satisfied, the offender is liable to be punished with imprisonment of either description for a term which may extend to seven years and is also liable to fine.

Voluntarily Causing Grievous Hurt to Extort Confession etc.

Section 120(2) deals with the offence of voluntarily causing grievous hurt to extort confession or to compel restoration of property.

Essentials and Punishment

- The offender must have committed the offence of voluntarily causing grievous hurt to a person.
- The offence of voluntarily causing hurt must have been caused for any one the purposes mentioned under Section 120(1).
- If the above-said conditions are satisfied, the offender is liable to be punished with imprisonment of either description for a term which may extend to ten years and is also liable to fine.

VOLUNTARILY CAUSING HURT OR GRIEVOUS HURT TO DETER PUBLIC SERVANT FROM HIS DUTY

(Note: ***Section 121*** *of the BNS corresponds to* ***Section 332, 333*** *of the IPC.*)

Voluntarily Causing Hurt to Deter Public Servant From His Duty

Section 121(1) deals with the offence of voluntarily causing hurt to deter a public servant from his duty.

Essentials and Punishment

- The offender must have committed the offence of voluntarily causing hurt against a public servant.
- The offence of voluntarily causing hurt must have been caused under any one of the following circumstances:
  - It must have been caused In the discharge of official duty of the public servant.
  - It must have been done with intent to prevent such public servant or any other public servant from discharging his official duty.
  - It must have been done in consequence of anything done or attempted to be done by the public servant in the lawful discharge of his official duty.
- If the above-said conditions are satisfied, the offender is liable to be punished with imprisonment of either description for a term which may extend to five years, or with fine, or with both.

Voluntarily Causing Grievous Hurt to Deter Public Servant From His Duty

Section 121(2) deals with the offence of voluntarily causing hurt to deter a public servant from his duty.

Essentials and Punishment

- The offender must have committed the offence of voluntarily causing grievous hurt against a public servant.
- The offence of voluntarily causing hurt must have been caused under any one of the following circumstances:
  - It must have been caused In the discharge of official duty of the public servant.
  - It must have been done with intent to prevent or deter such public servant or any other public servant from discharging his official duty.
  - It must have been done in consequence of anything done or attempted to be done by the public servant in the lawful discharge of his official duty.
- If the aforesaid conditions are satisfied, the offender is liable to be punished with imprisonment of either description for a term which shall not be less than one year but which may extend to ten years, and is also liable to fine.

VOLUNTARILY CAUSING HURT OR GRIEVOUS HURT ON PROVOCATION

(**Note:** ***Section 122*** *of the BNS corresponds to* ***Section 334, 335*** *of the IPC.*)

Voluntarily Causing Hurt on Provocation

Section 122(1) deals with the offence of voluntarily causing hurt on grave and sudden provocation. Section 122(1) is an exception to various forms of hurt enumerated in BNS and reduces the criminal liability of the offender.

Essentials and Punishment

- The offender must have committed the offence of voluntarily causing hurt.
- The offence of voluntarily causing hurt must have been committed by the offender due to grave and sudden provocation given to him by the person against whom it is committed.
- The offender must not have the intention or knowledge to cause hurt to any person other than the person who gave the provocation.
- If the aforesaid conditions are satisfied, the criminal liability of the offender is reduced and he is liable to be punished with imprisonment of either description for a term which may extend to one month, or with fine which may extend to five thousand rupees, or with both.

Voluntarily Causing Grievous Hurt on Provocation

Section 122(2) deals with the offence of voluntarily causing grevious hurt on grave and sudden provocation. Section 122(2) is an exception to various forms of hurt enumerated in BNS and reduces the criminal liability of the offender.

Essentials and Punishment

- The offender must have committed the offence of voluntarily causing grievous hurt.
- The offence of voluntarily causing grievous hurt must have been committed by the offender due to grave and sudden provocation given to him by the person against whom it is committed.
- The offender must not have the intention or knowledge to cause grievous hurt to any person other than the person who gave the provocation.
- If the aforesaid conditions are satisfied, the criminal liability of the offender is reduced and he is liable to be punished with imprisonment of either description for a term which may extend to five years, or with fine which may extend to ten thousand rupees, or with both.

EXCEPTIONS TO THE OFFENCE OF VOLUNTARILY CAUSING HURT OR GRIEVOUS HURT ON GRAVE AND SUDDEN PROVOCATION

The **Explanation of Section 122** declares that the section is subject to the same proviso as Exception 1 to Section 101 of BNS. Exception 1 of Section 101 declares grave and sudden provocation as one of the exceptions to the offence of murder. Therefore, in view of the provisions of Sections 101 and 122, grave and sudden provocation under Section 122 is subject to the following three exceptions/ limitations:

- It must not be sought or voluntarily provoked by the offender as an excuse for killing or doing harm to any person.
- It must not be given by anything done in obedience to the law, or by a public servant in the lawful exercise of the powers of such public servant.
- It must not be given by anything done in the lawful exercise of the right of private defence.

CAUSING HURT BY MEANS OF POISON, ETC., WITH INTENT TO COMMIT AN OFFENCE

(**Note:** ***Section 123*** *of the BNS corresponds to* ***Section 328*** *of the IPC.*)

Section 123 deals with the offence of Causing hurt by means of poison, etc., with intent to commit an offence.

Essentials and Punishment

- The offender must have administered to or caused to be taken by any person any poison or any stupefying, intoxicating or unwholesome drug, or other thing committed the offence of voluntarily causing grievous hurt.
- Any one of the above-said acts must have been done by the offender with any one of the following kinds of mens rea:
  - Intent to cause hurt to the person to whom poison etc was administered or who was made to take the poison etc.
  - Intent to commit or to facilitate the commission of an offence.
  - Knowledge that the offender will cause hurt by anyone of his aforesaid acts or
  - knowing it to be likely that he will thereby cause
- If the aforesaid conditions are satisfied, the offender is liable to be punished with imprisonment of either description for a term which may extend to ten years, and also liable to fine.

VOLUNTARILY CAUSING GRIEVOUS HURT BY USE OF ACID, ETC.

(**Note:** ***Section 124*** *of the BNS corresponds to* ***Section 326A-326B*** *of the IPC.*)

- A person who causes permanent or partial damage or deformity to, or burns or maims or disfigures or disables, any part or parts of the body of a person or causes grievous hurt
  - By throwing acid on or
  - By administering acid to that person, or
  - By using any other means
    - With the intention of causing or
    - With the knowledge that he is likely to cause such injury or hurt or
    - Causes a person to be in a permanent vegetative state

  is liable to be punished with imprisonment of either description for a term which shall not be less than ten years but which may extend to imprisonment for life, and with fine
- The fine imposed on the offender must be just and reasonable to meet the medical expenses of the treatment of the victim.
- The fine imposed under **Section 124(1)** shall be mandatorily paid to the victim.
- **Voluntarily Causing Grievous Hurt by Throwing or Attempting to Throw Acid:** A person who throws or attempts to throw acid on any person or attempts to administer acid to any person, or attempts to use any other means, with the intention of causing permanent or partial damage or deformity or burns or maiming or disfigurement or disability or grievous hurt to that person is liable to be punished with imprisonment of either description for a term which shall not be less than five years but which may extend to seven years, and is also liable to fine.
- **Explanation 1:** It is important to note that, for the pupose of **Section 124** of BNSS, "acid" includes any substance which has acidic or corrosive character or burning nature, that is capable of causing bodily injury leading to scars or disfigurement or temporary or permanent disability.
- **Explanation 2:** It is important to note that, for the purposes of **Section 124** of BNSS, permanent or partial damage or deformity or permanent vegetative state is not required to be irreversible.

ACT ENDANGERING LIFE OR PERSONAL SAFETY OF OTHERS

(**Note:** ***Section 125*** *of the BNS corresponds to* ***Sections 336, 337 & 338*** *of the IPC.*)

- **Section 125** deals with an act endangering life or personal safety of others. To invoke this, the offender must do an act so rashly or negligently as to endanger human life or the personal safety of others.
- If the aforesaid condition is fulfilled, the offender is liable to be punished with imprisonment of either description for a term which may extend to three months or with fine which may extend to two thousand five hundred rupees, or with both.
- However, if by such act
  - (a) Hurt is caused, the offender is liable to be punished with imprisonment of either description for a term which may extend to six months, or with fine which may extend to five thousand rupees, or with both.
  - (b) Grievous hurt is caused, the offender is liable to be punished with imprisonment of either description for a term which may extend to three years, or with fine which may extend to ten thousand rupees, or with both.

WRONGFUL RESTRAINT AND WRONGFUL CONFINEMENT

Wrongful restraint and wrongful confinement are offences related to the human body. Committing these two offences means the violation of the right of a person provided under **Articles 19 and 21** of the Constitution of India.

Though the offences of wrongful restraint and wrongful confinement may seem similar, they are significantly different. Understanding these distinctions is crucial, especially since the punishment for wrongful restraint is notably less severe compared to that for wrongful confinement.

Section 126 and 127 of the Bharatiya Nyaya Sanhita, 2023 (BNS) (Earlier, Section 339, 341, 340 and 342 of the IPC) deal with the 'Wrongful restraint and Wrongful Confinement'.

CHANGES IN BNS IN COMPARISON TO IPC

- **Section 126** of the BNS corresponding to Section 339 and 341 of the IPC has been changed as follows:
  - The fine has been **increased from Rs. 500 to Rs. 5000.**
- **Section 127** of the BNS corresponding to Sections 340, 342, 343, 344, 345, 346, 347 and 348 of the IPC has been modified as follows:
  - In **Section 127(2)**, the fine has been **increased from Rs. 1000 to Rs. 5000.**
  - In **Section 127(3),** prescribe the fine of **Rs. 10,000 (Newly added fine)** and enhances term of punishment from 2 years to 3 years
  - In **Section 127(4)**, prescribe the fine of **Rs. 10,000 (Newly added fine)** and enhances term of punishment from **3 years to 5 years**
  - In **Section 127(5)**, prescribe the fine also, earlier there was no provision of fine.
  - In **Section 127(6)**, enhances the punishment upto **3 years** in addition to any other punishment which the offender is liable for such wrongful confinement. Fine is also prescribed as a part of punishment.

COMPARATIVE CHART OF THE BNS AND IPC		
Bharatiya Nyaya Sanhita, 2023(BNS)	**Title**	**Indian Penal Code, 1860 (IPC)**
Section 126	Wrongful Restraint	Section 339
	EARLIER TITLE: (Punishment for wrongful restraint)	Section 341
Section 127	Wrongful Confinement	Section 340
	EARLIER TITLE: (Punishment for Wrongful confinement)	Section 342
	EARLIER TITLE: (Wrongful confinement for three or more days)	Section 343
	EARLIER TITLE: (Wrongful confinement for ten or more days)	Section 344
	EARLIER TITLE: (Wrongful confinement for of person for whose liberation writ has been issued)	Section 345
	EARLIER TITLE: (Wrongful confinement in secret)	Section 346
	EARLIER TITLE: (Wrongful confinement to extort property, or constrain to illegal act)	Section 347
	EARLIER TITLE: (Wrongful confinement to extort confession, or compel restoration of property	Section 348

Wrongful Restraint

(**Note:** ***Section 126*** *of the BNS corresponds to* ***Section 339*** *of the IPC*)

- **Section 126** of the BNS deals with the offence of wrongful restraint. The section provides that whoever voluntarily obstructs any person so as to prevent that person from proceeding in any direction in which that person has a right to proceed, is said wrongfully to restrain that person.
- Restraint means an abridgment of the liberty of a person against his will. Wrongful restraint means obstructing a man from moving from one place to another place where he has a right to be and wants to go. Wrongful restraint consists in preventing a man proceeding in some direction in which he wishes and has a right to proceed.
- **Ingredients**
  - A person causes obstruction to any person
  - Such obstruction is caused voluntarily
  - The obstruction must be such as to prevent that person from proceeding in any direction in which he has a right to proceed.
- **Exception to Section 126** provides that the obstruction of a private way over land or water which a person in good faith believes himself to have a lawful right to obstruct, is not an offence within the meaning of this section.
- **For Example**
  - A obstructs a path along which Z has a right to pass, A not believing in good faith that he has a right to stop the path. Z is thereby prevented from passing. A wrongfully restrains Z.
- **Punishment for Wrongful Restraint: Section 126(2)** provides that whoever wrongfully restrains any person shall be punished with simple imprisonment for a term which may extend to one month, or with fine which may extend to five thousand rupees, or with both.

WRONGFUL CONFINEMENT

(**Note:** ***Section 127*** *of the BNS corresponds to* ***Section 340, 342, 343, 344, 345, 346, 347, 348*** *of the IPC respectively*)

- **Section 127(1)** provides that whoever wrongfully restrains any person in such a manner as to prevent that person from proceeding beyond certain circumscribing limits, is said "wrongfully to confine" that person.
- Wrongful confinement occurs when a person is wrongfully restrained from proceeding beyond certain circumscribing limits.
- ***Ingredients:*** To invoke **Section 127** of BNS following ingredients are to be satisfied:
  - A person voluntarily restrains any person.
  - The act is done in such a manner as to prevent that person from proceeding beyond circumscribing limit
- This offence involves restricting someone's freedom of movement, effectively keeping them in a location against their will. Unlike wrongful restraint, which involves limiting someone's movement within a certain area, wrongful confinement implies a more severe restriction, often involving physical barriers or complete deprivation of liberty.
- **For Example**
  - A causes Z to go within a walled space, and locks Z in. Z is thus prevented from proceeding in any direction beyond the circumscribing line of the wall. A wrongfully confines Z.
  - A places men with firearms at the outlets of a building, and tells Z that they will fire at Z if Z attempts to leave the building. A wrongfully confines Z.
- **Punishment for Wrongful Confinement: Section 127(2)** provides that whoever wrongfully confines any person shall be punished with imprisonment of either description for a term which may extend to one year, or with fine which may extend to five thousand rupees, or with both.
- **Wrongful Confinement for Three or More Days: Section 127(3)** provides whoever wrongfully confines any person for three days, or more,
  - Shall be punished with imprisonment of either description for a term which may extend to three years, or with fine which may extend to ten thousand rupees, or with both.
- **Wrongful Confinement for Ten or More Days: Section 127(4)** provides that whoever wrongfully confines any person for ten days or more,
  - Shall be punished with imprisonment of either description for a term which may extend to five years, and shall also be liable to fine which shall not be less than ten thousand rupees.
- **Wrongful Confinement of Person for whose Liberation Writ has been issued: Section 127(5)** provides that whoever keeps any person in wrongful confinement, knowing that a writ for the liberation of that person has been duly issued,
  - Shall be punished with imprisonment of either description for a term which may extend to two years in addition to any term of imprisonment to which he may be liable under any other section of this Chapter and shall also be liable to fine.
- **Wrongful Confinement in Secret: Section 127(6)** provides that whoever wrongfully confines any person in such manner as to indicate an intention that the confinement of such person may not be known to any person interested in the person so confined, or to any public servant, or that the place of such confinement may not be known to or discovered by any such person or public servant as hereinbefore mentioned,
  - Shall be punished with imprisonment of either description for a term which may extend to three years in addition to any other punishment to which he may be liable for such wrongful confinement and shall also be liable to fine.

- **Wrongful Confinement to Extort Property, or Constrain to Illegal Act: Section 127(7)** provides that whoever wrongfully confines any person for the purpose of extorting from the person confined, or from any person interested in the person confined, any property or valuable security or of constraining the person confined or any person interested in such person to do anything illegal or to give any information which may facilitate the commission of an offence, shall be punished with imprisonment of either description for a term which may extend to three years, and shall also be liable to fine.
- **Wrongful Confinement to Extort Confession, or Compel Restoration of Property: Section 127(8)** provides that whoever wrongfully confines any person for the purpose of extorting from the person confined or any person interested in the person confined any confession or any information which may lead to the detection of an offence or misconduct, or for the purpose of constraining the person confined or any person interested in the person confined to restore or to cause the restoration of any property or valuable security or to satisfy any claim or demand, or to give information which may lead to the restoration of any property or valuable security, shall be punished with imprisonment of either description for a term which may extend to three years, and shall also be liable to fine.

DIFFERENCE BETWEEN WRONGFUL RESTRAINT AND WRONGFUL CONFINEMENT

Wrongful Restraint	Wrongful Confinement
Wrongful restraint is an obstructing a person from proceeding in a direction in which a person has a right to move or proceed.	Wrongful confinement is preventing a person to move in any direction by keeping him within circumscribing limits.
It is defined under Section 126(1) of BNS. Punishment: Imprisonment to one month, or fine of Rs. 5000, or with both.	It is defined under Section 127(1) of the BNS. Punishment: Imprisonment to one year, or fine of Rs. 5,000, or with both.
It is comparatively less serious offence as restraint is not in all the directions.	It is a serious offence as compared to wrongful restraint completely obstructing the liberty to move.
Wrongful restraint is a genus, meaning it is a generic term, a wider term.	Wrongful Confinement is a species as it is a type of wrongful restraint.
It is partial restraint. The person can move to any other direction.	It is complete or total restraint. The person, even if he wants, can not move in any other direction.

CRIMINAL FORCE AND ASSAULT

INTRODUCTION

Criminal force and assault are critical concepts within the framework of the Bharatiya Nyay Sanhita, 2023 that address the unlawful use of force and its various manifestations. These provisions are designed to safeguard individuals from physical harm and ensure their personal security.

Section 128 to 136 of BNS defines and deals with the offences of Criminal Force and Assault.

COMPARATIVE CHART OF THE BNS AND IPC		
Bharatiya Nyaya Sanhita, 2023 (BNS)	**Title**	**Indian Penal Code, 1860 (IPC)**
Section 128	Force	Section 349
Section 129	Criminal Force	Section 350
Section 130	Assault	Section 351
Section 131	Punishment for assault or criminal force otherwise than on grave provocation	Section 352
Section 132	Assault or criminal force to deter public servant from discharge of his duty	Section 353
Section 133	Assault or criminal force with intent to dishonor person, otherwise than on grave provocation	Section 355
Section 134	Assault or criminal force in attempt to commit theft of property carried by a person	Section 356
Section 135	Assault or criminal force in attempt to wrongfully confine a person	Section 357
Section 136	Assault or criminal force on grave provocation	Section 358

CHANGES IN BNS IN COMPARISON TO IPC

Section 131 of BNS corresponding to Section 352 of the IPC has been changes as follows:

- Amount of fine has been **enhanced** from **'five hundred rupees to one thousand rupees'.**

Section 135 of BNS corresponding to Section 357 of the IPC has been changes as follows:

- Amount of fine has been **enhanced** from **'one thousand rupees to five thousand rupees'.**

Section 136 of BNS corresponding to Section 358 of the IPC has been changes as follows:

- Amount of fine has been **enhanced** from **'two hundred rupees to one thousand rupees'.**

FORCE

- **Section 128** of BNS defines Force. A person is said to use force to another if he:
  - Causes motion, change of motion, or cessation of motion to that other, or
  - Causes to any substance such motion, or change of motion, or cessation of motion as brings that substance into contact with any part of that other's body, or with anything which that other is wearing or carrying, or with anything so situated that such contact affects that other's sense of feeling:

  Provided that the person causing the motion, or change of motion, or cessation of motion, causes that motion, change of motion, or cessation of motion in one of the three ways hereinafter described:

- **First:** By his own bodily power.
- **Secondly:** By disposing of any substance in such a manner that the motion or change or cessation of motion takes place without any further act of any other person or on the part of any other person.
- **Thirdly:** By inducing any animal to move on his part, to change its motion, or to cease to move.

- The force as defined in clause one contemplates the presence of the person to whom it is used. In other words, it takes into consideration both the presence of the person using the force and the person being used against.

CRIMINAL FORCE

- **Section 129** of BNS defines Criminal Force. It refers to the use of force against another person without their consent, and it must be used in a way that is intended to cause harm or apprehension.
- As per **Section 129,** whoever
  - Intentionally uses force to any person,
  - Without that person's consent,
    - In order to the committing of any offence, or
    - Intending by the use of such force to cause, or
    - Knowing it to be likely or use of such force he will cause injury, fear or annoyance to the person to whom the force is used, is said to use criminal force to that other.
- Criminal force is often a component of more serious offences, such as assault or battery, where it is combined with other elements like the intention to commit a specific crime.
- This section provides that force becomes criminal:
  - When it is used without consent and in order to the committing of an offence, or
  - When it is intentionally used to cause injury, fear or annoyance to another to whom the force is used.
  - To attract the definition of criminal force under **Section 129** of BNS there must be intentional use of force on any person, without that person's consent.
  - Such force must have been used to commit an offence, or with the intention of causing, or with knowledge that it is likely to cause, injury, fear or annoyance to the person on whom the force is used.
  - The term criminal force includes what in English law is called 'battery'.
- **Illustrations**
  - A incites a dog to spring upon Z, without Z's consent. Here, if A intends to cause injury, fear or annoyance to Z, he uses criminal force to Z.
  - Z is riding in a palanquin. A, intending to rob Z, seizes the pole and stops the palanquin. Here A has caused cessation of motion to Z, and he has done this by his own bodily power. A has therefore used force to Z; and as A has acted thus intentionally, without Z's consent, in order to the commission of an offence. A has used criminal force to Z.
  - 'A' intentionally pulls up a woman's veil. Here A intentionally uses force to her, and if he does so without her consent intending or knowing it to be likely that he may thereby injure, frighten or annoy her, he has used criminal force to her.

ASSAULT

Assault is a legal term used to describe an intentional act by one person that creates an apprehension of imminent harmful or offensive contact in another person. Unlike battery, which involves actual physical contact, assault is primarily concerned with the threat or fear of such contact. In most jurisdictions, assault is considered both a civil wrong (tort) and a criminal offence.

The Bharatiya Nyaya Sanhita, 2023 (BNS) deals with the provision of assault and its aggravated forms under **Section 130 to 136.** [Earlier, SEc-tion 351 to 358 of IPC]

ESSENTIAL INGREDIENTS OF ASSAULT

(**Note:** ***Section 130*** *of BNS corresponds to* ***Section 351*** *of the IPC*)

- **Section 130** provides that whoever makes any:
  - Gesture, or
  - Any preparation

  intending or knowing it to be likely that such gesture or preparation will cause any person present to apprehend that the person who makes that gesture or preparation is about to use criminal force to that person, is said to commit an assault.
- **Explanation** to **Section 130** provides that mere words do not amount to an assault. But the words which a person uses may give to his gestures or preparation such a meaning as may make those gestures or preparations amount to an assault.
- **Essential Ingredients:** The following essentials must be met for an act to be considered assault:
  - The accused must make a gesture or prepare to use criminal force.
  - The gesture or preparation must occur in the presence of the intended victim.
  - The accused must have known or intended to cause the victim to fear that criminal force would be used against them.
  - The victim must have genuinely feared that criminal force would be used against them.
- **Illustrations**
  - A shakes his fist at Z, intending or knowing it to be likely that he may thereby cause Z to believe that A is about to strike Z. A has committed an assault.
  - A begins to unloose the muzzle of a ferocious dog, intending or knowing it to be likely that he may thereby cause Z to believe that he is about to cause the dog to attack Z. A has committed an assault upon Z.
  - A takes up a stick, saying to Z, "I will give you a beating". Here, though the words used by A could in no case amount to an assault, and though the mere gesture, unaccompanied by any other circumstances, might not amount to an assault, the gesture explained by the words may amount to an assault.
- In the case of **Muneshwar Bux Singh v. State Through Raghunandan Prasad, (1955)**, the Court decided that an individual cannot be found guilty of assault if his actions or preparations do not raise the possibility of injury to another person.
- In the case of **AC Kama v. HF Morgan, (1864)** the Court decided that "only words" cannot constitute an attack if they manifestly indicate that using force was not the intended outcome.

Punishments for Assault and Criminal Force and Aggravated Forms

(**Note:** ***Sections 131, 132, 133, 134, 135 and 136*** *correspond to* ***Sections 352, 353, 355, 356, 357 and 358*** *of the IPC, respectively*)

- **Punishment for Assault and Criminal Force: Section 131** of BNS provides that whoever assaults or uses criminal force to any person otherwise than on grave and sudden provocation given by that person shall be punished with imprisonment or three minutes or fine, or both.

- **Assault on Public Servant: Section 132** of BNS provides that Assault on a public servant under Section 132 BNS occurs when a person assaults or uses criminal force on any person being a public servant in the execution of his duty. The intent might be to prevent or deter the public servant from discharging his duty.
  - The punishment includes imprisonment for a term that may extend to two years, a fine, or both.
  - **Example:** Physically obstructing a police officer from performing their duty during an arrest or investigation.
- **Intent to Dishonour otherwise than on Grave Provocation: Section 133** of BNS provides that Assault with the intent to dishonor under Section 133 BNS involves assaulting or using criminal force to any person intending to dishonour that person, other than on grave and sudden provocation given by that person.
  - The punishment includes imprisonment for a term that may extend to two years, a fine, or both.
  - **Example:** Engaging in an act that humiliates or disrespects an individual in public with the intention to cause dishonor.
- **Attempted Theft: Section 134** of BNS provides that assault or criminal force in attempting to commit theft under Section 134 BNS involves assaulting or using force while attempting to commit theft on any property carried by a person.
  - The punishment includes imprisonment for a term that may extend to two years, a fine, or both.
  - **Example:** Trying to forcefully snatch a bag or wallet from a person with the intent to steal.
- **Assault or Criminal Force in an Attempt to Wrongfully Confine a Person: Section 135** of BNS deals with assault or criminal force in an attempt to wrongfully confine a person.
  - The punishment includes imprisonment for a term that may extend to one year, a fine that may extend to five thousand rupees, or both.
  - **Example:** Restraining someone against their will, restricting their freedom of movement without legal justification.
- **Grave and Sudden Provocation: Section 136** of BNS provides that Assault on grave and sudden provocation under Section 136 BNS occurs when a person assaults or uses criminal force on another due to provocation provided by that person.
  - The punishment includes simple imprisonment for a term that may extend to one month, a fine that may extend to one thousand rupees, or both.
  - **Example:** Reacting violently in the heat of the moment to an immediate and serious provocation, such as a sudden physical attack.

❖❖❖

Chapter 14

KIDNAPPING AND ABDUCTION

INTRODUCTION

Kidnapping and abduction are serious offences under criminal law, often involving the unlawful taking or confinement of an individual against their will. These acts not only violate an individual's personal liberty but also instill fear and insecurity within society. Kidnapping typically involves the forcible removal of a person, particularly a child or someone of unsound mind, from their lawful guardianship. On the other hand, abduction refers to the act of compelling or deceiving a person to move from one place to another.

The Bharatiya Nyaya Sanhita, 2023 (BNS) provides specific provisions to address these crimes, outlining their definitions and legal consequences. **Section 137 to 146** of the BNS (Earlier, Section 359 to 374 of the Indian Penal Code, 1872) deals with the 'Kidnapping and Abduction'.

COMPARATIVE CHART OF THE BNS AND IPC

Bharatiya Nyaya Sanhita, 2023(BNS)	Title	Indian Penal Code, 1860 (IPC)
Section 137	Kidnapping	Section 359
	Kidnapping from India	Section 360
	Kidnapping from lawful guardianship	Section 361
Section 137(2)	Punishment for kidnapping	Section 363
Section 138	Abduction	Section 362
Section 139	Kidnapping or maiming a child for purposes of begging	Section 363A
Section 140	Kidnapping or abducting in order to murder	Section 364
	Kidnapping for ransom etc.	Section 364A
	Kidnapping or abducting with intent secretly and wrongfully to confine person	Section 365
	Kidnapping or abducting in order to subject a person to grievous hurt, slavery, etc.	Section 367
Section 141	Importation of girl from foreign country	Section 366B
Section 142	Wrongfully concealing or keeping in confinement, kidnapped or abducted person	Section 368
Section 143	Trafficking of person	Section 370
Section 144	Exploitation of a trafficked person	Section 370A
Section 145	Habitual dealing in slaves	Section 371
Section 146	Unlawful compulsory labour	Section 374

CHANGES IN BNS IN COMPARISON TO IPC

- **Section 137** of the BNS corresponds to Sections 359, 360, 361, 363 of IPC has been changed as follows:
  - The words "any minor under sixteen years of age if a male, or under eighteen years of age if a female, or any person of unsound mind" have been changed to **any child or any person of unsound mind.**
- **Section 139** corresponds to section 363A of IPC has been changed to following:
  - The "minor" have been changed to "**child**"
  - The "imprisonment of either description for a term which may extend to ten years, and shall also be liable to fine have been changed to **"rigorous imprisonment for a term which shall not be less than ten years but which may extend to imprisonment for life, and shall also be liable to fine."**
  - Punishment by way of maiming a child for the purpose of begging has been enhanced from imprisonment for life to imprisonment which shall not less than 20 years, but which may extend for the remainder of that person's natural life, and with fine.
- **Section 141** corresponds to **Section 366B** of IPC has been changed to following:
  - Section 141 is applicable to both boys and girls.
- **Section 143** corresponds to **Section 370** of IPC has been changed to following:
  - The word "minor" has been changed to "**child**".
- **Section 144** corresponds to **Section 370A** of IPC has been changed to following:
  - The word "minor" has been changed to "child"
  - Maximum imprisonment for sexual exploitation of trafficked child has been increased from **7 years to 10 years**
  - Maximum imprisonment for sexual exploitation of trafficked person has been increased from **7 years to 10 years.**

KIDNAPPING

(Note: ***Section 137*** *of the BNS corresponds to* ***Section 359, 360, 361 and 363*** *of the IPC*)

- As per **Section 137** of BNS, kidnapping are of two types:
  - Kidnapping from India, (**Section 137 (1) (a)**), and
  - Kidnapping from Lawful Guardianship. (**Section 137 (1)(b)**)
- There may be cases in which these two kinds overlap each other. For instance, a minor may be kidnapped from India as well as lawful guardianship.
- A simple reading of the provisions clearly shows that the legislature did not restrict the offence solely to cases where a child is taken from her place of residence; it also applies when the child is removed from the "lawful guardianship".

Kidnapping from India

(Notes: ***Section 137 (1)(a)*** *of the BNS corresponds to Section 360 of the IPC*)

- As per **Section 137(1)(a)** of BNS, whoever conveys any person beyond the limits of India without the consent of that person, or of some person legally authorized to consent on behalf of that person, is said to kidnap that person from India.
- The offence under this section may be committed in respect of any person, male or female, major or minor, irrespective of his nationality by conveying or taking him or her outside the geographical territory of India. To invoke this Section, following three things are to be met:
  - That the person kidnapped was at the time of offence in India.
  - That the person was conveyed beyond the limits of India.
  - Such conveying must be without the consent of that person.
- **Conveying without Consent:** Mere transporting an individual from one location

to another is not illegal. That act becomes criminal if he or she is conveyed without the consent. A person may be so conveyed as much by using force as by inducing him or her to give his or her consent by fraud or deception. Similarly, a consent loses its essential elements if it is given under fear duress, in which case it is submission and not consent.

Kidnapping from Lawful Guardianship

(Notes: ***Section 137 (1)(b)*** *of the BNS corresponds to* ***Section 361*** *of the IPC*)

- **Section 137(1)(b)** of BNS provides that whoever takes or entices:
  - Any child or
  - Any person of unsound mind,

  out of the keeping of the lawful guardian of such minor or person of unsound mind, without the consent of such guardian, is said to kidnap such minor or person from lawful guardianship.
- **Explanation:** The words "lawful guardian" in this section include any person lawfully entrusted with the care or custody of such minor or other person. The Explanation is intended to extend the protection given to parents to any person lawfully entrusted with the care or custody of the minor.
- The offence under this section may be committed in respect of either a minor or a person of unsound mind.
  - To kidnap an adult person of sound mind, therefore, would not amount to an offence under it. It may fall under Abduction.
- **Essentials:** The essential elements that are required for an act to be called as an offence under this section are:
  - A person must take or entice another person.
  - The person who is taken must be either a child, or a person of unsound mind.
  - The taking of the person must take place out of the lawful guardian who has the authority over that person.
  - There must not be any consent of the lawful guardian in the process of taking or enticing the person.
- **Takes or Entices**: In order to prove an offence under this section, the prosecution must show that the accused took some active part in the victim's leaving the guardians' custody and taking shelter with him. Without taking or enticing, there can be no kidnapping. Simply permitting or allowing a child to accompany a person will not amount to the offence. The word 'takes' implies absence of desire of the person taken.
- The Supreme Court considered the interpretation of expression 'takes or entices' in **S Varadarajan v. State of Madras, (1962) and State of Haryana v. Rajaram (1972)**
  - The expression 'takes' does not necessarily connote taking by force, and it is not necessary in such cases that force, actual or constructive, should be used as the only means of causing a person to go. 'Taking' in this section necessarily involves bodily removal.
  - A person who allows such a minor who is already out of the keeping of the guardian to accompany him commits no offence under Section 363 of the IPC (**Section 137 of BNS**).
- In **Chajju Ram v. State of Punjab (1968)** it was held that the offence of 'taking' is complete as soon as the minor is actually taken out of the custody of his or her guardian. The distance to which the minor is being taken away is immaterial.
- 'Taking' need not be constituted by a single act. A whole series of acts might together constitute the process of taking. When an actual taking has been completed is a question of fact. In **Deep Chand v. State (2000)**, where two girls were alleged to have been kidnapped from lawful guardians categorically stated that they persuaded the accused to take them for an outing, the accused was held not liable.

- **Takes or Entices an Unsound Mind**: If the person kidnapped is normally of sound mind but is made unconscious from poisoning, such a person cannot be said to be of unsound mind. For example, a person under anesthetic for an operation can hardly be said to be of unsound mind.
  - Where a girl aged 20 years had been made unconscious from *dhatura* poisoning when she was taken away, it was held that she could not be said to be a person of unsound mind, and the person taking her away could not be guilty of kidnapping.
  - The offence of kidnapping is not a continuing offence.
- **Without the Consent of Such Guardian:** In an offence of kidnapping, the consent of a person kidnapped is immaterial. What is material is the absence of the element of consent of the guardian. It is only the guardian's consent which takes the case out of purview of **Section 137** of BNS.
  - Moreover, the consent of the guardian after commission of offence would be of no value.
  - **Exception:** This section does not extend to the act of any person who in good faith believes himself to be the father of an illegitimate child, or who in good faith believes himself to be entitled to the lawful custody of such child, unless such act is committed for an immoral or unlawful purpose.
- **Father cannot be Guilty of Kidnapping:** In **Ashok Kumar v. State of Odisha (2003)**, the accused husband was charged with forcibly entering into House of his father-in-law and taking away minor child of the accused from custody of his wife.The court held that the father being natural guardian of a minor under Hindu law and since he was not specifically prohibited by court order not to have custody of his child, no prima facie case against his was made out of and therefore Cognizance of offence under **Section 361 (Section 137 of BNS)** against him was liable to be quashed.
- **Punishment for Kidnapping : Section 137(2)** provides that whoever kidnaps any person from India or from lawful guardianship, shall be punished with
  - Imprisonment of either description for a term which may extend to seven years, and shall also be liable to fine.
- In **Dutta Pradhan v. State of Orissa, (1985)**, where a married girl of 17 years of age was forcibly carried away by the accused and his companions from a jungle where she had gone with others to collect *mohua* flowers with a view to marrying her according to their tribal custom, it was held that such a custom, if any, could apply only to the cases of young unmarried men and women and had no application to to legalize the kidnapping of a married minor girl out of the keeping of her lawful guardian.
- In the case of **Kuldeep K. Mahato v. State of Bihar (1998)**, both the accused and the victim, a child, were living in the same village. The accused had allegedly eloped the victim when he went to a market and raped her. For the elopement, the accused first compelled the victim to sit in a tempo and kept her silent using a dagger. An FIR was lodged against the accused under Sections 363, 366 and 376 of the IPC. The Defence argued that the victim of her own free will came with the accused. However, the prosecution proved how the victim was threatened in tempo by presenting oral evidence. The Supreme Court upheld the conviction under Section 363 of the IPC.
- **Kidnapping or Maiming a Child for Purpose of Begging : Section 139** of BNS (Section 363A of the IPC) provides as follows:
  - **Section 139(1)** provides that whoever kidnaps any child or, not being the lawful guardian of such child, obtains the custody of the child, in order that such child may be employed or used for the purposes of begging shall be punishable with

- Rigorous imprisonment for a term which shall not be less than ten years but which may extend to imprisonment for life, and shall also be liable to fine.

- **Section 139(2)** provides that whoever maims any child in order that such child may be employed or used for the purposes of begging shall be punishable with
  - Imprisonment which shall not be less than twenty years, but which may extend to life which shall mean imprisonment for the remainder of that person's natural life, and with fine.
- **Section 139(3)** provides that where any person, not being the lawful guardian of a child employs or uses such child for the purposes of begging, it shall be presumed, unless the contrary is proved, that he kidnapped or otherwise obtained the custody of such child in order that such child might be employed or used for the purposes of begging.
- **Section 139(4)** provides that in this Section "begging" means:
  - Soliciting or receiving alms in a public place, whether under the pretense of singing, dancing, fortune telling, performing tricks or selling articles or otherwise;
  - Entering on any private premises for the purpose of soliciting or receiving alms;
  - Exposing or exhibiting, with the object of obtaining or extorting alms, any sore, wound, injury, deformity or disease, whether of himself or of any other person or of an animal;
  - Using such a child as an exhibit for the purpose of soliciting or receiving alms.

OTHER PROVISIONS RELATED TO KIDNAPPING AND ABDUCTION

- Kidnapping or abducting in order to murder or ransom etc. (**Section 140** of the BNS)
- Importation of girl or boy from foreign country (**Section 141** of the BNS)
- Wrongfully concealing or keeping in confinement, kidnapped or abducted person (**Section 142** of the BNS)

ABDUCTION

(**Note:** ***Section 138*** *of the BNS corresponds to* ***Section 362*** *of the IPC*)

- **Section 138** of BNS deals with Abduction. Abduction is not a substantive offence in itself unless coupled with some specific actions.
- It has been provided that whoever by force compels, or by any deceitful means induces, any person to go from any place, is said to abduct that person.
- The section requires following two requisites:
  - Forceful compulsion or inducement by deceitful means
  - The object of such compulsion or inducement must be the going of a person from any place.
- The expression "deceitful means" includes a misleading statement. It is, simply stating, a matter of intention. The intention of the accused is the basis and gravamen of the charge. The volition, the intention and conduct of the woman do not determine the offence.
- **Bahadur Ali v. King Emperor, (1923)**, in this case, the accused misrepresented himself as a police constable and kept a girl in his house for a certain time regarding money. The court in this case held that his act amounted to abduction.
- In the offence of abduction, there must be on the part of the offender, either an element of compulsion by force or an element of inducement by deceitful means. The word 'force' has the same meaning as given under Section 349 of the Sanhita. To induce means to lead into; there must

be an active suggestion on the part of the abductor making the victim agree to move to a place where he would not go but for this suggestion.

- The expression 'deceitful means' suggests that the means employed by the offender must be such as to practice deception on the victim. The expression has a wide import and includes a misleading statement.
- Mere abduction has not been made punishable under any section of the Sanhita. In other words, abduction by itself is not an offence.
- It is punishable only when it is coupled with one or the other intent as stated in certain subsequent sections. In cases of abduction committed by compulsion by force, actual force must be used and a mere threat of use of force is not enough.

DIFFERENCE BETWEEN KIDNAPPING AND ABDUCTION

Kidnapping	Abduction
Offence of kidnapping is defined under Section 137 of BNS.	Abduction is defined under Section 138 of BNS.
Kidnapping is committed only in respect of a child or a person of unsound mind.	Abduction in respect of a person of any age.
In kidnapping, the person kidnapped is removed out of lawful guardianship. A child without a guardian cannot be kidnapped.	Abduction has reference exclusively to the person abducted.
In kidnapping, consent of the person taken or enticed is immaterial.	In abduction, consent of the person moved, if freely and voluntarily given, condones abduction.
It is not a continuing offence. The offence is completed as soon as the minor is removed from the custody of the guardian.	It is a continuing offence. The offence continues as long as the abducted person's place continues changing.
Kidnapping is a substantive offence in itself.	Abduction simpliciter is not a substantive offence. To make it punishable it must be coupled with one or the other intent as stated in certain subsequent sections.

TRAFFICKING OF PERSON

(**Note:** ***Section 143*** *of the BNS corresponds to* ***Section 370*** *of the IPC*)

- **Section 143** of the BNS provides that whoever, for the purpose of exploitation, recruits, transports, harbours, transfers, or receives, a person or persons, by:
  - Using threats; or
  - Using force, or any other form of coercion; or
  - By abduction; or
  - By practicing fraud, or deception; or
  - By abuse of power; or
  - By inducement, including the giving or receiving of payments or benefits, in order to achieve the consent of any person having control over the person recruited, transported, harboured, transferred or received, commits the offence of trafficking.
- **Explanation 1** to **Section 143** provides that the expression "exploitation" shall include any act of physical exploitation or other form of sexual exploitation, slavery or practices similar to slavery, servitude, or the forced removal of organs.
- **Explanation 2** to **Section 143** provides that the consent of the victim is immaterial in determination of the offence of trafficking.
- In **People's Union for Democratic Rights v. Union of India**, (1982) , the Hon'ble Supreme Court defined forced labour, while discussing the scope of **Article 23** of the Constitution of India, stated:
- "The word force must therefore be construed to include not only physical or legal force but also force arising from the compulsion of economic circumstances which leaves no

choice of alternatives to a person in want and compels him to provide labour or service even though the remuneration received for it is less than the minimum wage."

- **Punishment for Trafficking: Section 143(2)** provides the punishment of trafficking as whoever commits the offence of trafficking shall be punished with
  - Rigorous imprisonment for a term which shall not be less than seven years, but which may extend to ten years, and shall also be liable to fine.
- **Punishment for Trafficking of Multiple Persons:** According to **Section 143(3)**, where the offence involves the trafficking of more than one person, it shall be punishable with
  - Rigorous imprisonment for a term which shall not be less than ten years but which may extend to imprisonment for life, and shall also be liable to fine.
- **Punishment for Trafficking of Minor:** According to **Section 143(4),** where the offence involves the trafficking of a child, it shall be punishable with
  - Rigorous imprisonment for a term which shall not be less than ten years, but which may extend to imprisonment for life, and shall also be liable to fine.
- **Punishment when Police Officer or Public Servant is Involved:** According to **Section 143(7)**, when a public servant or a police officer is involved in the trafficking of any person, then such public servant or police officer shall be punished with
  - Imprisonment for life, which shall mean imprisonment for the remainder of that person's natural life and shall also be liable to fine.

Exploitation of a Trafficked Person

(Note: ***Section 144*** *of the BNS corresponds to* ***Section 370A*** *of the IPC*)

- **Section 144(1)** provides that whoever, knowingly or having reason to believe that a child below the age of eighteen years has been trafficked, engages such child for sexual exploitation in any manner, shall be punished with
  - Rigorous imprisonment for a term which shall not be less than five years, but which may extend to ten years, and shall also be liable to fine.
- According to **Section 144 (2),** whoever, knowingly by or having reason to believe that a person has been trafficked, engages such person for sexual exploitation in any manner, shall be punished with
  - Rigorous imprisonment for a term which shall not be less than three years, but which may extend to seven years, and shall also be liable to fine.

Habitual Dealing in Slaves

(Note: ***Section 145*** *of the BNS corresponds to* ***Section 371*** *of the IPC*)

- According to **Section 145** of BNS, Whoever habitually imports, exports, removes, buys, sells, traffics or deals in slaves, shall be punished with
  - Imprisonment for life, or with imprisonment of either description for a term not exceeding ten years, and shall also be liable to fine.
- This section provides for the punishment of the slave trader who is habitually engaged in the traffic of buying and selling human beings. The preceding section dealt with the casual offender.

Unlawful Compulsory Labour

(Note: ***Section 146*** *of the BNS corresponds to* ***Section 372*** *of the IPC*)

Whoever unlawfully compels any person to labour against the will of that person, shall be punished with imprisonment of either description for a term which may extend to one year, or with fine, or with both.

❖❖❖

Chapter 15

OFFENCES AGAINST THE STATE

INTRODUCTION

Bharatiya Nyaya Sanhita, 2023 (BNS) deals with offences against the State under **Chapter VII Sections 147 to 158** (Earlier, Chapter VI from Section 121 to 130 of the IPC). The purpose of these provisions is to ensure the safety of the State as a whole. Strict penalties, like life imprisonment or the death penalty, can be applied to those who violate the laws in order to protect the state's existence, offences against the State as well as the government to disturb the public tranquility, public order and national integration.

Offences Against the State Fall into the Following Groups

- Waging, or attempting or conspiring to wage, or collecting men and ammunition to wage war against the Government of India falls under **Sections 147, 148, 149, 150** of BNS.
- As per **section 151** of BNS, Assaulting President, or Governor of a State with intent to compel or restrain the exercise of any lawful power.
- As per **section 152** of BNS, Act endangering sovereignty, unity, integrity of india.
- As per **section 153, 154** of BNS, Waging war against any foreign state at peace with Government of India or committing depredations on the territories of such power.
- As per **sections 156, 157, 158** of BNS, Permitting or aiding or negligently suffering the escape of, or rescuing or harboring, a State prisoner.

COMPARATIVE CHART OF THE BNS AND IPC

Bharatiya Nyaya Sanhita, 2023 (BNS)	Title	Indian Penal Code, 1860 (IPC)
Section 147	Waging, or attempting to wage war, or abetting waging of war, against the Government of India	Section 121
Section 148	Conspiracy to commit offences punishable by section 147	Section 121A
Section 149	Collecting arms etc with intention of waging war against the Government of India	Section 122
Section 150	Concealing with intent to facilitate design to wage war	Section 123
Section 151	Assaulting president governor etc with intent to compel or restrain the exercise of any lawful power	Section 124
Section 152	Act endangering sovereignty, unity, integrity of india	Section 124A
Section 153	Waging war against any foreign state at peace with Government of India	Section 125

Section 154	Committing depredation on territories of foreign state at peace with the Government of India	Section 126
Section 155	Receiving property taken by war or depredation mentioned in section 153 and 154	Section 127
Section 156	Public servant voluntarily allowing prisoner of state or war to escape	Section 128
Section 157	Public servant negligently suffering such prisoner to escape	Section 129
Section 158	Aiding escape of, rescuing or harboring such prisoner	Section 130

CHANGES IN BNS IN COMPARISONS TO IPC

- **Section 148** of the BNS corresponding to Section 121A of the IPC has been changed as follows:
  - Section 148 used the expression '**whoever within or without and beyond India**' instead of the expression 'within or without India'.
- **Offence of Sedition has been removed** from the BNS, a new offence under **Section 152** has been introduced as:
  - **'Act endangering sovereignty, unity, integrity of India'.**
- **Section 153** corresponding to Section 125 of the IPC has been changed as follows:
  - The scope of Section 153 has expanded as **'waging war against the government of any foreign state at peace with Government of India'** is also an offence.

Waging, or Attempting to Wage War, or Abetting Waging of War, Against the Government of India

(**Notes:** ***Section 147*** *of the BNS corresponds to* ***Section 121*** *of the IPC*)

- **Section 147 of BNS** defines, whoever,
  - Wages war against the Government of India or
  - Attempts to wage such war, or
  - Abets the waging of such war, shall be punished with:
    - Death, or imprisonment for life and shall also be liable to fine.
- **For Example**: A joins an insurrection against the Government of India. A has committed the offence defined in this section.
- In a republic, sovereignty vests in the people of the country and the lawfully elected government is simply the representative and a manifestation of the sovereign, that is, the people. Thus, the expression "Government of India", as appearing in **Section 147** of BNS, must be held to mean the State or interchangeably the people of the country as the repository of the sovereignty of India which is manifested and expressed through the elected Government as held in the case of **Mohd. Ajmal Amir Kasab v. State of Maharashtra (2012).**
- In **State (NCT of Delhi) v. Navjot Sandhu,** Supreme Court held that to constitute an offence of waging war under Section 121 of the IPC, the intention and purpose of the warlike operations directed against the government is *sine qua non*.
- The concept of 'waging war" should not be stretched too far. A balanced and realistic approach should be maintained while construing the offence committed, to find out whether it amounts to waging war against the State.

Conspiracy to Commit Offences Punishable by Section 147

(**Notes:** ***Section 148*** *of the BNS corresponds to* ***Section 121A*** *of the IPC*)

- **Section 148 of BNS** defines, whoever within or without India conspires to commit offences commit any of the offences punishable by **Section 147 of BNS**, or conspires to overawe, by means of criminal force or the show of criminal force, the Central Government or any State Government shall be punished with imprisonment for life, or with imprisonment of either description which may extend to ten years, and shall also be liable to fine.

- To constitute a conspiracy under this section, it is not necessary that any act or illegal omission shall take place in pursuance thereof.
- Explanation to **Section 148 of BNS** clarifies that it is not necessary that any act or illegal omission should take place pursuant to the conspiracy, in order to constitute the said offence. Thus, the criminal act done by the deceased terrorists in order to capture the Parliament House is an act that amounts to waging or attempting to wage war.
- The words 'conspires to overawe by means of criminal force or the show of criminal force, the Central Government, or any State Government' in this section clearly embrace not merely a conspiracy to raise a general insurrection, but also a conspiracy to overawe the Central Government or any State Government by the organization of a serious riot or a large and tumultuous unlawful assembly.

Collecting Arms, etc., with Intention of Waging War Against the Government of India

(Notes: *Section 149* *of the BNS corresponds to* *Section 122* *of the IPC*)

- **Section 149 of BNS,** Whoever collects men, arms or ammunition or otherwise prepares to wage war with the intention of either waging or being prepared to wage war against the "Government of India, shall be punished with imprisonment for life or imprisonment of either description for a term not exceeding ten years, "and shall also be liable to fine.
- This section is intended to put down with a heavy hand any preparation to wage war against the Government of India. The act made punishable by this section cannot be considered attempts; they are in truth preparations made for committing the offence of waging war.
- Preparation consists of devising or arranging the means or measures necessary for the commission of the offence. It differs widely from the attempt which is the direct movement towards the commission after preparations are made.

Concealing with Intent to Facilitate Design to Wage War

(Notes: *Section 150* *of the BNS corresponds to* *Section 123* *of the IPC*)

- As per **Section 150 of BNS,** Whoever, by any act, or by any illegal omission, conceals intent to facilitate the existence of a design to wage war against the Government of India, intending by such concealment to facilitate, or knowing it to be likely that such concealment will facilitate, the waging of such war, shall be punished with
  - imprisonment of either description for a term which may extend to ten years, and shall also be liable to fine.

Assaulting President, Governor etc., with Intent to Compel or Restrain the Exercise of any Lawful Power

(Notes: *Section 151* *of the BNS corresponds to* *Section 124* *of the IPC*)

- **Section 151 of BNS** provides that whoever, with the intention of inducing or compelling the President of India, or the "Governor of any State, to exercise or refrain from exercising in any manner any of the lawful power of such president or governor, assault or wrongfully restrained or attempts wrongfully to restrain or overawes by means of criminal force or the show of criminal force or attempts so to overawe, such president or governor shall be punished with:
  - Imprisonment of either description for a term which may extend to seven years, and also shall be liable to find.
- This section is an amplification of the third clause of **Section 148 of BNS**. It punishes severe assaults, etc., made on high officers of Government.

Endangering Sovereignty, Unity and Integrity of India

(Notes: *Section 152* of the *BNS corresponds to* *Section 124A* *of the IPC*)

- Section 124-A of the IPC was highly controversial, with numerous petitions challenging its constitutional validity. The state argues that sedition falls under 'public order' in Article 19(2), but balancing this with freedom of speech is challenging for the Court. There are series of cases from **Tara Singh v. The State, (1951)** to **Kedarnath Singh v. State of Bihar (1962)** to **S.G Vombatkare v. Union of India**, **(2022)** at present, the sedition has seen the twists and turns in its constitutionality, inclusive of the 1951 amendment.
- Recently, the Supreme Court, in **S.G. Vombatkare case**, has stayed the operation of **Section 124-A** of IPC, as a consequence of increasing petitions challenging the constitutionality of the law, the court has suspended all the proceedings, and trials with regard to **Section 124-A**, the Court had put a restriction on registration of any fresh FIR under the said law. The Court is of the opinion that the rigors of Section 124A of the IPC are not in tune with the current social issues and permitted reconsideration of the provision.
- The government asserts that it did not penalise the offence of sedition under the Bhartiya Nyaya Sanhita, 2023 which replaced IPC. This statement is colourably in-line with the public demand and the Supreme Court's order. However, in order to safeguard the sovereignty, unity and integrity of India, the new law penalise under **Section 152** of the BNS reads as follows:
- **Section 152** of the BNS provides that whoever, purposely or knowingly,
  - By words, either spoken or written, or
  - By signs, or
  - By visible representation, or
  - By electronic communication or
  - By use of financial mean, or otherwise,
- Excites or attempts to excite, secession or armed rebellion or subversive activities, or
- Encourages feelings of separatist activities or endangers sovereignty or unity and integrity of India; or
- Indulges in or commits any such act shall be punished with:
  - Imprisonment for life or with
  - Imprisonment which may extend to seven years and
  - Shall also be liable to fine.
- **Explanation to Section 152** provides that Comments expressing disapprobation of the measures, or administrative or other action of the Government with a view to obtain their alteration by lawful means without exciting or attempting to excite the activities referred to in this section.

Constitutional Validity of Section 124A Under IPC

- The Supreme Court in the case of **Kedar Nath Singh v. State of Bihar**, **(1962)** held that **Section 124A** is not unconstitutional and opined that only when it is construed that the words, written or spoken, etc, which have the pernicious tendency or intention of creating public disorder or disturbance of law and order the law steps in to prevent such activities in the interest of public order, then only the section strikes the correct balance between individual fundamental rights and the interest of public order.
- The Court also held that a citizen has a right to say or write whatever he likes about the Government, or its measures, by way of criticism or comment, so long as he does not incite people to violence against the Government established by law or with the intention of creating public disorder.
- Furthermore, the object of harm in **Section 124-A** of the IPC is the Government established by law. The Supreme Court defined the 'Government established by law' as the visible symbol of the State

necessary for its continuity and stability, differentiating it from individuals engaged in administrative tasks. This clarity served to define the specific object requiring protection and indicated the level of harm necessary to constitute sedition.

- Article 19(1)(a) includes the right to dissent, and it helps the democracy to grow. Public discussions, including dissents, are encouraged. The Court emphasized that every person has a fundamental right to form his own opinion. The State cannot prevent open discussion and open expression of views, however critical of its own views.
- Any such law like sedition could not restrict the citizen's right to dissent. Moreover, in the case of Balwant Singh, the Supreme Court determined that even chanting slogans like 'Khalistan Zindabad' cannot be restricted, as merely raising such slogans, without causing any disturbance or inciting people to create disorder is not restricted by Article 19(2).
- Futher in several leading judgments the court narrowly and strictly interpreted the effect that the restrictions must cause in order to make them 'reasonable'. Sedition was only allowed when the seditious act was intended to or has the tendency to cause public disorder, since it makes it 'reasonable' under Article 19(2).

Waging War Against any Asiatic Power in Alliance with Government of India

(**Notes:** ***Section 153*** *of the BNS corresponds to* ***Section 125*** *of the IPC*)

- **Section 153 of BNS,** Whoever wages war against the Government of any foreign state at peace with the Government of India or attempts to wage such war, or abets the waging of such war, shall with the Government of India be punished with
  - Imprisonment for life, to which fine may be added, or with
  - Imprisonment of either description for a term which may extend to seven years, to which fine may be added, or
  - With fine.

Committing Depredation on Territories of Power at Peace with Government of India

(**Notes:** ***Section 154*** *of the BNS corresponds to* ***Section 126*** *of the IPC*)

- **Section 154 of BNS,** Whoever commits depredation, or makes preparations to punished with depredation on commit depredation, on the territories of any foreign state at peace with Government of India, shall be the punished with:
  - Imprisonment of either description for a term which may extend to seven years, and
  - Shall also be liable to fine and to forfeiture of any property used or intended to be used in committing such depredation, or acquired by such depredation.

Receiving Property Taken by War or Depredation Mentioned Sections 153-154

(**Notes:** ***Section 155*** *of the BNS corresponds to* ***Section 127*** *of the IPC*)

- **Section 155 of BNS,** Whoever receives any property knowing the same to have been taken in the commission of any of the offences mentioned in **Sections 153 and 154** of BNS, shall be punished with:
  - Imprisonment of either description for a term which may extend to seven years, and
  - Shall also be liable to fine and to forfeiture of the property so received.

Public Servant Voluntarily Allowing Prisoner of State or War to Escape

(**Notes:** ***Section 156*** *of the BNS corresponds to* ***Section 128*** *of the IPC*)

- **Section 156 of BNS,** Whoever, being a public servant and having the custody of any state prisoner or prisoner of war voluntarily allows such prisoner or prisoner of war, voluntarily to escape from any place in which such prisoner is confined, shall be punished with:

- Imprisonment for life, or
- Imprisonment of either description for a term which may extend to ten years, and
- Shall also be liable to fine.

Public Servant Negligently Suffering such Prisoner to Escape

(Notes: ***Section 157*** *of the BNS corresponds to* ***Section 129*** *of the IPC*)

- **Section 157 of BNS,** Whoever, being a public servant and having the custody negligently suffering of any State prisoner or prisoner of war, negligently suffers such such prisoner to escape from any place of confinement in which such prisoner is confined, shall be punished with:
  - Simple imprisonment for a term which may extend to three years, and
  - Shall also be liable to fine.

Aiding Escape of, Rescuing or Harbouring such Prisoner

(Notes: ***Section 158*** *of the BNS corresponds to* ***Section 130*** *of the IPC*)

- **Section 158** provides that whoever knowingly aids or assists any State prisoner or prisoner of war in escaping from lawful custody, or rescues or attempts to rescue any such prisoner, or harbours or conceals any such prisoner who has escaped from lawful custody, or offers or attempts to offer any resistance to the recapture of such prisoner, shall be punished with:
  - Imprisonment for life, or with
  - Imprisonment of either description for a term which may extend to ten years, and
  - Shall also be liable to fine.
- **Explanation to Section 158** provides that a State prisoner or prisoner of war, who is permitted to be at large on his parole within certain limits in India, is said to escape from lawful custody if he goes beyond the limits within which he is allowed to be at large.

❖❖❖

Chapter 16

OFFENCES AGAINST PROPERTY

INTRODUCTION

Human society cannot control its governance without the protection of both people's property and person. The State must step in to prevent violent, nefarious, or fraudulent infringement of property rights.

Offences against property are covered under **Chapter XVII** from **Sections 303 to 334** of the Bharatiya Nyaya Sanhita, 2023 (BNS) (Earlier, Section 378 to 462 of the IPC). Offences relating to property are mainly divided into two parts, namely movable and immovable. Any offence which is committed in regard to any property whether it is movable or immovable is punishable under the provisions of BNS. The basic element common to all these offences is dishonesty. However, the manner in which dishonesty is exercised differs in different cases.

The offences against property has been categorised as follows:

- Theft (**Section 303-307** of the BNS)
- Extortion (**Section 308** of the BNS)
- Robbery and Dacoity (**Section 309-313** of the BNS)
- Criminal Misappropriation of Property (**Section 314- 315** of the BNS)
- Criminal Breach of Trust (**Section 316** of the BNS)
- Receiving Stolen Property (**Section 317** of the BNS)
- Cheating (**Section 318- 319** of the BNS)
- Mischief (**Section 324- 328** of the BNS)
- Criminal Trespass (**Section 329-334** of the BNS)

COMPARATIVE CHART OF THE BNS AND IPC		
Bharatiya Nyaya Sanhita, 2023 (BNS)	**Title**	**Indian Penal Code, 1860 (IPC)**
	THEFT	
Section 303 (1)	Theft	Section 378
Section 303 (2)	Theft **EARLIER TITLE:** (Punishment For Theft)	Section 379
Section 304	Snatching (New added section)	-
Section 305	Theft in a dwelling house, or means of transportation or place of worship etc. **EARLIER TITLE:** (Theft In Dwelling House)	Section 380
Section 306	Theft by clerk or servant of property in possession of master	Section 381
Section 307	Theft after preparation made for causing death, hurt or restraint in order to committing of theft	Section 382

COMPARATIVE CHART OF THE BNS AND IPC		
Bharatiya Nyaya Sanhita, 2023 (BNS)	**Title**	**Indian Penal Code, 1860 (IPC)**
EXTORTION		
Section 308 (1)	Extortion	Section 383
Section 308 (2)	Punishment of Extortion	Section 384
ROBBERY		
Section 309	Robbery	Section 390
Section 309	Robbery **EARLIER TITLE:** (Punishment for robbery)	Section 392
Section 309	Robbery **EARLIER TITLE:** (Attempt to commit robbery)	Section 393
Section 309	Robbery **EARLIER TITLE:** (Voluntarily causing hurt in committing robbery)	Section 394

DACOITY		
Section 310 (1)	Dacoity	Section 391
Section 310 (2)	Dacoity **EARLIER TITLE:** (Punishment for dacoity)	Section 395
Section 310 (3)	Dacoity **EARLIER TITLE:** (dacoity with murder)	Section 396
Section 310 (4)	Dacoity **EARLIER TITLE:** (Making preparation to commit dacoity)	Section 399
Section 310 (5)	Dacoity **EARLIER TITLE:** (Assembling for purpose of committing dacoity)	Section 402
Section 310 (6)	Dacoity **EARLIER TITLE:** (Punishment for belonging to gang of dacoits)	Section 400
Section 311	Robbery, or dacoity, with attempt to cause death or grievous hurt	Section 397
Section 312	Attempt to commit robbery or dacoity when armed with deadly weapon	Section 398
Section 313	Punishment for belonging to gang of robbers, dacoits, etc.	Section 401

CRIMINAL MISAPPROPRIATION OF PROPERTY		
Section 314	Dishonest Misappropriation of Property	Section 403
Section 315	Dishonest Misappropriation of Property Possessed by a Deceased	Section 404

COMPARATIVE CHART OF THE BNS AND IPC		
Bharatiya Nyaya Sanhita, 2023 (BNS)	**Title**	**Indian Penal Code, 1860 (IPC)**
CRIMINAL BREACH OF TRUST		
Section 316 (1)	Criminal Breach of Trust	Section 405
Section 316 (2)	Criminal Breach of Trust **EARLIER TITLE:** (Punishment for criminal breach of trust)	Section 406
Section 316 (3)	Criminal Breach of Trust **EARLIER TITLE:** (Criminal breach of trust by carrier, etc)	Section 407
Section 316 (4)	Criminal Breach of Trust **EARLIER TITLE:** (Criminal breach of trust by clerk or servant)	Section 408
Section 316 (5)	Criminal Breach of Trust **EARLIER TITLE:** (Criminal breach of trust by public servant, or by banker, merchant or agent)	Section 409

STOLEN PROPERTY		
Section 317	Stolen property	Section 410
Section 317(2)	Stolen property **EARLIER TITLE:** (Dishonestly receiving stolen property)	Section 411
Section 317(3)	Stolen property **EARLIER TITLE:** (Dishonestly receiving property stolen in the commission of a dacoity)	Section 412
Section 317(4)	Stolen property **EARLIER TITLE:** (Habitually dealing in stolen property)	Section 413
Section 317(5)	Stolen property **EARLIER TITLE:** (Assisting in concealment of stolen property)	Section 414

CHEATING		
Section 318(1)	Cheating	Section 415
Section 318(2)	Cheating **EARLIER TITLE:** (Punishment for cheating)	Section 417
Section 318(3)	Cheating **EARLIER TITLE:** (Cheating with knowledge that wrongful loss may ensue to person whose interest offender is bound to protect)	Section 418
Section 318(4)	Cheating **EARLIER TITLE:** (Cheating and dishonestly inducing delivery of property)	Section 420
Section 319(1)	Cheating by personation	Section 416
Section 319(2)	Cheating by personation **EARLIER TITLE:** (Punishment of cheating by personation)	Section 419

COMPARATIVE CHART OF THE BNS AND IPC		
Bharatiya Nyaya Sanhita, 2023 (BNS)	**Title**	**Indian Penal Code, 1860 (IPC)**
MISCHIEF		
Section 324	Mischief	Section 425
Section 324(2)	Mischief **EARLIER TITLE:** (Punishment for mischief)	Section 426
Section 324(4)	Mischief **EARLIER TITLE:** (Mischief causing damage to the amount of fifty rupees)	Section 427
Section 324(6)	Mischief **EARLIER TITLE:** (Mischief committed after preparation made for causing death or hurt)	Section 440
Section 325	Mischief by killing or maiming animal	Section 428
		Section 429
Section 326(a)	Mischief by injury, inundation, fire or explosive substance, etc. **EARLIER TITLE:** (Mischief by injury to works of irrigation or by wrongfully diverting water)	Section 430
Section 326(b)	Mischief by injury, inundation, fire or explosive substance, etc. **EARLIER TITLE:** (Mischief by injury to public road,bridge, river or channel)	Section 431
Section 326(c)	Mischief by injury, inundation, fire or explosive substance, etc. **EARLIER TITLE:** (Mischief by causing inundation or obstruction to public drainage attended with damage)	Section 432
Section 326(d)	Mischief by injury, inundation, fire or explosive substance, etc. **EARLIER TITLE:** (Mischief by destroying, moving or rendering less useful a light- house or sea-mark)	Section 433
Section 326(e)	Mischief by injury, inundation, fire or explosive substance, etc. **EARLIER TITLE:** (Mischief by destroying or moving, etc., a land-mark fixed by public authority)	Section 434
Section 326(f)	Mischief by injury, inundation, fire or explosive substance, etc. **EARLIER TITLE:** (Mischief by fire or explosive substance with intent to cause damage to amount of one hundred or (in case of agricultural produce) ten rupees)	Section 435
Section 326(g)	Mischief by injury, inundation, fire or explosive substance, etc. **EARLIER TITLE:** (Mischief by fire or explosive substance with intent to destroy house, etc)	Section 436

COMPARATIVE CHART OF THE BNS AND IPC		
Bharatiya Nyaya Sanhita, 2023 (BNS)	**Title**	**Indian Penal Code, 1860 (IPC)**
Section 329(1)	Criminal Trespass and House Trespass **EARLIER TITLE:** (Criminal Trespass)	Section 441
Section 329(2)	Criminal Trespass and House Trespass **EARLIER TITLE:** (House Trespass)	Section 442
Section 329(3)	Criminal Trespass and House Trespass **EARLIER TITLE:** (Punishment For Criminal Trespass)	Section 447
Section 329(4)	Criminal Trespass and House Trespass **EARLIER TITLE:** (Punishment For House Trespass)	Section 448
Section 330(1)	House Trespass and House breaking **EARLIER TITLE:** (lurking House Trespass)	Section 443
Section 330(2)	House Trespass and House breaking **EARLIER TITLE:** (House breaking)	Section 445
Section 331(1)	Punishment For House Trespass or House Breaking **EARLIER TITLE:** (Punishment For lurking House Trespass or House Breaking)	Section 453

CHANGES IN BNS IN COMPARISON TO IPC

- **Section 303** of the BNS corresponding to **Section 378** of the IPC has changes as follows:
  - The Proviso to Section 303 (2) is **newly added** and in case of second or subsequent conviction of any person under this section, he shall be punished with rigorous imprisonment for a term which shall not be less than one year but which may extend to five years and with fine and **"Community service"** as a punishment has been added under the Proviso of the Section 303 (2).
- **Section 305** of the BNS corresponding to Section 380 of the IPC has changes as follows:
  - The clauses (b), (c), (d) and (e) are added in the provision.
- **Section 308** of the BNS corresponding to **Section 383 to 389** of IPC has been changes as follows:
  - In Section 308(2) of the BNS, the imprisonment for extortion has been **increased** from **three years to seven years.**
- **Section 310** of the BNS corresponding to **Section 391-400** of IPC has been changes as follows:
  - Punishment for dacoity with murder under **Section 310(3)** changes to **'shall not be less than 10 years'.**
- **Section 313** of the BNS corresponding to Section 401 of the IPC has changes as follows:
  - Instead of thieves, the term "robbers" is used.
  - The word "thugs" has been **omitted**.
- **Section 314** of the BNS corresponding to Section 403 of the IPC has changes as follows:
  - **Section 314 of BNS** specifies a **minimum imprisonment of six months and includes a fine** whereas **Section 403 of IPC** does not mandate a minimum term and is less explicit about fines.
- **Section 316(2)** of the BNS corresponding to **Section 406** of the IPC has been changes as follows:

- Section 316(2) **increases** the maximum imprisonment term from **three years to five years** for general criminal breach of trust.

- **Section 317(1)** of the BNS corresponding to **Section 410** of the IPC has been changes as follows:
  - The term cheating has been added in Section 317(1).
- **Section 318(2)** of the BNS corresponding to **Section 417** of the IPC has been changes as follows:
  - Punishment for cheating has been **increased** from **one year to three years.**
- **Section 318(3)** of the BNS corresponding to **Section 418** of the IPC has been changes as follows:
  - Punishment by way of imprisonment for cheating a person whose interest the offender was bound to protect has been **increased** from **three years to five years.**
- **Section 319(3)** of the BNS corresponding to **Section 419** of the IPC has been changes as follows:
  - Punishments for cheating by personation are **increased** from **three years to five years.**
- **Section 324(2)** of the BNS corresponding to **Section 426** of the IPC has been changes as follows:
  - **Section 324(2) of BNS increases** the upper limit of imprisonment for general mischief from **three months to six months.**
- **Section 324(3)** is a newly added provision.
  - covering, "damage to government property with up to one year of imprisonment".
- **Section 324(4)** of the BNS corresponding to **Section 427** of the IPC has been changes as follows:
  - The monetary limit for the value of loss or damage caused by mischief is **increased** from **fifty to twenty thousand or more but less than one lakh.**
- **Section 325** of the BNS corresponding to **Section 428 and 429** of the IPC has been changes as follows:
  - Firstly, the maximum imprisonment term under Section 325 **increased** from **two years to five years** .
  - Secondly, **Section 325 of BNS** has a broader scope, encompassing any animal, whereas **Sections 428 and 429 of IPC** specify value thresholds and particular types of animals, such as cattle or animals valued at fifty rupees or more.
  - Under Section 325 irrespective of the value of animal killed, poisoned, maimed or rendered unless by mischief, punishment upto 5 years can be imposed.
- **Section 327** of the BNS corresponding to **Section 437** of the IPC has been changes as follows:
  - **Section 327 of BNS** introduces formal changes and expands the scope of mischief, explicitly including "rail" and "aircraft," which are absent in **Section 437 of IPC**.
  - It differentiates between standard mischief and that involving fire or explosives, aligning with **Section 438 of IPC** but emphasizing these specifics more clearly.
- **Section 329(3)** of the BNS corresponding to Section 447 of the IPC has changes as follows:
  - The fine for criminal trespass has now **increased** from "five hundred rupees" to **"five thousand rupees".**
- **Section 329(4)** of the BNS corresponding to Section 448 of the IPC has changes as follows:
  - The fine for house trespass has now **increased** from "one thousand rupees" to **"five thousand rupees".**
- **Section 331(1)** of the BNS corresponding to Section 456 of the IPC has changes as follows:
  - The word "by night" has been changed to **"after sunset and before sunrise"**.
- BNS has **omitted** the definition of 'Lurking house trespass by night' and 'House breaking by night'.

THEFT

(Note: ***Section 303(1)*** *of the BNS corresponds to* ***Section 378*** *of the IPC)*

- **Section 303(1) of BNS** provides that whoever, intending to take dishonestly any movable property out of the possession of any person without that person's consent, moves that property in order to such taking, is said to commit theft.
- **Explanation 1** provides that a thing so long as it is attached to the earth, not being movable property, is not the subject of theft; but it becomes capable of being the subject of theft as soon as it is severed from the earth.
  - **Illustration**: A cuts down a tree on Z's ground, with the intention of dishonestly taking the tree out of Z's possession without Z's consent. Here, as soon as A has severed the tree in order to such taking, he has committed theft.
- **Explanation 2** provides that a moving affected by the same act which affects the severance may be a theft.
- **Explanation 3** provides that a person is said to cause a thing to move by removing an obstacle which prevents it from moving or by separating it from any other thing, as well as by actually moving it.
- **Explanation 4** provides that a person, who by any means causes an animal to move, is said to move that animal, and to move everything which, in consequence of the motion so caused, is moved by that animal.
- **For Example:**
  - A puts bait for dogs in his pocket, and thus induces Z's dog to follow it. Here, if A's intention is dishonestly to take the dog out of Z's possession without Z's consent, A has committed theft as soon as Z's dog has begun to follow A.
  - A meets a bullock carrying a box of treasure. He drives the bullock in a certain direction, in order that he may dishonestly take the treasure. As soon as the bullock begins to move, A has committed theft of the treasure.
- **Explanation 5** provides that the consent mentioned in the definition may be express or implied, and may be given either by the person in possession, or by any person having for the purpose authority either express or implied.

Punishment for Theft

- **Section 303(2) of BNS** provides for punishment for theft: Whoever commits theft shall be punished with imprisonment of either description for a term which may extend to three years, or with fine, or with both.
  - In case of second or subsequent conviction of any person under this section, he shall be punished with rigorous imprisonment for a term which shall not be less than one year but which may extend to five years and with fine.
- **Proviso to Section 303(2)** provides that in cases of theft where the value of the stolen property is less than five thousand rupees, and a person is convicted for the first time, shall upon return of the value of property or restoration of the stolen property, shall be punished with **community service**.
- **Essential Ingredients of Theft:** The following are the essential ingredients of the offence of theft:
  - The property must be "movable" and not immovable;
  - Such property must be in possession of some person;
  - Existence of a "Dishonest Intention" to take that property out of that person's possession;
  - The said taking must be without that person's consent; and
  - The property must be "moved" in order to such taking.

Case laws:

- In **Bhaiyalal v. State of MP, (1993)** , It was held that the act of cutting trees standing on Government land amounts to theft.
- The Supreme Court in **Charanjit Singh v. Sudhir Mehra, (2000)** observed that in case of a hire-purchase transaction, when the financier seizes the vehicle as per the hire-purchase agreement for default in payment of installments by the hirer, the financer cannot be charged for an offence of theft under Section 378 of IPC (Section303(1) of BNS) because of absence of *mens rea.*
- As observed by Justice Subba Rao in **Pyarelal Bhargava v. State of Rajasthan, (1963)**, "To commit theft one need not take movable property permanently out of possession of another person with the intention not to return him. It would satisfy the definition if he took away any movable property out of possession of another person though he intends to return it later on."

OTHER PROVISIONS RELATED TO THEFT

Theft in a Dwelling House, or means of Transportation or Place of Worship, etc.

(Note: ***Section 305*** *of the BNS corresponds to* ***Section 380*** *of the IPC*)

- **Section 305** provides that whoever commits theft:
  - in any building, tent or vessel used as a human dwelling or used for the custody of property; or
  - of any means of transport used for the transport of goods or passengers; or
  - of any article or goods from any means of transport used for the transport of goods or passengers; or
  - of idol or icon in any place of worship; or
  - of any property of the Government or of a local authority, shall be punished
    - with imprisonment of either description for a term which may extend to seven years, and shall also be liable to fine.

Theft by clerk or servant of property in possession of master

(Note: ***Section 306*** *of the BNS corresponds to* ***Section 381*** *of the IPC*)

- **Section 306** provides that whoever, being a clerk or servant, or being employed in the capacity of a clerk or servant, commits theft in respect of any property in the possession of his master or employer, shall be punished with:
  - Imprisonment of either description for a term which may extend to seven years, and shall also be liable to fine

Theft after Preparation Made for Causing Death, Hurt or Restraint in Order to Committing of Theft

(Note: ***Section 307*** *of the BNS corresponds to* ***Section 382*** *of the IPC*)

- **Section 307** provides that whoever commits theft, having made preparation for causing death, or hurt, or restraint, or fear of death, or of hurt, or of restraint, to any person, in order to the committing of such theft, or in order to the effecting of his escape after the committing of such theft, or in order to the retaining of property taken by such theft, shall be punished with:
  - Rigorous imprisonment for a term which may extend to ten years, and shall also be liable to fine.
- **Illustrations:**
  - A commits theft on property in Z's possession; and while committing this theft, he has a loaded pistol under his garment, having provided this pistol for the purpose of hurting Z in case Z should resist. A has committed the offence defined in this section.
  - A picks Z's pocket, having posted several of his companions near him, in order that they may restrain Z, if Z should perceive what is passing and should resist, or should attempt to apprehend A. A has committed the offence defined in this section.

SNATCHING

- Snatching is a newly added offence which has been incorporated under the scheme of BNS.
- Snatching refers to the act of forcefully taking away someone's possessions. It's not merely a theft; it's an action that combines theft with assault, leaving the victim in shock and sometimes physical harm. The Indian legal system has been evolving to address this menace with a firm hand, ensuring that the law acts as a deterrent to curb such incidents. Hence, Snatching as an offence has been incroporated under Bharatiya Nyaya Sanhita, 2023 and dealt under **Section 304** of the BNS.
- **Section 304(1)** provides snatching. According to this section, Theft is snatching if, in order to commit theft,
  - the offender suddenly or quickly or forcibly seizes or secures or grabs or takes away from any person or from his possession any movable property.

Punishment of Snatching

- **Section 304(2)** lays down the punishment. Whoever commits snatching, shall be punished with
  - imprisonment of either description for a term which may extend to three years, and shall also be liable to fine.

EXTORTION

(Note: ***Section 308*** *of the BNS corresponds to* ***Section 383, 384, 385, 387, 386, 386, 389, 388*** *of the IPC*)

- As per **Section 308(1)** of BNS, Whoever intentionally puts any person in fear of any injury to that person, or to any other, and thereby dishonestly induces the person so put in fear to deliver to any person any property or valuable security or anything signed or sealed which may be converted into a valuable security, commits "extortion".
- **Illustration**: A threatens to publish a defamatory libel concerning Z unless Z gives him money. He thus induces Z to give him money. A has committed extortion.

Punishment for Extortion

- **Section 308(2)** lays down that whoever commits extortion shall be punished with:
  - Imprisonment of either description for a term which may extend to seven years, or with fine, or with both.

Putting Person in Fear of Injury in Order to Commit Extortion

- **Section 308(3)** provides that whoever, in order to the committing of extortion, puts any person in fear, or attempts to put any person in fear, of any injury, shall be punished with:
  - Imprisonment of either description for a term which may extend to two years, or with fine, or with both.

Putting Person in Fear of Death or of Grievous Hurt, in Order to Commit Extortion

- **Section 308(4)** provides that whoever, in order to the committing of extortion, puts or attempts to put any person in fear of death or of grievous hurt to that person or to any other, shall be punished with:
  - Imprisonment of either description for a term which may extend to seven years, and shall also be liable to fine.

Extortion by Putting a Person in Fear of Death or Grievous Hurt

- **Section 308(5)** provides that whoever commits extortion by putting any person in fear of death or of grievous hurt to that person or to any other, shall be punished with:
  - Imprisonment of either description for a term which may extend to ten years, and shall also be liable to fine.

Putting Person in Fear of Accusation of Offence, in Order to Commit Extortion

- **Section 308(6)** provides that whoever, in order to the committing of extortion, puts or attempts to put any person in fear of an accusation, against that person or any other, of having committed, or attempted to commit, an offence punishable with death or with imprisonment for life, or with imprisonment for a term which may extend to ten years, shall be punished with:
  - Imprisonment of either description for a term which may extend to ten years, and shall also be liable to fine.

Extortion by Threat of Accusation of an Offence Punishable with Death or Imprisonment for Life, etc

- **Section 308(7)** provides that whoever commits extortion by putting any person in fear of an accusation against that person or any other, of having committed or attempted to commit any offence punishable with death, or with imprisonment for life, or with imprisonment for a term which may extend to ten years, or of having attempted to induce any other person to commit such offence, shall be punished with:
  - Imprisonment of either description for a term which may extend to ten years, and shall also be liable to fine.
- **Essential Ingredients of Extortion** : The following are the essential ingredients of the offence of extortion:
  - Intentionally puts any person in fear of any injury;
  - Dishonestly inducing the person so put in fear, and
  - To deliver property or valuable security.
- **Intentionally Puts any Person in Fear of any Injury:** The act of extortion requires that the victim be purposefully made to fear harm, and that the "fear" be of a kind and intensity that disturbs the victim's equilibrium(state of mind) and removes the element of free will that is necessary for consent to be given.
- **Inducing a Person Dishonestly:** The main components of this offence are receiving property as a result of dishonest inducement. It is not enough that there be wrongful loss to a single person; there also needs to be an intention on the part of the person who is putting that person in danger of harm to cause wrongful loss. It cannot be claimed that the accused's attempt to retrieve the money was made with the intent to cause wrongful loss if he sincerely feels that it is his. Unless done with the intent to commit a crime, it is not illegal to cause fear of harm to another person.
- **To Deliver Property or Valuable Security:** The victim is induced to deliver or give the same to the accused or to any other person to whom the accused directs it to be given.

DIFFERENCE BETWEEN THEFT AND EXTORTION

Though obtaining property dishonestly is the common element in both, theft and extortion, but the two offences are different from one another in the following aspects:

- **Consent:** The property is taken by the offender without the consent of the possessor in case of a theft but extortion is committed by the wrongful obtaining of consent.
- **Element of Fear:** The element of fear does not exist in theft while it does exist in extortion.
- **Delivery of Property**: In theft, the accused himself removes the property and takes it, whereas in extortion, the victim is induced to deliver or give the same to the accused or to any other person to whom the accused directs it to be given.
- **Nature of Property**: In theft, the property which is subject of theft must be movable while in case of extortion, it may be movable or immovable and it may even be a valuable security.

ROBBERY

(Note: *Section 309* of the BNS corresponds to *Section 390, 392, 393, 394* of the IPC)

- Robbery means Property is taken away either with no consent or consent is obtained through threat, force, or intimidation.
- Robbery is a special and aggravated form of either theft or extortion. "There can be no case of robbery which does not fall within the definition either of theft or of extortion; but in practice it will perpetually be a matter of doubt whether a particular act of robbery was a theft or an extortion A large proportion of robberies will be half theft, half extortion."
- The chief distinguishing element in robbery is the presence of imminent fear of violence. **Section 309** of BNS deals with the Robbery.
- **Section 309 (1)** provides for Robbery,as per the section "In all robbery there is either theft or extortion."
- **When Theft is Robbery: Section 309(2)** provides theft is robbery if, in order to the committing of the theft, or in committing the theft, or in carrying away or attempting to carry way property obtained by the theft, the offender, for that end voluntarily causes or property to cause to any person death or hurt or wrongful restraint, or fear of instant death or of instant hurt, or of instant wrongful restraint.
- **When Extortion is Robbery: Section 309(3)** lays down Extortion is 'robbery' if the offender, at the time committing the extortion, is in the presence of the person put in fear, and commits the extortion by putting that person in fear of instant death, or instant hurt, or of instant wrongful restraint to that person or to some other person, and, by so putting in fear, induces the person so put in fear then and there to deliver up the thing extorted.
- **Explanation** to robbery provides that the offender is said to be present if he is sufficiently near to put the other person in fear of instant death, of instant hurt, or of instant wrongful restraint"
- **Illustrations**: A holds Z down, fraudulently takes Z's money and jewels from Z's clothes, without Z's consent. Here A has committed theft, and, in order to the committing of that theft, has voluntarily caused wrongful restraint to Z. A has therefore committed robbery.

Punishment for Robbery

- **Section 309(4)** provides that whoever commits robbery shall be punished with rigorous imprisonment for a term which may extend to ten years, and shall also be liable to fine; and, if the robbery be committed on the highway between sunset and sunrise, the imprisonment may be extended to fourteen years.

Attempt to Commit Robbery

- **Section 309(5)** provides that whoever attempts to commit robbery shall be punished with rigorous imprisonment for a term which may extend to seven years, and shall also be liable to fine.

Voluntarily Causing Hurt in Committing Robbery

- **Section 309(6)** provides if any person, in committing or in attempting to commit robbery, voluntarily causes hurt, such person, and any other person jointly concerned in committing or attempting to commit such robbery, shall be punished with imprisonment for life, or with rigorous imprisonment for a term which may extend to ten years, and shall also be liable to fine.
- **Essential Ingredients of Robbery**: The opening words of **Section 309 of BNS** shows that there cannot be any robbery, if there is no theft or extortion. It means robbery consists of either aggravated theft or aggravated extortion. The ingredients of either the offence of theft or of extortion, thus, must be present in the offence of robbery.

- **Extortion to Robbery**: When property is forced to be given to another person, robbery and extortion are related. When an individual (A) uses a phone to threaten another person (B) with dire consequences ('Unless you send the money demanded, you will be killed'), that is considered extortion even if B agrees to send the requested amount. However, if A enters B's room brandishing a weapon and threatens to kill him unless the money is given, and B agrees to give money in response, the extortion crime escalates into robbery.
  - When extortion is committed in the immediate presence of the victim, extortion is robbery because of the fear of instant death or instant hurt or instant wrongful restraint caused thereby. So, an attempt to commit extortion, in certain situations, will amount to attempt to commit robbery.
- **For that end:** Stealing must result in death, hurt, or wrongful restraint when it comes to taking away stolen property. The phrase "for that end" makes it very evident that the harm done by the offender must be intended to aid in the commission of theft, must occur while the offender is stealing, or must occur while the offender is attempting to steal or carrying away property.
- **Carrying Away:** Even if death, hurt or wrongful restraint, or fear of any of these, is caused after committing theft, in order to carry away the property obtained by theft, this offence would be committed. The words "to carry away the property obtained by theft" in the first part of the definition in Section 309 of BNS are important. The word "theft" involves wrongful gain or wrongful loss. Thus when a revolver is snatched to ward off being shot and the revolver later is abandoned and no element of any wrongful gain or wrongful loss is involved it cannot amount to robbery.
- **Voluntarily Causes:** These words indicate that a thief's offence will not be elevated to the level of robbery if they unintentionally cause harm to someone. Therefore, it was decided that theft, not robbery, had occurred in the case where someone accidentally cut the owner's wrist while cutting the string that held the basket while trying to steal it. The owner then fled with the basket. However, robbery is the crime committed when there is unquestionably an attempt to cause harm along with the intention to steal.

DACOITY

(Note: ***Section 310*** *of the BNS corresponds to* ***Section 391, 395, 396, 399, 400, 402*** *of the IPC*)

- **Section 310** of BNS provides that when five or more persons conjointly commit or attempt to commit a robbery, or where the whole number of persons conjointly committing or attempting to commit a robbery, and persons present and aiding such commission or attempt, amount to five or more, every person so committing, attempting or aiding, is said to commit "dacoity"

Punishment for Dacoity

- **Section 310(2)** provides Punishment for dacoity. According to this section, whoever commits dacoity shall be punished with
  - imprisonment for life, or with rigorous imprisonment for a term which may extend to ten years, and shall also be liable to fine.

Dacoity with Murder

- **Dacoity with Murder: Section 310(3)** provides if any one of five or more persons, who are conjointly committing dacoity, commits murder in so committing dacoity, every one of those persons shall be punished with:
  - Death, or imprisonment for life, or rigorous imprisonment for a term which shall not be less than ten years, and shall also be liable to fine.

Making Preparation to Commit Dacoity

- **Section 310(4)** provides that whoever makes any preparation for committing dacoity, shall be punished with rigorous imprisonment for a term which may extend to ten years, and shall also be liable to fine.

Assembling for Purpose of Committing Dacoity

- **Section 310(5)** provides that whoever is one of five or more persons assembled for the purpose of committing dacoity, shall be punished with rigorous imprisonment for a term which may extend to seven years, and shall also be liable to fine.
- **Section 310(6)** provides that whoever belongs to a gang of persons associated for the purpose of habitually committing dacoity, shall be punished with imprisonment for life, or with rigorous imprisonment for a term which may extend to ten years, and shall also be liable to fine
- Dacoity is nothing but robbery committed by five or more persons. The total number of persons involved at whatever level, either as the main persons or as aiders, should be five. They should be involved in either committing, attempting to commit or in aiding the commission of robbery. The gravity of the offence consists in the terror it causes by the presence of a number of offenders.
- **Essential Ingredients of Dacoity**
  - **Robbery by five or more:** Robbery must be committed in concert by at least five people. When a mob of more than five people attacks and takes property, it is called dacoity.
  - In **Ganesan v. State Rep. By Station House Officer, (2021)**, the Court while discussing the essential element of Section 391 of IPC (Section 310 of BNS) observed that the offence under Section 391 of IPC (Section 310 of BNS) punishable under Section 395(Section 310(3) of BNS) cannot be declared to not have been made out just because some of the accused fled and less than five individuals turned up to be punished in the trial. It is necessary to take into account that five or more people participated in and committed the robbery, not whether those people were put on trial. When five or more people jointly commit the robbery offence or attempt to commit the robbery, the case is brought under Section 391 of IPC (Section 310 of BNS) and is considered to be a "dacoity," depending on the evidence.
  - **Conjointly**: In assessing the liability to persons accused of the offence of dacoity, the word "conjointly" has an important significance/bearing on the ability of persons accused of an offence of dacoity. Mere presence of an accused amongst the robbers is not sufficient. The accused must be shown to have conjointly committed robbery or aided such commission.
    - While it may be true to say that "common intention" is no part of the offence of dacoity, the word "conjointly" used in Section 310 of BNS manifestly refers to united or concerted action of the persons participating in the transaction.

DISHONEST MISAPPROPRIATION OF PROPERTY

(Note: ***Section 314*** *of the BSA corresponds to* ***Section 403*** *of the IPC*)

- **Section 314** of the BNS deals with the offence of dishonest misappropriation of movable property.
- The core of the offence is that the accused dishonestly misappropriated or converts property to their own use, which belongs to another person.
- In **P. Dumgappa v. State of Mysore (1956)**, it was stated that, there must be actual misappropriation or conversion of the things.
- The word 'appropriate' means to set apart or assign the property to oneself or to another to the exclusion of the owner.

Dishonest Use of Property

- Section 2(7) of BNS defines dishonestly as doing anything with the intention of causing wrongful gain to one person or wrongful loss to another person.
- Dishonest intention involves using property as if it were one's own without the owner's consent, after initially coming into possession innocently or otherwise.
- In **Phulchand Dube v. Emperor (1929)**, where 'A' took possession of a stray cattle and it was not shown that the cattle was stolen property, and he dishonestly retained it, he was liable under **Section 314** of the BNS.

Legal Possession

- No entrustment is required for this offence; it suffices that the property belongs to another and is taken dishonestly by the accused for their own use.
- The offence is complete upon the dishonest misappropriation or conversion, irrespective of whether the property was lawfully acquired by the accused initially.

For Example

- Suppose, Initially believing a package delivered to his landlord's doorstep was meant for him due to a similar name, A took possession innocently.
- Upon realizing it belonged to the landlord, A decided to keep it for himself.
- **As per Section 314,** of the BNS, A's act of keeping the package after discovering it belongs to the landlord, without lawful justification or consent, constitutes criminal misappropriation.
- The section clarifies that even if A initially believed the property was rightfully his, his subsequent retention of it for personal use, knowing it belongs to another, is punishable.

Landmark Judgments

- In **Rama Krishna Mithan Lal v. Emperor (1888)**, where the court held that no entrustment is required for misappropriation; mere possession followed by dishonest conversion suffices.
- Similarly, in **Ramaswami Nadar v. State of Madras (1958)**, the Supreme Court highlighted the necessity of dishonest intention and personal use for constituting the offence.
- In **Mahabir Prasad Garodia v. State of Assam (1961)**, the Court states that, When the property of another person comes into the possession of the offender and is dishonestly converted or misappropriated by the offender for his own use, the offence is committed.

Dishonest Misappropriation of Property Possessed by a Deceased Person

(Note: ***Section 315*** *of the BSA corresponds to* ***Section 404*** *of the IPC*)

- **Section 315** of the BNS addresses the misappropriation of property that was in the possession of a deceased person at the time of their death and has not yet come into the possession of the legal heirs.
- The BNS prescribes a punishment of up to three years' imprisonment, or a fine, or both. If the offender is a servant or clerk of the deceased, the imprisonment term can extend to seven years.

Key Ingredients

- **Possession by Deceased:** The property must have been possessed by the deceased at the time of death.
- **No Legitimate Possession Post-Death**: Since the death of the deceased, the property must not have been legally possessed by any rightful heir or person entitled to it.
- **Dishonest Misappropriation:** The accused must have dishonestly misappropriated or converted the property for their own use.

- **Increased Punishment for Clerks/ Servants: Section 315** of the BNS enhances punishment to up to seven years if the offender was a clerk or servant of the deceased at the time of death, reflecting stricter consequences for breach of fiduciary duty.
- **Illustration**
  - B, a deceased person's trusted employee, finds jewelry in the deceased's possession. Instead of informing the legal heirs, B sells the jewelry for personal gain.
  - B's act of selling the jewelry, which belonged to the deceased and had not passed legally to any heir, constitutes dishonest misappropriation.
  - Since B was employed by the deceased and misused his position of trust to convert the deceased's property to personal use, **Section 315** of the BNS applies. It stipulates harsher penalties, up to seven years' imprisonment, for employees who misappropriate property of deceased persons.

Landmark Judgments

- In **Mahabir Prasad Garodia v. State of Assam (1961)**, where the court established that dishonest intention and possession by the deceased at the time of death are crucial for prosecution.
  - The case emphasized that the prosecution must prove the intent to misappropriate and the specific possession circumstances to secure a conviction.
- In **Ashok Kumar & Ors. v. The State of Jharkhand & Anr. (2014),** The Court held that being brothers and living jointly with the deceased, the petitioners were legally entitled to possession of his property.
  - Therefore, no offence under **Section 404** was made out against them.
  - The Court emphasized that possession by close relatives, even without ownership title, precludes application of **Section 404**, ensuring protection against misuse of legal process.

CRIMINAL BREACH OF TRUST

(Note: ***Section 316*** *of the BSA corresponds to* ***Section 405, 406, 407, 408, 409*** *of the IPC***)**

- According to **Section 316 of the BNS,** criminal breach of trust occurs when a person entrusted with property or control over it dishonestly misappropriates or violates legal directions or contracts regarding that trust.
- There must be entrustment of property, dishonest intent in misappropriating or using the property, and a violation of a legal direction, law, or contract related to the trust.
- For example, A, as the executor of a deceased person's will, is legally required to distribute the estate according to the will. Instead, A dishonestly appropriates the estate for personal use. This action constitutes a criminal breach of trust under **Section 316 of the BNS**, as A has violated the legal trust and direction.
- In **R.K. Dalmia v. Delhi Administration (1962)**, the Supreme Court emphasized the broad scope of "entrustment."
- It held that "entrustment" includes not just physical possession of property but also situations where a person has been given dominion or control over property in a fiduciary capacity.
- In **Challoor Mankkal Narayan Ituravi v. State of Travancore & Cochin, (1953)**, the Supreme Court clarified that for the offence of criminal breach of trust under **Section 405,** I.P.C., it must be proven that the accused was entrusted with property or had dominion over it, and that they dishonestly misappropriated or converted it for personal use.

Punishment for Criminal Breach of Trust

- For criminal breach of trust under **Section 316(2) of the BNS,** the punishment can include imprisonment of up to five years, a fine, or both, depending on the nature and severity of the offence.

- In **Kailash Kumar Sanwantia v. State of Bihar, (2003)**, the Supreme Court outlined the essential ingredients of criminal breach of trust as follows:
  - The accused must be entrusted with property or have dominion over it;
  - They must dishonestly misappropriated or convert the property for personal use, or dishonestly use, dispose of it, or allow another person to do so, contrary to legal directives or contractual obligations.
- For example, Rajesh, a financial advisor, misuses client funds entrusted for investment by diverting them into his personal accounts.
  - Upon discovery, Rajesh faces charges under **Section 406** of the IPC, risking up to three years' imprisonment and fines for simple breach of trust.
- In **Challoor Mankkal Narayan Ituravi v. State of Travancore and Cochin (1953)** highlighted the necessity of proving entrustment and dishonest misappropriation for conviction under these sections.

Criminal Breach of Trust by Carrier, etc.

- **Section 316(3) of the BNS** specifically addresses criminal breach of trust committed by carriers, wharfingers, or warehouse-keepers.
- If these individuals commit criminal breach of trust in relation to the property entrusted to them, the punishment can extend to imprisonment for up to seven years, along with a fine.
- The provision recognizes the significant responsibility these roles carry and prescribes a more severe penalty for breaches due to the entrusted nature of their duties.
- This section covers those responsible for the safe transport or storage of goods who misappropriate or misuse the property entrusted to them.
- For example, A warehouse manager, entrusted with storing valuable electronics, sells the goods for personal gain. Caught by inventory audits, the manager is charged under **Section 316(3) of the BNS** for breach of trust as a warehouse keeper, facing potential imprisonment for up to seven years and fines.
- In **Somnath v. State of Maharashtra, (1972),** a Traffic Assistant at Indian Airlines Corporation demanded extra trunk charges from passengers for seat reservations. After receiving the amount, he issued receipts on behalf of the Corporation but later falsified these receipts and misappropriated the excess funds. The Supreme Court found the accused guilty of criminal breach of trust.

Criminal Breach of Trust by Clerk or Servant

- Under **Section 316(4) of the BNS,** if a clerk, servant, or individual employed in a similar capacity commits criminal breach of trust, it pertains specifically to their role and responsibilities.
- The punishment for such a breach includes imprisonment for up to seven years and a fine.
- This section underscores the significant trust placed in clerks and servants, reflecting the severity of breaches committed in such positions.
- For example, Ravi, a cashier at a retail store, siphons off small amounts of cash over several months, using his position to cover up the theft. An audit reveals the shortfall.
  - Under **Section 316(4) of the BNS**, Ravi faces up to seven years of imprisonment and fines for misappropriating property entrusted to him.
- In **Emperor v. Bimal Charan Roy (1913)**, an inspector of water works misappropriated water supply for personal use, highlighting dominion over property.

Criminal Breach of Trust by Public Servant, or by Banker, Merchant or Agent

- Under **Section 316(5),** this provision addresses criminal breach of trust by individuals acting in their capacity as public servants, bankers, merchants, factors, brokers, attorneys, or agents.
- The punishment for committing criminal breach of trust in these roles can be imprisonment for life or up to ten years, along with a fine.
- The section acknowledges the heightened trust and responsibility associated with these positions, prescribing more severe penalties to reflect the gravity of breaches in such crucial roles.
- In **Mohd. Suliman v. Mohd. Ayub (1965),** The court clarified that mere civil disputes do not constitute criminal breach of trust unless there's clear dishonest misappropriation.
- In **Jaikrishandas Manohardas Desai v. State of Bombay (1960)**, the appellants, officials of Parikh Dyeing and Printing Mills Ltd., failed to return 130,000 yards of entrusted cloth to the Textile Commissioner.
  - The Supreme Court held that their failure to account for the cloth constituted criminal breach of trust under **section 409**, IPC, as it inferred dishonest misappropriation. The appeal was dismissed.

STOLEN PROPERTY

(Note: ***Section 317*** *of the BSA corresponds to* ***Section 410, 411, 412, 413, 414*** *of the IPC***)**

- **Section 317(1)** defines stolen property. According to this section, Property, the possession whereof has been transferred by theft or extortion or robbery or cheating, and property which has been criminally misappropriated or in respect of which criminal breach of trust has been committed, is designated as stolen property,
- Section 317(1) further lays down that whether the transfer has been made, or the misappropriation or breach of trust has been committed, within or without India, but, if such property subsequently comes into the possession of a person legally entitled to the possession thereof, it then ceases to be stolen property.

Punishment of Dishonestly Receives or Retains Stolen Property

- **Section 317(2)** provides that whoever dishonestly receives or retains any stolen property, knowing or having reason to believe the same to be stolen property,
  - shall be punished with imprisonment of either description for a term which may extend to three years, or with fine, or with both.

Dishonestly Receives or Retains Any Stolen Property in commission of dacoity

- **Section 317(3)** provides that whoever dishonestly receives or retains any stolen property, the possession whereof he knows or has reason to believe to have been transferred by the commission of dacoity, or dishonestly receives from a person, whom he knows or has reason to believe to belong or to have belonged to a gang of dacoits, property which he knows or has reason to believe to have been stolen,
  - shall be punished with imprisonment for life, or with rigorous imprisonment for a term which may extend to ten years, and shall also be liable to fine.

Habitually Dealing in Stolen Property

- **Section 317(4)** provides that whoever habitually receives or deals in property which he knows or has reason to believe to be stolen property,
  - shall be punished with imprisonment for life, or with imprisonment of either description for a term which may extend to ten years, and shall also be liable to fine.

Assisting in Concealment of Stolen Property

- **Section 317(5)** provides that whoever voluntarily assists in concealing or disposing of or making away with property which he knows or has reason to believe to be stolen property,
  - shall be punished with imprisonment of either description for a term which may extend to three years, or with fine, or with both.
- **Ingredients:**
  - **Stolen property:** A stolen property is one on which the possession of property is transferred by theft, extortion, robbery, cheating, criminal misappropriation, criminal breach of trust.
  - Whether the transfer has been made, or the misappropriation or breach of trust has been committed, within or without India.
  - When stolen property ceases to be "stolen property".
    - If such property subsequently comes into the possession of a person legally entitled to the possession thereof. of owner before its receipt by person
- **Stolen property ceases to be a stolen property**: The property which treated to be the stolen property will not longer a stolen property when the legally entitled person of that property, gets back possession of that property. When, the owner of the property gets the possession of the stolen property, before it is received by some other person, it ceases to be a stolen property, and if the other person, having known of the fact that the property was stolen receives that property, he cannot be held for receiving stolen property. Because, before, he received that, it ceased to be a stolen property.
- In the case of **Balinath v. state (1957)**, the court held that attention should be paid to the use of both the words 'received' and 'retained' in the section. The law makers have very cautiously imposed liability not only on those who receive stolen property, knowing it to be stolen, but also on those who receive the property honestly, but later on retain it dishonestly. Thus, the liability of a person who retains dishonestly a property that he received honestly, is no less than that of a person who receives it dishonestly.

CHEATING

(Note: ***Section 318*** *of the BSA corresponds to* ***Section 415, 417*** *of the IPC*)

- **Section 318 (1):** Defines cheating as the act of deceiving someone to fraudulently induce them to either deliver property, consent to retain property, or perform/omit an action which they wouldn't have done otherwise, causing or likely causing harm.
- **Section 318 (2):** Specifies that a person found guilty of cheating can be punished with imprisonment for up to three years, or fined, or both.
- In **Ram Das v. State of Uttar Pradesh (1974)**, the essential ingredients to constitute the offence of cheating are:
  - Fraudulent or dishonest inducement of a person by deceiving him;
  - (a) The deceived person should be induced to deliver any property or consent to retaining it, or (b) The deceived person should be intentionally induced to do or omit to do something he wouldn't if not deceived;
  - The act or omission should cause or likely cause damage or harm to the person in body, mind, reputation, or property.

Cheating by Personation

(Note: ***Section 319*** *of the BSA corresponds to* ***Section 416, 419*** *of the IPC*)

- **Section 319 (1):** Cheating by personation occurs when an individual pretends to be someone else, substitutes one person for another, or represents themselves or another person as someone different from who they truly are. This act of deception is considered cheating regardless of whether the person being impersonated is real or imaginary.

- **Explanation:** The offence is committed even if the person being impersonated does not exist or is fictional.
- **Section 319 (2):** If found guilty of cheating by personation, the person can be punished with imprisonment for up to five years, or a fine, or both.
- In **Mahadeo Prasad v. State of West Bengal (1954)**, it was held that selling adulterated groundnut oil as pure oil constitutes deception. To convict a person of cheating, there must be a direct nexus between the deception practiced and the parting of property. If the connection is too remote, there is no cheating.

Cheating with Knowledge that Wrongful Loss may Ensue

(Note: ***Section 318(3)*** *of the BSA corresponds to* ***Section 418*** *of the IPC***)**

- **Section 318 (3):** If the cheating is done with the knowledge that it is likely to cause wrongful loss to someone whose interests the cheat was legally or contractually bound to protect, the punishment is increased to imprisonment for up to five years, or a fine, or both.
- In **the case Queen Empress v. Moss (1894)**, it was established that a director of a banking company who presented a knowingly false and misleading balance sheet to shareholders, concealing the true financial position of the company, was held liable under the relevant legal section.
- In **Bhagwan Maharaj v. State of Andhra Pradesh (1999)**, it was held that Maharaj's claim of having divine healing powers, which induced a belief that he could cure a girl's congenital dumbness, constituted fraudulent inducement under the law.

Cheating and Dishonestly Inducing Delivery of Property

(Note: ***Section 318(4)*** *of the BSA corresponds to* ***Section 420*** *of the IPC***)**

- **Section 318 (4):** If the cheating involves inducing someone to deliver property or make, alter, or destroy valuable securities or documents capable of becoming valuable securities, the punishment can extend to seven years of imprisonment and a fine.
- In **Tulsi Ram v. State**, it was clarified that for a person to be convicted under **Section 420** of the IPC, it must be proven not only that they committed cheating but also that they dishonestly induced the deceived person to part with their property.

MISCHIEF

(Note: ***Section 324*** *of the BSA corresponds to* ***Section 425, 426, 427, 440*** *of the IPC***)**

- **Section 324 (1)** provides that mischief is committed when a person, with the intent to cause or knowing they are likely to cause wrongful loss or damage to the public or any individual, destroys or diminishes the value or utility of property. This includes any act that affects property injuriously.
- **Explanation 1:** It is not necessary for the offender to intend to cause loss to the specific owner of the property. It is sufficient if the act is likely to cause wrongful loss or damage to any person, even if the property harmed does not belong to that person.
- **Explanation 2:** Mischief can be committed against property owned by the person committing the act or shared jointly with others.
- **Mischief Causing Loss to Property Including Government Property: Section 324(3)** provides that if the mischief causes loss or damage to any property, including government or local authority property, the punishment can be imprisonment for up to one year, or a fine, or both.

- **Mischief Causing Damage Between 20,000 and 1 Lakh Rupees: Section 324(4)** provides that if the mischief results in damage or loss between twenty thousand rupees and less than one lakh rupees, the punishment can be imprisonment for up to two years, or a fine, or both.
- **Mischief Causing Damage of 1 Lakh Rupees or More: Section 324(5)** provides that for mischief causing damage or loss of one lakh rupees or more, the punishment can extend to five years of imprisonment, or a fine, or both.
- **Mischief with Intent to Cause Death or Injury: Section 324(6)** provides that if the mischief is committed with preparations to cause death, hurt, wrongful restraint, or fear of such harm, the punishment can be imprisonment for up to five years, and a fine.
- **For example,** If A intentionally vandalizes a competitor's office to undermine their business, such as smashing windows and damaging equipment, it constitutes mischief.
  - A's actions aim to cause wrongful loss or damage, demonstrating the offence under **Section 324 of the BSA** by affecting property value and utility.
- In **Punjaji Chandrabhan v. Maroti (1950)**, the Court ruled that no offence under **Section 425** of IPC occurred because the easement right to carry water through the accused's land did not cause harm to the complainant's tangible property.
- In **Sippattar Singh v. Krishna (1957)**, the Court distinguished theft from mischief.
  - The court distinguished mischief as an act that typically damages property but does not necessarily involve the dishonest appropriation of movable property.
  - The respondent was found guilty of cutting sugar cane from the petitioner's field and taking it away, constituting theft.

Ingredients of Mischief

- To constitute mischief, two key elements must be present:
  - Mens rea (guilty mind), and
  - Actus reus (guilty act).
- Mens rea involves intent or knowledge that one's actions are likely to cause wrongful loss or damage.
- Actus reus includes the physical act of causing destruction, change, or diminishment in property value or utility.
- In **Bhupinder Singh v. State of Punjab (1988)**, The Supreme Court clarified the ingredients of the offence, focusing on the intent and knowledge of likely harm.
- In **Indian Oil Corporation v. NEPC India Ltd. (2006)**, the Supreme Court clarified that ownership is irrelevant in determining liability for mischief, establishing that even owners can be held accountable under the law.

Punishment for Mischief

- **Section 324 (2)** provides that whoever commits mischief may be punished with imprisonment up to six months, or a fine, or both.
- Aggravated forms of mischief under **Sections 325 to 328 of the BNS** involve higher penalties based on the nature of the act and the extent of damage caused.

Aggravated Forms of Mischief

(Note: *Section* ***325*** *to* ***328*** *of the BSA corresponds to* ***Section 428 to 439*** *of the IPC*)

- **Mischief by Killing or Maiming an Animal: Section 325** of the BNS This deals with the aggravated offence of causing harm to animals through acts such as killing, poisoning, maiming, or rendering them useless. The punishment reflects the gravity of this offence, allowing for imprisonment of up to five years, a fine, or both.

- **Mischief Involving Injury, Inundation, Fire, or Explosive Substances: Section 326** of the BNS addresses aggravated forms of mischief, including acts that significantly disrupt public services or safety, such as reducing water supplies, obstructing transportation routes, causing flooding, tampering with navigation or landmark signs, and using fire or explosives to damage property. These offences are met with severe penalties, ranging from imprisonment of up to five years to life imprisonment, depending on the nature and impact of the act.
- **Mischief with Intent to Destroy or Render Unsafe Rail, Aircraft, or Vessel: Section 327** of the BNS criminalizes the intentional damage or sabotage of critical transportation infrastructure, such as railways, aircraft, or large vessels, with the aim of causing destruction or rendering them unsafe. The law prescribes imprisonment of up to ten years and a fine, with the possibility of life imprisonment if fire or explosives are involved, emphasizing the heightened danger posed by such actions.
- **Intentionally Running Vessel Aground or Ashore with Intent to Commit Theft, etc: Section 328** of the BNS focuses on the aggravated offence of arson, specifically targeting those who intentionally run vessels aground or ashore with the intent to commit theft or misappropriate property. The severity of this offence is reflected in the punishment of up to ten years of imprisonment and a fine, acknowledging the premeditated nature of the crime and its potential for causing significant harm.

CRIMINAL TRESPASS

(**Note:** ***Section 329*** *of the BNS corresponds to* ***Section 441*** *of the IPC*)

- **Criminal Trespass: Section 329(1)** provides for criminal trespass. According to this section, Whoever enters into or upon property in the possession of another with intent to commit an offence or to intimidate, insult or annoy any person in possession of such property or having lawfully entered into or upon such property, unlawfully remains there with intent thereby to intimidate, insult or annoy any such person or with intent to commit an offence is said to commit criminal trespass.
- **House Trespass: Section 329(2)** provides for house-trespass, Whoever commits criminal trespass by entering into or remaining in any building, tent or vessel used as a human dwelling or any building used as a place for worship, or as a place for the custody of property, is said to commit house-trespass.

Punishment for Criminal Trespass

- **Section 329(3)** provides punishment for criminal trespass. According to this section, Whoever commits criminal trespass shall be punished with imprisonment of either description for a term which may extend to three months, or with fine which may extend to five thousand rupees, or with both.

Punishment for House-Trespass

- **Section 329(4)** provides punishment for criminal trespass. According to this section, Whoever commits house-trespass shall be punished with imprisonment of either description for a term which may extend to one year, or with fine which may extend to five thousand rupees, or with both.
- The word 'possession' as used in **Section 329(1) of BNS** is wide enough to include not only actual and physical possession but also constructive possession.
- The intention is normally ascertained from the circumstances of the case. Intention and object are two different things. Purity of motive does not exculpate a man if his criminal intention in making the entry is otherwise proved.

- If there is no criminal intent involved, a trespass is not considered criminal. No trespassing offence was committed when a landlord entered a property sincerely thinking the tenant had left to regain possession. This is because it cannot be claimed that the landlord entered the property intending to break the law or to insult or annoy the tenant.
- According to **Section 329(1)**, it is not required for the entry to be illegal in order for it to be allowed. Even if the entry was allowed, it might turn illegal if the person in possession doesn't leave the property or stop using it by the deadline indicated in the notice when another person calls for them to do so in writing. Even though the entry was legal at first, it may turn illegal if he doesn't leave the property where the trespass was committed after receiving notice.
- **Essential Ingredient:** To constitute an offence of criminal trespass as defined in the **Section 329(1)** of BNS , the following essential ingredients must be satisfied:
  - Entry into or upon property in the possession of another,
  - Such entry should be with intent to commit an offence or to intimidate, insult or annoy any person in possession of such property.

HOUSE BREAKING

(Note: ***Section 330*** *of the BNS corresponds to* ***Section 445*** *of the IPC*)

- **Section 330(2) of BNS** provides that house breaking. According to this section, A person is said to commit "house-breaking" who commits house-trespass if he effects his entrance into the house or any part of it in only of the six ways hereinafter described; or if, being in the house or any part of it for the purpose of committing an offence, or having committed an offence therein, he quits the house or any part of it in any of following ways, that is to say:
  - **Firstly**; If he enters or quits through a passage made by himself, or by any abettor of the house-trespass, in order to the committing of the house-trespass.
  - **Secondly**: If he enters or quits through any passage not intended by any person, other than himself or an abettor of the offence, for human entrance, or through any passage to which he has obtained access by scaling or climbing over any wall or building.
  - **Thirdly**: If he enters or quits through any passage which he or any abettor of the house-trespass has opened, in order to the committing of the house-trespass by any means by which that passage was not intended by the occupier of the house to be opened.
  - **Fourthly:**If he enters or quits by opening any lock in order to the committing of the house trespass,or in order to the quitting of the house after a house trespass.
  - **Fifthly:** If he affects his entrance or departure by using criminal force or committing assault, or by threatening any person with assault.
  - **Sixthly**: If he enters or quits by any passage which he knows to have been fastened against such entrance or departure, and to have been unfastened by himself or by an abettor of the house-trespass.
- **Explanation**: Any out-house or building occupied with a house, and between which and such house there is an immediate internal communication, is part of the house within the meaning of this section.
- **Section 331(1) provides punishment for house breaking**. According to this section, Whoever commits lurking house-trespass or house-breaking, shall be punished with imprisonment of either description for a term which may extend to two years, and shall also be liable to fine.

- **Illustrations**
  - A commits house-trespass by making a hole through the wall of Z's house, and putting his hand through the aperture. This is house-breaking.
  - A commits house-trespass by creeping into a ship at a port hole between decks. This is a house-breaking.
  - A commits house-trespass by entering Z's house through a window. This is house-breaking.

Lurking House Trespass

- **Section 330(1)** lays down lurking house trespass. According to this section, whoever commits house-trespass having taken precautions to conceal such house-trespass from some person who has a right to exclude or eject the trespasser from the building, tent or vessel which is the subject of the trespass, is said to commit lurking house-trespass.

Punishment of Lurking House Trespass

- **Section 331(1)** provides that whoever commits lurking house-trespass or house-breaking, shall be punished with imprisonment of either description for a term which may extend to two years, and shall also be liable to fine.

Differences Between Criminal Trespass, House Trespass, House Breaking

- It is illegal to enter someone else's property with the intention of intimidate, insult or annoy them. The crime of criminal trespass changes to the crime of house trespass if the property is used as a place of residence for people. The crime of house trespassing, however, becomes house-breaking if the entry or departure is of a forceful character or occurs through a passageway not meant for human entry or departure.
- In all "house-breaking" there must be "house-trespass", and in all "house-trespass" there must be "criminal trespass". In order, therefore, to establish an offence either of house-breaking, or house-trespass, the intent necessary to prove "criminal trespass" must be present.

OTHER IMPORTANT PROVISIONS RELATED TO TRESPASS

- House-trespass in order to commit offence **(Section 332** of the BNS)
- House-trespass after preparation for hurt, assault or wrongful restraint **(Section 333** of the BNS)
- Dishonestly breaking open receptacle containing property **(Section 334** of the BNS)

❖ ❖ ❖

Chapter 17

OFFENCES RELATING TO DOCUMENTS

INTRODUCTION

Offences related to documents are punishable under Bharatiya Nyaya Sanhita, 2023 (BNS) under **Chapter XVIII** from **Sections 335 to 344** and Offences related to Property Marks are dealt from **Section 345 to 350** of the BNS. Earlier, Offences related to documents and of Property and Other Marks dealt under **Chapter XVIII** from **Sections 463 to 489E** of the Indian Penal Code, 1860 (IPC).

COMPARATIVE CHART OF THE BNS AND IPC		
Bhartiya Nyaya Sanhita, 2023 (BNS)	**Title**	**Indian Penal Code, 1860 (IPC)**
Section 335	Making a false document	Section 464
Section 336	Forgery	Section 463
		Section 465
		Section 468
		Section 469
Section 337	Forgery of record of Court or of public register, etc.	Section 466
Section 338	Forgery of valuable security, will, etc.	Section 467
Section 339	Having possession of document described in section 337 or section 338, knowing it to be forged and intending to use it as genuine.	Section 474
Section 340	Forged document or electronic record and using it as genuine.	Section 470
		Section 471
Section 345(1)	Property Mark	Section 479
Section 345(2)	Property Mark **EARLIER TITLE:** (Using a false property marks)	Section 481
Section 345(3)	Property Mark **EARLIER TITLE: (**Punishment for using a false property marks)	Section 482
Section 346	Tampering with property mark with intent to cause injury	Section 489
Section 347(1)	Counterfeiting a property mark used by another	Section 483
Section 347(2)	Counterfeiting a mark used by a public servant	Section 484
Section 348	Making or possession of any instrument for counterfeiting a property mark	Section 485
Section 349	Selling goods marked with a counterfeit property mark	Section 486
Section 350(1)	Making a false mark upon any receptacle containing goods	Section 487

Section 350(2)	Punishment of Making a false mark upon any receptacle containing goods **EARLIER TITLE:** (Punishment for making use of any such false mark)	Section 488

CHANGES IN BNS IN COMPARISON TO IPC

- **Section 336 of BNS** corresponding to **Sections 463, 465, 468,** and **469 of IPC** has been changes as follows:
  - The primary difference is the presentation in BNS, where sections are included as sub-sections without headings, while the IPC sections maintain distinct headings for each offence. The definitions, intents, and punishments are consistent across both, with no substantive changes in the legal framework.
- **Section 337 of BNS** corresponding to **Sections 466 of IPC** has been changes as follows:
  - **Section 337** of BNS introduces **"identity document issued by Government including voter identity card or Aadhaar Card,"** which is not present in Section 466 of IPC.
  - Additionally, **"baptism"** is excluded from the list in **Section 337**.
- **Section 340 of BNS** corresponding to **Sections 470 and 471 of IPC** has been changes as follows:
  - The heading of **Section 340** adds **"using it as genuine,"** which is not present in the **Section 470 and 471 of IPC** sections.
  - Section 340 also combines the definitions and penalties for both forging and using forged documents, whereas the IPC sections are split into separate provisions without a specific heading.

Making a False Document

(**Note:** ***Section 335*** *of the BNS corresponds to* ***Section 464*** *of the IPC*)

- **Section 335** provides that a person is said to make a false document or false electronic record:
  - **Making a False Document: Section 335 (A)** provides that who dishonestly or fraudulently:
    - (i) Makes, signs, seals or executes a document or part of a document;
    - (ii) Makes or transmits any electronic record or part of any electronic record;
    - (iii) Affixes any electronic signature on any electronic record;
    - (iv) Makes any mark denoting the execution of a document or the authenticity of the electronic signature,
  - With the intention of causing it to be believed that such document or part of document, electronic record or electronic signature was made, signed, sealed, executed, transmitted or affixed by or by the authority of a person by whom or by whose authority he knows that it was not made, signed, sealed, executed or affixed; or
  - **Unauthorized Alteration of Documents: Section 335 (B)** provides that who:
    - Without lawful authority,
    - Dishonestly or fraudulently,
    - By cancellation or otherwise.
  - Alters a document or an electronic record in any material part thereof, after it has been made, executed or affixed with electronic signature either by himself or by any other person, whether such person be living or dead at the time of such alteration; or
  - **Inducing Others to Sign or Alter Documents: Section 335 (C)** provides that who:
    - Dishonestly, or

- Fraudulently causes any person to sign, seal, execute or alter a document or an electronic record or to affix his electronic signature on any electronic record knowing that such person by reason of mental illness or intoxication cannot, or
- That by reason of deception practised upon him,
- He does not know the contents of the document or electronic record or the nature of the alteration.

- **Illustrations**
  - A has a letter of credit upon B for rupees 10,000, written by Z. A, in order to defraud B, adds a cipher to the 10,000, and makes the sum 1,00,000 intending that it may be believed by B that Z so wrote the letter. A has committed forgery.
  - A, without Z's authority, affixes Z's seal to a document purporting to be a conveyance of an estate from Z to A, with the intention of selling the estate to B and thereby of obtaining from B the purchase-money. A has committed forgery.
  - A picks up a cheque on a banker signed by B, payable to bearer, but without any sum having been inserted in the cheque. A fraudulently fills up the cheque by inserting the sum of ten thousand rupees. A commits forgery.
- **Explanation 1 of Section 335** provides that a man's signature of his own name may amount to forgery.
- **Illustrations**
  - A signs his own name to a bill of exchange, intending that it may be believed that the bill was drawn by another person of the same name. A has committed forgery.
  - A writes the word "accepted" on a piece of paper and signs it with Z's name, in order that B may afterwards write on the paper a bill of exchange drawn by B upon Z, and negotiate the bill as though it had been accepted by Z. A is guilty of forgery; and if B, knowing the fact, draws the bill upon the paper pursuant to A's intention, B is also guilty of forgery.
- **Explanation 2 of Section 335** the making of a false document in the name of a fictious person, intending it to be believed that the document was made by a real person, or in the name of a deceased person, intending it to be believed that the document was made by the person in his lifetime, may amount to forgery.
- **Illustration:** A draws a bill of exchange upon a fictious person, and fraudulently accepts the bill in the name of such fictitious person with intent to negotiate it. A commits forgery.
- **Explanation 3 of Section 335** provides that for the purposes of this section, the expression "affixing electronic signature" shall have the meaning assigned to it in clause (d) of sub-section (1) of **Section 2** of the Information Technology Act, 2000.

Definition and Provisions

- According to **Section 335**, a person is deemed to have made a false document or electronic record if they:
- **Dishonestly or Fraudulently**
  - Make, sign, seal, or execute a document or part of it.
  - Create or transmit any electronic record or part thereof.
  - Affix any electronic signature on an electronic record.
  - Make any mark that signifies the execution of a document or the authenticity of an electronic signature, intending to mislead others regarding its origin.

- Alter a document or electronic record without lawful authority, in a way that materially affects its content, whether done by themselves or another person.
- Cause another person to sign, seal, execute, or alter a document or electronic record, knowing that the person is unable to understand the contents due to unsoundness of mind, intoxication, or deception.
- In **Motisinh Gambhirsinh v. the State (1961)**, the Court held that for an attestation to amount to forgery, a critical element is that it must be made or signed by a person other than the one it purports to represent.

Illustrations of Offences

The section provides several illustrations to clarify what constitutes forgery under this law:

- **Example A**: A fraudulently alters a letter of credit to increase the amount from 10,000 to 1,00,000 rupees.
- **Example B**: A affixes Z's seal on a document without authorization, intending to sell property fraudulently.
- **Example C**: A fills in a blank cheque with an amount greater than authorized.

These examples demonstrate various scenarios of forgery, emphasizing the legal implications of creating or altering documents with fraudulent intent.

FORGERY

(Note: ***Section 336*** *of the BSA corresponds to* ***Section 463*** *of the IPC*)

- **Definition of Forgery: Section 336(1)** provides that forgery is committed when a person creates a false document or electronic record, or a part of it, with the intent to cause damage or injury to the public or an individual, to support any claim or title, to cause someone to part with property, to enter into a contract, or to commit fraud. This definition encompasses both physical and electronic forms of forgery, emphasizing the intent behind the act.
- **General Punishment for Forgery: Section 336(2)** provides that the general punishment for committing forgery is imprisonment of up to two years, a fine, or both. This provision covers cases where the forged document or record does not have a specific fraudulent purpose beyond the creation of the false document itself.
- **Forgery for the Purpose of Cheating: Section 336(3)** provides that if the forgery is committed with the intent that the forged document or electronic record will be used to cheat someone, the punishment is more severe, with imprisonment of up to seven years, along with a fine. This highlights the increased seriousness when forgery is directly linked to fraudulent schemes intended to deceive others.
- **Forgery Intended to Harm Reputation: Section 336(4)** provides that when forgery is committed with the intent to harm someone's reputation, or with the knowledge that the forged document or record is likely to be used for that purpose, the offender faces imprisonment of up to three years, along with a fine. This provision specifically targets forgery that aims to defame or damage the standing of individuals or entities.
- In **Ram Narain Popli v. Central Bureau of Investigation (2003)**, the Court clarified that "forgery" under the statute refers to its common and popular understanding. For an act to constitute forgery, the accused must create a false document with the intention to harm the public, a societal group, or a community.
- In **Mohammed Ibrahim and Ors. v. State of Bihar (2009)**, The Supreme Court distinguished between creating a false document and merely making a false representation, elaborating on the legal nuances of forgery.

TYPES OF FORGERY AND THEIR PUNISHMENTS

Forgery of Court Records or Public Registers

(**Note:** ***Section 337*** *of the BSA corresponds to* ***Section 466*** *of the IPC*)

- **Section 337 of the BNS** addresses the forgery of critical documents, including court records, government-issued identity documents (like Aadhaar cards), and official registers maintained by public servants.
- Forging such documents undermines public trust and legal integrity.
- The punishment for this offence is imprisonment of up to seven years, along with a possible fine.
- The section also clarifies that "register" includes electronic records, ensuring that digital documents receive the same legal protection as physical ones. This provision highlights the severity of tampering with official records and the strict penalties associated with such acts.
- In **the State of U.P. vs Ranjit Singh (1999)**, the court held that preparing a forged document falsely representing it as from a court of justice, leading to the unauthorized release of a person on bail, caused significant public harm. Therefore, any resulting damages must be compensated, highlighting the severity of using forged documents to manipulate legal proceedings and endanger public safety.

Forgery of Valuable Security, Wills, etc.

(**Note:** ***Section 338*** *of the BSA corresponds to* ***Section 467*** *of the IPC*)

- **Section 338 of the BNS** Act penalizes the forgery of critical documents like valuable securities, wills, or authorities related to financial transactions.
- Forging such documents can result in life imprisonment or imprisonment up to ten years, along with a fine.
- This emphasizes the serious consequences of tampering with high-value legal instruments.

Having Possession of Document Described in Section 337 or Section 338, Knowing it to be Forged and Intending to use it as Genuine

(**Note:** ***Section 339*** *of the BSA corresponds to* ***Section 474*** *of the IPC*)

- **Section 339 of the BNS,** deals with the possession of forged documents described in **Sections 337 and 338,** with the intent to use them as genuine.
- If a person knowingly possesses a forged document listed under **Section 337** (such as court records or identity documents), they can face imprisonment up to seven years, along with a fine.
- If the forged document falls under **Section 338 (like valuable securities or wills),** the punishment can extend to life imprisonment or up to seven years, in addition to a fine.
- This provision emphasizes the seriousness of possessing forged documents with fraudulent intent.

Forged Document or Electronic Record and using it as Genuine.

(**Note:** ***Section 340*** *of the BSA corresponds to* ***Section 470, 471*** *of the IPC*)

- A document or electronic record created, in whole or in part, through forgery is classified as a forged document or electronic record.
- Anyone who fraudulently or dishonestly uses a forged document or electronic record, knowing it to be forged or having reason to believe it is, will face the same penalties as if they had forged the document or record themselves. This ensures that the misuse of forged documents is penalized equivalently to the act of forgery itself.

PROPERTY MARK

(**Note:** ***Section 345*** *of the BSA corresponds to* ***Section 479, 481, 482*** *of the IPC*)

- **Section 345 (1)** of the BNS provides that a mark used for denoting that movable property belongs to a particular person is called a property mark.
- **Section 345 (2)** provides that whoever marks any movable property or goods or any case, package or other receptacle containing movable property or goods, or uses any case, package or other receptacle having any mark thereon, in a manner reasonably calculated to cause it to be believed that the property or goods so marked, or any property or goods contained in any such receptacle so marked, belong to a person to whom they do not belong, is said to use a false property mark.
- **Punishment of using False Property Marks: Section 345 (3)** provides that whoever uses any false property mark shall, unless he proves that he acted without intent to defraud, be punished with imprisonment of either description for a term which may extend to one year, or with fine, or with both.

Tampering with Property Mark with Intent to cause Injury

(**Note:** ***Section 346*** *of the BSA corresponds to* ***Section 489*** *of the IPC*)

Section 346 provides that whoever removes, destroys, defaces or adds to any property mark, intending or knowing it to be likely that he may thereby cause injury to any person, shall be punished with imprisonment of either description for a term which may extend to one year, or with fine, or with both.

Counterfeiting a Property Mark

(**Note:** ***Section 347*** *of the BSA corresponds to* ***Section 483, 484*** *of the IPC*)

- **Section 347 (1)** provides that whoever counterfeits any property mark used by any other person shall be punished with imprisonment of either description for a term which may extend to two years, or with fine, or with both.
- **Section 347 (2)** provides that whoever counterfeits any property mark used by a public servant, or any mark used by a public servant to denote that any property has been manufactured by a particular person or at a particular time or place, or that the property is of a particular quality or has passed through a particular office, or that it is entitled to any exemption, or uses as genuine any such mark knowing the same to be counterfeit, shall be punished with imprisonment of either description for a term which may extend to three years, and shall also be liable to fine

Making or Possession of any Instrument for Counterfeiting a Property Mark

(**Note:** ***Section 348*** *of the BSA corresponds to* ***Section 485*** *of the IPC*)

Section 348 provides that whoever makes or has in his possession any die, plate or other instrument for the purpose of counterfeiting a property mark, or has in his possession a property mark for the purpose of denoting that any goods belong to a person to whom they do not belong, shall be punished with imprisonment of either description for a term which may extend to three years, or with fine, or with both.

Selling Goods Marked with a Counterfeit Property Mark

(**Note:** ***Section 349*** *of the BSA corresponds to* ***Section 486*** *of the IPC*)

Section 349 provides that whoever sells, or exposes, or has in possession for sale, any goods or things with a counterfeit property mark affixed to or impressed upon the same or to or upon any case, package or other receptacle in which such goods are contained, shall, unless he proves:

(a) That, having taken all reasonable precautions against committing an offence against this section, he had at the time of the commission of the alleged offence no reason to suspect the genuineness of the mark; and

(b) That, on demand made by or on behalf of the prosecutor, he gave all the information in his power with respect to the persons from whom he obtained such goods or things; or

(c) That otherwise he had acted innocently, be punished with imprisonment of either description for a term which may extend to one year, or with fine, or with both.

Making a False Mark upon any Receptacle Containing Goods

(**Note:** ***Section 350*** *of the BSA corresponds to* ***Section 487, 488*** *of the IPC*)

- **Section 350(1)** provides that whoever makes:
  - Any false mark upon any case, package or other receptacle containing goods, in a manner reasonably calculated to cause any public servant or
  - Any other person to believe that such receptacle contains goods which it does not contain or that it does not contain goods which it does contain, or
  - That the goods contained in such receptacle are of a nature or quality different from the real nature or quality thereof,
  - Shall, unless he proves that he acted without intent to defraud, be punished with
    - Imprisonment of either description for a term which may extend to three years, or with fine, or with both.
- **Section 350(2)** provides that whoever makes use of any false mark in any manner prohibited under Section 350(1) shall, unless he proves that he acted without intent to defraud, be punished as if he had committed the offence under Section 350(1).

❖❖❖

Chapter 18

DEFAMATION

INTRODUCTION

"Every man is entitled to have his reputation preserved inviolate." **-Blackstone J.** The law of defamation is based upon the fundamental principle that the reputation of a member of society, the esteem in which he is held by it, the credit and trust it reposes on his intelligence, honour and integrity, all these constitute a valuable asset for him and it deserves protection at the hands of law.

The right of every person to the reputation which his conduct deserves stands on the same footing with the right to enjoyment of his life, liberty, health, property and all the comforts and advantages which appertains to a state of civil society in as much as security to reputation is indispensably essential to the enjoyment of every right and privilege incident to such a state.

Defamation is an injury to the reputation of a person. **Section 2 (14)** of Bhartiya Nyaya Sanhita (BNS) 2023 (Section 44 of IPC) defines "injury" as any harm whatsoever illegally caused to any person, in body, mind, reputation or property. The reputation of a person consists of the opinion of other people about him. A man's opinion of himself cannot be called his reputation. **Section 356** of the Bharatiya Nyaya Sanhita, 2023 (BNSS) deals with "Defamation". Earlier, **Section 499 to 502** of the Indian Penal Code, 1860 (IPC) dealt with defamation.

COMPARATIVE CHART OF THE BNS AND IPC

Bharatiya Nyaya Sanhita, 2023 (BNS)	Title	Indian Penal Code, 1860 (IPC)
Section 356	Defamation	Section 499
Section 356 (2)	**EARLIER TITLE:** (Punishment for Defamation)	Section 500
Section 356 (3)	**EARLIER TITLE:** (Printing or engraving matter known to be defamatory)	Section 501
Section 356 (4)	**EARLIER TITLE:** (Sale of printed or engraved substance containing defamatory matter)	Section 502

CHANGES IN BNS IN COMPARISON TO IPC

Section 356 (2) of the BNS corresponding to Section 500 of the IPC has been changed as follows:

- **Change in Punishment:** "Whoever defames another shall be punished with simple imprisonment for a term which may extend to two years, or with fine, or with both, or with **community service".** Community service is added as a new punishment.

DEFAMATION

- Defamation is the act of communicating false statements about a person that injure the reputation of that person when observed through the eyes of an ordinary man. Any false and unprivileged statement published or spoken deliberately, intentionally, knowingly with the intention to damage someone's reputation is defamation.

- Defamation gives rise to both civil and criminal action. The two remedies are not alternative but cumulative. The aggrieved person can bring a civil suit and also make a complaint before a criminal court at the same time.
- Even where the defendant has already been convicted by a criminal court under **Section 356** of BNS, the aggrieved person may still seek damages through a civil suit.

CIVIL DEFAMATION

- The civil law relating to defamation is not codified in India. Therefore, civil action against defamation is based on the English Common Law, subject to statutory exceptions.
- Civil defamation is the act of making a false statement about someone that damages their reputation. It allows the affected party to sue the person who made the false statement for damages in a civil court.
- The objective of civil defamation is to compensate the victim for any harm caused to their reputation.
- Intention is irrelevant in civil liability for defamation. Truth of the statement is a complete defence to a civil action for defamation.
- Criminal law of defamation is contained in **Section 356** of BNS (Section 499 of I.P.C and Section 502 of IPC) and is very exhaustive.
- Criminal defamation is a criminal offence wherein a person intentionally makes a false statement about someone else with the intent to harm their reputation.
- This false statement must be published or communicated to a third party.
- The punishment for criminal defamation can include two years simple imprisonment or a fine or community service as prescribed under section 356 (2) of the BNS.
- In criminal law intention is essential for liability. Good faith is a defence in criminal law. But truth as such is no defence in criminal defamation except under the first exception to Section 356 of BNS. It is necessary to prove further that the defamatory publication is for the public good.

What Constitute Defamation

(**Note:** ***Section 356 (1)*** *of the BNS correspond to* ***Sections 499*** *of the IPC*)

- As per **Section 356(1)** of BNS, whoever, by words:
  - Either spoken, or
  - Intended to be read, or
  - By signs, or
  - By visible representations

  Makes or publishes in any manner, any imputation concerning any person intending to harm, or knowing or having reason to believe that such imputation will harm, the reputation of such person, is said, except in the cases hereinafter excepted, to defame that person.
- An offence of defamation can be committed not only by spoken word or written statement but also by signs and visible representations. That means an offending cartoon or photograph may also give rise to action for defamation.
- **Illustration**
  - A says— "Z is an honest man; he never stole B's watch"; intending to cause it to be believed that Z did steal B's watch. This is defamation, unless it falls within one of the exceptions.
  - A is asked who stole B's watch. A points to Z, intending to cause it to be believed that Z stole B's watch. This is defamation, unless it falls within one of the exceptions.
  - A draws a picture of Z running away with B's watch, intending it to be believed that Z stole B's watch. This is defamation, unless it falls within one of the exceptions.
- There are four explanations to Section 356 of BNS:
  - **Explanation 1:** It may amount to defamation to impute anything to a deceased person, if the imputation would harm the reputation of that person if living, and is intended to be hurtful to the feelings of his family or other near relatives.

- **Explanation 2:** It may amount to defamation to make an imputation concerning a company or an association or collection of persons as such.
- **Explanation 3**: An imputation in the form of an alternative or expressed ironically, may amount to defamation.
- **Explanation 4:** No imputation is said to harm a person's reputation, unless that imputation directly or indirectly, in the estimation of others, lowers the moral or intellectual character of that person, or lowers the character of that person in respect of his caste or of his calling, or lowers the credit of that person, or causes it to be believed that the body of that person is in a loathsome state, or in a state generally considered as disgraceful.

Ingredients of the Offence of Defamation

- **Imputation Made Against Aggrieved Party:** An imputation concerning the specific person must have been made. It is not necessary for the person to be a single individual.
  - Imputation means an accusation against a person and implies an allegation of fact and not merely a term of abuse or insult.
- An imputation harms a person's reputation which in the estimation of others directly or indirectly, either:
  - Lowers his moral/ intellectual character, or
  - Lowers his character in respect of his caste or calling or his credit, or
  - Causes it to be believed that his body is in a loathsome state, or or in a state generally considered disgraceful.
- **Illustration:** A says that we should sympathatic with B because he is suffering from syphilis. This amounts to defamation unless it falls within one of the exceptions.
- In **CL Sagar v. Mayawati (2003),** it was alleged that a political party's Vice President defamed the complaint by declaring in a public assembly that the party's member with the long moustache was corrupt. He was not the only member of the party with a long moustache, as claimed in the complaint. Such a claim was not made in the press summary of the conference. There was therefore, no offence.
- Imputation Must Have Been Made by:
  - Words, uttered or intended to be read;
  - Signs/gestures; or
  - Visible representations.
- In **Jacob Mathew v. Manikantan, (2013),** the complainant claimed that four images of an event were published in a newspaper, one of which revealed the complainant more or less undressed, causing defamation and injury to him.
  - It was held that as the images were taken spontaneously to cover the event and not aimed to cover any particular person, it can never be said that the images were published in the newspaper with the intent, knowledge, or cause to think that they would hurt the complainant's reputation. Proceedings are liable to be quashed.
- **Imputation made in Alternative or Expressed Ironically:** As per **Explanation 3 of Section 356**, an imputation made in the form of an alternative or expressed ironically, may amount to defamation.
- It makes it clear that innuendos and ironical statements may also become cause of action if the complainant could prove that in the eyes of a person of ordinary intelligence, the imputation refers to him.
  - **Illustration**: A says Z is an honest man, he never stole B's watch intending to cause it to be believed that Z did steal B's watch; This is defamation, unless it falls within one of the exceptions.
- It is not the form of language used but the intent behind that language constitutes defamation. There may be defamation in the form of a questionnaire. Whether a

dispute of paternity will itself be *prima facie* defamation would depend upon the facts and circumstances of each case.

- **Malicious Intention and Knowledge:** The words, signs, and imputations made by the person must either be intended to injure the reputation of an individual, or the accused must rationally know that his or her behaviour might cause such injury to constitute defamation.
- In order to constitute the offence of defamation, it is not necessary that an injury to the reputation of the complainant must have been actually caused. It is enough if the offending statement is made with the intention of harming the reputation of the complainant or with knowledge or reason to believe that it will harm his reputation.
- In the case of **S Khushboo v. Kanniammal (2010)**, since the appellant's statement in the news magazine was a rather general acknowledgment of pre-marital sex and her comments were not directed at any individual or even a corporation, an association, or a collection of persons, it was held that it could not be construed as a personal attack on anyone's reputation.
- The essence of the offence of defamation is the intention or the knowledge that the allegation will harm the reputation of the person against whom they are made. If from the facts, it does not appear that the accused had the necessary intention or knowledge, it will not be proper to place him on trial for an offence under Section 356.
- In judging whether the accused had such intention or knowledge, the circumstances under which the main object with which the statement was made and the dispute between the parties should be considered.
- **Publication:** Publication of a defamatory statement is necessary to constitute the offence of defamation. Publication implies communication to atleast one person other than the person defamed. So, there can be no publication unless the subject matter of the libel is communicated to a third person.
    - Imputations on a charge sheet delivered to the employee, for example, do not constitute publishing. Furthermore, communicating an imputation merely to the individual who has been defamed is not the same as publishing.
- When the complainant containing the imputation is sent by the accused to the complainant by post in a registered cover addressed to the complainant himself, there is no publication and the offence of defamation is not committed.
- In **Sukhdeo v. State (1932),** the President of the Municipal Committee sent a letter under a Municipal Act to a specific person, who responded with defamatory claims against the President. The President filed this response in the official file, and the members of the committee reviewed it. The Court determined that the defamation had been published. The President's placement of the reply on the official file was not a spontaneous or voluntary act on his behalf; it was his responsibility, and the accused knew or must have known that the contents of his reply would be disclosed to committee members.
- **Making:** The law on defamation punishes not only those who publish but also those who partake in the making of defamatory statements. Defamation is a process and thus, the printer of a press may be punished for defamation alongwith the publisher and author of an Article.
- **Statement Must be Defamatory:** Whether a remark is defamatory or not is determined by how right-thinking people in the community interpret it.
- It is no defence to claim that the comment was not intended to be defamatory if the foreseeable impact was an injury to the plaintiff's reputation.
    - For example, the statement that 'A' is an honest man who has never stolen my watch in a sarcastic tone may be defamatory if the people who hear that, so believe that 'A' is a dishonest man who has stolen the watch.

- In **Goutam Sahu v. State of Orissa (1999)**, the appellant married the plaintiff in a temple by exchanging garlands. He stayed with her for several days before demanding money and describing her as an unchaste woman with bad looks. According to the Orissa High Court, the components of Section 500 (Section 356 (2) of BNS) were prima facie established, and the accused was consequently subject to prosecution.

Person Who May Be Defamed

- **Deceased Person:** A dead person ceases to be a person in the eyes of law. He is no longer a natural person and there is no question of inventing a legal fiction about him.
  - **Explanation 1 of Section 356** of BNS (Explanation 1 of Section 499 CrPC) says it may amount to defamation to impute anything to a deceased person, if the imputation would harm the reputation of that person if living, and is intended to be hurtful to the feelings of his family or other near relatives.
- The explanation does not provide for the defamation of a deceased person. The defamation contemplated therein relates to the effect of the statement concerning a deceased on the living members of the family.
- It may amount to defamation to impute anything to a deceased person, if the imputation would harm the reputation of that person if living and is intended to be harmful to the feelings of his family or other near relatives. The accusation must not only damage the person's reputation, were they living, but also be intended to emotionally harm their family or other relatives.
- **Defamation to Company or an Association or Collection of Persons: Explanation 2 of Section 356** provides that there can be defamation of a group or collection of persons. It says it may amount to defamation to make an imputation concerning a company or an association or collection of persons as such.
- In the case of **Sahib Singh v. State of UP (1965)**, the Supreme Court has held that imputations made against an identifiable group of persons, in this case the proctorial staff at Aligarh, a specified place, amounts to defamation.
- An association or collection of persons can maintain a complaint only when they are distinguishable from the rest of the community. A statement alleging generally that journalists are prone to undesirable influences may not be an offence.
  - But if the same imputation is made referring to, say the journalists of Hyderabad, it is against a well-defined group and therefore becomes an offence. Any journalist of Hyderabad can file a complaint even though he was not mentioned by his name.
- In the case of **Rahul Gandhi v. Purnesh Ishvarbhai Modi (2023)**, where Mr. Rahul Gandhi made a remark that "Why do all thieves have Modi in their names" the Gujarat High Court has found Rahul Gandhi guilty of defaming the 'Modi community' and observed that the case against Gandhi concerns a large identifiable class (Modi Community) and not just an individual. Gandhi is vested with a duty to ensure that the dignity and reputation of a large number of persons or any identifiable class is not "jeopardised" due to his political activities or utterances.

What Does Not Constitute Defamation

Once an imputation is proved to be defamatory, it is for the accused to show that he is protected by any of the exceptions to Section 356. The following are the exceptions as provided under Section 356 of the BNS:

Imputation of Truth which Public Good requires to be Made or Published

- **First Exception:** It is not defamation to impute anything which is true concerning any person, if it be for the 'public good' that the imputation should be made or published. Whether or not it is for the public good is a question of fact.
- A publication is said to be for public good if it has rendered or sought to render some benefit to the public or a section thereof.
- The defence that the statement is true is called the plea of justification. The accused should establish two ingredients to avail the benefit under this exception.
- Both these ingredients are questions of fact which are required to be proved strictly.
    - The first one is to prove that the imputation is true.
    - The second one is to prove that it is made for the public good.
- The truth of the imputation by itself is not sufficient in a criminal proceeding. Public good is also another ingredient that must have been involved. But in a civil suit, the truth of the defamatory statement is a complete defence.

Public Conduct of Public Servants

- **Second Exception:** It is not defamation to express in good faith any opinion regarding the conduct of a public servant in the discharge of his public functions or regarding his character, so far as his character appears in that conduct and no further.
- This exception, as is obvious, relates to the defence of fair comment. The statement made by the accused is an opinion and not a statement of fact. It must have been made in good faith and in public interest.
- When the comment is on the character of the aggrieved person, it must be related only to his conduct in public and the function he is performing.
- **Note:** The first exception deals with the allegation of facts while exception two deals with expression of opinion. In all exceptions except first what is protected is opinion and not assertion.

PLEA OF FAIR COMMENT

- Fair comment on a matter of public interest does not amount to Defamation.
    - The comment or criticism is said to be fair, if an ordinary set of men with ordinary judgement would think so and any matter that effects the public at large is a matter of public interest.
- In a plea of fair comment three points arise:
    - The comment relates to a matter of public interest.
    - It is only a comment and not a statement of fact.
    - The comment is fair.
- Conduct of persons in public office or sanitary conditions, public performances of dance, drama or publication of books or release of films for public exhibition etc., are all matters of public interest. Everyone is entitled to comment on such matters.
- Comment, being a matter of opinion, is enough if it is fair and honest. Others may agree with the comment but the commentator is not called upon by the law to justify it.
- However, criticism should not be actuated by malice. It should be a reasonable inference from the facts, which must be truly stated.

Conduct of Any Person Touching Any Public Question

- **Third Exception:** It is not defamation to express in good faith any opinion regarding the conduct of any person touching a public question, and regarding his character so far as his character appears in that conduct and no further.

- This exception also relates to fair comment. Only difference is that the opinion expressed relates to the conduct of a person touching a public question.

- So, as in the case of the second exception, the comment must have been made in good faith on a matter in which public interest is involved.
- **Illustration:** It is not defamation in A to express in good faith any opinion whatever respecting Z's conduct in petitioning Government on a public question, in signing a requisition for a meeting on a public question, in presiding or attending at such meeting, in forming or joining any society which invites the public support, in voting or canvassing for a particular candidate for any situation in the efficient discharge of the duties of which the public is interested.
- Fair comment cannot justify a defamatory statement which is untrue in fact nor can the comment based on such facts be said to be fair.

Publication of Reports of Proceedings of Court

- **Fourth Exception:** It is not defamation to publish a substantially true report of the proceedings of a court of justice or the result of any such proceedings.
- This exception comes under absolute privilege. Only thing is that it should be a mere report of the proceedings without any comment and it should be substantially true.
- In case of a newspaper report to judicial proceedings, it is not necessary in law that proceedings are to be published contemporaneously. All that is required in law that publication should be substantially a true report.

Merits of Case decided in Court or Conduct of Witnesses and Others Concerned

- **Fifth Exception:** It is not defamation to express in good faith any opinion regarding the merits of civil or criminal case, decided by a court of justice; or regarding the conduct of any person as party, witness or agent, in any such case; or regarding the character of such person, as far as the character appears in such performance and no further.
- This exception gives immunity to the publication of comments on the merits of the case which has already been decided by a court or comments relating to the conduct or character of any party, agent or witness. Only thing is that the opinion or comment is expressed in good faith.
- **Illustration**
  - A says—"I think Z's evidence on that trial is so contradictory that he must be stupid or dishonest". A is within this exception if he says this in good faith, in as much as the opinion which he expresses respects Z's character as it appears in Z's conduct as a witness, and no further.
  - But if A says—"I do not believe what Z asserted at that trial because I know him to be a man without veracity"; A is not within this exception, in as much as the opinion which expresses Z's character, is an opinion not founded on Z's conduct as a witness.

Merit of Public Performance

- **Sixth Exception:** It is not defamation to express in good faith any opinion regarding the merits of any performance which its author has submitted to the judgment of the public or regarding the character of the author, so far as the character appears in such performance, and no further.
- **Illustration**
  - A says of a book published by Z—"Z's book is foolish; Z must be a weak man. Z's book is indecent; Z must be a man of impure mind". A is within the exception, if he says this in good faith, in as much as the opinion which he expresses of Z respects Z's character only so far as it appears in Z's book, and no further.

- But if A says "I am not surprised that Z's book is foolish and indecent, for he is a weak man and a libertine". A is not within this exception, in as much as the opinion which he expresses of Z's character is an opinion not founded on Z's book.

- This exception safeguards the reviews, critiques of any artistic work or public performance. If the expression of the opinion is in good faith the newspaper or the journalist is not liable for action.
- Expression can either relate to the merits of such work or performance or the character of the author or performer in so far as such character appears in such work or performance.
    - In this exception, the expression "submitted to the judgment of the public" includes both expressed and implied submission.
- Publication of a book, public performance of a drama, music concert or release of a film are treated as implied submission to the public judgment, suffice that such expression of opinion should be in good faith.

Censure Passed in Good Faith by Person having Lawful Authority over Another

- **Seventh Exception:** It is not defamation if a person having authority over another, either conferred by law or arising out of a lawful contract, passes in good faith any censure on the conduct of that person.
    - This exception is not related to the work of a journalist and is related to an officer writing confidential reports about his subordinates.
- **Illustration**: A Judge censuring in good faith the conduct of a witness, or of an officer of the Court; a head of a department censuring in good faith those who are under his orders, a parent censuring in good faith a child in the presence of other children; a school master, whose authority is derived from a parent, censuring in good faith a pupil in the presence of other pupils; a master censuring a servant in good faith for remissness in service; a banker censuring in good faith the cashier of his bank for the conduct of such cashier as such cashier are within this exception.

Accusation Preferred in Good Faith to Authorised Person

- **Eight Exception:** It is not defamation to prefer in good faith an accusation against any person to those having lawful authority over that person, regarding the subject matter of accusation.
- In order to establish a defence under this exception, the accused would have to show that the person who lodged the complaint had legal authority over the person who was being charged in the situation at hand.
    - Besides, in a criminal defamation case, even defamatory allegations stated in a plaint are not completely protected.
- To be eligible for this exception, the charge must be made to a person in power over the person accused, and it must be made in good faith.
- **Illustration**: If A in good faith accuses Z before a Magistrate; if A in good faith complains of the conduct of Z, a servant, to Z's master; if A in good faith complains of the conduct of Z, a child, to Z's father, A is within this exception.

Imputation made in Good Faith by a Person for Protection of his or Other's Interests

- **Ninth Exception:** It is not defamation to make an imputation on the character of another, provided that the imputation be made in good faith for the protection of the interest of the person making it, or of any other person, or for the public good.

- Under this exception publication of matters concerning general public good are covered. If the public interest can be served by a private communication of the imputation, its publication is constructed by courts as indicating lack of good faith.
- **Illustration**: A, a shopkeeper, says to B, who manages his business—"Sell nothing to Z unless he pays you ready money, for I have no opinion of his honesty". A is within the exception, if he has made this imputation on Z in good faith for the protection of his own interests.
- In **Vedurumudi Rama Rao v. Chennuri Venkat Rao (1997),** a bank's regional manager sent a private circular to his region's branch managers, instructing them to exercise caution when dealing with people on the list, including the complainant. In the public interest and on orders from the Central Office, he published the directive in his executive capacity. According to the Court, the circular was protected under exception 9. As a result, even if the accusations in the complaint were true, no violation of Section 500 (Section 356(2) of BNS) would be established.
- In **Chaman Lal v. The State of Punjab, (1970),** the Hon'ble Supreme Court laid out when and how an exception of a statement made in good faith can be applied, as it fell under Section 499 of the IPC (Section 356(1) of BNS). It said, that "the interest of the person must be real and legitimate when communication is made in protection of the interest of the person making it. If that be so, then good faith is automatically drawn in and good faith obviously does not require logical infallibility."

Caution Intended for Good of Person to Whom Conveyed or for Public Good

- **Tenth Exception:** It is not defamation to convey a caution in good faith to one person against another, provided that such caution be intended for the good of the person to whom it is conveyed, or of some person in whom that person is interested, or for the public good.
  - Here again imputation published for the public good in good faith is accepted.

Punishment for Defamation

(**Note: Section 356 (2), (3) and (4)** of the BNS corresponds to **Section 500, 501, and 502** of the IPC, respectively)

- Defamation is punished under **Sections 356 (2), (3) and (4) of the BNS**. The offence is non-cognizable and bailable, according to the Bharatiya Nagrik Suraksha Sanhita 2023, which sets forth the procedural parts of the legislation.
- **Section 356 (2)** says whoever defames another shall be punished with:
  - Simple imprisonment for a term which may extend to two years, or
  - With fine, or
  - With both, or
  - With community service.
- **Printing or Engraving Matter Known to be Defamatory: Section 356 (3)** says whoever prints or engraves any matter, knowing or having good reason to believe that such matter is defamatory of any person, shall be punished with simple imprisonment for a term which may extend to two years, or with fine, or with both.
- **Sale of Printed or Engraved Substance Containing Defamatory Matter: Section 356 (4)** says whoever sells or offers for sale any printed or engraved substance

containing defamatory matter, knowing that it contains such matter, shall be punished with simple imprisonment for a term which may extend to two years, or with fine, or with both.

CONSTITUTIONALITY OF THE OFFENCE OF CRIMINAL DEFAMATION

- Freedom of speech is considered to be an absolute sacrosanct. This is the reason why the constitutionality of laws in relation to criminal defamation have been questioned several times at the touchstone of freedom of speech. However, like other rights, even this right is not absolute and is subject to certain reasonable restrictions as enumerated under **Article 19(6)** of the Constitution.
- If freedom of speech and expression is protected by **Article 19(1)(a)** of the Constitution, the right to reputation is also considered to be an inextricable part of the right to life protected by **Article 21** and balancing these two rights is a constitutional necessity.
- The laws of defamation aim to create this balance by punishing those who, in the garb of free speech, have hurt the reputation of another. But, at the same time protecting those who are communicating the truth or saying something in good faith.
- The Supreme Court's decision in the **Subramanian Swamy v. Union of India (2016),** is an important judgment in this regard. In this case, Dr. Subramanian Swamy alleged Ms. Jayalathitha of corruption in 2014. The Tamil Nadu State Government subsequently filed defamation suits against him. Following that, Dr. Swamy and other prominent politicians in India challenged the validity of Sections 499 and 500 (Section 356 of BNS) of the Indian Penal Code (IPC).
  - The Supreme Court observed that these sections are not arbitrary limitations on the right to freedom of speech and expression. Besides, it added that whatever affects a person, impacts society as a whole. As a result, it declared defamation to be a public wrong, supporting the legality of Sections 499 and 500.

❖❖❖

Chapter 19

ATTEMPT AND CRIMINAL INTIMIDATION

INTRODUCTION

Generally, the commission of crime consists of four successive stages, namely, (i) Intention, (ii) Preparation, (iii) Attempt, and (iv) Actual commission of the crime if the attempt is successful.

- The first stage is not punishable since it is very difficult to prove the mental state of a person and the Court cannot convict a person for something which it cannot know. The second stage consists of devising necessary means for commission of crime; it is generally perceived as a harmless act and is therefore, not punishable.
- In general legal sense, an attempt to commit a crime is the direct movement towards commission of the contemplated offence after the preparation is complete. A criminal attempt is an act or omission that the offender does for committing an offence but which fails due to circumstances beyond the control of the offender.
- The key difference between a criminal attempt and actual commission of an offence is with regard to accomplishment of intended objective. However, an attempt to commit a crime is considered as a substantive offence even though the intended offence is not committed.
- A criminal attempt is punishable because of the policy of the State to nip the crime right in the bud and to punish the offender for the steps taken by him ttowrds the commission of the contemplated offence. However, in view of the fact that a criminal attempt fails to attain its objective, it is considered an inchoate offence.

COMPARATIVE CHART OF THE BNS AND IPC		
Bharatiya Nyaya Sanhita, 2023 (BNS)	**Title**	**Indian Penal Code, 1860 (IPC)**
Section 62	Punishment For Attempting to Commit Offences Punishable With Imprisonment For Life or Other Imprisonment	Section 511

CRIMINAL ATTEMPT

(**Note:** *The observations given hereinafter pertain to* ***Section 511*** *of the IPC which corresponds to* ***Section 62*** *of the BNS*)

- The word "attempt" has nowhere been defined in the BNS. However, **Section 62** of the BNS punishes a person who "does any act towards the commission of the offence".
- In the case of **K Venkat Rao v. State of Andhra Pradesh (2004),** Hon'ble Apex Court has made the following observations with regard to criminal attempt:

  The word "attempt" is not itself defined, and must, therefore, be taken in its ordinary meaning. An attempt to commit an offence is an act, or a series of acts, which leads inevitably to the commission of the offence, unless something, which the doer of the act neither foresaw nor intended, happens to prevent this. An attempt may be described to be an act done in part execution of a criminal design, amounting to more than more preparation, but falling short of actual consummation, and, possessing, except for failure to consummate, all the elements of the substantive crime. In other words, an attempt consists in it the intent to commit a crime, falling short of, its actual commission or consummation/completion. It may consequently be defined as that which if not prevented would have resulted in the full consummation of the act attempted.

- In the case of **Arun Kumar v. State of Haryana (2004)**, Hon'ble Apex Court has inter alia observed that the stage of attempt "is reached when the accused takes deliberate overt or covert act or step towards the commission of the offence. Such step or act in order to be 'criminal' need not be penultimate act towards the commission of the offence. It is sufficient if such acts are reflection of the intention to commit offence aimed being reasonably proximate to the consummation of the offence".
- Therefore, the offence of criminal attempt consists of the following three essentials:
  - The offender must have an intention or mens rea to commit the contemplated offence.
  - He must have done some act or taken a step towards the commission of the contemplated offence. Such an act need not be a penultimate act towards the commission of offence but must be an act during the course of committing the offence.
  - The commission of the offence must have failed due to reasons beyond the control of the accused.
- Under the legislative scheme the BNS, criminal attempt has been dealt with in the following three ways:
  - **Same Punishment:** In the first category, commission of the offence as well as the attempt to commit it are dealt with in the same section and the extent of punishment prescribed for the both is the same. Offences such as waging or attempting to wage war against the Government of India are covered under this category
  - **Different Punishments:** In the second category, attempts to commit offences and commission of specific offences have been dealt with distinctly and distinct punishments have been provided for the attempts from those of the attempted offences. Some examples of this category are as under:
    - Attempt to commit murder, punishable under **Section 109** of BNS.
    - Attempt to commit culpable homicide not amounting to murder, punishable under **Section 110** of BNS.
    - Attempt to commit robbery under **Section 309**.
  - **General and Residuary Provision:** The third category relates to offences which are not covered by the aforesaid two categories. These attempts are governed by **Section 62** of the BNS. Section 62 contains general principles relating to criminal attempt and is residuary in nature.

Attempting to Commit Offences Punishable With Imprisonment for Life or Other Imprisonment

(Note: ***Section 62*** *of the BNS corresponds to* ***Section 511*** *of the IPC***)**

- **Section 62** deals with attempts to commit the offences which are punishable with life imprisonment or any other kind of imprisonment and prescribes punishment in respect thereof.
- The offence must be punishable with life imprisonment or any other kind of imprisonment.

- There must not be any express provision in the BNS for punishment of such an attempt.
- If the aforesaid conditions are fulfilled, the offender is liable to be punished with imprisonment of any description provided for the offence, for a term which may extend to one-half of life-imprisonment or one-half of the longest term of imprisonment provided for that offence, or with the fine provided for the offence, or with both.
- The offender must attempt to commit an offence punishable under the provisions of the BNS or must attempt to cause such offence to be committed. Moreover, in such an attempt, the offender must do any act towards the commission of the offence.
- There are two illustrations of **Section 62** which clarify that a person becomes liable for attempting to commit an impossible act if he, with intent to commit the intended offence, has done everything within his reach to commit the intended offence but his criminal objective could not be achieved due to circumstances unknown to him or beyond his control. These illustrations are as under:
  - **Illustration (a):** A makes an attempt to steal some jewels by breaking open a box, and finds after so opening the box, that there is no jewel in it. He has done an act towards the commission of theft, and therefore is guilty under this section.
  - **Illustration (b):** A makes an attempt to pick the pocket of Z by thrusting his hand into Z's pocket. A fails in the attempt in consequence of Z's having nothing in his pocket. A is guilty under this section.

THEORIES OF ATTEMPT

Proximity Rule

- According to this rule, for an act to be considered within the ambit of attempt, it has to be near the accomplishment of the substantive offence and not completely devoid of any connection or inclination towards the actual perpetration of the offence. The act doesn't need to be the last act towards the accomplishment of the offence, all it needs is the last act that was legally necessary for him to do.
- In the case of **Sudhir Kumar Mukherjee v. State of West Bengal, (1973)**, Hon'ble Apex Court has explained the proximity rule as under:
  - "... A person commits the offence of "attempt to commit a particular offence" when:
    - He intends to commit that particular offence and
    - He, having made preparations and with the intention of committing the offence, does an act towards its commission: such an act need not be the penultimate act towards the commission of that offence but must be an act during the course of committing that offence."

Doctrine of Locus Poenitentiae

- The literal meaning of the phrase *"locus poenitentiae" is* "Time for Repentance". The doctrine means that an act will amount to mere preparation if the offender, on his own accord, gives up his idea of committing a crime before the criminal act is done. As long as the steps taken by the accused leave scope for reasonable expectation that he, on his own accord- either due to fear of consequences that he might face or for any other reason, might desist from going further for the contemplated act, then in law, he will be treated at the stage of preparation and criminal lability will not be fastened on him.
- In the case of **Malkiat Singh v. State of Punjab**, Hon'ble Apex Court applied this doctrine and observed that, "the test for determining whether the act of the appellants constituted an attempt or preparation is whether the overt acts already done are such that if the offender changes his mind, and does not proceed further in its progress, the acts already done would be completely harmless."

Impossibility Test

- The impossibility test deals with criminal liability of the offender when he attempts to commit an impossible act. In earlier times, attempts deemed impossible were not subject to legal repercussions as they were equated with mere preparatory actions. Until the decision of **R v. William (1893 England),** it was observed that the offender was not guilty of an attempt to steal if he put his hands into the pocket of another person but found the pocket to be empty.
- However, the earlier legal position with regard to impossible attempts was overruled in the case of **R v. Ring (1892 England)** wherein the offender was held guilty of attempting to steal from the pocket of a lady although her pocket was found to be empty by him. The two illustrations of **Section 62** are based on the principles laid down in the case of **R vs. Ring**.

Social-Danger Test

- This test mandates that, in order to differentiate between an act of attempt and that of mere preparation, careful consideration needs to be given to the gravity of the offence attempted and the potential societal harm associated with it.
- For instance, where A provides pills to a pregnant woman with the intention of inducing an abortion but the pills prove to be innocuous and have no actual effect, A could still be held liable for an attempt to cause a miscarriage. This determination stems from the recognition that such an act, even if unsuccessful, has the potential to incite alarm within society and carry significant social ramifications.

Equivocality Test ("The Act must Speak for Itself")

- This theory means that to constitute an attempt, the act of the offender must be an unmistakable and unequivocal manifestation of his intention to commit the offence. If the actions undertaken provide irrefutable evidence that they are directed towards the ultimate goal in question, then they qualify as an attempt. Otherwise, if the evidence falls short of establishing clear intent and instead only signifies preliminary measures, it remains categorized as mere preparation.

CRIMINAL INTIMIDATION

Introduction

Chapter XIX of BNS, comprising Sections 351- 355, deals with the offences of criminal intimidation, intentional insult and annoyance [Earlier, Sections 503- 510 of the IPC]. BNS has brought about substantial changes in the provisions relating to these offences, e.g, the offence of misconduct committed in public by a drunken person has been addressed with changes in the amount of fine and the addition of community service as one of the punishments.

Comparative Chart of The BNS And IPC		
Bharatiya Nyaya Sanhita, 2023 (BNS)	**Title**	**Indian Penal Code, 1860 (IPC)**
Section 351	Criminal Intimidation	Section 503 Section 506 Section 507
Section 352	Intentional insult with intent to provoke breach of peace	Section 504
Section 353	Statements conducing to public mischief	Section 505
Section 354	Act caused by inducing person to believe that he will be rendered an object of the divine displeasure	Section 508
Section 355	Misconduct in public by a drunken person	Section 510

CHANGES IN BNS IN COMPARISON TO IPC

- **Section 351** of the BNS, corresponding to Sections 503, 506, 507 of the IPC, has introduced the following changes:
  - In Section 351(1), corresponding to Section 503 of the IPC, the words "by any means" have been added.
- **Section 352** of the BNS, corresponding to Section 504 of the IPC, has introduced the following changes:
  - The words "in any manner" have been added.
  - Twenty days to fifteen days.
- **Section 353** of the BNS, corresponding to Section 505 of the IPC, has introduced the following changes:
  - The words " false information" and "including through electronic means" have been added
- **Section 355** of the BNS, corresponding to Section 510 of the IPC, has introduced the following changes:
- The amount of fine has been increased from ten rupees to one thousand rupees and community service has been added as one of the punishments for the offence.

Criminal Intimidation

(**Note:** ***Section 351*** *of the BNS corresponds to* ***Sections 503, 506, 507*** *of the IPC*)

- **Section 351(1)** defines the offence of criminal intimidation.
- As per the definition, following are the essential ingredients of the criminal intimidation:
  - The accused must threaten another person with injury to his person, reputation or property, or to the person or reputation of any one in whom that another person is interested. The illustration appended to **Section 351(1)** further clarifies this legal position:
    - **Illustration:** A, for the purpose of inducing B to resist from prosecuting a civil suit, threatens to burn B's house. A is guilty of criminal intimidation.
  - The threat may be given by the accused by employing any means. Moreover, it is important to note that a threat to injure the reputation of any deceased person in whom the person threatened is interested comes within the purview of **Section 351.**
  - The threat must be given by the accused with intent to cause alarm to that person, or to cause that person to do any act which he is not legally bound to do, or to omit to do any act which that person is legally entitled to do, as the means of avoiding the execution of such threat.
- **Punishment for Criminal Intimidation Simpliciter: Section 351(2)** provides for the punishment of criminal intimidation simpliciter. As per the section, a person who commits the offence of criminal intimidation shall be punished with imprisonment of either description for a term which may extend to two years, or with fine, or with both.
- **Punishment for Aggravated Forms of Criminal Intimidation**
  - **Section 351(3)** provides that a person who commits the offence of criminal intimidation by threatening to cause death or grievous hurt, or to cause the destruction of any property by fire, or to cause an offence is liable to be punished with punishable with death, or life imprisonment, or with imprisonment up to seven years.
  - **Section 351(3)** provides that a person who commits the offence of criminal intimidation by threatening to impute unchastity to a woman, shall be punished with imprisonment of either description for a term which may extend to seven years, or with fine, or with both.
  - **Section 351(4)** provides that a person who commits the offence of criminal intimidation by anonymous communication, or having taken precaution to conceal the name or abode of the person from whom the threat comes,

shall be punished with imprisonment of either description for a term which may extend to two years. This punishment shall be in addition to the punishment provided for the offence under **Section 351(1).**

Intentional Insult with Intent to Provoke Breach of Peace

(**Note:** ***Section 352*** *of the BNS corresponds to* ***Section 504*** *of the IPC*)

- **Section 352** deals with the offence of intentional insult with intent to provoke breach of public peace.
- The accused must intentionally insult another person in any manner.
- The insult must give provocation to another person.
- The accused must intend or know such provocation will cause another person to break the public peace, or to commit any other offence.
- If the above-said conditions are satisfied, the accused is liable to be punished with imprisonment of either description for a term which may extend to two years, or with fine, or with both.

Statements Conducing To Public Mischief

(**Note:** ***Section 353*** *of the BNS corresponds to* ***Section 505*** *of the IPC*)

- **Section 353** deals with statements conducing to public mischief and inter alia punishes the dissemination of mischievous information with intent to cause public disturbance.
- **Section 353(1)** inter alia deals with the simpliciter form of the offence and can be summarized as under:
  - The accused must make, publish or circulate any statement, false information, rumor, or report through electronic means or through any other means.
  - The act of making, publishing or circulating must have any one of the following characters:
    - It must be done with intent to cause, or be likely to cause, any officer, soldier, sailor or airman in the Army, Navy or Air Force of India to mutiny or otherwise disregard or fail in his duty as such.
    - It must be done with intent to cause, or be likely to cause, fear or alarm to the public, or to any section of the public whereby any person may be induced to commit an offence against the State or against the public tranquility.
    - It must be done with intent to incite, or be likely to incite, any class or community of persons to commit any offence against any other class or community.
  - If the aforesaid conditions are satisfied, the accused is liable to be punished with imprisonment which may extend to three years, or with fine, or with both.
- **Statements Creating or Promoting Enmity, Hatred or Ill-will Between Classes: Section 353(2)** deals with an aggravated form of the offence and inter alia deals with the statements creating enmity between classes:
  - The accused must make, publish or circulate any statement or report containing false information, rumor or alarming news through electronic means or through any other means.
  - The accused must do so with intent to create or promote, or which is likely to create or promote, on grounds of religion, race, place of birth, residence, language, caste or community or any other ground whatsoever, feelings of enmity, hatred or ill will between different religious, racial, language or regional groups or castes or communities.
    - If the aforesaid conditions are satisfied, the accused is liable to be punished with imprisonment which may extend to three years, or with fine, or with both.

- **Commission of the offence under Section 353(2) in place of worship, etc.: Section 353(3)** deals with an aggravated form of the offence and provides that a person who commits the offence specified under Section 353(2) in any place of worship or in any assembly engaged in the performance of religious worship or religious ceremonies, is liable to be punished with imprisonment which may extend to five years and with to fine.

Act Caused By Inducing Person To Believe That He Will Be Rendered An Object of the Divine Displeasure

(**Note:** *Section 354 of the BNS corresponds to Section 508 of the IPC*)

- The accused must cause or attempt to cause any person to do anything which that person is not legally bound to do, or to omit to do anything which he is legally entitled to do.
- The accused must do so by inducing or attempting to induce that person to believe that he or any person in whom he is interested will become or will be rendered an object of Divine displeasure if he does not do or omit to do such thing as per the wishes of the accused.
- If the aforesaid conditions are satisfied, the accused is liable to be punished with imprisonment of either description for a term which may extend to one year, or with fine, or with both.
- The two illustrations appended to **Section 354** further clarify the provision.
  - **Illustration (a):** A sits dharna at Z's door with the intention of causing it to be believed that, by so sitting, he renders Z an object of Divine displeasure. A has committed the offence defined in this section.
  - **Illustration (b):** A threatens Z that, unless Z performs a certain act, A will kill one of A's own children, under such circumstances that the killing would be believed to render Z an object of Divine displeasure. A has committed the offence defined in this section.

Misconduct In Public By A Drunken Person

(**Note:** *Section 355 of the BNS corresponds to Section 510 of the IPC*)

- The accused must be in a state of intoxication and in such state, appear in any public place, or in any place which it is a trespass in him to enter,.
- At such a place, the accused must conduct himself in such a manner that he causes annoyance to any other person.
- If the aforesaid conditions are satisfied, the accused is liable to be punished with simple imprisonment for a term which may extend to twenty-four hours, or with fine which may extend to one thousand rupees, or with both or with community service.

❖ ❖ ❖

Chapter 20

MISCELLANEOUS PROVISIONS

INTRODUCTION

The Bharatiya Nyaya Sanhita (BNS) encompasses a diverse array of legal provisions designed to uphold justice, safeguard public welfare, and preserve societal order within India. Among its comprehensive framework, key provisions address critical offences that range from perjury and evidence fabrication to counterfeiting of currency and public nuisance. These provisions are integral to maintaining the integrity of judicial processes, ensuring economic stability, and fostering communal harmony by penalizing actions that undermine truth, financial security, and public peace.

COMPARATIVE CHART OF THE BNS AND IPC		
Bharatiya Nyaya Sanhita, 2023	**Title**	**Indian Penal Code, 1860**
OFFENCES RELATED TO FALSE EVIDENCE AND OFFENCES AGAINST PUBLIC JUSTICE		
Section 227	Giving false evidence	Section 191
Section 228	Fabricating false evidence	Section 192
Section 229	Punishment for false evidence	Section 193
Section 230	Giving or fabricating false evidence with intent to procure conviction of capital offence	Section 194
Section 231	Giving or fabricating false evidence with intent to procure conviction of offence punishable with imprisonment for life or imprisonment.	Section 195
Section 232	Threatening to give false evidence	Section 195A
OFFENCES RELATED TO COINS, CURRENCY NOTES, BANK NOTES AND STAMPS		
Section 178	Counterfeiting coins, Government stamps, currency-notes or banknotes.	Section 231
		Section 255
		Section 489A
Section 179	Using as a genuine, forged or counterfeit coin, Government stamp, currency-notes or bank-notes.	Section 237
		Section 238
		Section 239
		Section 240
		Section 241
		Section 250
		Section 251
		Section 254

Bharatiya Nyaya Sanhita, 2023	Title	Indian Penal Code, 1860
Section 179		Section 258
		Section 260
		Section 489B
Section 180	Possession of forged or counterfeit coin, Government stamp, currency-notes or bank-notes	Section 242
		Section 243
		Section 252
		Section 253
		Section 259
		Section 489C
Section 181	Making or possessing instruments or materials for forging or counterfeiting coin, Government stamp, currency-notes or banknotes.	Section 233
		Section 234
		Section 235
		Section 256
		Section 257
		Section 489D
Section 182	Making or using documents resembling currency-notes or banknotes.	Section 489E
Section 183	Effacing writing from substance bearing Government stamp, or removing from document a stamp used for it, with intent to cause loss to Government.	Section 261
Section 184	Using Government stamp known to have been used before.	Section 262
Section 185	Erasure of mark denoting that stamp has been used.	Section 263
Section 186	Prohibition of fictitious stamps.	Section 263-A
OFFENCES RELATED TO PUBLIC NUISANCE		
Section 270	Public Nuisance	Section 268
Section 292	Punishment for public nuisance in cases not otherwise provided for.	Section 290
Section 293	Continuance of nuisance after injunction to discontinue.	Section 291
Section 294	Sale, etc., of obscene books, etc.	Section 292
Section 295	Sale, etc., of obscene objects to child.	Section 293
Section 296	Obscene acts and songs.	Section 294
OFFENCES RELATED TO RELIGION		
Section 298	Injuring or defiling a place of worship with intent to insult religion of any class.	Section 295
Section 299	Deliberate and malicious acts, intended to outrage religious feelings of any class by insulting its religion or religious beliefs.	Section 295-A
Section 300	Disturbing religious assembly.	Section 296
Section 301	Trespassing on burial places, etc.	Section 297
Section 302	Uttering words, etc., with deliberate intent to wound religious feelings of any person.	Section 298

CHANGES IN BNS IN COMPARISON TO IPC

- **Section 229** of the BNS corresponding to Section 193 of the IPC has changes as follows:
  - Specifies fine amounts for false evidence in judicial proceedings **up to ten thousand rupees** and other **cases up to five thousand rupees,** whereas Section 193 of the IPC does not specify fine amounts.
- **Section 230** of the BNS corresponding to Section 194 of the IPC has changes as follows:
  - Specifies a fine amount of **up to fifty thousand rupees,** whereas Section 194 of the IPC does not specify a fine amount. The BNS uses slightly different wording for the additional punishment if an innocent person is executed, referring to **"the punishment specified in sub-section (1)" instead of "the punishment hereinbefore described."**
- In **Section 181** of the BNS corresponding to Section 256, 257 of the IPC has changes as follows:
  - 'Any coin, stamp issued by the Government for the purpose of revenue' is added.
- In **Section 182** of the BNS corresponding to Section 489E of the IPC has changes as follows:
  - The upper limit of fine is increased from one hundred to three hundred rupees and two hundred to six hundred rupees.
- Section 186 of the BNS corresponding to Section 263A of the IPC has changes as follows:
  - Section 263-A of the IPC includes the words **"and also in any part of Her Majesty's dominions"** in Sub-section (4). The **Section 186 of the BNS** excludes this phrase.
- In **Section 292** of the BNS corresponding to Section 290 of the IPC has changes as follows:
  - The upper limit of the fine is increased from two hundred to one thousand rupees.
- **Section 293** of the BNS corresponding to Section 291 of the IPC has changes as follows:
  - Fine is defined as up to five thousand rupees.
- **Section 294** of the BNS corresponding to Section 292 of the IPC has changes as follows:
  - The fine is increased from two thousand to five thousand rupees and from five thousand to ten thousand rupees on subsequent conviction. **"including display of any content in electronic form'" is added, "in whatever manner"** is also added.
- **Section 295** of the BNS corresponding to Section 292 of the IPC has changes as follows:
  - **"person under the age of twenty years"** is replaced by **"child",** thereby curtailing the scope of this provision.
- **Section 296** of the BNS corresponding to Section 294 of the IPC has changes as follows:
  - Fine is defined as up to one thousand rupees.

FALSE EVIDENCE

False evidence and fabricating evidence are grave offences under the Bharatiya Nyaya Sanhita (BNS), aimed at preserving the integrity of judicial proceedings and upholding public justice. These provisions are pivotal in maintaining trust and fairness within the legal system. **Chapter XIV** from **Section 227 to 269** of the BNS deals with the 'Offences related to False Evidence and Offences against Public Justice'.

Giving/Fabricating False Evidence

(Note: ***Section 227*** *of the BSA corresponds to* ***Section 191*** *of the IPC***)**

- False evidence refers to providing untrue statements while legally bound by oath or law to state the truth.
- This can be done either in written form or orally.
- A person is said to give false evidence if:
  - They are legally bound by an oath or an express provision of law to state the truth.
  - They make a false statement or a statement that they do not believe to be true or believe to be false.
- **For Example:**
  - If A, in support of a just claim which B has against Z for one thousand rupees, falsely swears in a trial that he heard Z admit the justice of B's claim, A has given false evidence.
  - If A, knowing the general character of Z's handwriting, states that he believes a certain signature to be the handwriting of Z, A in good faith believing it to be so, then A's statement is merely as to his belief and is true as to his belief, and therefore, although the signature may not be the handwriting of Z, A has not given false evidence.

Fabricated Evidence

(Note: ***Section 228*** *of the BNS corresponds to* ***Section 192*** *of the IPC***)**

- Fabricating evidence involves creating false entries in records or documents with the intent to use them as evidence in judicial proceedings.
- **Section 228** of BNS explains that a person fabricates false evidence if they cause any circumstance to exist, make any false entry in any book, record, or electronic record, or make any document or electronic record containing a false statement, intending for it to appear in evidence in a judicial proceeding.
- **Illustrations:**
  - A puts jewels into a box belonging to Z with the intention that they may be found in that box, causing Z to be convicted of theft. A has fabricated false evidence.
  - A, with the intention of causing Z to be convicted of a criminal conspiracy, writes a letter in imitation of Z's handwriting, purporting to be addressed to an accomplice in the criminal conspiracy, and places it where he knows the police are likely to search. A has fabricated false evidence.

Punishment for False Evidence

General Punishment

(Notes: ***Section 229*** *of the BNS corresponds to* ***Section 193*** *of the IPC***)**

- Under **Section 229(1)** of the BNS, giving or fabricating false evidence at any stage of a judicial proceeding attracts a punishment of imprisonment for up to seven years and a fine of up to Rs. 10,000.
- **Section 229(2)** of the BNS provides that if the false evidence is given in non-judicial proceedings, the imprisonment term can extend up to three years, with a fine of up to Rs. 5,000.
- In **S.H. Narendra Kumar Srivastava v. State of Bihar, (2019)**, Supreme Court iterated that a private complaint alleging an offence under this is not maintainable.
- In **Santokh Singh v. Izhar Hussain (1973),** The Supreme Court held that falsely identifying someone in a test identification parade, as done by the appellant, does not constitute an offence under Section 211 of IPC (Section 248 of BNS).
  - The Court emphasized that false evidence given during a trial is punishable under Section 193 of the IPC (Sections 229 of BNS) and Section 195 IPC (Section 231 of BNS) not Section 248.

False Evidence with Intent to Procure Conviction of Capital Offence

(**Note:** ***Section 230*** *of the BNS corresponds to* ***Section 194*** *of the IPC*)

- **Section 230 (1)** provides whoever gives or fabricates false evidence, intending thereby to cause, or knowing it to be likely that he will thereby cause, any person to be convicted of an offence which is capital by the law for the time being in force in India
  - Shall be punished with imprisonment for life, or with rigorous imprisonment for a term which may extend to ten years, and shall also be liable to fine which may extend to fifty thousand rupees.
- **Section 230 (2)** further provides that if an innocent person be convicted and executed in consequence of false evidence referred to in sub-section (1), the person who gives such false evidence
  - Shall be punished either with death or the punishment specified in sub-section (1).

False Evidence with Intent to Procure Conviction

(**Notes:** ***Section 231*** *of the BNS corresponds to* ***Section 195*** *of the IPC*)

- **Section 231** provides that if the false evidence leads to a conviction for a serious offence not punishable by death but by life imprisonment or a term of seven years or more, the person giving or fabricating the evidence will face the same punishment as the offence for which the wrongful conviction was made.
- Suppose, A person fabricates evidence to falsely accuse someone of dacoity, which is punishable by life imprisonment.
- The fabricator can be sentenced to life imprisonment, equivalent to the punishment for dacoity.

Threatening Any Person to Give False Evidence

(**Notes:** ***Section 232*** *of the BNS corresponds to* ***Section 195A*** *of the IPC*)

- **Section 232(1)** provides whoever threatens another with any injury to his person, reputation or property or to the person or reputation of any one in whom that person is interested, with intent to cause that person to give false evidence
  - Shall be punished with imprisonment of either description for a term which may extend to seven years, or with fine, or with both.
- **Section 232(2)** provides if innocent person is convicted and sentenced in consequence of false evidence referred to in sub-section (1), with death or imprisonment for more than seven years, the person who threatens
  - Shall be punished with the same punishment and sentence in the same manner and to the same extent such innocent person is punished and sentenced.

OTHER RELATED PROVISIONS

- Using evidence known to be false (**Section 233** of the BNS)
- Issuing or signing false certificate (**Section 234** of the BNS)
- Using as true a certificate known to be false (**Section 235** of the BNS)
- False Statement made in declaration which is by law receivable as evidence (**Section 236** of the BNS)
- Using as true such declaration knowing it to be false (**Section 237** of the BNS)
- Causing Disappearance of evidence of offence, or giving false information to screen offender (**Section 238** of the BNS)
- Intentional omission to give information of offence by person bound to inform.
- Giving false information respecting an offence committed (**Section 239** of the BNS)
- Destruction of document or electronic record to prevent its production as evidence (**Section 240** of the BNS)

- False Personation for the purpose of act or proceeding in suit or prosecution (**Section 241** of the BNS)
- False personation for purpose of act or proceeding in suit or prosecution (**Section 242** of the BNS)
- Fraudulent removal or concealment of property to prevent its seizure as forfeited or in execution (**Section 243** of the BNS)
- Fraudulent claim to property to prevent its seizure as forfeited or in execution (**Section 244** of the BNS)
- Fraudulently suffering decree for sum not due (**Section 245** of the BNS)
- Dishonestly making false claim in Court (**Section 246** of the BNS)
- Fraudulently obtaining decree for sum not due (**Section 247** of the BNS)
- False charge of offence made with intent to injure (**Section 248** of the BNS)
- Harbouring offender (**Section 249** of the BNS)
- Taking gift, etc., to screen an offender from punishment (**Section 250** of the BNS)
- Offering gift or restoration of property in consideration of screening offender (**Section 251** of the BNS)
- Taking gift to help to recover stolen property, etc (**Section 252** of the BNS)
- Harbouring offender who has escaped from custody or whose apprehension has been ordered (**Section 253** of the BNS)
- Penalty for harbouring robbers or dacoits (**Section 254** of the BNS)
- Public servant disobeying direction of law with intent to save person from punishment or property from forfeiture (**Section 255** of the BNS)
- Public servant framing incorrect record or writing with intent to save person from punishment or property from forfeiture (**Section 256** of the BNS)
- Public servant in judicial proceeding corruptly making report, etc., contrary to law. (**Section 257** of the BNS)
- Commitment for trial or confinement by person having authority who knows that he is acting contrary to law (**Section 258** of the BNS)
- Intentional omission to apprehend on part of public servant bound to apprehend (**Section 259** of the BNS)
- Intentional omission to apprehend on part of public servant bound to apprehend person under sentence or lawfully committed (**Section 260** of the BNS)
- Escape from confinement or custody negligently suffered by public servant (**Section 261** of the BNS)
- Resistance or obstruction by a person to his lawful apprehension (**Section 262** of the BNS)
- Resistance or obstruction to lawful apprehension of another person (**Section 263** of the BNS)
- Omission to apprehend, or sufferance of escape, on part of public servant, in cases not otherwise provided for (**Section 264** of the BNS)
- Resistance or obstruction to lawful apprehension or escape or rescue in cases not otherwise provided for (**Section 265** of the BNS)
- Violation of condition of remission of punishment (**Section 266** of the BNS)
- Intentional insult or interruption to public servant sitting in judicial proceeding (**Section 267** of the BNS)
- Personation of assessor (**Section 268** of the BNS)
    - Failure by person released on bail or bond to appear in Court (**Section 269** of the BNS)

OFFENCES RELATED TO COINS, CURRENCY NOTES, BANK NOTES AND STAMPS

Offences related to coins, currency notes, bank notes, and government stamps are dealt with in **Chapter X** from **Section 178 to 188** of the Bharatiya Nyaya Sanhita (BNS) (Earlier, Section 230 to 263A of the IPC). These offences threaten the economic stability of a nation and undermine public trust in the financial and governmental systems. The BNS sets out stringent penalties to deter and punish such acts.

Counterfeiting

(Note: ***Section 178*** *of the BNS corresponds to* ***Sections 246, 247, 248, 249, 255*** *of the IPC*)

- Counterfeiting involves the creation, alteration, or use of fake currency notes, coins, or government stamps that are intended to be passed off as genuine.
- This includes the entire process from production to the circulation of these counterfeit items, undermining the integrity of the financial system and legal processes.
- **Section 178** provides that Counterfeiting coins, currency notes, bank notes, or government stamps, or performing any part of the counterfeiting process, is a serious crime under Section 178 of the BNS.
- The punishment includes life imprisonment or imprisonment up to ten years, along with a fine.

Using Counterfeit Items

(Note: ***Section 179*** *of the BNS corresponds to* ***Sections 250, 251, 254, 260*** *of the IPC*)

- Under **Section 179,** using counterfeit coins, currency notes, bank notes, or government stamps, or engaging in their import, export, sale, or trafficking, knowing them to be counterfeit, is punishable by life imprisonment or imprisonment up to ten years, and a fine.

Possession of Counterfeit Items

(Note: ***Section 180*** *of the BNS corresponds to* ***Sections 252, 253*** *of the IPC*)

- **Section 180** deals with possession of counterfeit coins, currency notes, bank notes, or government stamps, with the intention to use them as genuine.
  - The punishment includes imprisonment up to seven years and a fine.
- **Explanation to Section 180** provides that if a person establishes the possession of the forged or counterfeit coin, stamp, currency-note or bank-note to be from a lawful source, it shall not constitute an offence under this section.

Making or Possessing Instruments for Counterfeiting

(Note: ***Section 181*** *of the BNS corresponds to* ***Sections 256, 257*** *of the IPC*)

- Making, mending, or possessing instruments or materials for the purpose of counterfeiting is covered under **Section 181.**
  - The punishment is life imprisonment or imprisonment up to ten years, along with a fine.

OTHER RELATED PROVISIONS

- Making or Using Documents Resembling Currency Notes (**Section 182** of the BNS)
- Effacing Writing from Stamps (**Section 183** of the BNS)
- Using Previously Used Stamps (**Section 184** of the BNS)
- Erasure of Marks on Stamps (**Section 185** of the BNS)
- Prohibition of Fictitious Stamps (**Section 186** of the BNS)
- Mint Offences (**Section 187 and 188** of the BNS)

Landmark Judgments

- In **Sri Kashi Prasad Saksena v. State of Uttar Pradesh (1966)**, the Court ruled that mere possession of instruments or materials for counterfeiting is sufficient to establish the accused's guilt.
  - Furthermore, the accused does not need to have ownership of the premises where the materials are discovered to be held liable.
- In **Abdul Kareem Telgi v. The State of Karnataka (2017)**, Telgi was convicted for a large-scale counterfeit stamp paper racket. The Supreme Court upheld the conviction under Sections 256 of IPC and Section 259 of IPC, emphasizing the substantial evidence linking Telgi to the manufacturing and circulation of fake stamps, which undermined public trust and financial integrity.

PUBLIC NUISANCE

(Note: ***Section*** *270 of the BNS, corresponds to* ***Section 268*** *of the IPC*)

- Public nuisance under Section 270 of the BNS, refers to any act or illegal omission that results in common injury, danger, or annoyance to the public or to people who reside or occupy property in the vicinity.
- It encompasses acts that affect public health, safety, comfort, or convenience.
- Public nuisance extends beyond mere inconvenience to impact the broader community or a significant portion thereof. It involves interference with public rights or amenities rather than individual grievances.
- Public nuisance is based on the principle "sic utere tuo ut alienum non laedas," meaning use your property in such a manner as not to injure that of others. It emphasizes responsible property use to avoid harm to public rights.
- **For example,** A factory near a residential area emits excessive noise and pollutants, causing widespread health issues and discomfort.
  - This constitutes a public nuisance as it affects the community's right to a clean and peaceful environment, potentially leading to legal action and penalties for the factory.
- In the case of **K. Ramakrishnan v. State of Kerala (1999)**, the Court set precedents for handling public health issues under the guise of public nuisance, highlighting the judiciary's proactive stance in safeguarding public interests.

Punishment for Public Nuisance

(**Note:** ***Sections 292, 293*** *of the BNS, corresponds to* ***Sections 290, 291*** *of the IPC respectively*)

- **Section 292** of BNS provides for the punishment of public nuisance. This section prescribes a monetary penalty as punishment for committing public nuisance.
- Offenders can be fined up to one thousand rupees upon conviction.
- The fine serves as a deterrent against behaviors that disturb public peace or comfort, imposing a financial consequence on offenders and signaling society's disapproval of such conduct.
- **Continuance of Nuisance after Injunction to Discontinue: Section 293** provides that whoever repeats or continues a public nuisance, having been enjoined by any public servant who has lawful authority to issue such injunction not to repeat or continue such nuisance,
  - Shall be punished with simple imprisonment for a term which may extend to six months, or with fine which may extend to five thousand rupees, or with both.
- **For example,** If an individual persistently organizes noisy events in a residential area

despite warnings and a subsequent court injunction, they may initially face a fine under **Section 292**.

- However, if the behavior continues despite the Court order, the person could face imprisonment under **Section 293**, alongside a higher fine.

Landmark Judgment

- In **Malton Board of Health v. Malton Manure Co.** (1879), the case is concerned the production of manure by the defendant company, which emitted vapors.
  - While it wasn't definitively proven that these vapors harmed healthy individuals or exacerbated illnesses, the Court ruled that their potential to release harmful or offensive substances affecting health justified regulatory intervention by the Board of Health.
- In **St. Helen's Smelting Co. v. Tipping (1865)**, the plaintiff's land neighboured a copper smelting factory emitting noxious gases, causing significant damage to trees. Despite the factory's lawful operation and the plaintiff's awareness upon settling nearby, the court upheld the plaintiff's right to claim against the nuisance.
  - This underscored that even established businesses can be liable for private nuisance if they cause tangible harm to others' property or well-being.

OBSCENE ACT

An obscene act, refers to any act, representation, or expression that is lascivious or appeals to prurient interest and has the potential to deprave and corrupt individuals who are likely to come across it. This includes content in various forms such as books, pamphlets, writings, drawings, paintings, electronic displays, etc. **Section 294 to 296** of the BNS deals with the Obscene Acts.

Analysis of Offences Related to Obscene

Acts Sale, etc., of Obscene Books, etc.

(Note: ***Section 294*** *of the BNS corresponds to* ***Section 292*** *of the IPC)*

- **Section 294 (1)** provides that for the purposes of sub-section (2), a book, pamphlet, paper, writing, drawing, painting, representation, figure or any other object, including display of any content in electronic form shall be deemed to be obscene if it is lascivious or appeals to the prurient interest or if its effect, or (where it comprises two or more distinct items) the effect of any one of its items, is, if taken as a whole, such as to tend to deprave and corrupt persons who are likely, having regard to all relevant circumstances, to read, see or hear the matter contained or embodied in it.
- Sub section (2) of **Section 294** provides, Whoever:
  - (a) Sells, lets to hire, distributes, publicly exhibits or in any manner puts into circulation, or for purposes of sale, hire, distribution, public exhibition or circulation, makes, produces or has in his possession any obscene book, pamphlet, paper, drawing, painting, representation or figure or any other obscene object whatsoever in whatever manner; or
  - (b) Imports, exports or conveys any obscene object for any of the purposes aforesaid, or knowing or having reason to believe that such object will be sold, let to hire, distributed or publicly exhibited or in any manner put into circulation; or
  - (c) Takes part in or receives profits from any business in the course of which he knows or has reason to believe that any such obscene objects are, for any of the purposes aforesaid, made produced, purchased, kept, imported, exported, conveyed, publicly exhibited or in any manner put into circulation; or

(d) Advertises or makes known by any means whatsoever that any person is engaged or is ready to engage in any act which is an offence under this section, or that any such obscene object can be procured from or through any person; or

(e) Offers or attempts to do any act which is an offence under this section, shall be punished on first conviction with imprisonment of either description for a term which may extend to two years, and with fine which may extend to five thousand rupees, and, in the event of a second or subsequent conviction, with imprisonment of either description for a term which may extend to five years, and also with fine which may extend to ten thousand rupees.

- **Exception:** This section does not extend to:
  (a) any book, pamphlet, paper, writing, drawing, painting, representation or figure:
  (i) The publication of which is proved to be justified as being for the public good on the ground that such book, pamphlet, paper, writing, drawing, painting, representation or figure is in the interest of science, literature, art or learning or other objects of general concern; or
  (ii) Which is kept or used bona fide for religious purposes;
- (b) any representation sculptured, engraved, painted or otherwise represented on or in:
  (i) Any ancient monument within the meaning of the Ancient Monuments and Archaeological Sites and Remains Act, 1958; or
  (ii) Any temple, or on any car used for the conveyance of idols, or kept or used for any religious purpose

Sale of Obscene Objects to Child

(Note: ***Section 295*** *of the BNS corresponds to* ***Section 293*** *of the IPC*)

Section 295 can be explained as follows:

- **Targeting Minors:** Specifically addresses the sale, distribution, or exhibition of obscene objects to children. This section prohibits the selling, letting to hire, distribute, exhibit or circulate to any child any such obscene object as is referred to in **Section 294**, or offers or attempts to do so.
- **Heightened Penalties:** The penalties for this section are more severe compared to those for adults, reflecting the importance of protecting children from harmful and corruptive materials. The offender shall be punished with:
  - On first conviction with imprisonment of either description for a term which may extend to three years, and with fine which may extend to two thousand rupees, and,
  - In the event of a second or subsequent conviction, with imprisonment of either description for a term which may extend to seven years, and also with fine which may extend to five thousand rupees.

Obscene Acts and Songs

(Note: ***Section 296*** *of the BNS corresponds to* ***Section 294*** *of the IPC*)

- **Section 296** of the BNS provides whoever, to the annoyance of others:
  - Does any obscene act in any public place; or
  - Sings, recites or utters any obscene song, ballad or words, in or near any public place,

  Shall be punished with imprisonment of either description for a term which may extend to three months, or with fine which may extend to one thousand rupees, or with both.

Landmark Judgments

- In **Miller v. California (1973),** the U.S. Supreme Court established the Miller test to determine obscenity. Melvin Miller was prosecuted for sending unsolicited explicit brochures, violating California law. The Miller test has three parts:
  - Whether the average person, applying contemporary community standards, finds the work appeals to prurient interest;
  - Whether the work depicts sexual conduct in a patently offensive way as defined by state law; and
  - Whether the work lacks serious literary, artistic, political, or scientific value.
- All three conditions must be met for material to be deemed obscene (Miller Test).
- In **Regina v. Hicklin (1868)**, the Court dealt with the issue of what constitutes obscenity.
  - The case centered around anti-Catholic pamphlets called The Confessional Unmasked, which criticized the Catholic Church.
  - Henry Scott, who sold these pamphlets, was accused of spreading obscene material.
  - The bureaucrat Benjamin Hicklin initially ordered their destruction, labeling them obscene.
  - However, Scott argued that his intention was not to corrupt public morals but to highlight issues with the Catholic Church.
  - The Court used this case to define obscenity as material that could corrupt or deprive those who see it, regardless of the creator's intention.
- The Hicklin Test was laid down by the Queen's Bench in **Regina v. Hicklin.** The test of obscenity is whether the tendency of the matter charged as obscenity is to deprave and corrupt those whose minds are open to such immoral influences and into whose hands a publication of this sort may fall. On application of the Hicklin test, a publication can be judged for obscenity based on isolated passages of a work considered out of context. Works can be judged by their apparent influence on most susceptible readers, such as children or weak-minded adults.
- In **Ranjit D. Udeshi v. State of Maharashtra (1964)**, the Supreme Court addressed obscenity under **Section 292** of the IPC (Now, Section 294 of BNS).
  - The case involved the book, Lady Chatterley's Lover.
  - The Court upheld the Victorian-era Hicklin test, which judged obscenity based on whether material could deprave and corrupt its readers.
  - The appellant argued that **Section 292** was overly vague and restricted freedom of speech under **Article 19(1)(a)** of the Indian Constitution.
  - The Court affirmed that **Section 292** was valid, emphasizing that while obscenity should be judged on context, it serves to uphold public decency and morality.
- In **Narendra H. Khurana and Ors. v. Commissioner of Police and Anr. (2003)**, the petitioners sought to quash an FIR related to obscene acts under **Section 294** IPC (Now, Section 296 of the BNS).
  - The case arose from a raid at Blue Nile Restaurant where cabaret dances were performed.
  - The petitioners argued that no annoyance was caused, as required by Section 294 IPC.
  - The Single Judge referred the matter to a larger bench, questioning if obscene acts in private venues with ticketed entry could constitute public annoyance under Section 294 IPC.

- Cabaret dances where indecent and obscene act per se is involved, would not attract the provision of Section 294 of the IPC without fulfillment of its essential ingredients i.e. Evidence pertaining to "annoyance to others"; and
- The hotels like the one where cabaret dances are performed and entry is restricted by purchase of the tickets, would still be the public places within the meaning of Section 294 of the IPC.

OFFENCES RELATED TO RELIGION

The Bharatiya Nyaya Sanhita (BNS) is a comprehensive legal framework aimed at maintaining law and order in India. Among its various provisions, it includes specific sections addressing offences related to religion. These sections are crucial for preserving communal harmony and ensuring that the religious sentiments of all citizens are respected. By penalizing actions that insult or outrage religious feelings, the BNS seeks to prevent communal tensions and promote peaceful coexistence among different religious communities. **Chapter XVI** from **Section 298 to 302** of the BNS deals with the 'Offences relating to Religion'.

Provisions Regarding Offences Related to Religion

(Notes: ***Sections 298, 299, 300, 301, 302*** *of the BNS corresponds to* ***Sections 295, 295A, 296, 297, 298*** *of the IPC respectively*)

- **Injuring or Defiling a Place of Worship with Intent to Insult Religion of Any Class: Section 298** provides that whoever destroys, damages or defiles any place of worship, or any object held sacred by any class of persons with the intention of thereby insulting the religion of any class of persons or with the knowledge that any class of persons is likely to consider such destruction, damage or defilement as an insult to their religion,
  - Shall be punished with imprisonment of either description for a term which may extend to two years, or with fine, or with both.
- This provision aims to protect religious places and objects from deliberate acts of insult or desecration, ensuring respect for religious sentiments and communal harmony.
- **Deliberate and Malicious Acts to Outrage Religious Feelings: Section 299** provides that acts intended to outrage the religious feelings of any class of citizens of India by words, spoken or written, gestures, visible representations, electronic means, or otherwise, shall be punishable with imprisonment of either description for a term which may extend to three years, or with fine, or with both.
  - This section targets deliberate acts aimed at hurting religious sentiments, whether through communication or symbolic gestures, emphasizing the protection of religious beliefs and communal peace.
- **Disturbing Religious Assembly: Section 300** provides that whoever voluntarily causes disturbance to any assembly lawfully engaged in the performance of religious worship, or religious ceremonies,
  - Shall be punished with imprisonment of either description for a term which may extend to one year, or with fine, or with both.
- This section protects the sanctity of religious gatherings from disruptions, ensuring the peaceful conduct of religious practices without interference.
- **Trespassing on Burial Places, etc.: Section 301** provides that whoever, with the:
  - Intention of wounding the feelings of any person, or
  - Insulting the religion of any person or

- With the knowledge that the feelings of any person are likely to be wounded, or
- That the religion of any person is likely to be insulted thereby,

commits any trespass in any place of worship or on any place of sepulture, or any place set apart for the performance of funeral rites or as a depository for the remains of the dead, or offers any indignity to any human corpse, or causes disturbance to any persons assembled for the performance of funeral ceremonies,

- Shall be punished with imprisonment of either description for a term which may extend to one year, or with fine, or with both.

- **Uttering Words, etc., to Wound Religious Feelings: Section 302** provides that whoever, deliberately uttering words, making sounds, gestures, or placing objects with the intent to wound the religious feelings of any person.
  - Shall be punished with imprisonment of either description for a term which may extend to one year, or with fine, or with both.
- Provision focuses on verbal and symbolic acts intended to provoke religious communities, aiming to prevent incitement of religious discord or hurt sentiments.
  - Shall be punished with imprisonment of either description for a term which may extend to one year, or with fine, or with both.

Landmark Judgments

- In **Ramji Lal Modi v. The State of U.P., (1956)**, the editor of 'Gaurakshak' was convicted under Section 295A of IPC for publishing an article that outraged Muslim religious sentiments.
  - The Supreme Court upheld the section, affirming its constitutionality in preventing public disorder arising from deliberate insults to religion.
- In **Joseph v. State of Kerala, (1963)**, accused were charged under Sections 295 of IPC for demolishing a prayer hall and removing Hindu idols. The courts found the accused had lawful possession and lacked intent to insult religion, leading to their acquittal. The case underscores legal protections for property rights and religious sentiments under Sections 295 of IPC.

❖❖❖

NOTES

NOTES